variety of organizations. The simple layout and businesslike graphics make it easy to scan quickly and find specific topics. Any organization that is seeking to evolve from a traditional waterfall approach toward a more agile methodology will find *Essential Scrum* a definitive guidebook for the journey."

—Julia Frazier, product manager

"Developing software is hard. Adopting a new way of working while in a project is even harder. This book offers a bypass of many of the pitfalls and will accelerate a team's ability to produce business value and become successful with Scrum. I wish I had this kind of book when I started using Scrum."

—Geir Hedemark, Development Manager, Basefarm AS

"I am convinced that *Essential Scrum* will become the foundation reference for the next generation of Scrum practitioners. Not only is it the most comprehensive introduction to Scrum available today, but it is also extremely well written and easy on the eye with its fantastic new visual Scrum language. If that isn't enough, Kenny shares a range of his valuable personal insights and experiences that we can all certainly learn from."

—Ilan Goldstein, Agile Solutions Manager, Reed Elsevier

"Scrum is elegantly simple, yet deceptively complex. In *Essential Scrum,* Kenny Rubin provides us with a step-by-step guide to those complexities while retaining the essential simplicity. Real-world experiences coupled with enlightening illustrations make Scrum come to life. For senior managers and team members alike, this is a must-read book if you are starting or considering whether to implement Scrum in your organization. This will certainly be a book recommended to my students."

—John Hebley, Hebley & Associates

"Kenny unpacks a wealth of wisdom and knowledge in *Essential Scrum,* providing valuable and comprehensive insights to the practical application of agile/Scrum. Whether you're new to agile or are looking to reach a greater maturity of continuous improvement in your organization, this is a definitive handbook for your toolbox."

—David Luzquiños, Head of Agile Enablement, Agile Coach, Betfair

"Kenny Rubin continues to provide clarity and insight into adopting agile in a pragmatic way. In one hand he holds the formal or ideal Scrum definition, and in the other, the pragmatic application of it. He brings the wisdom of his workshops and years of experience to the table for you to read in his latest book. If you are about to start out on your agile adoption journey or are seeking guidance midcourse, grab a copy."

—Cuan Mulligan, freelance coactive Agile coach

Praise for *Essential Scrum*

"Agile coaches, you're gonna be happy with this book. Kenny Rubin has created an indispensable resource for us. Do you have a manager who just doesn't 'get it'? Hand them this book and ask them to flip to Chapter 3 for a complete explanation of how Scrum is less risky than plan-driven management. It's written just for them—in management-speak. Want to help the team come to a common understanding of Scrum? The visual icon language used throughout this book will help you help them. These are just two ways this book can aid you to coach Scrum teams. Use it well."

—Lyssa Adkins, Coach of Agile Coaches, Agile Coaching Institute; author,
Coaching Agile Teams

"One of the best, most comprehensive descriptions of the core Scrum framework out there! *Essential Scrum* is for anyone—new to or experienced with Scrum—who's interested in the most important aspects of the process. Kenny does an excellent job of distilling the key tenets of the Scrum framework into a simple format with compelling visuals. As a Scrum coach for many teams, I continually reference the material for new ways to help teams that are learning and practicing the framework. I've seen Scrum continually misinterpreted and poorly implemented by big companies and tool vendors for more than ten years. Reading this book will help you get back to the basics and focus on what's important."

—Joe Balistrieri, Process Development Manager, Rockwell Automation

"Corporate IT leadership, which has been slow to embrace agile methods, would benefit immensely from giving a copy of this book to all of their project and delivery managers. Kenny Rubin has laid out in this book all the pragmatic business case and process materials needed for any corporate IT shop to successfully implement Scrum."

—John F. Bauer III, veteran of technical solution delivery in large corporate IT shops

"Kenny's extensive experience as a consultant, trainer, and past managing director of the Scrum Alliance is evident in this book. Along with providing the basics and introduction to Scrum, this book addresses the questions of masses—what happens to project managers? *Essential Scrum* helps us understand the big picture and guides how organization leaders can support and be involved with their Scrum teams for successful agile transformations."

—Sameer S. Bendre, CSM, PMP, Senior Consultant, 3i Infotech Inc.

"If you're new to agile development or to Scrum, this book will give you a flying start. The examples and descriptions are clear and vivid, and you'll often find yourself asking a question just before the book addresses that very topic."

—Johannes Brodwall, Principal Solution Architect, Steria Norway

"Kenny's well-structured explanations have a clarity to them that echoes the sensibilities of Smalltalk—the development environment with which he worked for years and from which both Scrum and Extreme Programming were born. This book pulls together a thorough set of agile management principles that really hit the mark and will no doubt guide you toward a more effective agile approach."

—Rowan Bunning, Founder, Scrum WithStyle

"There are lots of books on Scrum these days, but this book takes a new angle: a reality check for software practitioners. Kenny uses real-world examples and clear illustrations to show what makes a solid foundation for successful agile development. Readers will understand the value of building quality in, and the reality that we can't get everything right up front; we must work incrementally and learn as we go. It might have 'Scrum' in the title, but the book leverages effective practices from the larger agile universe to help managers and their teams succeed."

—Lisa Crispin, coauthor, *Agile Testing*

"Kenny Rubin managed to write the book that I want everyone associated with Scrum development to read! He covers everything you'll need to know about Scrum and more!"

—Martine Devos, European Scrum Pioneer and Certified Scrum Trainer

"I've reviewed a number of agile books in the past few years, so the question of 'Do we really need another one?' always comes to my mind. In the case of Kenny's book, I very much believe the answer is 'yes.' Getting the benefit of different, experienced perspectives on commonly encountered and needed material is valuable. Kenny has one of those valuable perspectives. One unique aspect of the book is an interesting 'iconography'—a new icon language for Scrum and agile that Kenny has created. I believe you'll find value-added material in this book to expand your ideas for how Scrum can be applied."

—Scott Duncan, Agile/Scrum coach and trainer

"Anyone who has had Scrum training or has been part of a Scrum team will find *Essential Scrum* to be a great follow-up read. It dives into the details of how to become more agile through implementing Scrum processes, and it explains exactly how to break down complex projects into manageable initiatives (or 'sprints'). Kenny Rubin provides a wealth of relevant case studies on what worked—or what didn't—in a

ESSENTIAL SCRUM

ESSENTIAL SCRUM

A PRACTICAL GUIDE TO THE MOST POPULAR AGILE PROCESS

KENNETH S. RUBIN

✦ Addison-Wesley

Upper Saddle River, NJ • Boston • Indianapolis • San Francisco
New York • Toronto • Montreal • London • Munich • Paris • Madrid
Capetown • Sydney • Tokyo • Singapore • Mexico City

Many of the designations used by manufacturers and sellers to distinguish their products are claimed as trademarks. Where those designations appear in this book, and the publisher was aware of a trademark claim, the designations have been printed with initial capital letters or in all capitals.

The author and publisher have taken care in the preparation of this book, but make no expressed or implied warranty of any kind and assume no responsibility for errors or omissions. No liability is assumed for incidental or consequential damages in connection with or arising out of the use of the information or programs contained herein.

The publisher offers excellent discounts on this book when ordered in quantity for bulk purchases or special sales, which may include electronic versions and/or custom covers and content particular to your business, training goals, marketing focus, and branding interests. For more information, please contact:

U.S. Corporate and Government Sales
(800) 382-3419
corpsales@pearsontechgroup.com

For sales outside the United States, please contact:

International Sales
international@pearson.com

Visit us on the Web: informit.com/aw

Library of Congress Cataloging-in-Publication Data
Rubin, Kenneth S.
    Essential Scrum : a practical guide to the most popular agile process / Kenneth S. Rubin.
        p.   cm.
    Includes bibliographical references and index.
    ISBN 978-0-13-704329-3 (pbk. : alk. paper)—ISBN 0-13-704329-5 (pbk. : alk. paper)
  1. Scrum (Computer software development) 2. Agile software development. 3. Project management. I. Title.
    QA76.76.D47R824 2012
    005.1—dc23
                                                                            2012010892

ISBN-13: 978-0-13-704329-3
ISBN-10:   0-13-704329-5
Text printed in the United States on recycled paper at Edwards Brothers Malloy in Ann Arbor, Michigan.
Sixth printing, January 2015

To my wife, Jenine, for all your loving support

To my sons, Jonah and Asher, for inspiring me

To my father, Manny, for teaching me the value of hard work
(may his memory be a blessing)

To my mother, Joyce, for showing me what real courage looks like
(may her memory be a blessing)

CONTENTS

PART II   Roles   163

LIST OF FIGURES

FOREWORD
BY MIKE COHN

I had lunch today at a Burger King. A sign on the wall proclaimed the restaurant the "Home of the Whopper" and then proceeded to tell me there were over a million different ways to order a Whopper. If various combinations of extra or no pickles, tomatoes, lettuce, cheese, and so on can lead to over a million ways to make a hamburger, there must be billions of possible ways to implement Scrum. And while there is no single right way, there are better and worse ways to implement Scrum.

In *Essential Scrum*, Kenny Rubin helps readers find the better ways. His isn't a prescriptive book—he doesn't say, "You must do this." Instead, he teaches the essential principles underlying success with Scrum and then gives us choices in how we live up to those principles. For example, there is no one right way for all teams to plan a sprint. What works in one company or project will fail in another. And so Kenny gives us choices. He describes an overall structure for why Scrum teams plan sprints and what must result from sprint planning, and he gives us a couple of alternative approaches that will work. But ultimately the decision belongs to each team. Fortunately for those teams, they now have this book to help them.

An unexpected benefit of *Essential Scrum* is the visual language Kenny introduces for communicating about Scrum. I found these images very helpful in following along with the text, and I suspect they will become commonplace in future discussions of Scrum.

The world has needed this book for a long time. Scrum started as a small concept. The first book to talk about it—*Wicked Problems, Righteous Solutions* in 1990 by DeGrace and Stahl—did so in six pages. But in the more than 20 years since that book appeared, Scrum has expanded. New roles, meetings, and artifacts have been introduced and refined. With each new piece that was added, we were at risk of losing the heart of Scrum, that part of it that is about a team planning how to do something, doing some small part of it, and then reflecting on what the team members did and how well they did it together.

With *Essential Scrum*, Kenny brings us back to the heart of Scrum. And from there teams can begin to make the decisions necessary to implement Scrum, making it their own. This book serves as an indispensable guide, helping teams choose among the billions of possible ways of implementing Scrum and finding one that leads to success.

—Mike Cohn
   Author of *Succeeding with Agile*, *Agile Estimating and Planning*, and *User Stories Applied*
   www.mountaingoatsoftware.com

FOREWORD
BY RON JEFFRIES

When Kenny asked me to write a foreword for *Essential Scrum*, I was thinking, "This will be quick and easy; it must be a short book going straight to a simple description of what Scrum is." I knew Kenny's work, so I knew it would be a good read, and short, too. What could be better!

Imagine my surprise and delight when I found that this book covers just about everything you'll need to know about Scrum, on the first day or years into your use of Scrum. And Kenny doesn't stop there. He starts with the central ideas, including the agile principles that underlie all the agile methods, and a quick view of the Scrum framework. Then he drills in, deeper and deeper. It's still a good read, and it's quite comprehensive as well.

Kenny covers planning in good detail, looking at requirements, stories, the backlog, estimation, velocity. Then he takes us deeper into the principles and helps us deal with all the levels of planning and all the time horizons. He describes how sprints are planned, executed, reviewed, and improved. And throughout, he gives us more than the basics, highlighting key issues that you may encounter as you go along.

My own focus in Scrum and agile is on the necessary developer skills to ensure that teams can deliver real, running, business-focused software, sprint after sprint. Kenny helps us understand how to use ideas like velocity and technical debt safely and well. Both of these are critical topics, and I commend them to your attention.

Velocity tells us how much the team is delivering over time. We can use it to get a sense of how much we're getting done and whether we're improving. Kenny warns us, however, that using velocity as a performance measure is damaging to our business results, and he helps us understand why.

Technical debt has become a very broad term, referring to almost everything that could go wrong in the code. Kenny helps us tease apart all the various meanings and helps us understand why we care about these seemingly technical details. In particular, I like his description of how putting a team under pressure will inevitably damage our prospects of getting a good product on time.

Scrum, like all agile methods, relies on an exploratory approach with rapid feedback. Kenny tells a story of his brief use of punch cards, and it reminded me of my earliest experience with computing, many years before Kenny saw his first punch card.

As a college student, I was lucky enough to get a job as a sort of intern at Strategic Air Command headquarters in Omaha. In those days all computing was on cards. My cards got sent down several floors underground at SAC HQ and run on the computer that would run the war, if we ever had one. I was lucky to get one or two runs a day.

As soon as my security clearance came through, I would go down to the computer room in the middle of the night. I would sweet-talk Sergeant Whittaker into letting me run my own programs, sitting at the console of the machine—yes, the machine whose main job was to launch a nuclear attack. Rest easy, though: The red button was not in that room.

Working hands-on with the machine, I got ten times as much work done as when I had to wait for my cards to be taken down and my listings to be brought back up. Feedback came faster, I learned faster, and my programs worked sooner.

That's what Scrum is about. Instead of waiting months or even years to find out what the programmers are doing, in Scrum we find out every couple of weeks. A Scrum product owner with a really good team will be seeing actual features taking shape every few days!

And that is what Kenny's book is about. If you're new to Scrum, read it through from beginning to end. Then keep it nearby. If you've been doing Scrum for a while, scan it, then keep it nearby.

When you find yourself thinking about something that's happening to your team, or wondering about different things to try, pick up this book and look around. Chances are you'll find something of value.

—Ron Jeffries

PREFACE

This book discusses Essential Scrum—the things you have to know if you're going to be successful when using Scrum to develop innovative products and services.

What Is Essential Scrum?

Scrum is based on a small set of core **values**, **principles**, and **practices** (collectively the **Scrum framework**). Organizations using Scrum should embrace the Scrum framework in its entirety, perhaps not through the entire organization all at once, but certainly within the initial teams that will use Scrum. Embracing all of Scrum does not mean, however, that organizations must implement Scrum according to some cookie-cutter, one-size-fits-all formula. Rather, it means that organizations should always stay true to the Scrum framework while choosing an appropriate blend of **approaches** for their Scrum implementations.

Essential Scrum combines the values, principles, and practices of Scrum with a set of tried-and-true approaches that are consistent with, but not mandated by, the Scrum framework. Some of these approaches will be appropriate to your situation; others will not. Any approach will need to be inspected and adapted to your unique circumstances.

Origins of This Book

As an agile/Scrum coach and trainer, I am frequently asked for a reference book for Scrum—one that provides a comprehensive overview of the Scrum framework and also presents the most popular approaches for applying Scrum. Because I have been unable to find a single book that covers these topics at a level deep enough to be useful to today's practitioners, I found myself recommending a collection of books: a few that discuss the Scrum framework but are out of date or incomplete; several highly regarded agile books that do not focus solely on Scrum; and a handful that are focused on a specific aspect of Scrum or a specific approach but do not cover the full Scrum framework in depth. That's a lot of books for someone who just wants a single, stand-alone resource that covers the essentials of Scrum!

The originators of Scrum (Jeff Sutherland and Ken Schwaber) do have a Scrum-specific publication called "The Scrum Guide." This short document (about 15 pages) is described by its authors as the "definitive rule book of Scrum and the documentation of Scrum itself" (Schwaber and Sutherland 2011). They equate their document to the rules of the game of chess, "describing how the pieces move, how turns are taken, what is a win, and so on." Although useful as a Scrum overview or rule book, "The Scrum Guide" is by design not intended to be a comprehensive source of essential Scrum knowledge. Extending the authors' analogy, giving a new Scrum team just "The Scrum Guide" and expecting good results would be like giving a new chess player a 15-page description of the rules of chess and expecting her to be able to play a reasonable game of chess after reading it. It just isn't a stand-alone resource.

This book, *Essential Scrum,* is an attempt to be the missing single source for essential Scrum knowledge. It includes an in-depth discussion of Scrum's principles, values, and practices—one that in most cases agrees with other agile thought leaders and "The Scrum Guide." (Where this book offers a different perspective from what is widely promoted elsewhere, I point it out and explain why.) This book also describes approaches that are consistent with the Scrum framework and that have been used successfully by me and teams I have coached. I did not intend for this book to replace other books that provide a deep vertical treatment of a given Scrum practice or approach. Such books are complementary to and extend this book. Rather, think of *Essential Scrum* as the starting point on the journey of using Scrum to delight customers.

Intended Audience

For the many thousands of people who have taken my Working on a Scrum Team, Certified ScrumMaster, and Certified Scrum Product Owner classes, and the many teams I have coached, this book will refresh and perhaps even clarify topics we have already discussed. And for the even larger number of people with whom I have not yet had the pleasure of working, this book will either be your first introduction to Scrum and agile or it will be a chance to look at Scrum in a different light and perhaps even improve how you perform Scrum.

I did not write this book for any one specific role—this is not a book specifically for product owners, or ScrumMasters, or members of the development team. Instead, it is a book intended to give everyone involved with Scrum, from all the members of the Scrum team to those with whom they interact in the organization, a common understanding of Scrum based on a core set of concepts with a clear vocabulary for discussing them. With this shared foundation my hope is that your organization will be in a better position to successfully use Scrum to deliver business value.

I imagine that every Scrum team member would have a copy of this book on her desk open to a chapter relevant to the work at hand. I also envision managers at all levels of the organization reading it to understand why Scrum can be an effective approach for managing work and to understand the type of organizational change that may be necessary to successfully implement Scrum. Organizations using or planning to use an agile approach other than Scrum will also find the information relevant and helpful to their specific agile adoption.

Organization of This Book

This book begins with a brief introduction to Scrum (Chapter 1) and concludes with a discussion of where you might go next (Chapter 23). The remaining chapters are organized into four parts:

- Part I—Core Concepts (Chapters 2–8): Scrum framework, agile principles, sprints, requirements and user stories, product backlog, estimating and velocity, and technical debt
- Part II—Roles (Chapters 9–13): product owner, ScrumMaster, development team, Scrum team structures, and managers
- Part III—Planning (Chapters 14–18): Scrum planning principles, multilevel planning, portfolio planning, envisioning/product planning, and release planning
- Part IV—Sprinting (Chapters 19–22): sprint planning, sprint execution, sprint review, and sprint retrospective

How to Use This Book

As you would expect, I wrote the book assuming that most people would read it linearly from front to back. If you are new or newer to Scrum, you should take this approach because the chapters do tend to build on one another. That being said, if you are looking for one place to get an end-to-end overview of the Scrum framework (a highly visual Scrum primer), read and reference Chapter 2.

For those who are more familiar with Scrum, you can use this book as a Scrum reference guide. If you're interested in sprint retrospectives, jump directly to Chapter 22. If you are interested in exploring the nuances of the product backlog, jump directly to Chapter 6. I highly recommend, however, that everyone, even those familiar with Scrum, read Chapter 3 in its entirety. The principles laid out there form the foundation of the Scrum framework and the rest of the book. It is not simply a restatement of the values and principles of the Agile Manifesto (Beck et al. 2001) that is common in many other written descriptions of Scrum.

Visual AGILExicon

I am proud to include in this book the Visual AGILExicon (pronounced "visual agile lexicon"), a language for describing and communicating core agile and Scrum concepts in a graphically rich and visually appealing manner. The Visual AGILExicon was used to create many of the more than 200 graphics in this book. This visual language is composed of a vocabulary of icons that have been designed to capture essential Scrum roles, artifacts, and activities. The Visual AGILExicon is an effective way to communicate concepts and improves the overall shared understandability of Scrum. If you are interested in obtaining and using the full-color images in the Visual AGILExicon (this book is printed in only two colors), visit www.innolution.com for details. This website also hosts a variety of resources and discussions related to this book.

Let's Get Started

So, whatever your role, whatever your situation, you have picked up this book for a reason. Spend a little time getting to know Scrum. In the pages that follow you just might find a powerful framework that you can make your own, allowing you to substantially improve the way you develop and deliver products and services to delight your customers.

ACKNOWLEDGMENTS

This book would not have been possible without the input of many people, including the thousands of people who have attended my agile-related classes and coaching sessions. By mentioning some people by name, I run the risk of failing to mention others. To those whose names I fail to mention, please know that all of our discussions and email exchanges have been invaluable to me and have definitely influenced this book!

There are three people in particular I would like to thank: Mike Cohn, Rebecca Traeger, and Jeff Schaich. Without the unique involvement of each, this book would be a mere shadow of itself.

Mike Cohn has been a friend and colleague since we first worked together at Genomica in 2000. He was gracious enough to include my book in the Mike Cohn Signature Series; by being affiliated with Mike and the other prestigious authors in that book series, "I look good by the company that I keep," as my parents would say. Mike was my go-to person whenever I wanted to bounce around ideas or discuss book strategies. He always made time in his insane schedule to review each chapter and give me his thoughtful feedback. Working with Mike all these years has been a very rewarding experience—one that I hope will continue long into the future.

Rebecca Traeger has been my personal editor on this book. We have worked together since my days as managing director of the Scrum Alliance in 2007. At that time Rebecca was the editor of the Scrum Alliance website and through that work (and much more since) became the industry's foremost editor on agile-related materials. Early on in writing this book I reached out to Rebecca and asked if she would work with me again, and to my good fortune, she agreed. Nobody saw any chapter unless Rebecca had seen it first. At times her feedback would make me blush, because she frequently improved how I said something, making it sound both more understandable and approachable. If you just love a section of this book, you can be sure Rebecca had her hands in it. If you don't, I probably foolishly chose to ignore her recommendations.

Jeff Schaich is an artist/designer extraordinaire. We have worked on so many different art projects that I can't recall them all. Early on in the formulation of this book I wanted to create an agile/Scrum icon vocabulary to use as the basis for my training presentations and many of the over 200 figures in the book. I knew that I needed a great designer to pull off this feat. Jeff agreed to take on the challenge. There are times when this book seemed like two different projects—writing the content and creating the artistic concepts. I'm honestly not sure which took more time. I am sure, however, that without Jeff's artistic input, this book would have suffered immeasurably.

I am deeply honored to have both Mike Cohn and Ron Jeffries, two luminaries in the agile community, write forewords for the book! In their own unique ways each has done a great job of properly placing the book in context and opening the door for a discussion of Essential Scrum. Also, Mike, stop eating at Burger King, and Ron, thanks for not pushing the red button!

I'd also like to thank the many people who took time out of their busy schedules to review chapters and send me their feedback. Let me start by mentioning reviewers who provided extensive feedback: Joe Balistrieri, Johannes Brodwall, Leyna Cotran, Martine Devos, Scott Duncan, Ilan Goldstein, John Hebley, Geir Hedemark, James Kovacs, Lauri Mackinnon, Robert Maksimchuk, and Kevin Tureski.

In addition, I would like to thank other reviewers who provided excellent feedback on select chapters: Lyssa Adkins, John Bauer, Sameer Bendre, Susan Briscoe, Pawel Brodzinski, Rowan Bunning, Josh Chappell, Lisa Crispin, Ward Cunningham, Cornelius Engelbrecht, Julia Frazier, Brindusa Gabur, Caroline Gordon, Drew Jemilo, Mike Klimkosky, Tom Langerhorst, Bjarne Larsen, Dean Leffingwell, Maurice le Rutte, David Luzquiños, Lv Yi, Shay McAulay, Armond Mehrabian, Sheriff Mohamed, Cuan Mulligan, Greg Pease, Roman Pichler, Jacopo Romei, Jens Schauder, Bill Schroeder, Yves Stalgies, Branko Stojaković, Howard Sublett, Julie Sylvain, Kevin Tambascio, Stephen Wolfram, and Michael Wollin.

I would also like to thank the staff at Pearson who were great partners in this project. They tolerated my delays with patience and always offered encouragement. Special thanks to Chris Guzikowski, who oversaw the whole thing from soup to nuts. He was there from my first Pearson meeting at a pub in Lexington, MA, through the final production. I would also like to thank Olivia Basegio for adeptly handling logistics and Julie Nahil who did a fantastic job overseeing the project. In addition, thanks to Barbara Wood for the great job of helping polish the manuscript and Gail Cocker for pulling all of the art together into a coherent and beautiful whole.

I am also grateful to my assistant, Lindsey Kalicki, to whom I was able to offload many important tasks so that I could stay focused on book development. I am lucky to be able to work with such a skilled professional.

Most of all, I would like to acknowledge my family—Jenine, Jonah, and Asher—and the critical role that they played. I have asked so very much from them during the long effort of creating this book. No amount of gratitude can make up for the family pressure it caused and our lost time together.

Jenine is my loving soulmate and has stuck by me through all of the ups and downs of writing this book. The sacrifices she made so that I could write would double the size of this book if I tried to list them all. I couldn't have done it without her!

Funny thing is, a year after we were married in 1993, I published my first book, *Succeeding with Objects*. At that time Jenine made me promise that I would never write another book again. Luckily for me, after 15 years memories fade and the crushing workload doesn't seem as bad in hindsight, so when she urged me to write this one I was surprised to say the least! She hasn't yet told me I can't do book number three, but I suspect it might be 15 more years before the memory of this one fades enough for either of us to want me to write another one!

I also deeply appreciate the loving support from my sons, Jonah and Asher. They gave up time with their dad so that I could write. They were always there to bounce around ideas and to give input on the book. A number of their content and art suggestions have made their way into the book—and it's better because of them! I hope they learned the value of perseverance and that even the most daunting work can be completed if you take it a step at a time and don't give up.

Finally, I would like to acknowledge my parents, Joyce and Manny Rubin, for all of the love and support they gave me. Without their influence this book would never have been possible. Sadly, neither survived to see its publication. Mom passed away in January 2012 and Dad passed away in July 2012, leaving a void in my life and the lives of their family that can never be filled. They were very special people to the many whose lives they touched. Mom and Dad, I miss you more than I can possibly express.

About the Author

Kenny Rubin provides Scrum and agile training and coaching to help companies develop products in an effective and economically sensible way. A Certified Scrum Trainer, Kenny has trained more than 19,000 people on agile and Scrum, Smalltalk development, managing object-oriented projects, and transition management. He has coached over 200 companies, ranging from start-ups to Fortune 10.

Kenny was the first Managing Director of the worldwide Scrum Alliance, a non-profit organization focused on the successful adoption of Scrum. In addition to this book, Kenny is also the coauthor of the 1995 book *Succeeding with Objects: Decision Frameworks for Project Management*. He received his B.S. in Information and Computer Science from the Georgia Institute of Technology and his M.S. in Computer Science from Stanford University.

Kenny's background is rooted in the object-oriented technology community. He started as a Smalltalk developer on a NASA-funded project back in 1985 and developed the first blackboard expert system outside of LISP. In 1988 he was fortunate to join ParcPlace Systems, a start-up company formed as a Xerox PARC spin-off, whose charter was to bring object-oriented technology out of the research labs and release it to the world. As a Smalltalk development consultant with many different organizations in the late 1980s and throughout the 1990s, Kenny was an early adopter of agile practices. His first use of Scrum was in 2000 for developing bioinformatics software.

In the course of his career, Kenny has held many roles, including successful stints as a Scrum product owner, ScrumMaster, and member of development teams. In addition, he has held numerous executive management roles: CEO, COO, VP of Engineering, VP of Product Management, and VP of Professional Services. He has also overseen the development of five commercial software product suites, generating over $200M in aggregate revenue. In addition, he has been directly involved in raising over $150M in venture capital funding and assisted in taking two companies public on the NASDAQ.

His multifaceted background gives Kenny the ability to understand (and explain) Scrum and its implications equally well from multiple perspectives: from the development team to the executive board.

Chapter 1

INTRODUCTION

On June 21, 2000, I was employed as Executive Vice President at Genomica, a bio-informatics company in Boulder, Colorado. I remember the date because my son Asher was born at one o'clock that morning.

His birth was a good start to the day. Asher was actually born on his predicted due date (in the United States this happens about 5% of the time). So we (really my wife, Jenine) had finished our nine-month "project" on schedule. And to top things off, Asher had a very high Apgar score, indicating that we had produced a healthy, good-quality result! Our biggest stakeholder, our older son, Jonah, was thrilled to have a younger brother. On time, high quality, and delighted stakeholders—it truly was a good day!

After a brief nap, I checked email and saw that the CEO of Genomica had sent an urgent message asking me to be at a board of directors' meeting at 8:00 a.m. that same day. Begrudgingly, I left the hospital and went to the meeting.

When I arrived, I was told that the VP of Engineering had been fired the night before and I had now inherited the 90-person engineering team. I wasn't surprised. For several months the executive team and board had been discussing Genomica's inability to deliver valuable products on time and with acceptable quality, and the VP of Engineering was at the center of that discussion.

It was now my responsibility to oversee the effort of substantially improving the results of our product development organization. I remember being struck by the irony of that day's successful delivery and my new responsibilities.

Because I was already quite busy overseeing sales and marketing, I was told that at my discretion I could hire a new VP of Engineering to report to me. The person I chose to hire was Mike Cohn (Cohn 2004; Cohn 2006; Cohn 2010), and Scrum was the approach that we decided to use.

What Is Scrum?

Scrum is an **agile** approach for developing innovative products and services. Figure 1.1 shows a simple, generic, agile development approach.

With an agile approach, you begin by creating a **product backlog**—a prioritized list of the features and other capabilities needed to develop a successful product. Guided by the product backlog, you always work on the most important or highest-priority items first. When you run out of resources (such as time), any work that didn't get completed will be of lower priority than the completed work.

FIGURE 1.1   Agile development overview

   The work itself is performed in short, timeboxed **iterations**, which usually range from a week to a calendar month in length. During each iteration, a self-organizing, **cross-functional team** does all of the work—such as designing, building, and testing—required to produce completed, working features that could be put into production.

   Typically the amount of work in the product backlog is much greater than can be completed by a team in one short-duration iteration. So, at the start of each iteration, the team plans which high-priority subset of the product backlog to create in the upcoming iteration. In Figure 1.1, for example, the team has agreed that it can create features A, B, and C.

   At the end of the iteration, the team reviews the completed features with the stakeholders to get their feedback. Based on the feedback, the product owner and team can alter both what they plan to work on next and how the team plans to do the work. For example, if the stakeholders see a completed feature and then realize that another feature that they never considered must also be included in the product, the product owner can simply create a new item representing that feature and insert it into the product backlog in the correct order to be worked on in a future iteration.

   At the end of each iteration, the team should have a potentially shippable product (or increment of the product), one that can be released if appropriate. If releasing after each iteration isn't appropriate, a set of features from multiple iterations can be released together.

As each iteration ends, the whole process is begun anew with the planning of the next iteration.

Scrum Origins

Scrum's rich history can be traced back to a 1986 *Harvard Business Review* article, "The New New Product Development Game" (Takeuchi and Nonaka 1986). This article describes how companies such as Honda, Canon, and Fuji-Xerox produced world-class results using a scalable, team-based approach to **all-at-once product development**. It also emphasizes the importance of empowered, self-organizing teams and outlines management's role in the development process.

The 1986 article was influential in weaving together many of the concepts that gave rise to what today we call Scrum. Scrum is not an acronym, but rather a term borrowed from the sport of rugby, where it refers to a way of restarting a game after an accidental infringement or when the ball has gone out of play. Even if you are not a rugby aficionado, you have probably seen a scrum where the two sets of forwards mass together around the ball with locked arms and, with their heads down, struggle to gain possession of the ball.

Takeuchi and Nonaka used the metaphors of rugby and the scrum to describe product development:

> The . . . "relay race" approach to product development . . . may conflict with the goals of maximum speed and flexibility. Instead a holistic or "rugby" approach—where a team tries to go the distance as a unit, passing the ball back and forth—may better serve today's competitive requirements.

In 1993, Jeff Sutherland and his team at Easel Corporation created the Scrum process for use on a software development effort by combining concepts from the 1986 article with concepts from object-oriented development, empirical process control, iterative and incremental development, software process and productivity research, and complex adaptive systems. In 1995, Ken Schwaber published the first paper on Scrum at OOPSLA 1995 (Schwaber 1995). Since then, Schwaber and Sutherland, together and separately, have produced several Scrum-specific publications, including *Agile Software Development with Scrum* (Schwaber and Beedle 2001), *Agile Project Management with Scrum* (Schwaber 2004), and "The Scrum Guide" (Schwaber and Sutherland 2011).

Though Scrum is most commonly used to develop software products, the core values and principles of Scrum can and are being used to develop different types of products or to organize the **flow** of various types of work. For example, I have worked with organizations that have successfully used Scrum for organizing and managing the work associated with hardware development, marketing programs, and sales initiatives.

Why Scrum?

So what made an agile approach like Scrum a good choice for Genomica? First, it was clear that Genomica's previous approach to development simply wasn't working. That was the bad news; the good news was that most everyone agreed.

Genomica operated in a complex domain where more was unknown than known. We built products that had never been built before. Our focus was on bleeding-edge, continuously evolving, state-of-the-art, discovery informatics platforms that research scientists would use to help discover the next blockbuster molecule. We needed a way of developing that would allow us to quickly explore new ideas and approaches and learn fast which solutions were viable and which were not. We had a strategic corporate partner to whom we needed to show working results every few weeks or so to get feedback, because our product had to integrate with its core line of DNA sequencers. This need for rapid exploration and feedback did not mesh well with the detailed, up-front planning we had been doing.

We also wanted to avoid big up-front architecture design. A previous attempt to create a next generation of Genomica's core product had seen the organization spend almost one year doing architecture-only work to create a grand, unified bioinformatics platform. When the first real scientist-facing application was put on top of that architecture, and we finally validated design decisions made many months earlier, it took 42 seconds to tab from one field on the screen to the next field. If you think a typical user is impatient, imagine a molecular biologist with a Ph.D. having to wait 42 seconds! It was a disaster. We needed a different, more balanced approach to design, which included some design up front combined with a healthy dose of emergent, just-in-time design.

We also wanted our teams to be more cross-functional. Historically Genomica operated like most organizations. Development would hand off work to the test teams only after it was fully completed. We now had a desire for all team members to synchronize frequently—daily was the goal. In the past, errors were compounded because important issues were being discussed too late in the development effort. People in different areas weren't communicating frequently enough.

For these reasons, and others, we determined that Scrum would be a good fit for Genomica.

Genomica Results

When we chose to embrace Scrum, it was not well known; the first Scrum book didn't appear until the following year (Schwaber and Beedle 2001). However, we pulled together the available information and did the best we could, which was substantially better than we had done before (see Table 1.1).

From an effort perspective, with Scrum development we required one-tenth the amount of effort (calculated in person-months) compared to our previous use of a

TABLE 1.1   Genomica Scrum Results

Measure	Waterfall	Scrum
Effort	10x	1x
Velocity	1x	7x
Customer satisfaction	Poor	Excellent

plan-driven, **waterfall-style** approach to develop a comparable amount of product functionality. Equally important, the Scrum development progressed at seven times the velocity of the waterfall development, meaning that per unit of time, the Scrum development produced about seven times more valuable features than the waterfall development. Even more compelling was that we delivered the software to our partner in a time frame that met the expectations for the launch of its new hardware platform. This enabled us to reinforce a long-term partnership that substantially increased the shareholder value of Genomica.

Can Scrum Help You?

The Genomica pre-Scrum experience of building features that nobody wanted and delivering those features late and with poor quality is not uncommon. Genomica, like many other organizations, had survived by being no worse than its competitors. I saw the same problems when I first started working in commercial software development in the mid-1980s. And for many, after nearly 30 years, the situation hasn't improved.

Today, if you gathered together your business people and developers and asked them, "Are you happy with the results of our software development efforts?" or "Do you think we deliver good customer value in a timely, economical, and quality manner?" what would they say?

More often than not, the people I meet during my worldwide training and coaching answer both questions with a resounding "No." This is followed by a chorus of "Project failure rate is unacceptably high"; "Deliverables are late"; "Return on investment frequently falls short of expectations"; "Software quality is poor"; "Productivity is embarrassing"; "No one is accountable for outcomes"; "Employee morale is low"; "Employee turnover is too high." Then there's the under-the-breath snicker that accompanies the tongue-in-cheek "There must be a better way."

Yet even with all this discontent, most people seem resigned to the fact that dissatisfaction is just part of the reality of software development. It doesn't have to be.

Organizations that have diligently applied Scrum are experiencing a different reality (see Figure 1.2).

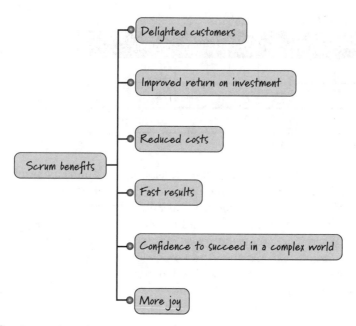

FIGURE 1.2   Scrum benefits

   These organizations are repeatedly delighting their customers by giving them what they really want, not just the features they might have specified on the first day when they knew the least about their true needs. They are also seeing an improved return on investment by delivering smaller, more frequent **releases**. And, by relentlessly exposing organizational dysfunction and **waste**, these organizations are able to reduce costs.

   Scrum's focus on delivering working, integrated, tested, business-valuable features each iteration leads to results being delivered fast. Scrum is also well suited to help organizations succeed in a complex world where they must quickly adapt based on the interconnected actions of competitors, customers, users, regulatory bodies, and other stakeholders. And Scrum provides more joy for all participants. Not only are customers delighted, but also the people doing the work actually enjoy it! They enjoy frequent and meaningful collaboration, leading to improved interpersonal relationships and greater mutual trust among team members.

   Don't get me wrong. Though Scrum is an excellent solution for many situations, it is not the proper solution in all circumstances. The **Cynefin** framework (Snowden and Boone 2007) is a sense-making framework that helps us understand the situation in which we have to operate and decide on a situation-appropriate approach. It defines and compares the characteristics of five different domains: **simple**, **complicated**, **chaotic**, **complex**, and a fifth domain, **disorder**, which occurs when you don't know which other domain you are in (see Figure 1.3). I will use the Cynefin framework to discuss situations in which Scrum is and is not a good fit.

First, it is important to realize that the many facets of software development and support will not fit nicely into just one Cynefin domain. Software development is a rich endeavor, with aspects that overlap and activities that fall into all of the different domains (Pelrine 2011). So, while most software development work falls in the domains of complicated or complex, to boldly claim that software development is a complex domain would be naive, especially if we define software development to include the spectrum of work ranging from innovative new-product development, ongoing software product maintenance, and operations and support.

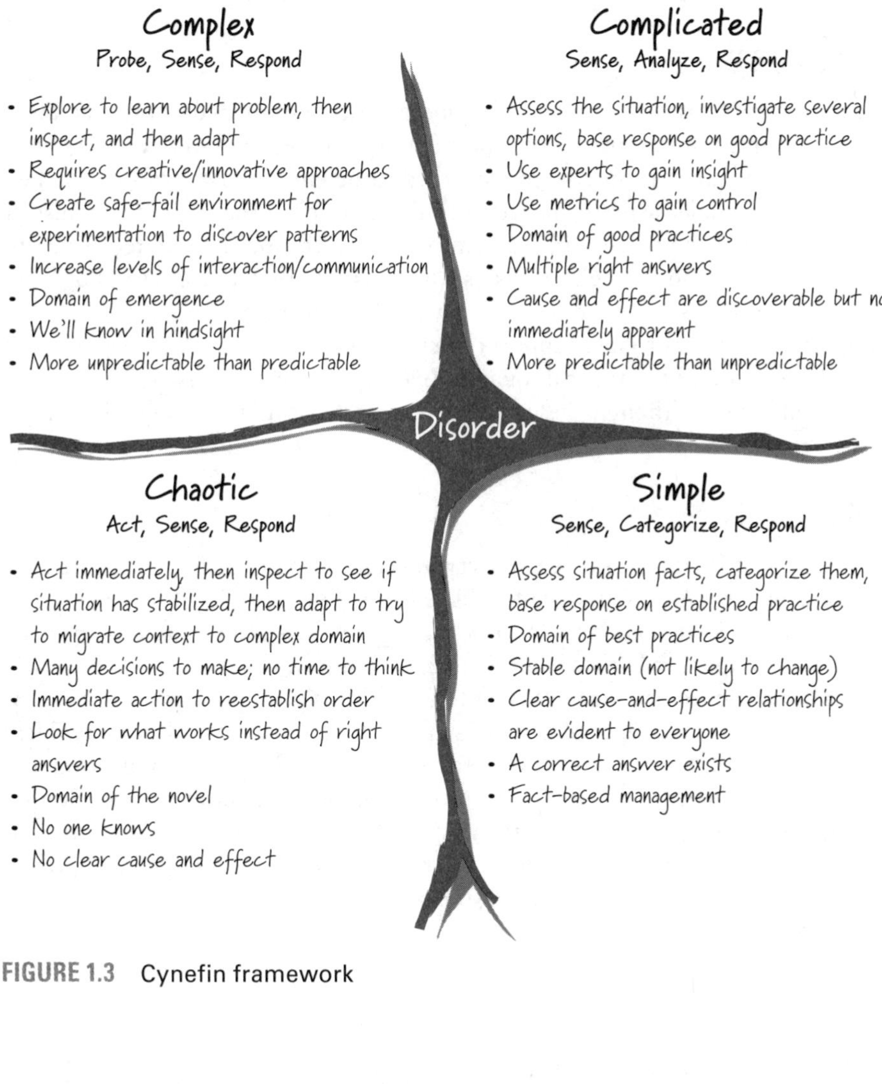

Complex
Probe, Sense, Respond

- Explore to learn about problem, then inspect, and then adapt
- Requires creative/innovative approaches
- Create safe-fail environment for experimentation to discover patterns
- Increase levels of interaction/communication
- Domain of emergence
- We'll know in hindsight
- More unpredictable than predictable

Complicated
Sense, Analyze, Respond

- Assess the situation, investigate several options, base response on good practice
- Use experts to gain insight
- Use metrics to gain control
- Domain of good practices
- Multiple right answers
- Cause and effect are discoverable but not immediately apparent
- More predictable than unpredictable

Disorder

Chaotic
Act, Sense, Respond

- Act immediately, then inspect to see if situation has stabilized, then adapt to try to migrate context to complex domain
- Many decisions to make; no time to think
- Immediate action to reestablish order
- Look for what works instead of right answers
- Domain of the novel
- No one knows
- No clear cause and effect

Simple
Sense, Categorize, Respond

- Assess situation facts, categorize them, base response on established practice
- Domain of best practices
- Stable domain (not likely to change)
- Clear cause-and-effect relationships are evident to everyone
- A correct answer exists
- Fact-based management

FIGURE 1.3   Cynefin framework

Complex Domain

When dealing with complex problems, things are more unpredictable than they are predictable. If there is a right answer, we will know it only with hindsight. This is the domain of **emergence**. We need to explore to learn about the problem, then **inspect and adapt** based on our learning. Working in complex domains requires creative and innovative approaches. Routine, cookie-cutter solutions simply don't apply. We need to create a safe-fail environment for experimentation so that we can discover important information. In this environment high levels of interaction and communication are essential. Innovative new-product development falls into this category as does enhancing existing products with innovative new features.

Scrum is particularly well suited for operating in a complex domain. In such situations our ability to probe (explore), sense (inspect), and respond (adapt) is critical.

Complicated Domain

Complicated problems are the domain of good practices dominated by experts. There might be multiple right answers, but expert diagnosis is required to figure them out. Although Scrum can certainly work with these problems, it might not be the best solution. For example, a performance optimization effort that calls for adjusting parameters to find the best overall system performance would be better served by assembling experts and letting them assess the situation, investigate several options, and base their response on good practice. Much of day-to-day software maintenance (dealing with a flow of product support or defect issues) falls into this category. This is also where many of the tactical, quantitative approaches like Six Sigma are particularly well suited, although these tactical approaches can also apply with simple domains.

Simple Domain

When dealing with simple problems, everyone can see cause and effect. Often the right answer is obvious and undisputed. This is the domain of legitimate best practices. There are known solutions. Once we assess the facts of our situation, we can determine the proper predefined solution to use. Scrum can be used for simple problems, but it may not be the most efficient tool for this type of problem. Using a process with a well-defined, repeatable set of steps that are known to solve the problem would be a better fit. For example, if we want to reproduce the same product over and over again, a well-defined assembly-line process would be a better fit than Scrum. Or deploying the same commercial-off-the-shelf (COTS) product into the 100th customer environment might best be completed by repeating a well-defined and proven set of steps for installing and configuring the product.

Chaotic Domain

Chaotic problems require a rapid response. We are in a crisis and need to act immediately to prevent further harm and reestablish at least some order. For example, suppose a university published an article stating that our product has a flawed algorithm that is producing erroneous results. Our customers have made substantial business investments based on the results from our product, and they are filing lawsuits against us for large damages. Our lead algorithm designer is on holiday in the jungles of Borneo and can't be reached for two more weeks. Scrum is not the best solution here. We are not interested in prioritizing a backlog of work and determining what work to perform in the next iteration. We need the ability to act immediately and decisively to stem the bleeding. With chaotic problems, someone needs to take charge of the situation and act.

Disorder

You are in the disorder domain when you don't know which of the other domains you are in. This is a dangerous place to be because you don't know how to make sense of your situation. In such cases, people tend to interpret and act according to their personal preference for action. In software development, many people are familiar with and therefore have a personal preference for phase-based, sequential approaches that work well in simple domains. Unfortunately, as I will discuss in Chapter 3, these tend to be a rather poor fit for much of software development. When you are in the disorder domain, the way out is to break down the situation into constituent parts and assign each to one of the other four domains. You are not trying to apply Scrum in the disorder domain; you are trying to get out of this domain.

Interrupt-Driven Work

Scrum is not well suited to highly interrupt-driven work. Say you run a customer support organization and you want to use Scrum to organize and manage your support activities. Your product backlog is populated on a continuous basis as you receive support requests via phone or email. At no point in time do you have a product backlog that extends very far into the future, and the content and order of your backlog could change frequently (perhaps hourly or every few minutes).

In this situation, you will not be able to reliably plan iterations of a week or more because you won't know what the work will be that far into the future. And, even if you think you know the work, there is a very good likelihood that a high-priority support request will arrive and preempt any such forward-looking plans.

In interrupt-driven environments you would be better off considering an alternative agile approach called **Kanban**. Kanban is not a stand-alone process solution, but instead an approach that is overlaid on an existing process. In particular, Kanban advocates that you

- Visualize how the work flows through the system (for example, the steps that the support organization takes to resolve a support request)
- Limit the work in process (WIP) at each step to ensure that you are not doing more work than you have the capacity to do
- Measure and optimize the flow of the work through the system to make continuous improvements

The sweet spots for Kanban are the software maintenance and support areas. Some Kanban practitioners point out that Kanban's focus on eliminating overburden (by aligning WIP with capacity) and reducing variability in flow while encouraging an evolutionary approach to change makes it appropriate to use in complex domains as well.

Scrum and Kanban are both agile approaches to development, and each has strengths and weaknesses that should be considered once you make sense of the domain in which you are operating. In some organizations both Scrum and Kanban can be used to address the different system needs that coexist. For example, Scrum can be used for new-product development and Kanban for interrupt-driven support and maintenance.

Closing

Scrum is not a silver bullet or a magic cure. Scrum can, however, enable you to embrace the changes that accompany all complex **product development efforts**. And it can, and has, worked for Genomica and many other companies that decided to employ an approach to software development that better matched their circumstances.

Although the Scrum framework is simple, it would be a mistake to assume that Scrum is easy and painless to apply. Scrum doesn't prescriptively answer your process questions; instead, it empowers teams to ask and answer their own great questions. Scrum doesn't give individuals a cookbook solution to all of their organizational maladies; instead, Scrum makes visible the dysfunctions and waste that prevent organizations from reaching their true potential.

These realizations can be painful for many organizations. However, if they move past the initial discomfort and work to solve the problems Scrum unearths, organizations can take great strides in terms of both their software development process and products and their levels of employee and customer satisfaction.

The rest of the book is devoted to discussing the essential aspects of Scrum. I will begin with a description of the entire Scrum framework, including its roles, activities, artifacts, and **rules**. Who knows; if you use Scrum in the right way and in the proper conditions, perhaps you too will deliver value as successfully as my wife did on that fateful day back in 2000.

PART I

CORE CONCEPTS

Chapter 2

SCRUM FRAMEWORK

This chapter provides an overview of the Scrum framework with a primary focus on its practices, including roles, activities, and artifacts. Subsequent chapters will provide a deeper treatment of each of these practices, including an in-depth look at the principles that underlie the practices.

Overview

Scrum is not a standardized process where you methodically follow a series of sequential steps that are guaranteed to produce, on time and on budget, a high-quality product that delights customers. Instead, Scrum is a **framework** for organizing and managing work. The Scrum framework is based on a set of values, principles, and practices that provide the foundation to which your organization will add its unique implementation of relevant engineering practices and your specific approaches for realizing the Scrum practices. The result will be a version of Scrum that is uniquely yours.

To better grasp the framework concept, imagine that the Scrum framework is like the foundation and walls of a building. The Scrum values, principles, and practices would be the key structural components. You can't ignore or fundamentally change a value, principle, or practice without risking collapse. What you can do, however, is customize inside the structure of Scrum, adding fixtures and features until you have a process that works for you.

Scrum is a refreshingly simple, people-centric framework based on the values of honesty, openness, courage, respect, focus, trust, empowerment, and collaboration. Chapter 3 will describe the Scrum principles in depth; subsequent chapters will highlight how specific practices and approaches are rooted in these principles and values.

The Scrum practices themselves are embodied in specific roles, activities, artifacts, and their associated rules (see Figure 2.1).

The remainder of this chapter will focus on Scrum practices.

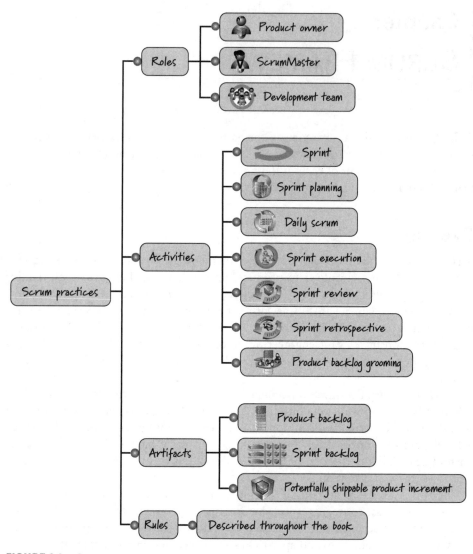

FIGURE 2.1   Scrum practices

Scrum Roles

Scrum development efforts consist of one or more **Scrum teams**, each made up of three Scrum roles: **product owner, ScrumMaster,** and the **development team** (see Figure 2.2). There can be other roles when using Scrum, but the Scrum framework requires only the three listed here.

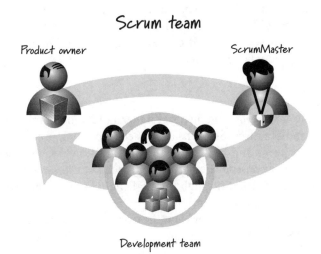

Scrum team

Product owner

ScrumMaster

Development team

FIGURE 2.2   Scrum roles

The product owner is responsible for what will be developed and in what order. The ScrumMaster is responsible for guiding the team in creating and following its own process based on the broader Scrum framework. The development team is responsible for determining how to deliver what the product owner has asked for.

If you are a manager, don't be concerned that "manager" doesn't appear as a role in Figure 2.2; managers still have an important role in organizations that use Scrum (see Chapter 13). The Scrum framework defines just the roles that are specific to Scrum, not all of the roles that can and should exist within an organization that uses Scrum.

Product Owner

The product owner is the empowered central point of product leadership. He[1] is the single authority responsible for deciding which features and functionality to build and the order in which to build them. The product owner maintains and communicates to all other participants a clear vision of what the Scrum team is trying to achieve. As such, the product owner is responsible for the overall success of the solution being developed or maintained.

It doesn't matter if the focus is on an external product or an internal application; the product owner still has the obligation to make sure that the most valuable work possible, which can include technically focused work, is always performed. To

---

1. In this book the product owner will always be referred to as "he" or "him" and the ScrumMaster as "she" or "her." This is consistent with the visual representation of each role within the figures.

ensure that the team rapidly builds what the product owner wants, the product owner actively collaborates with the ScrumMaster and development team and must be available to answer questions soon after they are posed. See Chapter 9 for a detailed description of the product owner role.

ScrumMaster

The ScrumMaster helps everyone involved understand and embrace the Scrum values, principles, and practices. She acts as a coach, providing process leadership and helping the Scrum team and the rest of the organization develop their own high-performance, organization-specific Scrum approach. At the same time, the Scrum-Master helps the organization through the challenging change management process that can occur during a Scrum adoption.

As a facilitator, the ScrumMaster helps the team resolve issues and make improvements to its use of Scrum. She is also responsible for protecting the team from outside interference and takes a leadership role in removing **impediments** that inhibit team productivity (when the individuals themselves cannot reasonably resolve them). The ScrumMaster has no authority to exert control over the team, so this role is not the same as the traditional role of project manager or development manager. The Scrum-Master functions as a leader, not a manager. I will discuss the roles of functional manager and project manager in Chapter 13. See Chapter 10 for more details on the ScrumMaster role.

Development Team

Traditional software development approaches discuss various job types, such as architect, programmer, tester, database administrator, UI designer, and so on. Scrum defines the role of a development team, which is simply a diverse, cross-functional collection of these types of people who are responsible for designing, building, and testing the desired product.

The development team self-organizes to determine the best way to accomplish the goal set out by the product owner. The development team is typically five to nine people in size; its members must collectively have all of the skills needed to produce good-quality, working software. Of course, Scrum can be used on development efforts that require much larger teams. However, rather than having one Scrum team with, say, 35 people, there would more likely be four or more Scrum teams, each with a development team of nine or fewer people. See Chapter 11 for more details on the development team role and Chapter 12 for more details on coordinating multiple teams.

Scrum Activities and Artifacts

Figure 2.3 illustrates most of the Scrum activities and artifacts and how they fit together.

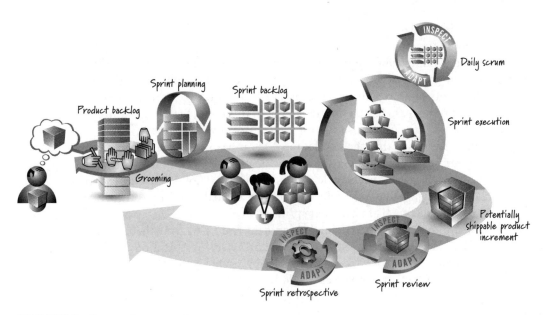

FIGURE 2.3   Scrum framework

Let's summarize the diagram, starting on the left side of the figure and working clockwise around the main looping arrow (the sprint).

The product owner has a vision of what he wants to create (the big cube). Because the cube can be large, through an activity called **grooming** it is broken down into a set of features that are collected into a prioritized list called the product backlog.

A sprint starts with sprint planning, encompasses the development work during the sprint (called sprint execution), and ends with the review and retrospective. The sprint is represented by the large, looping arrow that dominates the center of the figure. The number of items in the product backlog is likely to be more than a development team can complete in a short-duration sprint. For that reason, at the beginning of each sprint, the development team must determine a subset of the product backlog items it believes it can complete—an activity called sprint planning, shown just to the right of the large product backlog cube.

As a brief aside, in 2011 a change in "The Scrum Guide" (Schwaber and Sutherland 2011) generated debate about whether the appropriate term for describing the result of sprint planning is a **forecast** or a **commitment**. Advocates of the word *forecast* like it because they feel that although the development team is making the best estimate that it can at the time, the estimate might change as more information becomes known during the course of the sprint. Some also believe that a commitment on the part of the team will cause the team to sacrifice quality to meet the commitment or will cause the team to "under-commit" to guarantee that the commitment is met.

I agree that all development teams should generate a forecast (estimate) of what they can deliver each sprint. However, many development teams would benefit from using the forecast to derive a commitment. Commitments support mutual trust between the product owner and the development team as well as within the development team. Also, commitments support reasonable short-term planning and decision making within an organization. And, when performing multiteam product development, commitments support synchronized planning—one team can make decisions based on what another team has committed to do. In this book, I favor the term *commitment*; however, I occasionally use *forecast* if it seems correct in context.

To acquire confidence that the development team has made a reasonable commitment, the team members create a second backlog during sprint planning, called the sprint backlog. The sprint backlog describes, through a set of detailed **tasks**, how the team plans to design, build, integrate, and test the selected subset of features from the product backlog during that particular sprint.

Next is sprint execution, where the development team performs the tasks necessary to realize the selected features. Each day during sprint execution, the team members help manage the flow of work by conducting a synchronization, inspection, and adaptive planning activity known as the daily scrum. At the end of sprint execution the team has produced a potentially shippable product increment that represents some, but not all, of the product owner's vision.

The Scrum team completes the sprint by performing two inspect-and-adapt activities. In the first, called the sprint review, the stakeholders and Scrum team inspect the product being built. In the second, called the sprint retrospective, the Scrum team inspects the Scrum process being used to create the product. The outcome of these activities might be adaptations that will make their way into the product backlog or be included as part of the team's development process.

At this point the Scrum sprint cycle repeats, beginning anew with the development team determining the next most important set of product backlog items it can complete. After an appropriate number of sprints have been completed, the product owner's vision will be realized and the solution can be released.

In the remainder of this chapter I will discuss each of these activities and artifacts in greater detail.

Product Backlog

Using Scrum, we always do the most valuable work first. The product owner, with input from the rest of the Scrum team and stakeholders, is ultimately responsible for determining and managing the sequence of this work and communicating it in the form of a prioritized (or ordered) list known as the **product backlog** (see Figure 2.4). On new-product development the product backlog items initially are features required to meet the product owner's vision. For ongoing product development, the product backlog might also contain new features, changes to existing features, defects needing repair, technical improvements, and so on.

The product owner collaborates with internal and external stakeholders to gather and define the product backlog items. He then ensures that product backlog items

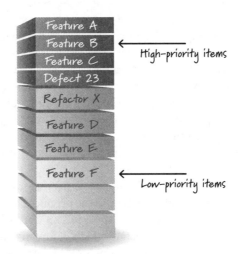

FIGURE 2.4   Product backlog

are placed in the correct sequence (using factors such as value, cost, knowledge, and risk) so that the high-value items appear at the top of the product backlog and the lower-value items appear toward the bottom. The product backlog is a constantly evolving artifact. Items can be added, deleted, and revised by the product owner as business conditions change, or as the Scrum team's understanding of the product grows (through feedback on the software produced during each sprint).

Overall the activity of creating and refining product backlog items, estimating them, and prioritizing them is known as grooming (see Figure 2.5).

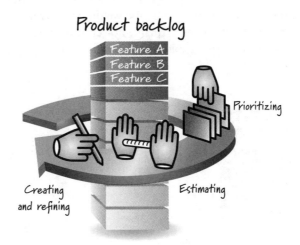
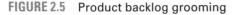

FIGURE 2.5   Product backlog grooming

As a second brief aside, in 2011 there was another debate as to whether the appropriate term for describing the sequence of items in the product backlog should be *prioritized* (the original term) or *ordered*, the term used in "The Scrum Guide" (Schwaber and Sutherland 2011). The argument was that prioritizing is simply one form of ordering (and, according to some, not even the most appropriate form of ordering). The issue of how to best sequence items in the product backlog, however, is influenced by many factors, and a single word may never capture the full breadth and depth of the concept. Although there may be theoretical merit to the ordered-versus-prioritized debate, most people (including me) use the terms interchangeably when discussing the items in the product backlog.

Before we finalize prioritizing, ordering, or otherwise arranging the product backlog, we need to know the size of each item in the product backlog (see Figure 2.6).

Size equates to cost, and product owners need to know an item's cost to properly determine its priority. Scrum does not dictate which, if any, size measure to use with product backlog items. In practice, many teams use a **relative size measure** such as **story points** or **ideal days**. A relative size measure expresses the overall size of an item in such a way that the absolute value is not considered, but the relative size of an item compared to other items is considered. For example, in Figure 2.6, feature C is size 2 and feature E is size 8. What we can conclude is that feature E is about four times larger than feature C. I will discuss these measures further in Chapter 7.

Sprints

In Scrum, work is performed in iterations or cycles of up to a calendar month called **sprints** (see Figure 2.7). The work completed in each sprint should create something of tangible value to the customer or user.

Sprints are **timeboxed** so they always have a fixed start and end date, and generally they should all be of the same duration. A new sprint immediately follows the completion of the previous sprint. As a rule we do not permit any goal-altering changes in scope or personnel during a sprint; however, business needs sometimes make adherence to this rule impossible. I will describe sprints in more detail in Chapter 4.

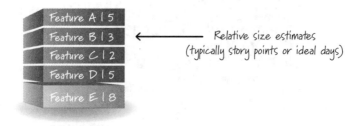

FIGURE 2.6   Product backlog item sizes

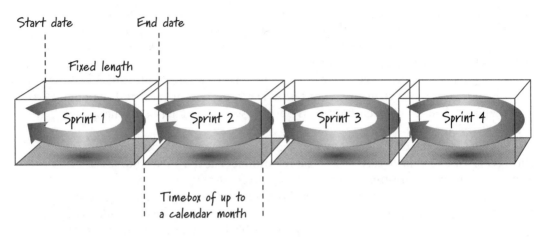

FIGURE 2.7   Sprint characteristics

Sprint Planning

A product backlog may represent many weeks or months of work, which is much more than can be completed in a single, short sprint. To determine the most important subset of product backlog items to build in the next sprint, the product owner, development team, and ScrumMaster perform **sprint planning** (see Figure 2.8).

During sprint planning, the product owner and development team agree on a **sprint goal** that defines what the upcoming sprint is supposed to achieve. Using this

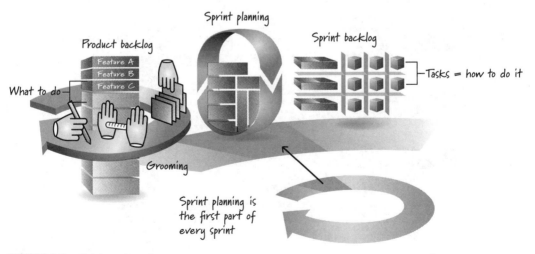

FIGURE 2.8   Sprint planning

goal, the development team reviews the product backlog and determines the high-priority items that the team can realistically accomplish in the upcoming sprint while working at a **sustainable pace**—a pace at which the development team can comfortably work for an extended period of time.

To acquire confidence in what it can get done, many development teams break down each targeted feature into a set of tasks. The collection of these tasks, along with their associated product backlog items, forms a second backlog called the **sprint backlog** (see Figure 2.9).

The development team then provides an estimate (typically in hours) of the effort required to complete each task. Breaking product backlog items into tasks is a form of design and **just-in-time** planning for how to get the features done.

Most Scrum teams performing sprints of two weeks to a month in duration try to complete sprint planning in about four to eight hours. A one-week sprint should take no more than a couple of hours to plan (and probably less). During this time there are several approaches that can be used. The approach I use most often follows a simple cycle: Select a product backlog item (whenever possible, the next-most-important item as defined by the product owner), break the item down into tasks, and determine if the selected item will reasonably fit within the sprint (in combination with other items targeted for the same sprint). If it does fit and there is more capacity to complete work, repeat the cycle until the team is out of capacity to do any more work.

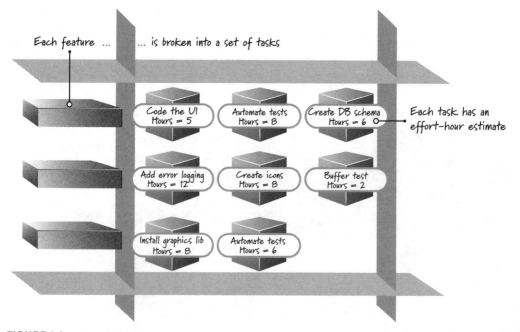

FIGURE 2.9   Sprint backlog

An alternative approach would be for the product owner and team to select all of the target product backlog items at one time. The development team alone does the task breakdowns to confirm that it really can deliver all of the selected product backlog items. I will describe each approach in more detail in Chapter 19.

Sprint Execution

Once the Scrum team finishes sprint planning and agrees on the content of the next sprint, the development team, guided by the ScrumMaster's coaching, performs all of the task-level work necessary to get the features done (see Figure 2.10), where "done" means there is a high degree of confidence that all of the work necessary for producing good-quality features has been completed.

Exactly what tasks the team performs depends of course on the nature of the work (for example, are we building software and what type of software, or are we building hardware, or is this marketing work?).

Nobody tells the development team in what order or how to do the task-level work in the sprint backlog. Instead, team members define their own task-level work and then self-organize in any manner they feel is best for achieving the sprint goal. See Chapter 20 for more details on sprint execution.

Daily Scrum

Each day of the sprint, ideally at the same time, the development team members hold a timeboxed (15 minutes or less) **daily scrum** (see Figure 2.11). This inspect-and-adapt activity is sometimes referred to as the **daily stand-up** because of the common practice of everyone standing up during the meeting to help promote brevity.

FIGURE 2.10   Sprint execution

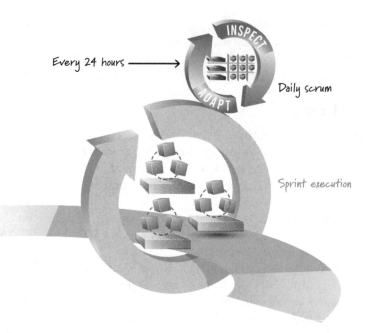

Every 24 hours ⟶

INSPECT

ADAPT

Daily scrum

Sprint execution

FIGURE 2.11   Daily scrum

A common approach to performing the daily scrum has the ScrumMaster facilitating and each team member taking turns answering three questions for the benefit of the other team members:

- What did I accomplish since the last daily scrum?
- What do I plan to work on by the next daily scrum?
- What are the obstacles or impediments that are preventing me from making progress?

By answering these questions, everyone understands the big picture of what is occurring, how they are progressing toward the sprint goal, any modifications they want to make to their plans for the upcoming day's work, and what issues need to be addressed. The daily scrum is essential for helping the development team manage the fast, flexible flow of work within a sprint.

The daily scrum is not a problem-solving activity. Rather, many teams decide to talk about problems after the daily scrum and do so with a small group of interested people. The daily scrum also is not a traditional status meeting, especially the kind historically called by project managers so that they can get an update on the project's status. A daily scrum, however, can be useful to communicate the status of sprint backlog items among the development team members. Mainly, the daily scrum is an inspection, synchronization, and adaptive daily planning activity that helps a self-organizing team do its job better.

Although their use has fallen out of favor, Scrum has used the terms "**pigs**" and "**chickens**" to distinguish who should participate during the daily scrum versus who simply observes. The farm animals were borrowed from an old joke (which has several variants): "In a ham-and-eggs breakfast, the chicken is involved, but the pig is committed." Obviously the intent of using these terms in Scrum is to distinguish between those who are involved (the chickens) and those who are committed to meeting the sprint goal (the pigs). At the daily scrum, only the pigs should talk; the chickens, if any, should attend as observers.

I have found it most useful to consider everyone on the Scrum team a pig and anyone who isn't, a chicken. Not everyone agrees. For example, the product owner is not required to be at the daily scrum, so some consider him to be a chicken (the logic being, how can you be "committed" if you aren't required to attend?). This seems wrong to me, because I can't imagine how the product owner, as a member of the Scrum team, is any less committed to the outcome of a sprint than the development team. The metaphor of pigs and chickens breaks down if you try to apply it within a Scrum team.

Done

In Scrum, we refer to the sprint results as a **potentially shippable product increment** (see Figure 2.12), meaning that whatever the Scrum team agreed to do is really done according to its agreed-upon definition of done. This definition specifies the degree

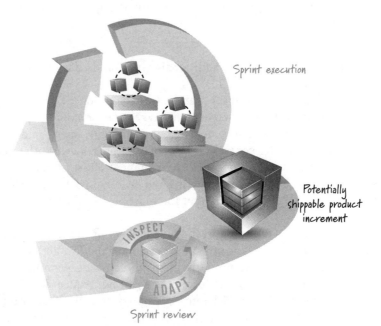

FIGURE 2.12   Sprint results (potentially shippable product increment)

of confidence that the work completed is of good quality and is potentially shippable. For example, when developing software, a bare-minimum definition of done should yield a complete slice of product functionality that is designed, built, integrated, tested, and documented.

An aggressive definition of done enables the business to decide each sprint if it wants to ship (or deploy or release) what got built to internal or external customers.

To be clear, "potentially shippable" does not mean that what got built must actually be shipped. Shipping is a business decision, which is frequently influenced by things such as "Do we have enough features or enough of a customer workflow to justify a customer deployment?" or "Can our customers absorb another change given that we just gave them a release two weeks ago?"

Potentially shippable is better thought of as a state of confidence that what got built in the sprint is actually done, meaning that there isn't materially important undone work (such as important testing or integration and so on) that needs to be completed before we can ship the results from the sprint, if shipping is our business desire.

As a practical matter, over time some teams may vary the definition of done. For example, in the early stages of game development, having features that are potentially shippable might not be economically feasible or desirable (given the exploratory nature of early game development). In these situations, an appropriate definition of done might be a slice of product functionality that is sufficiently functional and usable to generate feedback that enables the team to decide what work should be done next or how to do it. See Chapter 4 for more details on the definition of done.

Sprint Review

At the end of the sprint there are two additional inspect-and-adapt activities. One is called the **sprint review** (see Figure 2.13).

The goal of this activity is to inspect and adapt the product that is being built. Critical to this activity is the conversation that takes place among its participants, which include the Scrum team, stakeholders, sponsors, customers, and interested members of other teams. The conversation is focused on reviewing the just-completed features in the context of the overall development effort. Everyone in attendance gets clear visibility into what is occurring and has an opportunity to help guide the forthcoming development to ensure that the most business-appropriate solution is created.

A successful review results in bidirectional information flow. The people who aren't on the Scrum team get to sync up on the development effort and help guide its direction. At the same time, the Scrum team members gain a deeper appreciation for the business and marketing side of their product by getting frequent feedback on the convergence of the product toward delighted customers or users. The sprint review therefore represents a scheduled opportunity to inspect and adapt the product. As a

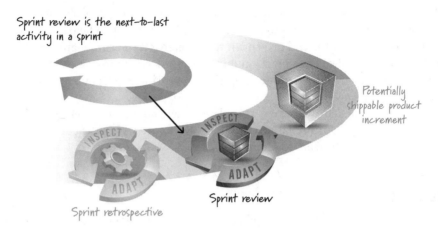

Sprint review is the next-to-last activity in a sprint

Potentially shippable product increment

Sprint review

Sprint retrospective

FIGURE 2.13 Sprint review

matter of practice, people outside the Scrum team can perform intra-sprint feature reviews and provide feedback to help the Scrum team better achieve its sprint goal. See Chapter 21 for more details on the sprint review.

Sprint Retrospective

The second inspect-and-adapt activity at the end of the sprint is the **sprint retrospective** (see Figure 2.14). This activity frequently occurs after the sprint review and before the next sprint planning.

Whereas the sprint review is a time to inspect and adapt the product, the sprint retrospective is an opportunity to inspect and adapt the process. During the sprint retrospective the development team, ScrumMaster, and product owner come together

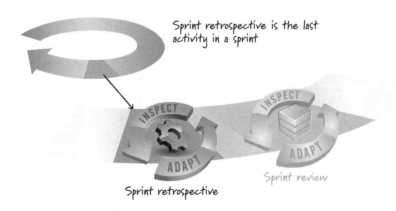

Sprint retrospective is the last activity in a sprint

Sprint retrospective

Sprint review

FIGURE 2.14 Sprint retrospective

to discuss what is and is not working with Scrum and associated technical practices. The focus is on the continuous process improvement necessary to help a good Scrum team become great. At the end of a sprint retrospective the Scrum team should have identified and committed to a practical number of process improvement actions that will be undertaken by the Scrum team in the next sprint. See Chapter 22 for details on the sprint retrospective.

After the sprint retrospective is completed, the whole cycle is repeated again—starting with the next sprint-planning session, held to determine the current highest-value set of work for the team to focus on.

Closing

This chapter described core Scrum practices, focusing on an end-to-end description of the Scrum framework's roles, activities, and artifacts. There are other practices, such as higher-level planning and progress-tracking practices, that many Scrum teams use. These will be described in subsequent chapters. In the next chapter, I will provide a description of the core principles on which Scrum is based. This will facilitate the deeper exploration of the Scrum framework in subsequent chapters.

Chapter 3
AGILE PRINCIPLES

Before we delve deeper into the mechanics of Scrum, it will be helpful to understand the underlying principles that drive and inform those mechanics.

This chapter describes the agile principles that underlie Scrum and compares them with those of traditional, plan-driven, sequential product development. In doing so, the chapter sets the stage for understanding how Scrum differs from more traditional forms of product development and for a more detailed analysis of Scrum practices in subsequent chapters.

Overview

I find it instructive to introduce Scrum's underlying principles by comparing them with the beliefs that drive more traditional, plan-driven, sequential development. Doing so makes it easier for people to understand how Scrum is similar to or different from something they know and understand.

The goal of comparing agile principles with traditional development principles is not to make the case that plan-driven, sequential development is bad and that Scrum is good. Both are tools in the professional developer's toolkit; there is no such thing as a bad tool, rather just inappropriate times to use that tool. As I described briefly in the context of the Cynefin framework in Chapter 1, Scrum and traditional, plan-driven, sequential development are appropriate to use on different classes of problems.

In making the comparison between the two approaches, I am using the pure or "textbook" description of plan-driven, sequential development. By taking this perspective when describing traditional development, I am better able to draw out the distinctions and more clearly illustrate the principles that underlie Scrum-based development.

One pure form of traditional, plan-driven development frequently goes by the term **waterfall** (see Figure 3.1). However, that is just one example of a broader class of **plan-driven** processes (also known as **traditional**, **sequential**, **anticipatory**, **predictive**, or **prescriptive development processes**).

Plan-driven processes are so named because they attempt to plan for and anticipate up front all of the features a user might want in the end product, and to determine how best to build those features. The idea here is that the better the planning, the better the understanding, and therefore the better the execution. Plan-driven processes are often called sequential processes because practitioners perform, in sequence, a complete requirements analysis followed by a complete design followed in turn by coding/building and then testing.

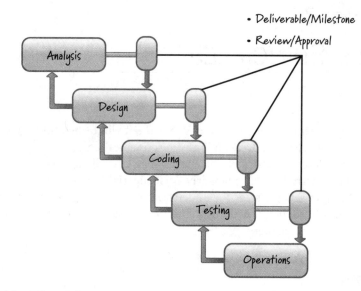

FIGURE 3.1   Waterfall process

Plan-driven development works well if you are applying it to problems that are well defined, predictable, and unlikely to undergo any significant change. The problem is that most product development efforts are anything but predictable, especially at the beginning. So, while a plan-driven process gives the impression of an orderly, accountable, and measurable approach, that impression can lead to a false sense of security. After all, developing a product rarely goes as planned.

For many, a plan-driven, sequential process just makes sense, understand it, design it, code it, test it, and deploy it, all according to a well-defined, prescribed plan. There is a belief that it *should* work. If applying a plan-driven approach doesn't work, the prevailing attitude is that we must have done something wrong. Even if a plan-driven process repeatedly produces disappointing results, many organizations continue to apply the same approach, sure that if they just do it better, their results will improve. The problem, however, is not with the execution. It's that plan-driven approaches are based on a set of beliefs that do not match the uncertainty inherent in most product development efforts.

Scrum, on the other hand, is based on a different set of beliefs—ones that do map well to problems with enough uncertainty to make high levels of predictability difficult. The principles that I describe in this chapter are drawn from a number of sources, including the Agile Manifesto (Beck et al. 2001), lean product development (Reinertsten 2009b; Poppendieck and Poppendieck 2003), and "The Scrum Guide" (Schwaber and Sutherland 2011).

These principles are organized into several categories as shown in Figure 3.2.

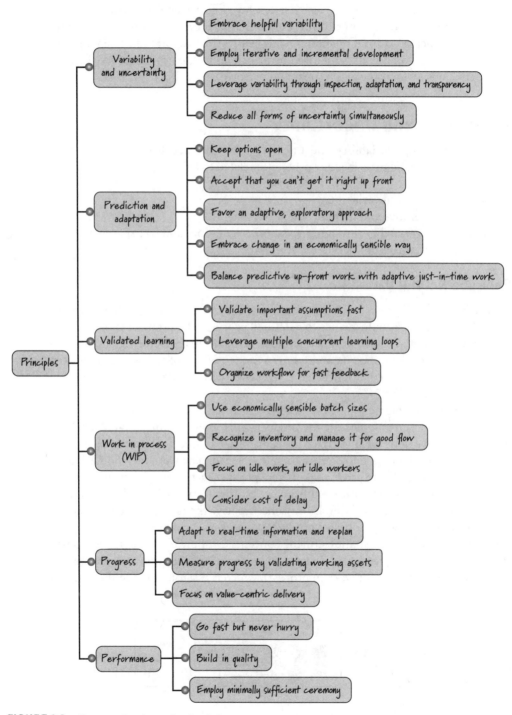

FIGURE 3.2 Categorization of principles

I start by discussing principles that leverage the variability and uncertainty inherent in product development. This is followed by a discussion of principles that deal with balancing up-front prediction with just-in-time adaptation. Then, I discuss principles focused on learning, followed by principles for managing the work in process. I conclude by focusing on progress and performance principles.

Variability and Uncertainty

Scrum leverages the **variability** and **uncertainty** in product development to create innovative solutions. I describe four principles related to this topic:

- Embrace helpful variability.
- Employ iterative and incremental development.
- Leverage variability through inspection, adaptation, and transparency.
- Reduce all forms of uncertainty simultaneously.

Embrace Helpful Variability

Plan-driven processes treat product development like manufacturing—they shun variability and encourage conformance to a **defined process**. The problem is that product development is not at all like product manufacturing. In manufacturing our goal is to take a fixed set of requirements and follow a sequential set of well-understood steps to manufacture a finished product that is the same (within a defined variance range) every time (see Figure 3.3).

In product development, however, the goal is to create the unique *single instance* of the product, not to *manufacture* the product. This single instance is analogous to a unique recipe. We don't want to create the same recipe twice; if we do, we have wasted our money. Instead, we want to create a unique recipe for a new product. Some amount of variability is necessary to produce a different product each time. In fact, every feature we build within a product is different from every other feature within that product, so we need variability even at this level. Only once we have the recipe do we manufacture the product—in the case of software products, as easily as copying bits.

That being said, some manufacturing concepts do apply to product development and can and should be leveraged. For example, as I will discuss shortly, recognizing and managing **inventory** (or work in process), which is essential to manufacturing, is

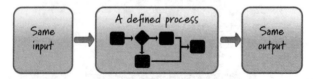

FIGURE 3.3   Defined process

also essential in product development. By the very nature of the work involved, however, product development and product manufacturing are not at all the same thing and as such require very different processes.

Employ Iterative and Incremental Development

Plan-driven, sequential development assumes that we will get things right up front and that most or all of the product pieces will come together late in the effort.

Scrum, on the other hand, is based on **iterative and incremental development**. Although these two terms are frequently used as if they were a single concept, iterative development is actually distinct from incremental development.

Iterative development acknowledges that we will probably get things wrong before we get them right and that we will do things poorly before we do them well (Goldberg and Rubin 1995). As such, iterative development is a planned rework strategy. We use multiple passes to improve what we are building so that we can converge on a good solution. For example, we might start by creating a prototype to acquire important knowledge about a poorly known piece of the product. Then we might create a revised version that is somewhat better, which might in turn be followed by a pretty good version. In the course of writing this book, for example, I wrote and rewrote each of the chapters several times as I received feedback and as my understanding of how I wanted to communicate a topic improved.

Iterative development is an excellent way to improve the product as it is being developed. The biggest downside to iterative development is that in the presence of uncertainty it can be difficult up front to determine (plan) how many improvement passes will be necessary.

Incremental development is based on the age-old principle of "Build some of it before you build all of it." We avoid having one large, *big-bang-style* event at the end of development where all the pieces come together and the entire product is delivered. Instead, we break the product into smaller pieces so that we can build some of it, learn how each piece is to survive in the environment in which it must exist, adapt based on what we learn, and then build more of it. While writing this book, I wrote a chapter at a time and sent each chapter out for review as it was completed, rather than trying to receive feedback on the entire book at once. This gave me the opportunity to incorporate that feedback into future chapters, adjusting my tone, style, or delivery as needed. It also gave me the opportunity to learn incrementally and apply what I learned from earlier chapters to later chapters.

Incremental development gives us important information that allows us to adapt our development effort and to change how we proceed. The biggest drawback to incremental development is that by building in pieces, we risk missing the big picture (we see the trees but not the forest).

Scrum leverages the benefits of both iterative and incremental development, while negating the disadvantages of using them individually. Scrum does this by using both ideas in an adaptive series of timeboxed iterations called sprints (see Figure 3.4).

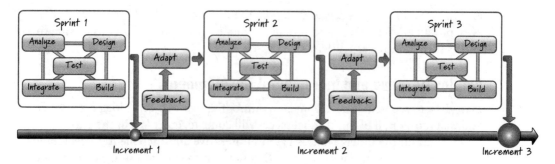

FIGURE 3.4   Scrum uses iterative and incremental development.

During each sprint we perform all of the activities necessary to create a working product increment (some of the product, not all of it). This is illustrated in Figure 3.4 by showing that some analysis, design, build, integration, and test work is completed in each sprint. This all-at-once approach has the benefit of quickly validating the assumptions that are made when developing product features. For example, we make some design decisions, create some code based on those decisions, and then test the design and code—all in the same sprint. By doing all of the related work within one sprint, we are able to quickly rework features, thus achieving the benefits of iterative development, without having to specifically plan for additional iterations.

A misuse of the sprint concept is to focus each sprint on just one type of work—for example, sprint 1 (analysis), sprint 2 (design), sprint 3 (coding), and sprint 4 (testing). Such an approach attempts to overlay Scrum with a waterfall-style work breakdown structure. I often refer to this misguided approach as **WaterScrum**, and I have heard others refer to it as **Scrummerfall**.

In Scrum, we don't work on a phase at a time; we work on a feature at a time. So, by the end of a sprint we have created a valuable product increment (some but not all of the product features). That increment includes or is integrated and tested with any previously developed features; otherwise, it is not considered done. For example, increment 2 in Figure 3.4 includes the features of increment 1. At the end of the sprint, we can get feedback on the newly completed features within the context of already completed features. This helps us view the product from more of a big-picture perspective than we might otherwise have.

We receive feedback on the sprint results, which allows us to adapt. We can choose different features to work on in the next sprint or alter the process we will use to build the next set of features. In some cases, we might learn that the increment, though it technically fits the bill, isn't as good as it could be. When that happens, we can schedule rework for a future sprint as part of our commitment to iterative development and continuous improvement. This helps overcome the issue of not knowing up front exactly how many improvement passes we will need. Scrum does not require that we predetermine a set number of iterations. The continuous stream of feedback will guide us to do the appropriate and economically sensible number of iterations while developing the product incrementally.

Leverage Variability through Inspection, Adaptation, and Transparency

Plan-driven processes and Scrum are fundamentally different along several dimensions (see Table 3.1, based on dimensions suggested by Reinertsen 2009a).

A plan-driven, sequential development process assumes little or no output variability. It follows a well-defined set of steps and uses only small amounts of feedback late in the process. In contrast, Scrum embraces the fact that in product development, some level of variability is required in order to build something new. Scrum also assumes that the process necessary to create the product is complex and therefore would defy a complete up-front definition. Furthermore, it generates early and frequent feedback to ensure that the right product is built and that the product is built right.

At the heart of Scrum are the principles of **inspection, adaptation,** and **transparency** (referred to collectively by Schwaber and Beedle 2001 as **empirical process control**). In Scrum, we inspect and adapt not only what we are building but also how we are building it (see Figure 3.5).

To do this well, we rely on transparency: all of the information that is important to producing a product must be available to the people involved in creating the product. Transparency makes inspection possible, which is needed for adaptation. Transparency also allows everyone concerned to observe and understand what is happening. It leads to more communication and it establishes trust (both in the process and among team members).

TABLE 3.1   Comparison of Plan-Driven and Scrum Processes

Dimension	Plan-Driven	Scrum
Degree of process definition	Well-defined set of sequential steps	Complex process that would defy a complete up-front definition
Randomness of output	Little or no output variability	Expect variability because we are not trying to build the same thing over and over
Amount of feedback used	Little and late	Frequent and early

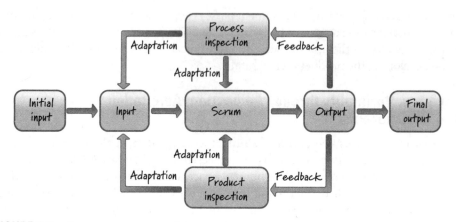

FIGURE 3.5 Scrum process model

Reduce All Forms of Uncertainty Simultaneously

Developing new products is a complex endeavor with a high degree of uncertainty. That uncertainty can be divided into two broad categories (Laufer 1996):

- **End uncertainty** (*what* uncertainty)—uncertainty surrounding the features of the final product
- **Means uncertainty** (*how* uncertainty)—uncertainty surrounding the process and technologies used to develop a product

In particular environments or with particular products there might also be **customer uncertainty** (*who* uncertainty). For example, start-up organizations (including large organizations that focus on novel products) may only have assumptions as to who the actual customers of their products will be. This uncertainty must be addressed or they might build brilliant products for the wrong markets.

Traditional, sequential development processes focus first on eliminating all end uncertainty by fully defining up front what is to be built, and only then addressing means uncertainty.

This simplistic, linear approach to uncertainty reduction is ill suited to the complex domain of product development, where our actions and the environment in which we operate mutually constrain one another. For example:

- We decide to build a feature (our action).
- We then show that feature to a customer, who, once he sees it, changes his mind about what he really wants, or realizes that he did not adequately convey the details of the feature (our action elicits a response from the environment).

- We make design changes based on the feedback (the environment's reaction influences us to take another unforeseen action).

In Scrum, we do not constrain ourselves by fully addressing one type of uncertainty before we address the next type. Instead, we take a more holistic approach and focus on simultaneously reducing all uncertainties (end, means, customer, and so on). Of course, at any point in time we might focus more on one type of uncertainty than another. Simultaneously addressing multiple types of uncertainty is facilitated by iterative and incremental development and guided by constant inspection, adaptation, and transparency. Such an approach allows us to opportunistically probe and explore our environment to identify and learn about the **unknown unknowns** (the things that we don't yet know that we don't know) as they emerge.

Prediction and Adaptation

When using Scrum, we are constantly balancing the desire for prediction with the need for adaptation. I describe five agile principles related to this topic:

- Keep options open.
- Accept that you can't get it right up front.
- Favor an adaptive, exploratory approach.
- Embrace change in an economically sensible way.
- Balance predictive up-front work with adaptive just-in-time work.

Keep Options Open

Plan-driven, sequential development requires that important decisions in areas like requirements or design be made, reviewed, and approved within their respective phases. Furthermore, these decisions must be made before we can transition to the next phase, even if those decisions are based on limited knowledge.

Scrum contends that we should never make a premature decision just because a generic process would dictate that now is the appointed time to make one. Instead, when using Scrum, we favor a strategy of keeping our options open. Often this principle is referred to as the **last responsible moment** (**LRM**) (Poppendieck and Poppendieck 2003), meaning that we delay commitment and do not make important and irreversible decisions until the last responsible moment. And when is that? When the cost of not making a decision becomes greater than the cost of making a decision (see Figure 3.6). At that moment, we make the decision.

To appreciate this principle, consider this. On the first day of a product development effort we have the least information about what we are doing. On each subsequent day of the development effort, we learn a little more. Why, then, would we ever choose to make all of the most critical, and perhaps irreversible, decisions on the first

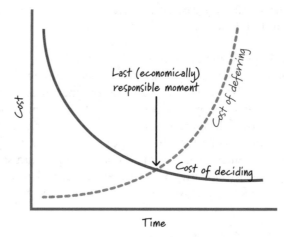

FIGURE 3.6   Make decisions at the last responsible moment.

day or very early on? Most of us would prefer to wait until we have more information so that we can make a more informed decision. When dealing with important or irreversible decisions, if we decide too early and are wrong, we will be on the exponential part of the cost-of-deciding curve in Figure 3.6. As we acquire a better understanding regarding the decision, the cost of deciding declines (the likelihood of making a bad decision declines because of increasing market or technical certainty). That's why we should wait until we have better information before committing to a decision.

Accept That You Can't Get It Right Up Front

Plan-driven processes not only mandate full requirements and a complete plan; they also assume that we can "get it right" up front. The reality is that it is very unlikely that we can get all of the requirements, or the detailed plans based on those requirements, correct up front. What's worse is that when the requirements do change, we have to modify the baseline requirements and plans to match the current reality (more about this in Chapter 5).

In Scrum, we acknowledge that we can't get all of the requirements or the plans right up front. In fact, we believe that trying to do so could be dangerous because we are likely missing important knowledge, leading to the creation of a large quantity of low-quality requirements (see Figure 3.7).

This figure illustrates that when using a plan-driven, sequential process, a large number of requirements are produced early on when we have the least cumulative knowledge about the product. This approach is risky, because there is an illusion that we have eliminated end uncertainty. It is also potentially very wasteful when our understanding improves or things change (as I will describe shortly).

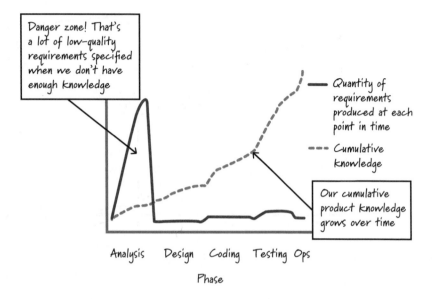

FIGURE 3.7   Plan-driven requirements acquisition relative to product knowledge

With Scrum, we still produce some requirements and plans up front, but just sufficiently, and with the assumption that we will fill in the details of those requirements and plans as we learn more about the product we are building. After all, even if we think we're 100% certain about what to build and how to organize up front the work to build it, we will learn where we are wrong as soon as we subject our early incremental deliverables to the environment in which they must exist. At that point all of the inconvenient realities of what is really needed will drive us to make changes.

Favor an Adaptive, Exploratory Approach

Plan-driven, sequential processes focus on using (or exploiting) what is currently known and predicting what isn't known. Scrum favors a more adaptive, trial-and-error approach based on appropriate use of exploration.

Exploration refers to times when we choose to gain knowledge by doing some activity, such as building a prototype, creating a proof of concept, performing a study, or conducting an experiment. In other words, when faced with uncertainty, we buy information by exploring.

Our tools and technologies significantly influence the cost of exploration. Historically software product development exploration has been expensive, a fact that favored a more predictive, try-to-get-it-right-up-front approach (see Figure 3.8).

As an example, in my freshman year at Georgia Tech (early 1980s), I (briefly) used punch cards—a tool that, like a typewriter, made you loathe to make any

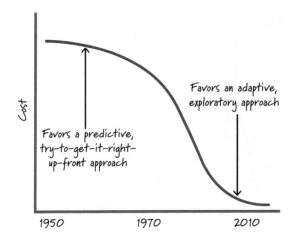

FIGURE 3.8   Historical cost of exploration

mistakes or modifications. It was hard to embrace the concept of "Let's quickly try that out and see what happens" when, with each potential solution, you had to painstakingly create punch cards, get in the queue for the mainframe, and wait up to 24 hours to get validation of your solution. Even the cost of a simple typo was at least a day in the schedule. A waterfall-style process that allowed for careful consideration of current knowledge and prediction in the presence of uncertainty in an attempt to arrive at a good solution just made economic sense.

Fortunately, tools and technologies have gotten better and the cost of exploring has come way down. There is no longer an economic disincentive to explore. In fact, nowadays, it's often cheaper to adapt to user feedback based on building something fast than it is to invest in trying to get everything right up front. Good thing, too, because the context (the surrounding technologies) in which our solutions must exist is getting increasingly more complex.

In Scrum, if we have enough knowledge to make an informed, reasonable step forward with our solution, we advance. However, when faced with uncertainty, rather than trying to predict it away, we use low-cost exploration to buy relevant information that we can then use to make an informed, reasonable step forward with our solution. The feedback from our action will help us determine if and when we need further exploration.

Embrace Change in an Economically Sensible Way

When using sequential development, change, as we have all learned, is substantially more expensive late than it is early on (see Figure 3.9, based on Boehm 1981).

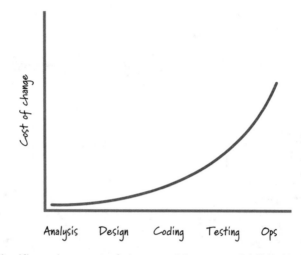

FIGURE 3.9 Significant late cost of change with sequential development

As an example, a change made during analysis might cost $1; that same change made late during testing might cost $1,000. Why is this so? If we make a mistake during analysis and find it during analysis, it is an inexpensive fix. If that same error is not found until design, we have to fix not only the incorrect requirement, but potentially parts of our design based on the wrong requirement. This compounding of the error continues through each subsequent phase, making what might have been a small error to correct during analysis into a much larger error to correct in testing or operations.

To avoid late changes, sequential processes seek to carefully control and minimize any changing requirements or designs by improving the accuracy of the predictions about what the system needs to do or how it is supposed to do it.

Unfortunately, being excessively predictive in early-activity phases often has the opposite effect. It not only fails to eliminate change; it actually contributes to deliveries that are late and over budget as well. Why this paradoxical truth? First, the desire to eliminate expensive change forces us to overinvest in each phase—doing more work than is necessary and practical. Second, we're forced to make decisions based on important assumptions early in the process, before we have validated these assumptions with feedback from our stakeholders based on our working assets. As a result, we produce a large inventory of work products based on these assumptions. Later, this inventory will likely have to be corrected or discarded as we validate (or invalidate) our assumptions, or change happens (for example, requirements emerge or evolve), as it always will. This fits the classic pattern of a self-fulfilling prophecy (see Figure 3.10).

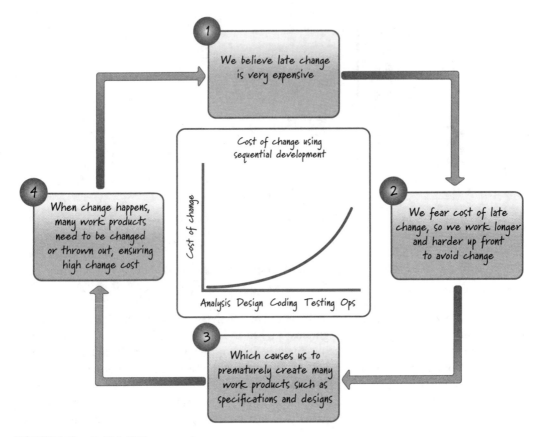

FIGURE 3.10   Self-fulfilling prophecy

In Scrum, we assume that change is the norm. We believe that we can't predict away the inherent uncertainty that exists during product development by working longer and harder up front. Thus, we must be prepared to embrace change. And when that change occurs, we want the economics to be more appealing than with traditional development, even when the change happens later in the product development effort.

Our goal, therefore, is to keep the cost-of-change curve flat for as long as possible—making it economically sensible to embrace even late change. Figure 3.11 illustrates this idea.

We can achieve that goal by managing the amount of work in process and the flow of that work so that the cost of change when using Scrum is less affected by time than it is with sequential projects.

Regardless of which product development approach we use, we want the following relationship to be true: a small change in requirements should yield a proportionally

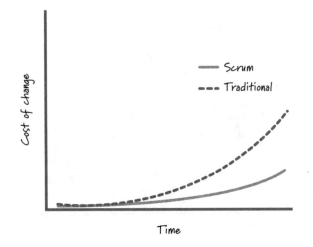

FIGURE 3.11   Flattening the cost-of-change curve

small change in implementation and therefore in cost (obviously we would expect a larger change to cost more). Another desirable property of this relationship is that we want it to be true regardless of *when* the change request is made.

With Scrum, we produce many work products (such as detailed requirements, designs, and test cases) in a just-in-time fashion, avoiding the creation of potentially unnecessary artifacts. As a result, when a change is made, there are typically far fewer artifacts or constraining decisions based on assumptions that might be discarded or reworked, thus keeping the cost more proportional to the size of the requested change.

Using sequential development, the early creation of artifacts and push for premature decision making ultimately mean that the cost of a change rises rapidly over time as inventory grows. This causes the inflection point (where the line begins to aggressively climb up) on the traditional curve in Figure 3.11 to occur early. When developing with Scrum, there does come a time when the cost of change will no longer be proportional to the size of the request, but this point in time (as illustrated by the inflection point on the Scrum curve in Figure 3.11) occurs later.

Balance Predictive Up-Front Work with Adaptive Just-in-Time Work

A fundamental belief of plan-driven development is that detailed up-front requirements and planning are critical and should be completed before moving on to later stages. In Scrum, we believe that up-front work should be helpful without being excessive.

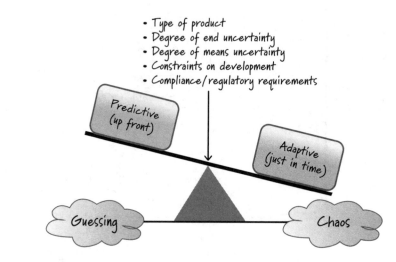

FIGURE 3.12   Balancing predictive and adaptive work

With Scrum, we acknowledge that it is not possible to get requirements and plans precisely right up front. Does that mean we should do no requirements or planning work up front? Of course not! Scrum is about finding balance—balance between predictive up-front work and adaptive just-in-time work (see Figure 3.12, adapted from a picture by Cohn 2009).

When developing a product, the balance point should be set in an economically sensible way to maximize the amount of ongoing adaptation based on fast feedback and minimize the amount of up-front prediction, while still meeting compliance, regulatory, and/or corporate objectives.

Exactly how that balance is achieved is driven in part by the type of product being built, the degree of uncertainty that exists in both what we want to build (end uncertainty) and how we want to build it (means uncertainty), and the constraints placed on the development. Being overly predictive would require us to make many assumptions in the presence of great uncertainty. Being overly adaptive could cause us to live in a state of constant change, making our work feel inefficient and chaotic. To rapidly develop innovative products we need to operate in a space where adaptability is counterbalanced by just enough prediction to keep us from sliding into chaos. The Scrum framework operates well at this balance point of order and chaos.

Validated Learning

When using Scrum, we organize the work to quickly create **validated learning** (a term proposed by Ries 2011). We acquire validated learning when we obtain knowledge that confirms or refutes an assumption that we have made. I describe three agile principles related to this topic:

- Validate important assumptions fast.
- Leverage multiple concurrent learning loops.
- Organize workflow for fast feedback.

Validate Important Assumptions Fast

An **assumption** is a guess, or belief, that is assumed to be true, real, or certain even though we have no validated learning to know that it is true. Plan-driven development is much more tolerant of long-lived assumptions than Scrum. Using plan-driven development, we produce extensive up-front requirements and plans that likely embed many important assumptions, ones that won't be validated until a much later phase of development.

Assumptions represent a significant development **risk**. In Scrum, we try to minimize the number of important assumptions that exist at any time. We also don't want to let important assumptions exist without validation for very long. The combination of iterative and incremental development along with a focus on low-cost exploration can be used to validate assumptions fast. As a result, if we make a fundamentally bad assumption when using Scrum, we will likely discover our mistake quickly and have a chance to recover from it. In plan-driven, sequential development, the same bad assumption if validated late might cause a substantial or total failure of the development effort.

Leverage Multiple Concurrent Learning Loops

There is learning that occurs when using sequential development. However, an important form of learning happens only after features have been built, integrated, and tested, which means considerable learning occurs toward the end of the effort. Late learning provides reduced benefits because there may be insufficient time to leverage the learning or the cost to leverage it might be too high.

In Scrum, we understand that constant learning is a key to our success. When using Scrum, we identify and exploit feedback loops to increase learning. A recurring pattern in this style of product development is to make an assumption (or set a goal), build something (perform some activities), get feedback on what we built, and then use that feedback to inspect what we did relative to what we assumed. We then make adaptations to the product, process, and/or our beliefs based on what we learned (see Figure 3.13).

Scrum leverages several predefined **learning loops**. For example, the daily scrum is a daily loop and the sprint review is an iteration-level loop. I will describe these and others in subsequent chapters.

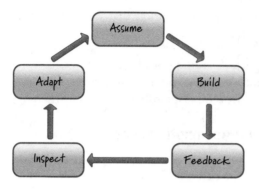

FIGURE 3.13   Learning loop pattern

The Scrum framework is also flexible enough to embrace many other learning loops. For example, although not specified by Scrum, technical practice feedback loops, such as pair programming (feedback in seconds) and test-driven development (feedback in minutes), are frequently used with Scrum development.

Organize Workflow for Fast Feedback

Being tolerant of long-lived assumptions also makes plan-driven processes tolerant of late learning, so **fast feedback** is not a focus. With Scrum, we strive for fast feedback, because it is critical for helping truncate wrong paths sooner and is vital for quickly uncovering and exploiting time-sensitive, emergent opportunities.

In a plan-driven development effort, every activity is planned to occur at an appointed time based on the well-defined phase sequence. This approach assumes that earlier activities can be completed without the feedback generated by later activities. As a result, there might be a long period of time between doing something and getting feedback on what we did (hence closing the learning loop).

Let's use component **integration** and testing as an example. Say we are developing three components in parallel. At some time these components have to be integrated and tested before we have a shippable product. Until we try to do the integration, we really don't know whether we have developed the components correctly. Attempting the integration will provide critical feedback on the component development work.

Using sequential development, integration and testing wouldn't happen until the predetermined downstream phase, where many or all components would be integrated. Unfortunately, the idea that we can develop a bunch of components in parallel and then later, in an integration phase, smoothly bring them together into a cohesive whole is unlikely to work out. In fact, even with well-conceived interfaces defined before we develop the components, it's likely that something will go wrong when we integrate them (see Figure 3.14).

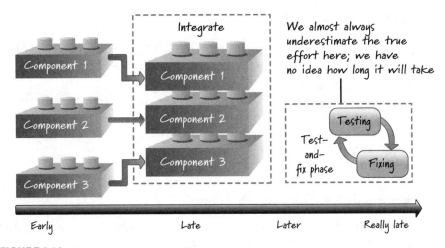

FIGURE 3.14   Component integration

Feedback-generating activities that occur a long time after development have unfortunate side effects, such as turning integration into a large test-and-fix phase, because components developed disjointedly from each other frequently don't integrate smoothly. How long it will take and how much it will cost to fix the problem can only be guessed at this point.

In Scrum, we organize the flow of work to move through the learning loop in Figure 3.13 and get to feedback as quickly as possible. In doing so, we ensure that feedback-generating activities occur in close time proximity to the original work. Fast feedback provides superior economic benefits because errors compound when we delay feedback, resulting in exponentially larger failures.

Let's look again at our component integration example. When we designed the components, we made important assumptions about how they would integrate. Based on those assumptions, we proceeded down a design path. We do not, at this point, know whether the selected design path is right or wrong. It's just our best guess.

Once we choose a path, however, we then make many other decisions that are based on that choice. The longer we wait to validate the original design assumption, the greater the number of dependent decisions. If we later determine (via feedback during the integration phase) that the original assumption was wrong, we'll have a large, compounded mess on our hands. Not only will we have many bad decisions that have to be reworked; we'll also have to do it after a great deal of time has passed. Because people's memories will have faded, they will spend time getting back up to speed on the work they did earlier.

When we factor in the total cost of reworking potentially bad dependent decisions, and the cost of the delay to the product, the economic benefits of fast feedback are very compelling. Fast feedback closes the learning loop quickly, allowing us to truncate bad development paths before they can cause serious economic damage.

Work in Process (WIP)

Work in process (or **WIP**) refers to the work that has been started but not yet finished. During product development WIP must be recognized and properly managed. I describe four agile principles related to this topic:

- Use economically sensible batch sizes.
- Recognize inventory and manage it for good flow.
- Focus on idle work, not idle workers.
- Consider cost of delay.

Use Economically Sensible Batch Sizes

Another core belief underlying plan-driven, sequential development processes is that it is preferable to batch up all of one type of work and perform it in a single phase. I refer to this as the **all-before-any** approach, where we complete all (or substantially all) of one activity before starting the next. Let's say we create all of the requirements during the analysis phase. Next, we move the batch of requirements into the design phase. Because we generated the complete set of requirements, our **batch size** in this example is 100%.

The all-before-any approach is, in part, a consequence of believing that the old manufacturing principle of economies of scale applies to product development. This principle states that the cost of producing a unit will go down as we increase the number of units (the batch size) that are produced. So, the sequential development belief is that larger batches in product development will also realize economies of scale.

In Scrum, we accept that although economies-of-scale thinking has been a bedrock principle in manufacturing, applying it dogmatically to product development will cause significant economic harm.

As counterintuitive as it might sound, working in smaller batches during product development has many benefits. Reinertsen discusses batch-size issues in depth, and Table 3.2 includes a subset of the small-batch-size benefits that he describes (Reinertsen 2009b).

If small batches are better than large batches, shouldn't we just use a batch size of one, meaning that we work on only one requirement at a time and flow it through all of the activities until it is done and ready for a customer? Some people refer to this as **single-piece flow**. As I will show in later chapters, a batch size of one might be appropriate in some cases, but assuming that "one" is the goal might suboptimize the flow and our overall economics.

TABLE 3.2   Reinertsen Benefits of Small Batch Sizes

Benefit	Description
Reduced cycle time	Smaller batches yield smaller amounts of work waiting to be processed, which in turn means less time waiting for the work to get done. So, we get things done faster.
Reduced flow variability	Think of a restaurant where small parties come and go (they flow nicely through the restaurant). Now imagine a large tour bus (large batch) unloading and the effect that it has on the flow in the restaurant.
Accelerated feedback	Small batches accelerate fast feedback, making the consequences of a mistake smaller.
Reduced risk	Small batches represent less inventory that is subject to change. Smaller batches are also less likely to fail (there is a greater risk that a failure will occur with ten pieces of work than with five).
Reduced overhead	There is overhead in managing large batches—for example, maintaining a list of 3,000 work items requires more effort than a list of 30.
Increased motivation and urgency	Small batches provide focus and a sense of responsibility. It is much easier to understand the effect of delays and failure when dealing with small versus large batches.
Reduced cost and schedule growth	When we're wrong on big batches, we are wrong in a big way with respect to cost and schedule. When we do things on a small scale, we won't be wrong by much.

Recognize Inventory and Manage It for Good Flow

Throughout this chapter, I have been reminding you that manufacturing and product development are not the same thing and thus should be approached differently. There is, however, one lesson that manufacturing has learned that we should apply to product development and yet often do not. That lesson has to do with the high cost of inventory, also known as work in process or WIP. The lean product development community has known for many years of the importance of WIP (Poppendieck and Poppendieck 2003; Reinertsen 2009b), and Scrum teams embrace this concept.

Manufacturers are acutely aware of their inventories and the financial implications of those inventories. How can they not be? Inventory quickly starts to pile up on the floor, waiting to be processed. Not only is factory inventory physically visible; it is also financially visible. Ask the CFO of a manufacturing company how much inventory (or WIP) he has in the factory or how much it has changed in the past month and he can give a definitive answer.

No competent manufacturer sits on a large quantity of inventory. Parts that are sitting on the factory floor waiting to be put into finished goods are depreciating on the financial books. Worse yet, what happens if we purchase a truckload of parts, and then change the design of the product? What do we do with all of those parts? Maybe we rework the parts so that they fit into the new design. Or worse, maybe we discard the parts because they can no longer be used. Or, to avoid incurring waste on the parts we already purchased, are we going to not change our design (even though doing so would be the correct design choice) so we can use those parts—at the risk of producing a less satisfying product?

It's obvious that if we sit on a lot of inventory and then something changes, we experience one or more forms of significant waste. To minimize risks, competent manufacturers manage inventory in an economically sensible way—they keep some inventory on hand but use a healthy dose of just-in-time inventory management.

Product development organizations, generally speaking, are not nearly as cognizant of their work in process. Part of the problem stems from the fact that in product development we deal with knowledge assets that aren't physically visible in the same way as parts on the factory floor. Knowledge assets are far less intrusive, such as code on a disk, a document in a file cabinet, or a visual board on the wall.

Inventory in product development is also typically not financially visible. Ask a CFO of a product development organization how much inventory exists in the product development organization and he will likely give you a puzzled look and say, "None." While the financial team is tracking other measures of a product development effort, it won't likely be tracking product development inventory of this type.

Unfortunately, inventory (WIP) is a critical variable to be managed during product development, and the traditional approaches to product development don't focus on managing it. As I mentioned in the discussion of batch sizes, by setting the batch size to be quite large (frequently 100%), traditional development actually favors the creation of large amounts of inventory. An important consequence of having a lot of WIP in product development is that it significantly affects the cost-of-change curve I described earlier (see Figure 3.9).

Although we need some requirements if we are going to start development, we don't need to have *all* of the requirements. If we have too many requirements, we will likely experience inventory waste when requirements change. On the other hand, if we don't have enough requirements inventory, we will disrupt the fast flow of work, which is also a form of waste. In Scrum, our goal is to find the proper balance between just enough inventory and too much inventory.

It is important to realize that requirements are just one form of inventory that exists in product development. There are many different places and times during product development where we have WIP. We need to proactively identify and manage those as well.

Focus on Idle Work, Not Idle Workers

In Scrum, we believe that idle work is far more wasteful and economically damaging than idle workers. **Idle work** is work that we want to do (such as building or testing something) but can't do because something is preventing us. Perhaps we are blocked waiting on another team to do something, and until that team completes its work, we can't do ours. Or maybe we just have so much work to do that it can't all be done at once. In this case, some of the work sits idle until we become available to work on it. **Idle workers**, on the other hand, are people who have available **capacity** to do more work because they are not currently 100% utilized.

Many product development organizations focus more on eliminating the waste of idle workers than on the waste of idle work. For example, in traditional thinking, if I hire you to be a tester, I expect you to spend 100% of your time testing. If you spend less than 100% of your time testing, I incur waste (you're idle when you could be testing). To avoid this problem, I will find you more testing work to do—perhaps by assigning you to multiple projects—to get your utilization up to 100%.

Unfortunately, this approach reduces one form of waste (idle-worker waste) while simultaneously increasing another form of waste (idle-work waste). And, most of the time, the cost of the idle work is far greater than the cost of an idle worker. Let's explore why this is true.

To illustrate the issue, let's apply the keep-workers-100%-busy strategy to the 4 × 100-meter relay race at the Olympics. Based on the keep-them-busy strategy, this race seems highly inefficient. I pay people to run and they seem to be running only one-quarter of the time. The rest of the time they are just standing around. Well, that's not right! I pay them 100% salary so I want them to run 100% of the time. How about if when they're not carrying the baton, they just run up and down the stands or perhaps run another race on an adjacent track? That way they will be utilized 100% at running.

Of course, we all know that you don't win the relay gold medal by keeping the runners 100% busy. You win the gold medal by getting the baton across the finish line first. So, the important takeaway is "Watch the baton, not the runners" (Larman and Vodde 2009). In the context of product development, the baton sitting on the ground equates to work that is ready to be performed but is blocked waiting for necessary resources. You don't win the race (deliver products) when the baton is on the ground. (I really like the baton and runner analogy because it nicely illustrates that we should watch the work and not the workers. However, like any analogy, it has its limits. In this case, the relay-race approach to handing off work is precisely one aspect of traditional, sequential product development that we would like to avoid!)

Also, everyone knows the consequences of keeping a resource 100% busy. If we borrow a graph from queuing theory, we can see the obvious damage caused when striving for 100% utilization (see Figure 3.15).

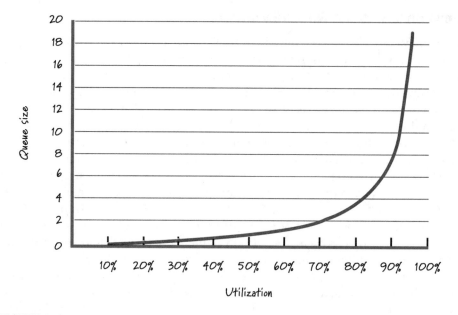

FIGURE 3.15   How utilization affects queue size (delay)

Anyone who owns a computer understands this graph. What happens if you run your computer at 100% (full processor and memory utilization)? It starts to thrash and every job on the computer slows down. In other words, the computer is working on more things and actually gets less productive work completed. Once you get into that state, it is very difficult to get out of it (you probably have to start killing jobs or reboot the machine). Your computer would be much more efficient if you ran it at closer to 80% utilization. In Figure 3.15, **queue** size equates to delay and delay to the baton sitting on the ground.

The idle work (delayed work) grows exponentially once we get into the high levels of utilization. And that idle work can be very expensive, frequently many times more expensive than the cost of idle workers (see the next section on cost of delay for an example). So, in Scrum, we are acutely aware that finding the bottlenecks in the flow of work and focusing our efforts on eliminating them is a far more economically sensible activity than trying to keep everyone 100% busy.

Consider Cost of Delay

Cost of delay is the financial cost associated with delaying work or delaying achievement of a milestone. Figure 3.15 illustrates that as capacity utilization increases, queue size and delay also increase. Therefore, by reducing the waste of idle workers (by increasing their utilization), we simultaneously increase the waste associated with idle work (work sitting in queues waiting to be serviced). Using cost of delay, we can calculate which waste is more economically damaging.

Unfortunately, 85% of organizations don't quantify cost of delay (Reinertsen 2009b). Combine that with the fact that most development organizations don't realize they have accumulated work (inventory) sitting in queues, and it is easy to see why their default behavior is to focus on eliminating the visible waste of idle workers.

Here is a simple example to illustrate why the cost of idle work is typically much greater than the cost of idle workers. Consider this question: Should we assign a documenter to the team on the first day of development or at the end of development? Table 3.3 illustrates a comparison of these two options (there are other options we could use).

Assume that we assign the documenter full-time for 12 months to work on this product, even if he is not needed 100% of the time. Doing so costs an incremental $75K (think of this as idle worker waste) above what it would cost if we brought him on for two months at the end once the product reaches the state of "all but documented."

If we assign the documenter to do all of the documentation at the end, we will need him full-time for only two months, but we will also delay the delivery of the

TABLE 3.3   Example Cost-of-Delay Calculation

Parameter	Value
Duration with full-time documenter	12 months
Duration with documenter assigned at the end (when we reach the state of "all but documented")	14 months
Cycle-time cost for doing documentation at the end	2 months
Cost of delay, per month	$250K
Total cost of delay	**$500K**
Annual fully burdened cost of documenter	$90K
Monthly fully burdened cost of documenter	$7.5K
Cost for full-time documenter	$90K
Cost for documenter if assigned at end	$15K
Incremental cost for full-time documenter	**$75K**

product by the same two months. If we delay shipping the product by two months, the calculated cost of delay in terms of lifecycle profits is $500K (**lifecycle profits** are the total profit potential of a product over its lifetime; in this example, that potential decreases by $500K).

In this example, the cost of the idle worker is $75K and the cost of the idle work is $500K. If we focus on optimizing the utilization of the documenter, we will substantially suboptimize the economics of the overall product. During product development we are presented with these types of trade-offs on a continuous basis; cost of delay will be one of the most important variables to consider when making economically sensible decisions.

Progress

When using Scrum, we measure progress by what we have delivered and validated, not by how we are proceeding according to the predefined plan or how far we are into a particular phase or stage of development. I describe three agile principles related to this topic:

- Adapt to real-time information and replan.
- Measure progress by validating working assets.
- Focus on value-centric delivery.

Adapt to Real-Time Information and Replan

In a plan-driven, sequential process, the plan is the authoritative source on how and when work should occur. As such, conformance to the plan is expected. In contrast, in Scrum we believe that unbridled faith in the plan will frequently blind us to the fact that the plan might be wrong.

On a Scrum development effort our goal is not to conform to some plan, some up-front prediction of how we thought things might go. Instead, our goal is to rapidly replan and adapt to the stream of economically important information that is continuously arriving during the development effort.

Measure Progress by Validating Working Assets

Progress during a sequential, plan-driven development effort is demonstrated by completing a phase and being permitted to enter the next phase. As a result, if each phase starts and completes as expected, the product development effort might seem to be progressing quite well. Yet in the end, the product we created in full accordance with the plan might deliver far less customer value than anticipated. Can we really claim success if we finish on time and on budget and yet fail to meet customer expectations?

With Scrum, we measure progress by building working, validated assets that deliver value and that can be used to validate important assumptions. This gives us the feedback to know what the right next step is. In Scrum, it's not about how much work we start; it's all about what customer-valuable work we finish.

Focus on Value-Centric Delivery

Plan-driven, sequential development focuses on diligently following the process. By its very structure, the integration and delivery of features during sequential development happen at the end of the effort (see Figure 3.16). With this approach there is a risk that we will run out of resources (time or money) before we deliver all of the important value to our customers.

A related belief of traditional development is that the planning and document artifacts that get produced en route to delivering features are themselves valuable. If these artifacts are indeed valuable, most of the time they are valuable only to the downstream process and not the customers. And, if they are valuable to the customer, that value accrues only if a desirable product is ultimately delivered to the customer. Until that happens, these artifacts provide no direct customer value.

Scrum, on the other hand, is a customer-value-centric form of development. It is based on a prioritized, incremental model of delivery in which the highest-value features are continuously built and delivered in the next iteration. As a result, customers get a continuous flow of high-value features sooner.

In Scrum, value is generated by delivering working assets to customers, by validating important assumptions, or by acquiring valuable knowledge. In Scrum, we believe that the intermediate artifacts provide no perceived customer value and are merely a means to an end if they themselves cannot be used to generate important feedback or acquire important knowledge.

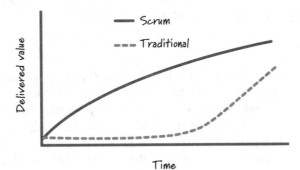

FIGURE 3.16   Deliver high-value features sooner.

Performance

There are specific performance-related characteristics we expect when using Scrum. I describe three agile principles related to this topic:

- Go fast but never hurry.
- Build in quality.
- Employ minimally sufficient ceremony.

Go Fast but Never Hurry

Plan-driven development believes that if we follow the plan and do things right the first time, we'll avoid costly and time-consuming rework. Moving from step to step quickly is of course desirable, but it isn't a principal goal.

In Scrum, one core goal is to be nimble, adaptable, and speedy. By going fast, we deliver fast, we get feedback fast, and we get value into the hands of our customers sooner. Learning and reacting quickly allow us to generate revenue and/or reduce costs sooner.

Do not, however, mistake going fast for being hurried. In Scrum, time is of the essence, but we don't rush to get things done. Doing so would likely violate the Scrum principle of **sustainable pace**—people should be able to work at a pace that they can continue for an extended period of time. In addition, hurrying will likely come at the expense of quality.

An example might help clarify the difference between fast and hurried. I study Muay Thai (Thai kickboxing). As is true of most martial arts, Muay Thai performance is enhanced with speed. Being able to swiftly and accurately perform katas or sparring enhances the pleasure of the sport and the outcome. However, hurrying through the movements with the intent of getting done substantially reduces their effectiveness and could cause serious bodily harm during sparring. When performing Muay Thai, you move swiftly, nimbly, and deliberately while quickly adapting to the situation. In other words, you need to be fast, but never hurried.

Build In Quality

During plan-driven development, the belief is that through careful, sequential performance of work we get a high-quality product. However, we can't actually verify this quality until we do the testing of the integrated product, which occurs during a late phase of the process. If testing should indicate that the quality is lacking, we then must enter the costly test-and-fix phase in an attempt to test quality in. Also, because a different team frequently works on each phase, the testing team is often viewed as owning the quality of the result.

In Scrum, quality isn't something a testing team "tests in" at the end; it is something that a cross-functional Scrum team owns and continuously builds in and verifies every sprint. Each increment of value that is created is completed to a high level of confidence and has the potential to be put into production or shipped to customers (see Chapter 4 for a deeper discussion of the definition of done). As a result, the need for any significant late testing to tack on quality is substantially reduced.

Employ Minimally Sufficient Ceremony

Plan-driven processes tend to be high-**ceremony**, document-centric, process-heavy approaches. A side effect of Scrum's being value-centric is that very little emphasis is put on process-centric ceremonies. I don't mean to imply that all ceremony is bad. For example, a "ceremony" of going to the pub to socialize and bond every Friday after work would be a good ceremony. I am referring to ceremony that is **unnecessary formality**. Some might call it "process for the sake of process." Such ceremony has a cost but adds little or no value (in other words, it's a type of waste).

Example ceremonies that might be unnecessary formality include the following:

- A three-day, heavyweight process is required for approving and migrating code from the development environment to the QA environment before we are allowed to start testing.
- All anomalies have to be logged into a software tool so that they can be tracked and reported, even if I could just tap on the shoulder of the person sitting next to me and say, "Hey, this isn't working; could you fix it?" and have him make a fix so I can continue my work.
- I write a document because now is the prescribed time to write that document, even though nobody can say why that document is necessary or valuable.

In Scrum, our goal is to eliminate unnecessary formality. Therefore, we set the ceremonial bar at a low level, one that is minimally sufficient (some call it barely sufficient) or good enough. Of course, what constitutes minimally sufficient or good enough can differ from organization to organization. If we're building a new social media website, our need for ceremony might be exceptionally low. On the other hand, if we're building a pacemaker and are subject to numerous governmental regulations that require specific types of ceremonies, the minimally sufficient bar will be set higher (see Figure 3.17).

Frequently the Scrum focus on minimally sufficient ceremony is misinterpreted to mean things like "Scrum is anti-documentation." Scrum isn't anti-documentation. Rather, when using Scrum, we adopt an economic perspective and carefully review which documents we create. If we write a document that is shelfware and adds no value, we have wasted our time and money creating a dead document. However, not all documents are dead. For example, we will likely write a document if

- It is a deliverable as part of the product (for example, installation instructions, user's guide, and so on)

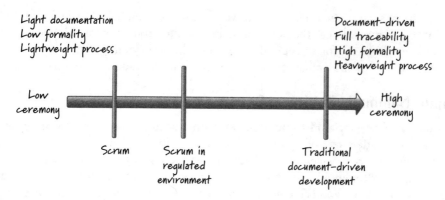

FIGURE 3.17   Ceremony scale

- Our goal is to capture an important discussion, decision, or agreement so that in the future we will have a clear recollection of what was discussed, decided, or agreed to
- It is the high-value way of helping new team members come up to speed quickly
- There is a regulatory requirement that a certain document be written (a cost of doing business in a regulated industry)

What we are trying to avoid is work that adds no short-term or long-term economic value. In Scrum, we believe that time and money are better spent delivering customer value.

Closing

In this chapter I focused on describing core agile principles—the fundamental beliefs that drive how we develop with Scrum. In doing so, I compared how these beliefs are different from the beliefs that underlie textbook, traditional, plan-driven, sequential development (which are summarized in Table 3.4).

My goal of making this comparison is not to convince you that waterfall is bad and that Scrum is good. Instead, my goal is to illustrate that the underlying beliefs of waterfall make it more appropriate to a different class of problem than Scrum. You can evaluate for yourself what type of problems your organization addresses and therefore which is the more appropriate tool to use. The subsequent chapters of this book will provide a detailed description of how these principles reinforce one another, providing a powerful approach to product development.

TABLE 3.4 Comparison Summary of Plan-Driven and Agile Principles

Topic	Plan-Driven Principle	Agile Principle
Similarity between development and manufacturing	Both follow a defined process.	Development isn't manufacturing; development creates the recipe for the product.
Process structure	Development is phase-based and sequential.	Development should be iterative and incremental.
Degree of process and product variability	Try to eliminate process and product variability.	Leverage variability through inspection, adaptation, and transparency.
Uncertainty management	Eliminate end uncertainty first, and then means uncertainty.	Reduce uncertainties simultaneously.
Decision making	Make each decision in its proper phase.	Keep options open.
Getting it right the first time	Assumes we have all of the correct information up front to create the requirements and plans.	We can't get it right up front.
Exploration versus exploitation	Exploit what is currently known and predict what isn't known.	Favor an adaptive, exploratory approach.
Change/emergence	Change is disruptive to plans and expensive, so it should be avoided.	Embrace change in an economically sensible way.
Predictive versus adaptive	The process is highly predictive.	Balance predictive up-front work with adaptive just-in-time work.
Assumptions (unvalidated knowledge)	The process is tolerant of long-lived assumptions.	Validate important assumptions fast.
Feedback	Critical learning occurs on one major analyze-design-code-test loop.	Leverage multiple concurrent learning loops.
Fast feedback	The process is tolerant of late learning.	Organize workflow for fast feedback.

continues

TABLE 3.4 Comparison Summary of Plan-Driven and Agile Principles (*Continued*)

Topic	Plan-Driven Principle	Agile Principle
Batch size (how much work is completed before the next activity can start)	Batches are large, frequently 100%—all before any. Economies of scale should apply.	Use smaller, economically sensible batch sizes.
Inventory/work in process (WIP)	Inventory isn't part of the belief system so is not a focus.	Recognize inventory and manage it to achieve good flow.
People versus work waste	Allocate people to achieve high levels of utilization.	Focus on idle work, not idle workers.
Cost of delay	Cost of delay is rarely considered.	Always consider cost of delay.
Conformance to plan	Conformance is considered a primary means of achieving a good result.	Adapt and replan rather than conform to a plan.
Progress	Demonstrate progress by progressing through stages or phases.	Measure progress by validating working assets.
Centricity	Process-centric—follow the process.	Value-centric—deliver the value.
Speed	Follow the process; do things right the first time and go fast.	Go fast but never hurry.
When we get high quality	Quality comes at the end, after an extensive test-and-fix phase.	Build quality in from the beginning.
Formality (ceremony)	Formality (well-defined procedures and checkpoints) is important to effective execution.	Employ minimally sufficient ceremony.

Chapter 4

SPRINTS

Scrum organizes work in iterations or cycles of up to a calendar month called sprints. This chapter provides a more detailed description of what sprints are. It then discusses several key characteristics of sprints: They are timeboxed, have a short and consistent duration, have a goal that shouldn't be altered once started, and must reach the end state specified by the team's definition of done.

Overview

Sprints are the skeleton of the Scrum framework (see Figure 4.1).

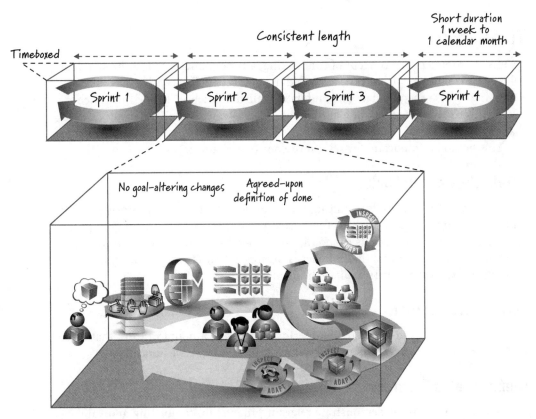

FIGURE 4.1 Sprints are the skeleton of the Scrum framework.

The gray main looping arrow in the figure, which stretches from the product backlog through the sprint execution loop and encompasses the Scrum team members, represents the sprint, on which the other Scrum artifacts and activities are shown oriented by their relative time of occurrence within the sprint. Although sprint execution is frequently confused with being "the sprint," it's really just one activity that occurs during the sprint, along with sprint planning, sprint review, and the sprint retrospective.

All sprints are timeboxed, meaning they have fixed start and end dates. Sprints must also be short, somewhere between one week and a calendar month in length. Sprints should be consistent in length, though exceptions are permitted under certain circumstances. As a rule, no goal-altering changes in scope or personnel are permitted during a sprint. Finally, during each sprint, a potentially shippable product increment is completed in conformance with the Scrum team's agreed-upon definition of done.

Although each organization will have its own unique implementation of Scrum, these sprint characteristics, with a few exceptions that we'll explore, are meant to apply to every sprint and every team. Let's look at each in detail so that we can understand why this is so.

Timeboxed

Sprints are rooted in the concept of **timeboxing**, a time-management technique that helps organize the performance of work and manage scope. Each sprint takes place in a time frame with specific start and end dates, called a timebox. Inside this timebox, the team is expected to work at a sustainable pace to complete a chosen set of work that aligns with a sprint goal.

Timeboxing is important for several reasons (see Figure 4.2).

Establishes a WIP Limit

Timeboxing is a technique for limiting the amount of WIP (work in process). WIP represents an inventory of work that is started but not yet finished. Failing to properly manage it can have serious economic consequences. Because the team will plan to work on only those items that it believes it can start and finish within the sprint, timeboxing establishes a WIP limit each sprint.

Forces Prioritization

Timeboxing forces us to prioritize and perform the small amount of work that matters most. This sharpens our focus on getting something valuable done quickly.

Demonstrates Progress

Timeboxing also helps us demonstrate relevant progress by completing and validating important pieces of work by a known date (the end of the sprint). This type of

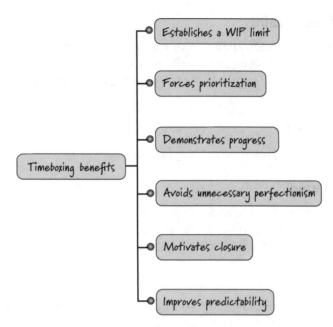

FIGURE 4.2   The benefits of timeboxing

progress reduces organizational risk by shifting the focus away from unreliable forms of progress reporting, such as conformance to plan. Timeboxing also helps us demonstrate progress against big features that require more than one timebox to complete. Completing some work toward those features ensures that valuable, measurable progress is being made each sprint. It also helps the stakeholders and team learn exactly what remains to be done to deliver the entire feature.

Avoids Unnecessary Perfectionism

Timeboxing helps avoid unnecessary perfectionism. At one time or another we have all spent too much time trying to get something "perfect" or to do "gold plating" when "good enough" would suffice. Timeboxing forces an end to potentially unbounded work by establishing a fixed end date for the sprint by which a good solution must be done.

Motivates Closure

Timeboxing also motivates closure. My experience is that things are more likely to get done when teams have a known end date. The fact that the end of the sprint brings with it a hard deadline encourages team members to diligently apply themselves to complete the work on time. Without a known end date, there is less of a sense of urgency to complete the job.

Improves Predictability

Timeboxing improves predictability. Although we can't predict with great certainty exactly the work we will complete a year from now, it is completely reasonable to expect that we can predict the work we can complete in the next short sprint.

Short Duration

Short-duration sprints provide many benefits (see Figure 4.3).

Ease of Planning

Short-duration sprints make it easier to plan. It is easier to plan a few weeks' worth of work than six months' worth of work. Also, planning on such short time horizons requires far less effort and is far more accurate than longer-horizon planning.

Fast Feedback

Short-duration sprints generate fast feedback. During each sprint we create working software and then have the opportunity to inspect and adapt what we built and how we built it. This fast feedback enables us to quickly prune unfavorable product paths or development approaches before we compound a bad decision with many follow-on

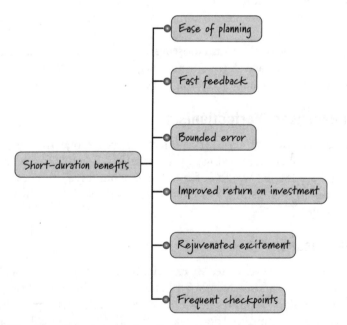

FIGURE 4.3   The benefits of short-duration sprints

decisions that are coupled to the bad decision. Fast feedback also allows us to more quickly uncover and exploit time-sensitive emergent opportunities.

Improved Return on Investment

Short-duration sprints not only improve the economics via fast feedback; they also allow for early and more frequent deliverables. As a result, we have the opportunity to generate revenue sooner, improving the overall return on investment (see Chapter 14 for an example).

Bounded Error

Short-duration sprints also bound error. How wrong can we be in a two-week sprint? Even if we fumble the whole thing, we have lost only two weeks. We insist on short-duration sprints because they provide frequent coordination and feedback. That way, if we're wrong, at least we're wrong in a small way.

Rejuvenated Excitement

Short-duration sprints can help rejuvenate excitement. It is human nature for interest and excitement to decline the longer we have to wait for gratification (see Figure 4.4).

If we work on a very long-duration project, not only are we more likely to fail; we are also more likely to eventually lose enthusiasm for the effort. (When I worked at IBM, we used to call these the "boil-the-ocean" projects, because they would

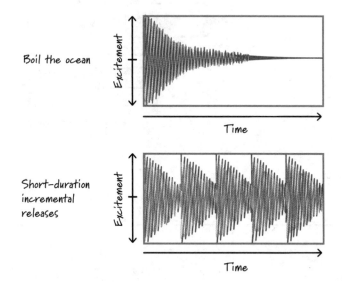

FIGURE 4.4   Excitement over time

take a really long time and a lot of effort to complete, if ever, like trying to boil an ocean.) With no visible progress and no end in sight, people begin to grow disinterested. Toward the end, they may be willing to *pay* someone to get moved to a different product!

Short-duration sprints keep participant excitement high by delivering working assets frequently. The gratification from early and frequent deliverables rejuvenates our interest and our desire to continue working toward the goal.

Frequent Checkpoints

Short-duration sprints also provide multiple, meaningful checkpoints (see Figure 4.5).

One valued aspect of sequential projects is a well-defined set of milestones. These milestones provide managers with known project-lifecycle checkpoints that are usually tied to go/no-go funding decisions for the next phase. Although potentially useful from a governance perspective, as I discussed in Chapter 3 these milestones give an unreliable indication of the true status of customer value delivery.

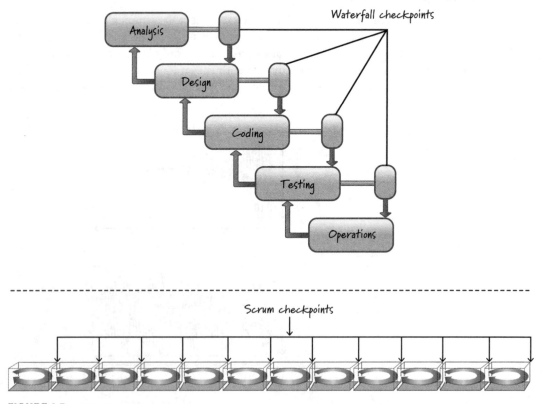

FIGURE 4.5   Checkpoint comparison

Scrum provides managers, stakeholders, product owners, and others with many more checkpoints than they would have with sequential projects. At the end of each short sprint there is a meaningful checkpoint (the sprint review) that allows everyone to base decisions on demonstrable, working features. People are better able to deal with a complex environment when they have more actionable checkpoint opportunities to inspect and adapt.

Consistent Duration

As a rule, on a given development effort, a team should pick a consistent duration for its sprints and not change it unless there is a compelling reason. Compelling reasons might include the following:

- You are considering moving from four-week sprints to two-week sprints in order to obtain more frequent feedback but want to try a couple of two-week sprints before making a final decision.
- The annual holidays or end of the fiscal year make it more practical to run a three-week sprint than the usual two-week sprint.
- The product release occurs in one week, so a two-week sprint would be wasteful.

The fact that the team cannot get all the work done within the current sprint length is not a compelling reason to extend the sprint length. Neither is it permissible to get to the last day of the sprint, realize you are not going to be done, and lobby for an extra day or week. These are symptoms of dysfunction and opportunities for improvement; they are not good reasons to change the sprint length.

As a rule, therefore, if a team agrees to perform two-week sprints, all sprints should be two weeks in duration. As a practical matter, most (but not all) teams will define two weeks to mean ten calendar weekdays. If there is a one-day holiday or training event during the sprint, it reduces the team's capacity for that sprint but doesn't necessitate a sprint length change.

Using the same sprint length also leverages the benefits of cadence and simplifies planning.

Cadence Benefits

Sprints of the same duration provide us with **cadence**—a regular, predictable rhythm or heartbeat to a Scrum development effort. A steady, healthy heartbeat allows the Scrum team and the organization to acquire an important rhythmic familiarity with when things need to happen to achieve the fast, flexible flow of business value. In my experience, having a regular cadence to sprints enables people to "get into the zone," "be on a roll," or "get into a groove." I believe this happens because regular cadence makes the mundane but necessary activities habitual, thereby freeing up mental capacity to stay focused on the fun, value-added work.

Having a short sprint cadence also tends to level out the intensity of work. Unlike a traditional sequential project where we see a steep increase in intensity in the latter phases, each sprint has an intensity profile that is similar to that of the other sprints. As I will discuss in Chapter 11, sprint cadence enables teams to work at a sustainable pace.

Sprinting on a regular cadence also significantly reduces coordination overhead. With fixed-length sprints we can predictably schedule the sprint-planning, sprint review, and sprint retrospective activities for many sprints at the same time. Because everyone knows when the activities will occur, the overhead required to schedule them for a large batch of sprints is substantially reduced.

As an example, if we do two-week sprints on a yearlong development effort, we can send out the recurring event on everyone's calendar for the next 26 sprint reviews. If we allowed sprint durations to vary from sprint to sprint, imagine the extra effort we would need to coordinate the schedules of the stakeholders on what might be just one or two weeks' notice for an upcoming sprint review! That assumes that we could even find a time that worked for the core set of stakeholders, whose schedules are likely filled up many weeks ahead.

Finally, if we have multiple teams on the same project, having all teams with a similar sprint cadence allows for synchronization of the work across all of the teams (see Chapter 12 for a more detailed discussion).

Simplifies Planning

Using a consistent duration also simplifies planning activities. When all sprints are the same length (even when they might have a day or less capacity per sprint because of a holiday), the team gets comfortable with the amount of work that it can accomplish in a typical sprint (referred to as its **velocity**). Velocity is typically normalized to a sprint. If the length of the sprint can vary, we really don't have a normalized sprint unit. It wouldn't be meaningful to say things like "The team has an average velocity of 20 points per sprint."

While it is certainly possible to compute a team's velocity even if it uses variable-length sprints, it is more complicated. Sticking with a consistent sprint duration simplifies the computations we perform on a team's historical velocity data.

Consistent sprint durations also simplify the rest of the planning math. For example, if we are working on a **fixed-date release**, and we have consistent-duration sprints, calculating the number of sprints in the release is simply an exercise in calendar math (we know today's date, we know the release date, and we know that all sprints are the same length). If the sprint durations were allowed to vary, calculating the number of sprints in the release could be significantly more challenging (because we would have to do extensive early planning), involve unnecessary overhead, and likely be far less reliable than with consistent sprint durations.

No Goal-Altering Changes

An important Scrum rule states that once the sprint goal has been established and sprint execution has begun, no change is permitted that can materially affect the sprint goal.

What Is a Sprint Goal?

Each sprint can be summarized by a sprint goal that describes the business purpose and value of the sprint. Typically the sprint goal has a clear, single focus, such as

- Support initial report generation.
- Load and curate North America map data.
- Demonstrate the ability to send a text message through an integrated software, firmware, and hardware stack.

There are times when a sprint goal might be multifaceted, for example, "Get basic printing working and support search by date."

During sprint planning, the development team should help refine and agree to the sprint goal and use it to determine the product backlog items that it can complete by the end of the sprint (see Chapter 19 for more details). These product backlog items serve to further elaborate the sprint goal.

Mutual Commitment

The sprint goal is the foundation of a mutual commitment made by the team and the product owner. The team commits to meeting the goal by the end of the sprint, and the product owner commits to not altering the goal during the sprint.

This mutual commitment demonstrates the importance of sprints in balancing the needs of the business to be adaptive to change, while allowing the team to concentrate and efficiently apply its talent to create value during a short, fixed duration. By defining and adhering to a sprint goal, the Scrum team is able to stay focused (in the zone) on a well-defined, valuable target.

Change versus Clarification

Although the sprint goal should not be materially *changed*, it is permissible to *clarify* the goal. Let me differentiate the two.

What constitutes a change? A change is any alteration in work or resources that has the potential to generate economically meaningful waste, harmfully disrupt the flow of work, or substantially increase the scope of work within a sprint. Adding or removing a product backlog item from a sprint or significantly altering the scope of a product backlog item that is already in the sprint typically constitutes change. The following example illustrates a change:

> Product owner: "Oh, when I said that we need to be able to search the police database for a juvenile offender, I didn't just mean by last name and first name. I also meant we should be able to search the database based on a picture of the suspect's body tattoos!"

Adding the ability to search based on a picture likely represents substantially more effort and almost certainly would affect the team's ability to meet a commitment to deliver search based on last name and first name. In this case, the product owner should consider creating a new product backlog item that captures the search-by-picture feature and adding it to the product backlog to be worked on in a subsequent sprint.

What constitutes a clarification? Clarifications are additional details provided during the sprint that assist the team in achieving its sprint goal. As I will discuss in Chapter 5, all of the details associated with product backlog items might not be fully known or specified at the start of the sprint. Therefore, it is completely reasonable for the team to ask clarifying questions during a sprint and for the product owner to answer those questions. The following example illustrates a clarification:

> Development team: "When you said the matches for a juvenile offender search should be displayed in a list, did you have a preference for how that list is to be ordered?"
>
> Product owner: "Yes, sort them alphabetically by last name."
>
> Development team: "OK, we can do that."

In this manner, the product owner can and should provide clarification during the sprint.

Consequences of Change

It may appear that the no-goal-altering-change rule is in direct conflict with the core Scrum principle that we should embrace change. We do embrace change, but we want to embrace it in a balanced, economically sensible way.

The economic consequences of a change increase as our level of investment in the changed work increases (see Figure 4.6).

We invest in product backlog items to get them ready to be worked on in a sprint. However, once a sprint starts, our investment in those product backlog items has increased (because we spent time during sprint planning to discuss and plan them at a task level). If we want to make a change after sprint planning has occurred, we not only jeopardize the planning investment, but we also incur additional costs for having to replan any changes during the sprint.

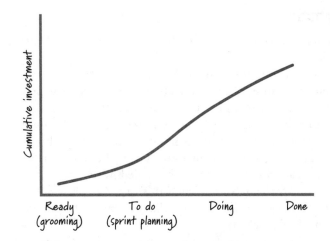

FIGURE 4.6   Cumulative investment at different states

In addition, once we begin sprint execution, our investment in work increases even more as product backlog items transition through the states of to do (work not yet started), doing (work in process), and done (work completed).

Let's say we want to swap out feature X, currently part of the sprint commitment, and substitute feature Y, which isn't part of the existing commitment. Even if we haven't started working on feature X, we still incur planning waste. In addition, feature X might also have dependencies with other features in the sprint, so a change that affects feature X could affect one or more other features, thus amplifying the effect on the sprint goal.

If work on feature X has already begun, in addition to the already-mentioned waste, we could have other potential wastes. For example, all of the work already performed on feature X might have to be thrown away. And we might have the additional waste of removing the partially completed work on feature X, which we may never use in the future (we're not going to include partially completed work in a potentially shippable product increment at the end of the sprint).

And, of course, if feature X is already completed, we might have wasted the full investment we made in feature X. All of this waste adds up!

In addition to the direct economic consequences of waste, the economics can be indirectly affected by the potential deterioration of team motivation and trust that can accompany a change. When the product owner makes a commitment to not alter the goal and then violates the commitment, the team naturally will be demotivated, which will almost certainly affect its desire to work diligently to complete other product backlog items. In addition, violating the commitment can harm the trust within the Scrum team, because the development team will not trust that the product owner is willing to stick to his commitments.

Being Pragmatic

The no-goal-altering-change rule is just that—a rule, not a law. The Scrum team has to be pragmatic.

What if business conditions change in such a way that making a change to the sprint goal seems warranted? Say a competitor launches its new product during our sprint. After reviewing the new product, we conclude that we need to alter the goal we established for our current sprint because what we are doing is now economically far less valuable given what our competitor has done. Should we blindly follow the rule of no goal-altering changes and not alter our sprint? Probably not.

What if a critical production system has failed miserably and some or all of the people on our team are the only ones who can fix it? Should we not interrupt the current sprint to fix it? Do we tell the business that we will fix the production failure first thing next sprint? Probably not.

In the end, being pragmatic trumps the no-goal-altering-change rule. We must act in an economically sensible way. Everyone on the Scrum team can appreciate that. If we change the current sprint, we will experience the negative economic consequences I previously discussed. However, if the economic consequences of the change are far less than the economic consequences of deferring the change, making the change is the smart business decision. If the economics of changing versus not changing are immaterial, no change to the sprint goal should be made.

As for team motivation and trust, in my experience, when a product owner has a frank, economically focused discussion with the team about the necessity of the change, most teams understand and appreciate the need, so the integrity of motivation and trust is upheld.

Abnormal Termination

Should the sprint goal become completely invalid, the Scrum team may decide that continuing with the current sprint makes no sense and advise the product owner to abnormally terminate the sprint. When a sprint is abnormally terminated, the current sprint comes to an abrupt end and the Scrum team gathers to perform a sprint retrospective. The team then meets with the product owner to plan the next sprint, with a different goal and a different set of product backlog items.

Sprint termination is used when an economically significant event has occurred, such as a competitor's actions that completely invalidate the sprint or product funding being materially changed.

Although the product owner reserves the option to cancel each and every sprint, in my experience it is rare that product owners invoke this option. Often there are less drastic measures that a Scrum team can take to adjust to the situation at hand. Remember, sprints are short, and, on average, the team will be about halfway through a sprint when a change-causing situation arises. Because there may be only a week or so of time left in the sprint when the change occurs, the economics of terminating may be less favorable than just staying the course. And many times it is possible to make a less dramatic change, such as dropping a feature to allow time to fix a critical production failure, instead of terminating the sprint.

It is important to realize that terminating the sprint early, in addition to having a negative effect on morale, is a serious disruption of the fast, flexible flow of features and negates many of the benefits of consistent-duration sprints I mentioned earlier. Terminating a sprint should be the last resort.

If a sprint is terminated, the Scrum team will have to determine the length of the next sprint (see Figure 4.7).

There are three apparent options:

1. Stay with the original sprint length. This has the advantage of keeping a uniform sprint length throughout development (except for the terminated sprint, of course). If multiple Scrum teams are collaborating on the same development effort, using the original sprint length will put the Scrum team that terminated its sprint out of sync with the other teams.
2. Make the next sprint just long enough to get to the end date of the terminated sprint. For example, if the Scrum team terminated a two-week sprint at the end of the first week, the next sprint would be one week to get the team resynchronized to its original sprint cadence.
3. Make the next sprint bigger than a normal sprint to cover the remaining time in the terminated sprint plus the time for the next full sprint. So, in the previous example, make the next sprint three weeks in order to get the team resynchronized to its original sprint cadence.

In a multiteam development effort, either option 2 or option 3 would be preferred. In all cases, you will need to consider your specific context to know which option is best.

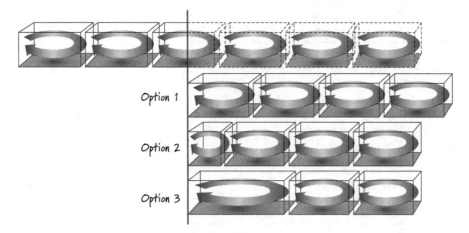

FIGURE 4.7   Deciding on the next sprint length after sprint termination

Definition of Done

In Chapter 2, I discussed how the result of each sprint should be a potentially shippable product increment. I also mentioned that "potentially shippable" doesn't mean that what was built must actually be shipped. Shipping is a business decision that often occurs at a different cadence; in some organizations it may not make sense to ship at the end of every sprint.

Potentially shippable is better thought of as a state of confidence that what got built in the sprint is actually done, meaning that there isn't materially important undone work (such as important testing or integration and so on) that needs to be completed before we could ship the results from the sprint, if shipping was our business desire. To determine if what got produced is potentially shippable, the Scrum team must have a well-defined, agreed-upon definition of done.

What Is the Definition of Done?

Conceptually the **definition of done** is a checklist of the types of work that the team is expected to successfully complete before it can declare its work to be potentially shippable (see Table 4.1).

TABLE 4.1   Example Definition-of-Done Checklist

	Definition of Done
❏	Design reviewed
❏	Code completed
❏	Code refactored
❏	Code in standard format
❏	Code is commented
❏	Code checked in
❏	Code inspected
❏	End-user documentation updated
❏	Tested
❏	Unit tested
❏	Integration tested
❏	Regression tested
❏	Platform tested
❏	Language tested
❏	Zero known defects
❏	Acceptance tested
❏	Live on production servers

Obviously the specific items on the checklist will depend on a number of variables:

- The nature of the product being built
- The technologies being used to build it
- The organization that is building it
- The current impediments that affect what is possible

Most of the time, a bare-minimum definition of done should yield a complete slice of product functionality, one that has been designed, built, integrated, tested, and documented and would deliver validated customer value. To have a useful checklist, however, these larger-level work items need to be further refined. For example, what does tested mean? Unit tested? Integration tested? System tested? Platform tested? Internationalization tested? You can probably think of many other forms of testing that are specific to your product. Are all of those types of testing included in the definition of done?

Keep in mind that if you don't do an important type of testing every sprint (say, performance testing), you'll have to do it sometime. Are you going to have some specialized sprint in the future where the only thing you do is performance testing? If so, and performance testing is essential to being "done," you really don't have a potentially shippable product increment each sprint. And even worse, when you actually do the performance testing at a later time and it doesn't go quite as planned, not only will you discover a critical problem very late in the process, but you will also have to spend much more time and money to fix it at that time than if you had done the performance testing earlier.

Sometimes the testing might take longer than the duration of a sprint. If this occurs because the development team has accrued a huge manual testing debt, the team needs to start automating its tests so that the testing can be completed within a sprint. If this occurs because of the nature of the test, we will need to accept starting the test in one sprint and finishing it in some future sprint. For example, one organization I coached was building a device composed of hardware, firmware, and software. One of its standard tests was the 1,500-hour burn-in test, where the device was run flat-out for that amount of time to see if it would fail. That test can't be completed in a two-week sprint, so the Scrum team adjusted the definition of done so that a sprint could be deemed done even if the 1,500-hour test was not yet completed.

Often I am asked, "What if there is a significant defect that remains on the last day of the sprint; is the product backlog item done?" No, it's not done! And because, as a rule, we don't extend sprints beyond the end of the planned timebox, we wouldn't extend the sprint by a day or two to fix the defect in the current sprint. Instead, at the planned end of the sprint, the incomplete product backlog item is taken from the current sprint and reinserted into the product backlog in the proper order based on the other items that are currently in the product backlog. The incomplete item might then be finished in some future sprint.

Scrum teams need to have a robust definition of done, one that provides a high level of confidence that what they build is of high quality and can be shipped. Anything less robs the organization of the business opportunity of shipping at its discretion and can lead to the accrual of technical debt (as I will discuss in Chapter 8).

Definition of Done Can Evolve Over Time

You can think of the definition of done as defining the state of the work at the end of the sprint. For many high-performance teams, the target end state of the work enables it to be potentially shippable—and that end state remains relatively constant over the development lifecycle.

For example, when I was product owner for the Scrum Alliance website redesign project in 2007, we performed one-week sprints. The end state of our definition of done could be summarized as "live on the production servers." The team and I determined that this was a perfectly reasonable state for us to achieve every sprint. We defined this end state at the beginning of the development effort; that target end state didn't change during the time I was product owner for the site.

Many teams, however, start out with a definition of done that doesn't end in a state where all features are completed to the extent that they could go live or be shipped. For some, real impediments might prevent them from reaching this state at the start of development, even though it is the ultimate goal. As a result, they might (necessarily) start with a lesser end state and let their definition of done evolve over time as organizational impediments are removed.

For example, I visited an organization that builds a clinical informatics system. Its product is installed in a medical clinic and collects a variety of clinical data (some even directly from the machines that perform diagnostic tests). The team knew that clinical testing, which involved installing the product in a clinical lab to make sure it worked with clinical hardware, would be required before they could ship. However, because they didn't have regular access to a lab, the team didn't at first include clinical testing in its definition of done. Instead, it included clinical-testing sprints at the end of each release.

In our discussions, I learned that marketing and the team hated these prerelease clinical tests. No one could predict how many sprints it would take to work out all of the defects, and the product couldn't be released until the defects were removed. As we were brainstorming potential solutions, the VP of Engineering chimed in. He asked his team, "If you had access to a clinical lab, would you be able to do clinical testing each sprint?"

The team members discussed his question and responded, "Yes, but it will mean we complete fewer features each sprint." The VP agreed to remove the impediment by getting the team access to a local university clinical lab. The product owner agreed that having fewer features completed each sprint was a sensible trade-off for knowing that the features that were delivered had been clinically tested. At that point the team was able to evolve its definition of done to actually achieve "potentially shippable," giving everyone involved a higher degree of confidence in the work completed each sprint.

Other times a team might have an impediment that it knows can't be removed right away. As a result, it knows that the definition of done during its product development effort will necessarily evolve. A common example is a product that includes hardware and software. I have seen Scrum applied to the development of many such products, and frequently I'll hear the software people say, "The hardware always arrives late!" In cases like this, if the team is building software and it doesn't have the actual hardware on which to test the software, it can't really claim that the results produced at the end of the sprint are potentially shippable. At best it might claim "emulator done," because testing during the early sprints is typically performed against a software emulator of the actual hardware. Later, when the actual hardware is available, the definition of done will evolve to mean potentially shippable or at least something closer to it.

Definition of Done versus Acceptance Criteria

The definition of done applies to the product increment being developed during the sprint. The product increment is composed of a set of product backlog items, so each backlog item must be completed in conformance with the work specified by the definition-of-done checklist.

As I will discuss in Chapter 5, each product backlog item that is brought into the sprint should have a set of **conditions of satisfaction** (item-specific acceptance criteria), specified by the product owner. These **acceptance criteria** eventually will be verified in **acceptance tests** that the product owner will confirm to determine if the backlog item functions as desired. For example, if the product backlog item is "Allow a customer to purchase with a credit card," the conditions of satisfaction might be "Works with AmEx, Visa, and MasterCard." So each product backlog item will have its own appropriate set of acceptance criteria. These item-specific criteria are in addition to, not in lieu of, the done criteria specified by the definition-of-done checklist, which apply to all product backlog items.

A product backlog item can be considered done only when both the item-specific acceptance criteria (for example, "works with all of the credit cards") and the sprint-level definition-of-done (for example, "live on the production server") items have been met.

If it is confusing to refer to product backlog items that pass their acceptance criteria as *done*, call them *completed* or *accepted*.

Done versus Done-Done

Some teams have adopted the concept of "done" versus "done-done." Somehow done-done is supposed to be more done than done! Teams shouldn't need two different concepts, but I have to admit to using both terms with my son and his homework. I used to ask my son if he was "done" with his homework and he would tell me yes. Then I went to parent-teacher night at his school, and during a discussion with his teacher I asked, "So, when he turns in his homework, is it done?" She said, "Not really!"

After a more probing discussion with my son, I came to understand that his definition of done was "I did as much work as I was prepared to do!" So, from that point forward I started using the term *done-done*, which we both agreed would mean "done to the point where your teacher would think you are done."

Teams that are unaccustomed to really getting things done early and often are more likely to use done-done as a crutch. For them, using done-done makes the point that being done (doing as much work as they are prepared to do) is a different state from done-done (doing the work required for customers to believe it is done). Teams that have internalized that you can be done only if you did all the work necessary to satisfy customers don't need to have two states; to them, done means done-done!

Closing

In this chapter I emphasized the crucial role of sprints in the Scrum framework. Sprints provide the essential Scrum skeleton on which most other activities and artifacts can be placed. Sprints are short, timeboxed, and consistent in duration. They are typically defined by a sprint goal, a goal that should not be altered without good economic cause. Sprints should produce a potentially shippable product increment that is completed in conformance with an agreed-upon definition of done. In the next chapter I will focus on the inputs to the sprints—requirements and their common representation, user stories.

Chapter 5

REQUIREMENTS AND USER STORIES

In this chapter I discuss how requirements on a Scrum project are handled differently than on a traditional project. With this context in place, I describe the role of user stories as a common format for representing items of business value. I focus on what user stories are, how they can represent business value at multiple levels of abstraction, and how to determine when the user stories are good. I then describe how to handle nonfunctional requirements and knowledge-acquisition work on a Scrum project. I end by detailing two techniques for gathering user stories.

Overview

Scrum and sequential product development treat requirements very differently. With sequential product development, requirements are nonnegotiable, detailed up front, and meant to stand alone. In Scrum, the details of a requirement are negotiated through conversations that happen continuously during development and are fleshed out *just in time* and *just enough* for the teams to start building functionality to support that requirement.

With sequential product development, requirements are treated much as they are in manufacturing: They are required, nonnegotiable specifications to which the product must conform. These requirements are created up front and given to the development group in the form of a highly detailed document. It is the job of the development group, then, to produce a product that conforms to the detailed requirements.

When a change from the original plan is deemed necessary, it is managed through a formal change control process. Because conformance to specifications is the goal, these deviations are undesirable and expensive. After all, much of the work in process (WIP), in the form of highly detailed requirements (and all work based on them), might need to be changed or discarded.

In contrast, Scrum views requirements as an important degree of freedom that we can manipulate to meet our business goals. For example, if we're running out of time or money, we can drop low-value requirements. If, during development, new information indicates that the cost/benefit ratio of a requirement has become significantly less favorable, we can choose to drop the requirement from the product. And if a new high-value requirement emerges, we have the ability to add it to the product, perhaps discarding a lower-value requirement to make room.

We have probably all had the experience of writing a "complete" requirements document at the beginning of development, only to discover later that an important requirement was missing. When we discovered that missing requirement, the conversation probably sounded something like this:

> Customer: "Now that I see these built features, I realize I need this other feature that isn't in the requirements document."
>
> Developers: "If you wanted that feature, why didn't you specify it up front?"
>
> Customer: "Well, I didn't realize I needed that feature until I saw the product coming together."
>
> Developers: "Well, if you had thought longer and harder about the requirements up front, you would have found that feature then instead of now."

The fact is, when developing innovative products, you can't create complete requirements or designs up front by simply working longer and harder. Some requirements and design will always emerge once product development is under way; no amount of comprehensive up-front work will prevent that.

Thus, when using Scrum, we don't invest a great deal of time and money in fleshing out the details of a requirement up front. Because we expect the specifics to change as time passes and as we learn more about what we are building, we avoid overinvesting in requirements that we might later discard. Instead of compiling a large inventory of detailed requirements up front, we create placeholders for the requirements, called **product backlog items** (PBIs). Each product backlog item represents desirable business value (see Figure 5.1).

Initially the product backlog items are large (representing large swaths of business value), and there is very little detail associated with them. Over time, we flow these product backlog items through a series of conversations among the stakeholders, product owner, and development team, refining them into a collection of smaller, more detailed PBIs. Eventually a product backlog item is small and detailed enough to move into a sprint, where it will be designed, built, and tested. Even during the sprint, however, more details will be exposed in conversations between the product owner and the development team.

As I will discuss in Chapter 6, the product backlog is simply a snapshot of the current collection of product backlog items and their associated details.

While Scrum doesn't specify any standard format for these product backlog items, many teams represent PBIs as user stories. You don't have to. Some teams prefer use cases, and others choose to represent their PBIs in their own custom formats.

In this book, I employ user stories as the principal representation of product backlog items. I will discuss the details of user stories later in this chapter. Even if you choose to use something else, you'll still find the discussion of user stories helpful in understanding what characteristics you'll want from any other representation.

Product backlog over time

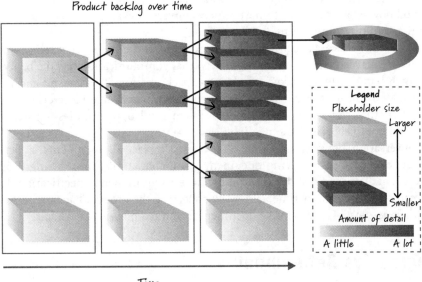

Time

FIGURE 5.1   Scrum uses placeholders for requirements.

Using Conversations

As a communication vehicle, requirements facilitate a shared understanding of what needs to be built. They allow the people who understand what should be created to clearly communicate their desires to the people who have to create it.

Sequential product development relies heavily on written requirements, which look impressive but can easily be misunderstood. I recall a conversation with a VP of Product Management at a company I visited. I asked this person, who managed all of the company's business analysts, how they handled requirements. He said by way of illustration, "On January 1 my team provides the engineering organization with the requirements document, and on December 31 we show up and see what we got."

I asked him who from his team would be available during the year to answer questions and clarify requirements for the developers. He said, "No one. All of the time my group had to invest in this project was spent writing the requirements document. My analysts are off working on the requirements documents for other projects. But don't worry, we wrote a good document, and any questions the developers or testers have can be answered by carefully reading the document."

It seemed unlikely to me that there would be no ambiguities in his 150-page, detailed use case document for a new electronic medical records system. English just isn't that precise; even if it were, people just aren't that precise with their writing.

A way to better ensure that the desired features are being built is for the people who know what they want to have timely conversations with the people who are designing, building, and testing those features.

In Scrum, we leverage conversation as a key tool for ensuring that requirements are properly discussed and communicated. Verbal communication has the benefit of being high-bandwidth and providing fast feedback, making it easier and cheaper to gain a shared understanding. In addition, conversations enable bidirectional communication that can spark ideas about problems and opportunities—discussions that would not likely arise from reading a document.

Conversation, however, is just a tool. It doesn't replace all documents. In Scrum, the product backlog is a "living document," available at all times during product development. Those who still want or must have a requirements specification document can create one at any time, simply by collecting the product backlog items and all of their associated details into a document formatted however they like.

Progressive Refinement

With sequential product development all requirements must be at the same level of detail at the same time. In particular, the approved requirements document must specify each and every requirement so that the teams doing the design, build, and test work can understand how to conform to the specifications. There are no details left to be added.

Forcing all requirements to the same level of detail at the same time has many disadvantages:

- We must predict all of these details early during product development when we have the least knowledge that we'll ever have.
- We treat all requirements the same regardless of their priority, forcing us to dedicate valuable resources today to create details for requirements that we may never build.
- We create a large inventory of requirements that will likely be very expensive to rework or discard when things change.
- We reduce the likelihood of using conversations to elaborate on and clarify requirements because the requirements are already "complete."

As Figure 5.1 illustrates, when using Scrum, not all requirements have to be at the same level of detail at the same time. Requirements that we'll work on sooner will be smaller and more detailed than ones that we won't work on for some time. We employ a strategy of **progressive refinement** to disaggregate, in a just-in-time fashion, large, lightly detailed requirements into a set of smaller, more detailed items.

What Are User Stories?

User stories are a convenient format for expressing the desired business value for many types of product backlog items, especially features. User stories are crafted in a way that makes them understandable to both business people and technical people. They are structurally simple and provide a great placeholder for a conversation. Additionally, they can be written at various levels of granularity and are easy to progressively refine.

As well adapted to our needs as user stories might be, I don't consider them to be the only way to represent product backlog items. They are simply a lightweight approach that dovetails nicely with core agile principles and our need for an efficient and effective placeholder. I use them as the central placeholder to which I will attach any other information that I think is relevant and helpful for detailing a requirement. If I find that user stories are a forced fit for a particular situation (such as representing certain defects), I'll use another approach. For example, I once saw a team write the following user story: "As a customer I would like the system to not corrupt the database." I think we can all agree that a user story is probably not the best way to represent this issue. Perhaps a simple reference to the defect in the defect-tracking system would be more appropriate.

So what exactly are user stories? Ron Jeffries offers a simple yet effective way to think about user stories (Jeffries 2001). He describes them as the three Cs: card, conversation, and confirmation.

Card

The card idea is pretty simple. People originally wrote (and many still do) user stories directly on 3 × 5-inch index cards or sticky notes (see Figure 5.2).

A common template format for writing user stories (as shown on the left in Figure 5.2) is to specify a class of users (the user role), what that class of users wants to achieve (the goal), and why the users want to achieve the goal (the benefit) (Cohn 2004). The "so that" part of a user story is optional, but unless the purpose of the

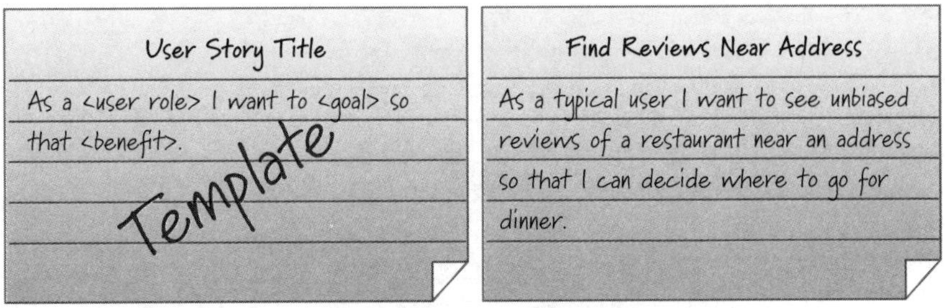

User Story Title	Find Reviews Near Address
As a <user role> I want to <goal> so that <benefit>. *Template*	As a typical user I want to see unbiased reviews of a restaurant near an address so that I can decide where to go for dinner.

FIGURE 5.2   A user story template and card

story is completely obvious to everyone, we should include it with every user story. The right side of Figure 5.2 shows an example of a user story based on this template.

The card isn't intended to capture all of the information that makes up the requirement. In fact, we deliberately use small cards with limited space to promote brevity. A card should hold a few sentences that capture the essence or intent of a requirement. It serves as the placeholder for more detailed discussions that will take place among the stakeholders, product owner, and development team.

Conversation

The details of a requirement are exposed and communicated in a conversation among the development team, product owner, and stakeholders. The user story is simply a promise to have that conversation.

I say "that conversation," but in actuality, the conversation is typically not a one-time event, but rather an ongoing dialogue. There can be an initial conversation when the user story is written, another conversation when it's refined, yet another when it's estimated, another during sprint planning (when the team is diving into the task-level details), and finally, ongoing conversations while the user story is being designed, built, and tested during the sprint.

One of the benefits of user stories is that they shift some of the focus away from writing and onto conversations. These conversations enable a richer form of exchanging information and collaborating to ensure that the correct requirements are expressed and understood by everyone.

Although conversations are largely verbal, they can be and frequently are supplemented with documents. Conversations may lead to a UI sketch, or an elaboration of business rules that gets written down. For example, I visited an organization that was developing medical imaging software. One of its stories is shown in Figure 5.3.

Notice that the user story references an entire article for future reading and conversation.

So we're not tossing out all of our documents in favor of user stories and their associated story cards. User stories are simply a good starting point for eliciting the initial essence of what is desired, and for providing a reminder to discuss

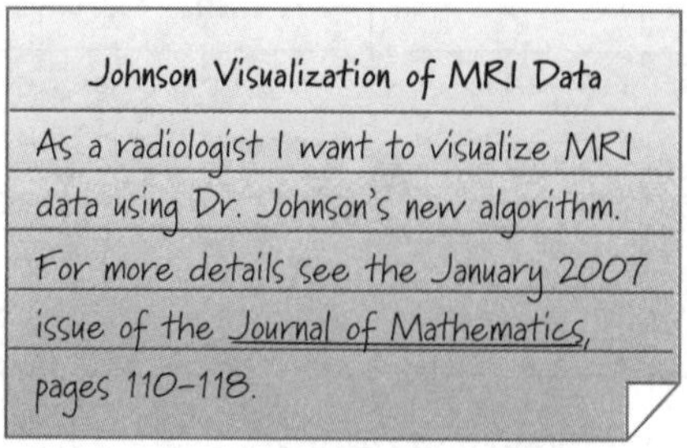

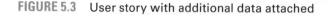

> Johnson Visualization of MRI Data
>
> As a radiologist I want to visualize MRI data using Dr. Johnson's new algorithm.
>
> For more details see the January 2007 issue of the *Journal of Mathematics*, pages 110–118.

FIGURE 5.3   User story with additional data attached

requirements in more detail when appropriate. However, user stories can and should be supplemented with whatever other written information helps provide clarity regarding what is desired.

Confirmation

A user story also contains confirmation information in the form of conditions of satisfaction. These are acceptance criteria that clarify the desired behavior. They are used by the development team to better understand what to build and test and by the product owner to confirm that the user story has been implemented to his satisfaction.

If the front of the card has a few-line description of the story, the back of the card could specify the conditions of satisfaction (see Figure 5.4).

These conditions of satisfaction can be expressed as high-level acceptance tests. However, these tests would not be the only tests that are run when the story is being developed. In fact, for the handful of acceptance tests that are associated with a user story, the team will have many more tests (perhaps 10 to 100 times more) at a detailed technical level that the product owner doesn't even know about.

The acceptance tests associated with the story exist for several reasons. First, they are an important way to capture and communicate, from the product owner's perspective, how to determine if the story has been implemented correctly.

These tests can also be a helpful way to create initial stories and refine them as more details become known. This approach is sometimes called **specification by example** or **acceptance-test-driven development** (**ATTD**). The idea is fairly intuitive. Discussions about the stories can and frequently do focus on defining specific examples or desired behaviors. For example, in the "Upload File" story in Figure 5.4, the conversation likely went something like this:

> Initially, let's limit uploaded file sizes to be 1 GB or less. Also, make sure that we can properly load common text and graphics files. And for legal reasons we can't have any files with digital rights management (DRM) restrictions loaded to the wiki.

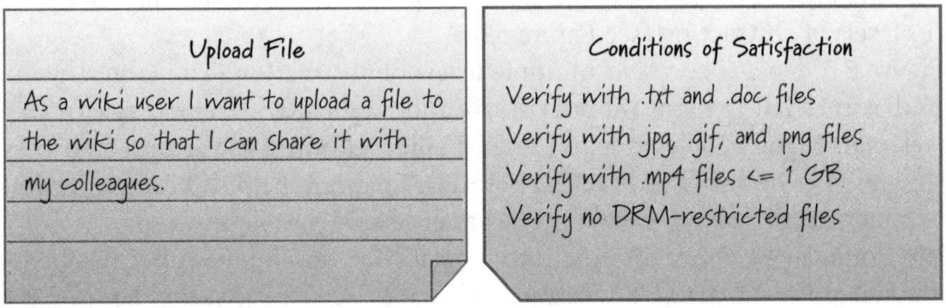

Upload File	Conditions of Satisfaction
As a wiki user I want to upload a file to the wiki so that I can share it with my colleagues.	Verify with .txt and .doc files Verify with .jpg, .gif, and .png files Verify with .mp4 files <= 1 GB Verify no DRM-restricted files

FIGURE 5.4 User story conditions of satisfaction

TABLE 5.1   Automated Test Example

Size	Valid()
0	True
1,073,741,824	True
1,073,741,825	False

If we were using a tool like Fit or FitNesse, we could conveniently define these tests in a table like Table 5.1, which shows examples of different file sizes and whether or not they are valid.

By elaborating on specific examples like these, we can drive the story creation and refinement process and have (automated) acceptance tests available for each story.

Level of Detail

User stories are an excellent vehicle for carrying items of customer or user value through the Scrum value-creation flow. However, if we have only one story size (the size that would comfortably fit within a short-duration sprint), it will be difficult to do higher-level planning and to reap the benefits of progressive refinement.

Small stories used at the sprint level are too small and too numerous to support higher-level product and release planning. At these levels we need fewer, less detailed, more abstract items. Otherwise, we'll be mired in a swamp of mostly irrelevant detail. Imagine having 500 very small stories and being asked to provide an executive-level description of the proposed product to secure your funding. Or try to prioritize among those 500 really small items to define the next release.

Also, if there is only one (small) size of story, we will be obligated to define all requirements at a very fine-grained level of detail long before we should. Having only small stories precludes the benefit of progressively refining requirements on a just-enough, just-in-time basis.

Fortunately, user stories can be written to capture customer and user needs at various levels of abstraction (see Figure 5.5).

Figure 5.5 depicts stories at multiple levels of abstraction. The largest would be stories that are a few to many months in size and might span an entire release or multiple releases. Many people refer to these as **epics**, alluding to the idea that they are *Lord of the Rings* or *War and Peace* size stories. Epics are helpful because they give a very big-picture, high-level overview of what is desired (see Figure 5.6).

We would never move an epic into a sprint for development because it is way too big and not very detailed. Instead, epics are excellent placeholders for a large

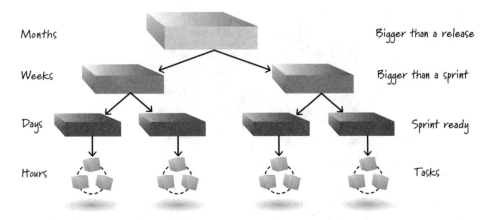

Months — Bigger than a release
Weeks — Bigger than a sprint
Days — Sprint ready
Hours — Tasks

FIGURE 5.5   User story abstraction hierarchy

> **Preference Training Epic**
>
> As a typical user I want to train the system on what types of product and service reviews I prefer so it will know what characteristics to use when filtering reviews on my behalf.

FIGURE 5.6   Example epic

collection of more detailed stories to be created at an appropriate future time. I will illustrate the use of epics during the discussion of product planning in Chapter 17.

The next-size stories in Figure 5.5 are those that are often on the order of weeks in size and therefore too big for a single sprint. Some teams might call these **features**.

The smallest forms of user stories are those I typically refer to as **stories**. To avoid any confusion with epics, features, or other larger items, which are also "stories," some people call these stories either **sprintable stories** or **implementable stories** to indicate that they are on the order of days in size and therefore small enough to fit into a sprint and be implemented. Figure 5.2 provides an example of a sprintable story.

Some teams also use the term **theme** to refer to a collection of related stories. Themes provide a convenient way to say that a bunch of stories have something in common, such as being in the same functional area. In Figure 5.7, the theme represents the collection of stories that will provide the details of how to perform keyword training.

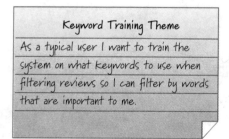

> Keyword Training Theme
>
> As a typical user I want to train the system on what keywords to use when filtering reviews so I can filter by words that are important to me.

FIGURE 5.7   Example theme

I often think of a theme as the summary card for a bunch of note cards stacked together with a rubber band around them to indicate that they are similar to one another in an area that we think is important.

Tasks are the layer below stories, typically worked on by only one person, or perhaps a pair of people. Tasks typically require hours to perform. When we go to the task layer, we are specifying *how* to build something instead of *what* to build (represented by epics, features, and stories). Tasks are not stories, so we should avoid including task-level detail when writing stories.

It is important to keep in mind that terms like *epic, feature, story,* and *theme* are just labels of convenience, and they are not universally shared. It really doesn't matter what labels you use as long as you use them consistently. What does matter is recognizing that stories can exist at multiple levels of abstraction, and that doing so nicely supports our efforts to plan at multiple levels of abstraction and to progressively refine big items into small items over time.

INVEST in Good Stories

How do we know if the stories that we have written are good stories? Bill Wake has offered six criteria (summarized by the acronym INVEST) that have proved useful when evaluating whether our stories are fit for their intended use or require some additional work (Wake 2003).

The **INVEST** criteria are *Independent, Negotiable, Valuable, Estimatable, Small* (sized appropriately), and *Testable*. When we combine the information derived from applying each criterion, we get a clear picture of what, if any, additional changes we might want to make to a story. Let's examine each criterion.

Independent

As much as is practical, user stories should be *independent* or at least only loosely coupled with one another. Stories that exhibit a high degree of interdependence complicate estimating, prioritizing, and planning. For example, on the left side of Figure 5.8, story #10 depends on many other stories.

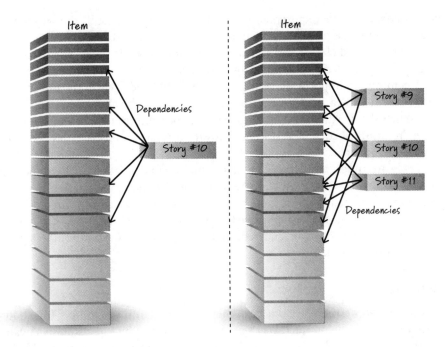

FIGURE 5.8   Highly dependent stories

Before we can work on story #10, we must first develop all of the dependent sto-ries. In this single case that might not be so bad. However, imagine that you have many different stories with a high degree of interdependence, as illustrated by the right side of Figure 5.8. Trying to determine how to prioritize all of these stories and deciding which stories to work on in a sprint would be difficult to say the least.

When applying the *independent* criteria, the goal is not to eliminate all depen-dencies, but instead to write stories in a way that minimizes dependencies.

Negotiable

The details of stories should also be *negotiable*. Stories are not a written contract in the form of an up-front requirements document. Instead, stories are placeholders for the conversations where the details will be negotiated.

Good stories clearly capture the essence of what business functionality is desired and why it is desired. However, they leave room for the product owner, the stakehold-ers, and the team to negotiate the details.

This negotiability helps everyone involved avoid the us-versus-them, finger-pointing mentality that is commonplace with detailed up-front requirements docu-ments. When stories are negotiable, developers can't really say, "Hey, if you wanted it, you should have put it in the document," because the details are going to be negoti-ated with the developers. And the business people can't really say, "Hey, you obviously didn't understand the requirements document because you built the wrong thing," because the business people will be in frequent dialogue with the developers to make sure there is shared clarity. Writing negotiable stories avoids the problems associated with up-front detailed requirements by making it clear that a dialogue is necessary.

A common example of where negotiability is violated is when the product owner tells the team *how* to implement a story. Stories should be about what and why, not how. When the *how* becomes nonnegotiable, opportunities for the team to be innovative are diminished. The resulting **innovation waste** could have devastating economic consequences.

There are times, however, when *how* something is built is actually important to the product owner. For example, there might be a regulatory obligation to develop a feature in a particular way, or there might be a business constraint directing the use of a specific technology. In such cases the stories will be a bit less negotiable because some aspect of the "how" is required. That's OK; not all stories are fully negotiable, but most stories should be.

Valuable

Stories need to be *valuable* to a customer, user, or both. Customers (or choosers) select and pay for the product. Users actually use the product. If a story isn't valuable to either, it doesn't belong in the product backlog. I can't imagine saying, "Story #10 isn't valuable to anyone, but let's build it anyway." We wouldn't do that. We would either rewrite the story to make it valuable to a customer or user, or we would just discard it.

How about stories that are valuable to the developers but aren't of obvious value to the customers or users? Is it OK to have **technical stories** like the one shown in Figure 5.9?

The fundamental problem with technical stories is that the product owner might not perceive any value in them, making it difficult if not impossible to prioritize them against business-valuable stories. For a technical story to exist, the product owner should understand why he is paying for it and therefore what value it will ultimately deliver.

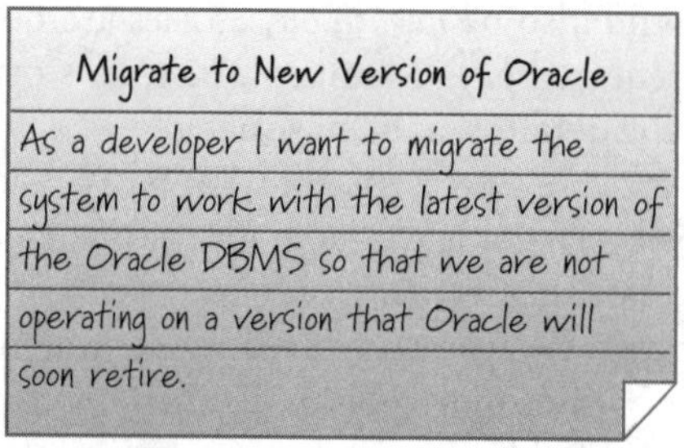

> Migrate to New Version of Oracle
>
> As a developer I want to migrate the system to work with the latest version of the Oracle DBMS so that we are not operating on a version that Oracle will soon retire.

FIGURE 5.9   Example technical story

In the case of the "Migrate to New Version of Oracle" story, the product owner might not initially understand why it is valuable to change databases. However, once the team explains the risks of continuing to develop on an unsupported version of a database, the product owner might decide that migrating databases is valuable enough to defer building some new features until the migration is done. By understanding the value, the product owner can treat the technical story like any other business-valuable story and make informed trade-offs. As a result, this technical story might be included in the product backlog.

In practice, though, most technical stories (like the one in Figure 5.10) should not be included in the product backlog.

Instead, these types of stories should be tasks associated with getting business-valuable stories done. If the development team has a strong definition of done, there should be no need to write stories like these, because the work is implied by the definition of being done.

The crux of the *valuable* criteria is that all stories in the backlog must be valuable (worth investing in) from the product owner's perspective, which represents the customer and user perspectives. Not all stories are independent, and not all stories are fully negotiable, but they all must be valuable.

Estimatable

Stories should be *estimatable* by the team that will design, build, and test them. Estimates provide an indication of the size and therefore the effort and cost of the stories (bigger stories require more effort and therefore cost more money to develop than smaller stories).

Knowing a story's size provides actionable information to the Scrum team. The product owner, for example, needs to know the cost of a story to determine its final priority in the product backlog. The Scrum team, on the other hand, can determine from the size of the story whether additional refinement or disaggregation is required. A large story that we plan to work on soon will need to be broken into a set of smaller stories.

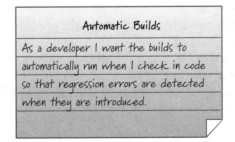

FIGURE 5.10   Undesirable technical story

If the team isn't able to size a story, the story is either just too big or ambiguous to be sized, or the team doesn't have enough knowledge to estimate a size. If it's too big, the team will need to work with the product owner to break it into more manageable stories. If the team lacks knowledge, some form of exploratory activity will be needed to acquire the information (I will discuss this topic shortly).

Sized Appropriately (Small)

Stories should be *sized appropriately* for when we plan to work on them. Stories worked on in sprints should be *small*. If we're doing a several-week sprint, we want to work on several stories that are each a few days in size. If we have a two-week sprint, we don't want a two-week-size story, because the risk of not finishing the story is just too great.

So ultimately we need small stories, but just because a story is large, that doesn't mean it's bad. Let's say we have an epic-size story that we aren't planning to work on for another year. Arguably that story is sized appropriately for when we plan to work on it. In fact, if we spent time today breaking that epic down into a collection of smaller stories, it could easily be a complete waste of our time. Of course, if we have an epic that we want to work on in the next sprint, it's not sized appropriately and we have more work to do to bring it down to size. You must consider *when* the story will be worked on when applying this criterion.

Testable

Stories should be *testable* in a binary way—they either pass or fail their associated tests. Being testable means having good acceptance criteria (related to the conditions of satisfaction) associated with the story, which is the "confirmation" aspect of a user story that I discussed earlier.

Without testable criteria, how would we know if the story is done at the end of the sprint? Also, because these tests frequently provide important story details, they may be needed before the team can even estimate the story.

It may not always be necessary or possible to test a story. For example, epic-size stories probably don't have tests associated with them, nor do they need them (we don't directly build the epics).

Also, on occasion there might be a story that the product owner deems valuable, yet there might not be a practical way to test it. These are more likely to be nonfunctional requirements, such as "As a user I want the system to have 99.999% uptime." Although the acceptance criteria might be clear, there may be no set of tests that can be run when the system is put into production that can prove that this level of uptime has been met, but the requirement is still valuable as it will drive the design.

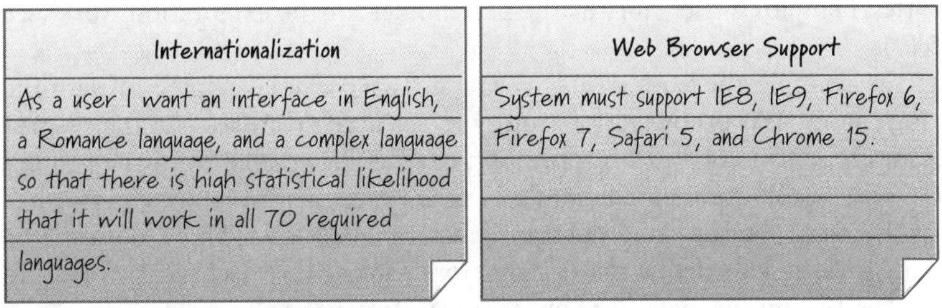

Internationalization	Web Browser Support
As a user I want an interface in English, a Romance language, and a complex language so that there is high statistical likelihood that it will work in all 70 required languages.	System must support IE8, IE9, Firefox 6, Firefox 7, Safari 5, and Chrome 15.

FIGURE 5.11 Nonfunctional requirements

Nonfunctional Requirements

Nonfunctional requirements represent system-level constraints. I frequently write nonfunctional requirements as user stories (see the left side of Figure 5.11), but I feel no obligation to do so, especially if it seems awkward or more convenient to write them in a different format (right side of Figure 5.11).

As system-level constraints, nonfunctional requirements are important because they affect the design and testing of most or all stories in the product backlog. For example, having a "Web Browser Support" nonfunctional requirement (right side of Figure 5.11) would be common on any website project. When the team develops the website features, it must ensure that the site features work with all of the specified browsers.

The team must also decide when to test all of the browsers. Each nonfunctional requirement is a prime target for inclusion in the team's definition of done. If the team includes the "Web Browser Support" nonfunctional requirement in the definition of done, the team will have to test any new features added in the sprint with all of the listed browsers. If it doesn't work with all of them, the story isn't done.

I recommend that teams try to include as many of the nonfunctional requirements in their definitions of done as they possibly can. Waiting to test nonfunctional requirements until late in the development effort defers getting fast feedback on critical system performance characteristics.

Knowledge-Acquisition Stories

Sometimes we need to create a product backlog item that focuses on knowledge acquisition. Perhaps we don't have enough exploitable knowledge about the product or the process of building the product to move forward. So, as I discussed in Chapter 3, we need to explore. Such exploration is known by many names: *prototype, proof of concept, experiment, study, spike,* and so on. They are all basically exploration activities that involve buying information.

Often I employ a user story as the placeholder for the exploration work (see Figure 5.12).

In the example, the team wants to evaluate two possible architectures for the new filtering engine. It is proposing to prototype both architectures and then run speed, scale, and type tests against both prototypes. The deliverable from the prototyping activity will be a short memo that describes the experiments that were performed, the results that were obtained, and the team's recommendation for how to proceed.

This specific knowledge-acquisition story looks like a technical story, and as I said earlier, the business value of any technical story has to be justifiable to the product owner. Because product owners think in economic terms, there needs to be an economic justification for doing this prototyping work. There is likely a compelling technical argument for doing a knowledge-acquisition story because the team is typically blocked from making forward progress until it has the knowledge produced by the story. The question for the Scrum team is whether the value of the acquired information exceeds the cost of getting it.

Here is how a Scrum team could approach answering that question. First, we need to know the cost of the prototyping. No good product owner will authorize unbounded exploration. The team might not be able to answer particular questions until an architectural decision has been made, but it must be able to answer the question of how much effort it wants to spend to buy the information necessary to make the architectural decision. So, we ask the team to size the prototyping story.

Let's say that the size estimate indicates that the full team would need to work on the story for one sprint. We know who is on the team and the length of the sprint, so we also know the cost of acquiring the information. (Let's say it is $10K.) Now we need to know the value of the information.

Here is one way we might estimate the value. Imagine that I flip a coin. If it comes up heads, we'll do architecture A; if it comes up tails, we'll do architecture B. Now, I ask the team to estimate the cost of being wrong. For example, if I flip the coin and it comes up heads and we start building business features on top of architecture A, and architecture A turns out to be the wrong approach, what would be the cost to unwind

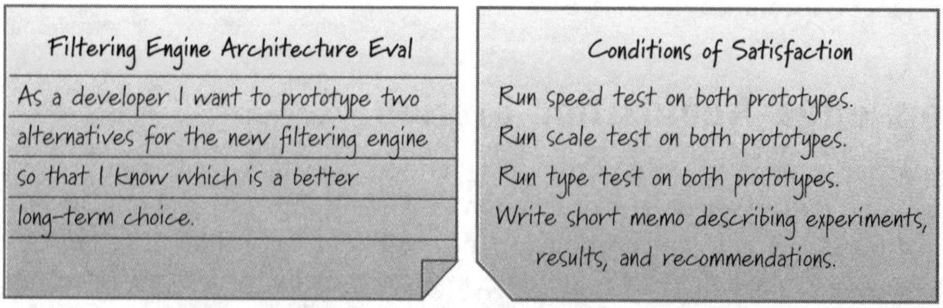

Filtering Engine Architecture Eval	Conditions of Satisfaction
As a developer I want to prototype two alternatives for the new filtering engine so that I know which is a better long-term choice.	Run speed test on both prototypes. Run scale test on both prototypes. Run type test on both prototypes. Write short memo describing experiments, results, and recommendations.

FIGURE 5.12   Knowledge-acquisition story

the bad decision and rebuild everything on top of architecture B? Let's say the team estimates the cost to be $500K.

Now we have enough information to make a sensible economic decision. Are we willing to spend $10K to purchase information that has an expected value of $250K (half the time we flip the coin we would be correct)? Sure, that seems like a sensible business decision. Now the product owner can justify why this story is in the backlog.

As a final illustration of using economics to justify knowledge-acquisition stories, let's alter the numbers. What if the team's response to "What would it cost if we were wrong?" is $15K? In this case it would be a bad decision to do the prototyping story. Why spend $10K to buy information that has an expected value of $7.5K? We would be better off just flipping the coin (or making an educated guess) and, if we're wrong, simply redoing the work using the other architecture. Actually, given today's ever-advancing technologies, this scenario is not as far-fetched as it may sound. It's an example of what some people call a **fail-fast** strategy (try something, get fast feedback, and rapidly inspect and adapt).

Gathering Stories

How do user stories come into existence? Traditional approaches to requirements gathering involve asking the users what they want. I have never been very successful with that approach. In my experience, users are far better critics than they are authors.

So, if you ask a user, "What do you want?" she may or may not be able to answer. Even if she does answer the question and we build exactly what she asked for, she may say, "Yep, you gave me exactly what I asked for, and now that I see it, I want something different." I'm sure we have all had such an experience.

A better approach is to involve the users as part of the team that is determining what to build and is constantly reviewing what is being built. To promote this level of participation, many organizations prefer to employ user-story-writing workshops as a principal means of generating at least the initial set of user stories. Some also employ story mapping to organize and provide a user-centered context to their stories. I will briefly describe each technique.

User-Story-Writing Workshop

The goal of a **user-story-writing workshop** is to collectively brainstorm desired business value and create user story placeholders for what the product or service is supposed to do.

The workshop frequently includes the product owner, ScrumMaster, and development team, in conjunction with internal and external stakeholders. Most workshops last anywhere from a few hours to a few days. I have rarely seen them go longer, nor do I think they should. The goal isn't to generate a full and complete set of user stories up front (akin to a complete requirements specification on a sequential development project). Instead, the workshop typically has a specific focus. For example, I frequently do a workshop in conjunction with initial release planning to generate a candidate set of stories for the upcoming release (see Chapter 18 for more details).

If it is the first workshop, I usually start by performing user role analysis. The goal is to determine the collection of user roles that can be used to populate the **user role** part of our stories ("As a <user role>, I want to . . ."). Of course, marketing or market research people might have created a good definition of our users in a separate activity prior to the story-writing workshop.

We might also have **personas**, which are prototypical individuals that represent core characteristics of a role. For example, "Lilly," along with her associated description, might be the persona corresponding to the role of the seven- to nine-year-old female player of a young girl's video game. Once Lilly is defined, we would write stories with Lilly in the user role position, instead of a more abstract role such as "Young Female Player." For example, "As Lilly, I want to select from among many different dresses so that I can customize my avatar to my liking."

During the workshop there is no standard way of generating user stories. Some teams prefer to work top-down and others prefer to work bottom-up. The top-down approach involves the team starting with a large story (like an epic) and then concentrating its efforts on generating a reasonable collection of smaller stories associated with the epic.

An alternative is to work more bottom-up and start immediately brainstorming stories that are associated with the next release of an existing system. There isn't a right or wrong approach; use whatever approach works well, or switch approaches to get the best of both.

Story Mapping

Story mapping is a technique popularized by Jeff Patton (Patton 2009) that takes a user-centric perspective for generating a set of user stories. The basic idea is to decompose high-level user activity into a workflow that can be further decomposed into a set of detailed tasks (see Figure 5.13).

Patton uses terms like *activity*, *task*, and *subtask* to describe the hierarchy inside a story map. To be consistent with the terminology I introduced earlier, I use *epic*, *theme*, and *sprintable story*.

At the highest level are the epics, representing the large activities of measurable economic value to the user—for example, the "Buy a Product" epic.

Next we think about the sequence or common workflow of user tasks that make up the epic (represented by themes—collections of related stories). We lay out the themes along a timeline, where themes in the workflow that would naturally occur sooner are positioned to the left of the ones that would occur later. For example, the "Search for Product" theme would be to the left of the "Manage Shopping Cart" theme.

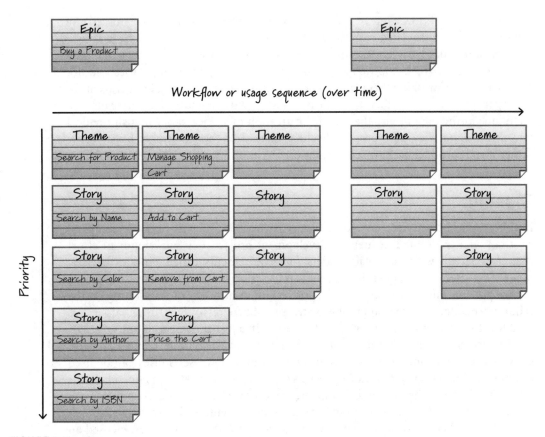

FIGURE 5.13   Story map

Each theme is then decomposed into a set of implementable stories that are arranged vertically in order of priority (really desirability because it is unlikely that the stories have been estimated yet and we can't really know final priority until we know cost). Not all stories within a theme need to be included in the same release. For example, the "Search by Color" story might not be slated for the first release, whereas the "Search by Name" story probably would be.

Story mapping combines the concepts of user-centered design with story decomposition. Good story maps show a flow of activities from the users' perspective and provide a context for understanding individual stories and their relationship to larger units of customer value.

Even if you don't do formal story mapping, I still find the idea of using workflows to be helpful during my story-writing workshops. They focus the discussion on writing stories within the context of delivering a complete workflow of value to the user.

By having the workflow context, it is easier for us to determine if we have missed any important stories associated with the workflow.

One difference between traditional story-writing workshops and story mapping is that during the workshop we are primarily focused on generating stories and not so focused on prioritizing them (the vertical position of implementable stories within a story map). So, we might use story mapping as a complement to the workshop, as a technique for helping to visualize the prioritization of stories. Story maps provide a two-dimensional view of a product backlog instead of the traditional linear (one-dimensional) product backlog representation.

Closing

In this chapter I discussed how requirements are treated differently on a Scrum project than on a traditional, sequential development project. On a development effort that uses Scrum we create placeholders for requirements called product backlog items. These items are frequently expressed as user stories and are flowed through the Scrum process with a distinct focus on conversations as a way of elaborating on the requirements details. We also employ a strategy of progressively refining larger, less detailed stories into smaller, more detailed stories in a just-in-time fashion.

I then formally introduced user stories by describing them in the context of "card, conversation, and confirmation." I went on to discuss how user stories can be used to represent business value at multiple levels of abstraction. Next I explained how the INVEST criteria are helpful in determining whether we have good user stories. Then I introduced ways to deal with nonfunctional requirements and knowledge-acquisition activities. I concluded with a discussion of how to gather user stories, focused on user-story-writing workshops and story mapping. In the next chapter I will discuss the product backlog.

Chapter 6

PRODUCT BACKLOG

In this chapter I describe the important role that the product backlog plays on a Scrum development project. I begin by describing the different types of items that typically populate a product backlog. Next I discuss four characteristics of a good product backlog and how good backlog grooming helps ensure that those characteristics are achieved. I then describe why the product backlog is a key element in managing fast, flexible flow at both the release and sprint level. I end by discussing how we determine which and how many product backlogs we should have.

Overview

The product backlog is a prioritized list of desired product functionality. It provides a centralized and shared understanding of what to build and the order in which to build it. It is a highly visible artifact at the heart of the Scrum framework that is accessible to all project participants (see Figure 6.1).

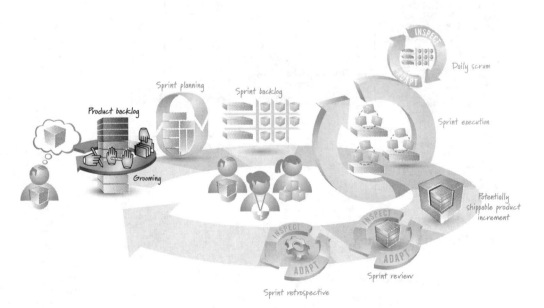

FIGURE 6.1   The product backlog is at the heart of the Scrum framework.

As long as there is a product or system being built, enhanced, or supported, there is a product backlog.

Product Backlog Items

The product backlog is composed of backlog items, which I refer to as PBIs, backlog items, or simply items (see Figure 6.2).

Most PBIs are features, items of functionality that will have tangible value to the user or customer. These are often written as user stories (although Scrum does not specify the format of PBIs). Examples of features include something brand-new (a login screen for a new website), or a change to an existing feature (a more user-friendly login screen for an existing website). Other PBIs include defects needing repair, technical improvements, knowledge-acquisition work, and any other work the product owner deems valuable. See Table 6.1 for examples of the different types of PBIs.

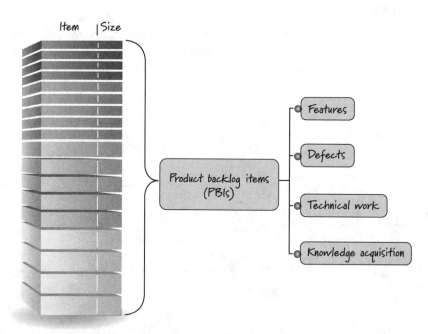

FIGURE 6.2   Product backlog items

TABLE 6.1 Example Product Backlog Items

PBI Type	Example
Feature	As a customer service representative I want to create a ticket for a customer support issue so that I can record and manage a customer's request for support.
Change	As a customer service representative I want the default ordering of search results to be by last name instead of ticket number so that it's easier to find a support ticket.
Defect	Fix defect #256 in the defect-tracking system so that special characters in search terms won't make customer searches crash.
Technical improvement	Move to the latest version of the Oracle DBMS.
Knowledge acquisition	Create a prototype or proof of concept of two architectures and run three tests to determine which would be a better approach for our product.

Good Product Backlog Characteristics

Good product backlogs exhibit similar characteristics. Roman Pichler (Pichler 2010) and Mike Cohn coined the acronym **DEEP** to summarize several important characteristics of good product backlogs: *Detailed appropriately, Emergent, Estimated,* and *Prioritized.* Much as the INVEST criteria (see Chapter 5) are useful for judging the quality of a user story, the DEEP criteria are useful for determining if a product backlog has been structured in a good way.

Detailed Appropriately

Not all items in a product backlog will be at the same level of detail at the same time (see Figure 6.3).

PBIs that we plan to work on soon should be near the top of the backlog, small in size, and very detailed so that they can be worked on in a near-term sprint. PBIs that we won't work on for some time should be toward the bottom of the backlog, larger in size, and less detailed. That's OK; we don't plan to work on those PBIs anytime soon.

As we get closer to working on a larger PBI, such as an epic, we will break that story down into a collection of smaller, sprint-ready stories. This should happen in a just-in-time fashion. If we refine too early, we might spend a good deal of time figuring out the details, only to end up never implementing the story. If we wait too long, we will impede the flow of PBIs into the sprint and slow the team down. We need to find the proper balance of just enough and just in time.

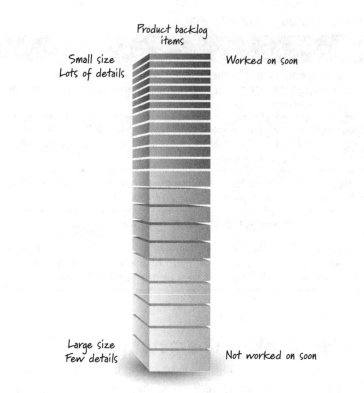

Product backlog
items

Small size
Lots of details

Worked on soon

Large size
Few details

Not worked on soon

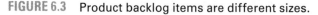

FIGURE 6.3   Product backlog items are different sizes.

Emergent

As long as there is a product being developed or maintained, the product backlog is never complete or frozen. Instead, it is continuously updated based on a stream of economically valuable information that is constantly arriving. For example, customers might change their mind about what they want; competitors might make bold, unpredictable moves; or unforeseen technical problems might arise. The product backlog is designed to adapt to these occurrences.

The structure of the product backlog is therefore constantly emerging over time. As new items are added or existing items are refined, the product owner must rebalance and reprioritize the product backlog, taking the new information into account.

Estimated

Each product backlog item has a size estimate corresponding to the effort required to develop the item (see Figure 6.4).

The product owner uses these estimates as one of several inputs to help determine a PBI's priority (and therefore position) in the product backlog. Also, a high-priority,

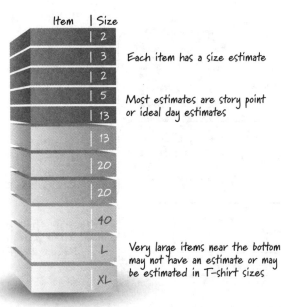

Item | Size

| 2

| 3   Each item has a size estimate

| 2

| 5   Most estimates are story point

| 13   or ideal day estimates

| 13

| 20

| 20

| 40

L   Very large items near the bottom
may not have an estimate or may
XL   be estimated in T-shirt sizes

FIGURE 6.4   Product backlog items are estimated.

large PBI (near the top of the backlog) signals to the product owner that additional refinement of that item is necessary before it can be moved into a near-term sprint.

As I will discuss in more detail in Chapter 7, most PBIs are estimated in either story points or ideal days. These size estimates need to be reasonably accurate without being overly precise. Because items near the top of the backlog are smaller and more detailed, they will have smaller, more accurate size estimates. It may not be possible to provide numerically accurate estimates for larger items (like epics) located near the bottom of the backlog, so some teams might choose to not estimate them at all, or to use T-shirt-size estimates (L, XL, XXL, etc.). As these larger items are refined into a set of smaller items, each of the smaller items would then be estimated with numbers.

Prioritized

Although the product backlog is a prioritized list of PBIs, it is unlikely that *all* of the items in the backlog will be prioritized (see Figure 6.5).

It is useful to prioritize the near-term items that are destined for the next few sprints. Perhaps it is valuable to prioritize as far down in the backlog as we think we can get in Release 1. Going beyond that point at anything other than a gross level of prioritization is likely not worth our time.

For example, we might declare that an item is destined for Release 2 or Release 3 according to our product roadmap. However, if we are early in the development of

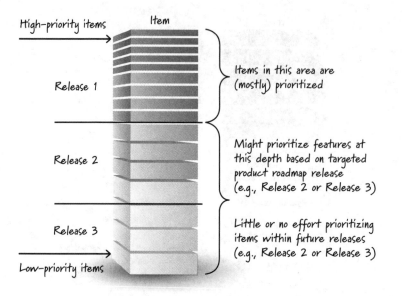

FIGURE 6.5   Product backlog items are prioritized.

Release 1 features, spending any of our valuable time worrying about how to prioritize features that we might work on someday in Release 2 or Release 3 is likely not a good investment. We might never end up actually doing a Release 2 or Release 3, or our ideas surrounding those releases might change significantly during the development of Release 1. So time spent prioritizing that far out has a high probability of being wasted.

Of course, as new items emerge during the course of development, the product owner is responsible for inserting them in the correct order based on the items that currently exist in the backlog.

Grooming

To get a good, DEEP product backlog, we must proactively manage, organize, administer, or, as it has commonly come to be referred to, groom the product backlog.

What Is Grooming?

Grooming refers to a set of three principal activities: creating and refining (adding details to) PBIs, estimating PBIs, and prioritizing PBIs.

Figure 6.6 illustrates some specific grooming tasks and how they affect the structure of the product backlog.

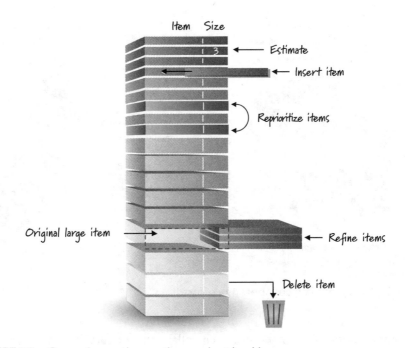

FIGURE 6.6 Grooming reshapes the product backlog.

At the appropriate time, all PBIs need to be estimated to help determine their order in the backlog and to help decide whether additional refinement work is warranted. Also, as important information becomes available, new items are created and inserted into the backlog in the correct order. Of course, if priorities shift, we'll want to reorder items in the backlog. And as we get closer to working on a larger item, we'll want to refine it into a collection of smaller items. We also might decide that a particular backlog item is just not needed, in which case we'll delete it.

Who Does the Grooming?

Grooming the product backlog is an ongoing collaborative effort led by the product owner and including significant participation from internal and external stakeholders as well as the ScrumMaster and development team (see Figure 6.7).

Ultimately there is one grooming decision maker: the product owner. However, good product owners understand that collaborative grooming fosters an important dialogue among all participants and leverages the collective intelligence and perspectives of a diverse group of individuals, thereby revealing important information that might otherwise be missed. Good product owners also know that by involving the diverse team members in the grooming, they ensure that everyone will have a clearer, shared understanding of the product backlog, so less time will be wasted

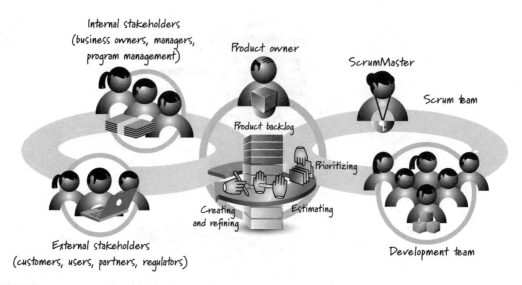

FIGURE 6.7   Grooming is a collaborative effort.

in miscommunications and handoffs. Such collaborative efforts also go a long way toward bridging the historical gap between the business people and the technical people.

Stakeholders should allocate a sufficient amount of time to grooming based on the nature of the organization and the type of project. As a general rule, the development team should allocate up to 10% of its time each sprint to assisting the product owner with grooming activities. The team will use this time to help create or review emergent product backlog items as well as progressively refine larger items into smaller items. The team will also estimate the size of product backlog items and help the product owner prioritize them based on technical dependencies and resource constraints.

When Does Grooming Take Place?

The Scrum framework only indicates that grooming needs to happen; it doesn't specify *when* it should happen. So when does grooming actually take place?

Using sequential development, we try to capture a complete and detailed description of the requirements up front, so little or no requirements grooming is scheduled after the requirements have been approved. In many organizations these baselined requirements may be changed only via a separate change control process, which is discontinuous to the primary development flow (see Figure 6.8).

As such, grooming during sequential development is an exceptional, unplanned, outside-of-primary-flow activity that we invoke only if we need to, making it disruptive to the fast flow of delivered business value.

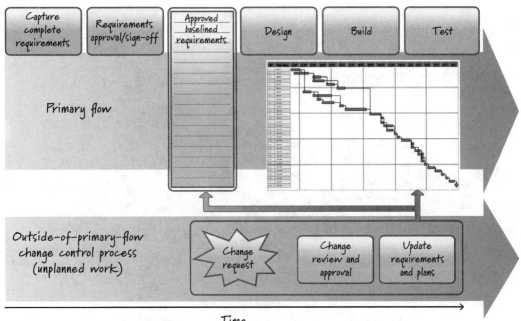

FIGURE 6.8 Outside-of-primary-flow grooming with sequential projects

Using Scrum, we assume an uncertain environment and therefore must be prepared to constantly inspect and adapt. We expect the product backlog to evolve constantly rather than being locked down early and changed only through a secondary process for handling exceptional, undesirable occurrences. As a result, we must ensure that our grooming activities are an essential, intrinsic part of how we manage our work.

Figure 6.9 illustrates the various times when grooming might be performed.

Initial grooming occurs as part of the release-planning activity (see Chapter 18 for details). During product development, the product owner meets with the stakeholders at whatever frequency makes sense to perform ongoing grooming.

When working with the development team, the product owner might schedule either a weekly or a once-a-sprint grooming workshop during sprint execution. Doing so ensures that grooming occurs on a regular schedule and enables the team to account for that time during sprint planning. It also reduces the waste of trying to schedule ad hoc meetings (for example, determining when people are available, finding available space, and so on).

Sometimes teams prefer to spread out the grooming across the sprint, rather than block out a predetermined period of time. They take a bit of time after their daily scrums to do some incremental grooming. This grooming doesn't have to include all of the team members. For example, after a daily scrum the product owner might ask for help refining a large story. Team members who are knowledgeable and interested

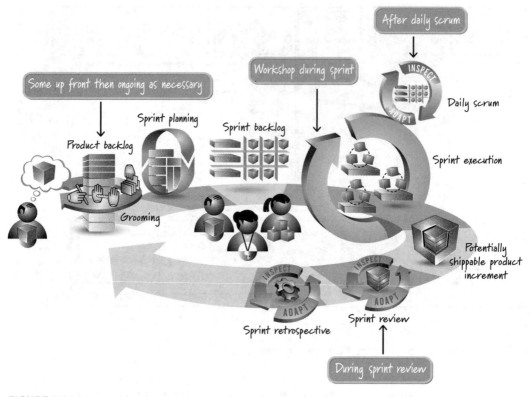

FIGURE 6.9   When grooming happens

stick around and assist the product owner. The next time, different team members might assist.

Even if teams have regularly scheduled workshops or take some time each day to look at the backlog, most teams find that they naturally do some grooming as part of the sprint review. As everyone involved gains a better understanding of where the product is and where it is going, new PBIs are often created or existing PBIs are reprioritized, or deleted if they are no longer needed.

When the grooming happens is less important than making sure it is well integrated into the Scrum development flow, to ensure flexible and fast delivery of business value.

Definition of Ready

Grooming the product backlog should ensure that items at the top of the backlog are ready to be moved into a sprint so that the development team can confidently commit and complete them by the end of a sprint.

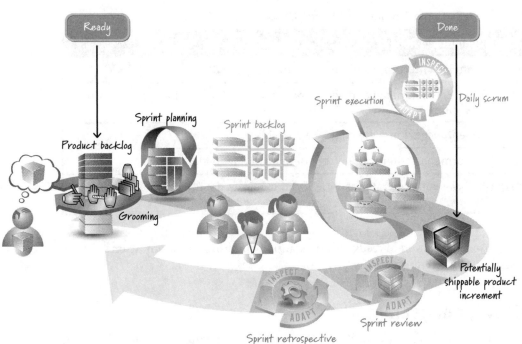

FIGURE 6.10   Definition of ready

Some Scrum teams formalize this idea by establishing a **definition of ready.** You can think of the definition of ready and the definition of done (see Chapter 4) as two states of product backlog items during a sprint cycle (see Figure 6.10).

Both the definition of done and the definition of ready are checklists of the work that must be completed before a product backlog item can be considered to be in the respective state. An example of a definition-of-ready checklist for product backlog items is given in Table 6.2.

TABLE 6.2   Example Definition-of-Ready Checklist

Definition of Ready
❑ Business value is clearly articulated.
❑ Details are sufficiently understood by the development team so it can make an informed decision as to whether it can complete the PBI.
❑ Dependencies are identified and no external dependencies would block the PBI from being completed.

continues

TABLE 6.2 Example Definition-of-Ready Checklist (*Continued*)

	Definition of Ready
❑	Team is staffed appropriately to complete the PBI.
❑	The PBI is estimated and small enough to comfortably be completed in one sprint.
❑	Acceptance criteria are clear and testable.
❑	Performance criteria, if any, are defined and testable.
❑	Scrum team understands how to demonstrate the PBI at the sprint review.

A strong definition of ready will substantially improve the Scrum team's chance of successfully meeting its sprint goal.

Flow Management

The product backlog is a crucial tool that enables the Scrum team to achieve fast, flexible value-delivery flow in the presence of uncertainty. Uncertainty cannot be eliminated from product development. We must assume that a stream of economically important information will be constantly arriving and that we need to organize and manage the work (manage the product backlog) so that this information can be processed in a rapid, cost-effective way while maintaining good flow. Let's examine the role of the product backlog in supporting good release flow and sprint flow.

Release Flow Management

The product backlog must be groomed in a way that supports ongoing release planning (the flow of features within a release). As illustrated in Figure 6.5, a release can be visualized as a line through the product backlog. All of the PBIs above the release line are targeted to be in that release; the items below the line are not.

I have found it useful to actually partition the product backlog using two lines for each release, as illustrated in Figure 6.11.

These two lines partition the backlog into three areas: *must have, nice to have,* and *won't have*. The **must-have features** represent the items that we simply must have in the upcoming release or else we don't have a viable customer release. The **nice-to-have features** represent items we are targeting for the next release and would like to include. If, however, we run short of time or other resources, we could drop nice-to-have features and still be able to ship a viable product. The **won't-have features** are items that we're declaring won't be included in the current release. The second line,

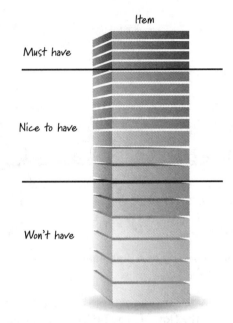

Item

Must have

Nice to have

Won't have

FIGURE 6.11   Release-level view of the product backlog

the one that separates the won't-have items from the others, is the same as the Release 1 line shown in Figure 6.5.

Maintaining the backlog in this fashion helps us better perform ongoing release planning, as I will discuss in Chapter 18.

Sprint Flow Management

Product backlog grooming is essential for effective sprint planning and the resulting flow of features into a sprint. If the product backlog has been detailed appropriately, the items at the top of the backlog should be clearly described and testable.

When grooming for good sprint flow, it is helpful to view the product backlog as a pipeline of requirements that are flowing into sprints to be designed, built, and tested by the team (see Figure 6.12).

In this figure we see that larger, less-well-understood requirements are being inserted into the pipeline. As they progress through the pipeline and move closer to the time when they will flow out to be worked on, they are progressively refined through the grooming activity. At the right side of the pipeline is the team. By the time an item flows out of the pipeline, it must be ready—detailed enough that the team can understand it and be comfortable delivering it during a sprint.

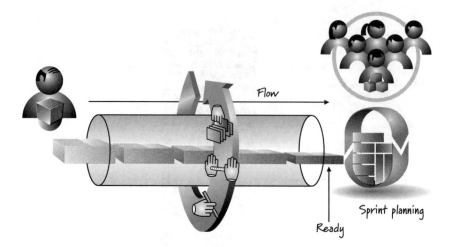

FIGURE 6.12   The product backlog as a pipeline of requirements

If there is ever a mismatch or unevenness between the inflow and outflow of items, we have a problem. If the flow of groomed, detailed, ready-to-implement items is too slow, eventually the pipeline will run dry and the team won't be able to plan and execute the next sprint (a major flow disruption or waste in Scrum). On the other hand, putting too many items into the pipeline for refinement creates a large inventory of detailed requirements that we may have to rework or throw away once we learn more (a major source of waste). Therefore, the ideal situation is to have just enough product backlog items in inventory to create an even flow but not so many as to create waste.

One approach that Scrum teams use is to have an appropriate inventory of groomed and ready-to-implement items in the backlog. A heuristic that seems to work for many teams is to have about two to three sprints' worth of stories ready to go. So, for example, if the team can normally do about 5 PBIs per sprint, the team grooms its backlog to always have about 10 to 15 PBIs ready to go at any point in time. This extra inventory ensures that the pipeline won't run dry, and it also provides the team with flexibility if it needs to select PBIs out of order for capacity reasons or other sprint-specific constraints (see Chapter 19 for a deeper discussion of this topic).

Which and How Many Product Backlogs?

When deciding on which and how many product backlogs to form, I start with a simple rule: one product, one product backlog, meaning that each product should have its own single product backlog that allows for a product-wide description and prioritization of the work to be done.

There are, however, some occasions when we need to exercise care when applying this rule to ensure that we end up with a practical, workable product backlog structure. For example, in some cases, it's not always clear what constitutes a product; some products are very large; sometimes we have multiple teams that aren't interchangeable; other times there are multiple products and a single team. Let's examine each of these special instances to see how they affect our single-backlog rule.

What Is a Product?

An issue with the one-product-one-product-backlog rule is that it isn't always clear exactly what constitutes a product. Is Microsoft Word the product, or is it simply one facet of a larger product called Microsoft Office? If we sell only the product suite, do we have a product backlog for the suite, or do we have a product backlog for each individual application in the suite (see Figure 6.13)?

When I worked at IBM, the customer-facing answer to the question "What is a product?" was "Whatever has its own unique product ID (PID) number." The beauty

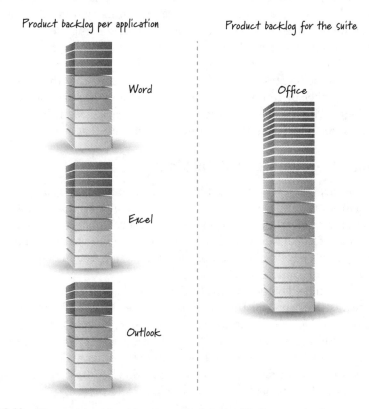

FIGURE 6.13   The product backlog is associated with the product.

of that answer was its simplicity. IBM sold products from a catalog, so if you could put a PID on it, salespeople could include it on an order form and therefore it was a "product." Although the IBM answer may seem overly simplistic, I suggest that we use it as our starting point. A product is something of value that a customer would be willing to pay for and something we're willing to package up and sell.

Using this rule becomes more complicated if we form **component teams** whose purpose is to create one component of a larger product that a customer would buy (see Chapter 12 for a deeper discussion of component teams). For example, when I purchased my portable GPS, I didn't buy the routing algorithm; I purchased a portable device that would give me accurate graphical and auditory turn-by-turn directions. The routing "component" was simply one of many that came together to create a device that a customer like me would be willing to buy.

If the GPS manufacturer created a routing team to develop the routing component, is there a product backlog for that component? Or is there just one product backlog corresponding to the entire GPS, with the routing features woven into that product backlog?

And to make things even more interesting, what if the same routing component could be placed into multiple GPS products (each with its own PID)? Would we be more inclined to create a separate product backlog for a component if it could be shared among various device products?

As you can see, once we start asking these questions, we can go a long way down the rabbit hole. To help extricate ourselves, it helps to remember that our goal is to minimize the number of component teams and therefore the need for component product backlogs. Think about what you create that is packaged, delivered, and adds end-customer value. Then align your product backlog with that offering.

Large Products—Hierarchical Backlogs

Whenever possible, I prefer one product backlog even for a large product like Microsoft Office. However, we need to be practical when applying this rule. On a large product development effort to create something like a cell phone, we can have many tens or hundreds of teams whose work must all come together to create a marketable device. Trying to put the PBIs from all of these teams into one manageable product backlog isn't practical (or necessary).

To begin with, not all of these teams work in related areas. For example, we might have seven teams that work on the audiovisual player for the phone, and another eight teams that work on the web browser for the phone. Each of these areas delivers identifiable value to the customer, and the work in each area can be organized and prioritized at a detail level somewhat independent of the other areas.

Based on these characteristics, most organizations address the large-product problem by creating hierarchical backlogs (see Figure 6.14).

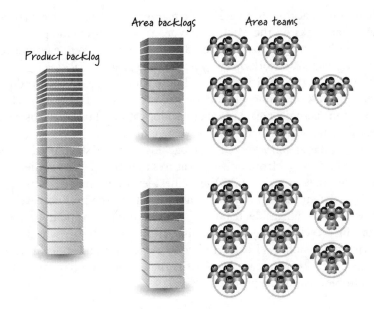

FIGURE 6.14   Hierarchical product backlogs

At the top of the hierarchy we still have the one product backlog that describes and prioritizes the large-scale features (perhaps epics) of the product. There would also be one chief product owner, as I will discuss in Chapter 9, at this level. Each of the related feature areas then has its own backlog. So the audiovisual player area has a backlog that contains the PBIs for the seven teams that work in that area. The PBIs at the feature-area level will likely be smaller in scale (feature or story size) than the corresponding items in the product backlog. In Chapter 12 I will discuss the release train concept that is based on a three-level enterprise backlog model: the portfolio backlog (containing epics), the program backlog (containing features), and the team backlogs (containing sprintable user stories).

Multiple Teams—One Product Backlog

The one-product-one-product-backlog rule is designed to allow all of the teams working on the product to share a product backlog. Aligning all of the teams to a single backlog enables us to optimize our economics at the full-product level. We get this benefit because we put all of the features into one backlog and make them compete for priority against all other features, ensuring that the highest-priority features from the full-product perspective are identified and prioritized to be worked on first.

If all of our teams are interchangeable, so that any team can work on any PBI in the one shared backlog, we actually get to realize the prioritization benefit enabled by the single product backlog. But what if the teams aren't interchangeable? For example, a team that works on the Microsoft Word text-layout engine probably can't be assigned to work on the Microsoft Excel calculation engine. While not ideal, in some cases, not every team can work on every item in the product backlog.

To work within this reality, we must know which items in the product backlog each team can work on. Conceptually, we need team-specific backlogs. In practice, however, we don't actually create product backlogs at the team level. Instead, we have team-specific views of the shared backlog (see Figure 6.15).

As shown in Figure 6.15, there is one backlog, but it is structured in such a way that teams see and choose from only the features that are relevant to their skill sets.

Notice, too, that in Figure 6.15 the highest-level item in the team C backlog is derived from an item that is not a very high priority in the product-level backlog. If the teams were interchangeable, team C's backlog would correspond to much higher-priority product-level backlog items. This lack of flexibility is why many organizations strive for a high level of shared code ownership and more interchangeable teams, so that they too can reap the benefits that come from having teams that can work on multiple areas of the product.

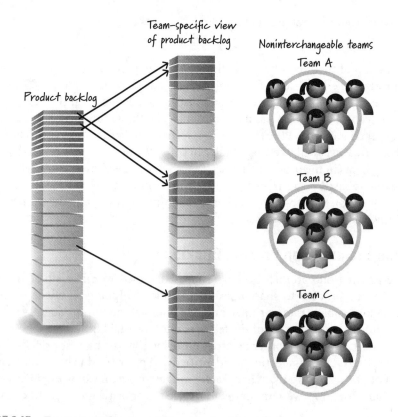

FIGURE 6.15 Team-specific view of the product backlog

One Team—Multiple Products

If an organization has multiple products, it will have multiple product backlogs. The best way to handle multiple product backlogs is to assign one or more teams to work exclusively on each product backlog (see the left side of Figure 6.16).

In some instances, however, one team ends up working from multiple product backlogs (see the right side of Figure 6.16). As I will discuss in Chapter 11, our goal should be to minimize the amount of multi-projecting that teams or team members perform. The first, and often the best, solution is to have the team work on one product at a time. In each sprint the team works only on the items from one product backlog.

However, if organizational impediments force us to have the single team work on multiple products concurrently, we might consider merging the PBIs for all three products into one product backlog. This would require that the product owners for the three products come together and reach a single prioritization across all of the products.

Even if we choose to maintain three separate product backlogs, every sprint someone (presumably the product owner for the team) will need to assemble a

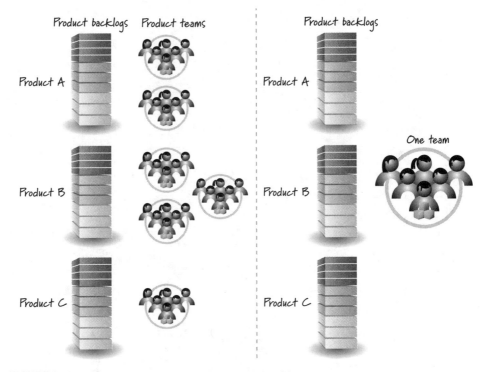

FIGURE 6.16   Scenarios for multiple product backlogs

prioritized set of PBIs from the three backlogs (perhaps based on a preallocation of the team's time to each product during the sprint) and present those to the team for its consideration and commitment.

Closing

In this chapter I discussed the crucial role of the product backlog in achieving fast, flexible value-delivery flow in the presence of uncertainty. I emphasized a number of structural and process issues surrounding the product backlog, such as what types of items are in the product backlog and how to groom the product backlog to obtain several desirable product backlog characteristics. I concluded by addressing the issue of which and how many product backlogs we should have. In the next chapter I will discuss how product backlog items are estimated and how those estimates are used to measure velocity.

Chapter 7

ESTIMATION AND VELOCITY

In this chapter I describe the concepts of estimation and velocity. I begin with an overview of the important roles that estimation and velocity play in agile planning. I then discuss the various items that we estimate and when and how we estimate them. The bulk of the chapter focuses on how to estimate product backlog items, including how to choose a unit of measure and use Planning Poker. Next I move on to the concept of velocity and how using a velocity range is essential for planning. I discuss how new teams can forecast velocity in the absence of historical data. I conclude with ways we can influence velocity and how velocity can be misused.

Overview

When planning and managing the development of a product, we need to answer important questions such as "How many features will be completed?" "When will we be done?" and "How much will this cost?" To answer these questions using Scrum, we need to estimate the size of what we are building and measure the velocity or rate at which we can get work done. With that information, we can derive the likely product development duration (and the corresponding cost) by dividing the estimated size of a set of features by the team's velocity (see Figure 7.1).

Given the product backlog in Figure 7.1, how much time do we need to create the features in Release 1? To answer that question, we must first gauge the size of Release 1. We can do this by adding the individual size estimates for each PBI targeted for Release 1. (In our example, the sum of the PBI estimates is 200 points.)

Once we know the approximate size of the release, we turn our attention to the team's velocity, how much work the team typically gets done each sprint. Velocity is easy to measure. At the end of each sprint, we simply add the size estimates of every item that was completed during the sprint; if an item isn't done, it doesn't count toward velocity. The sum of the sizes of all the completed product backlog items in a sprint is the team's velocity for that sprint. The graph in Figure 7.1 shows the team's velocity data for the prior seven sprints. Note that the average velocity is 20.

Now that we have estimated size and measured velocity, we are in a position to calculate (derive) the duration. To do this, we simply divide the size by the velocity. If the size of Release 1 is 200 points and the team can, on average, complete 20 points of work each sprint, it should take the team 10 sprints to complete Release 1 (see

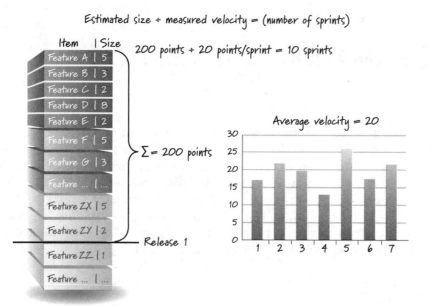

FIGURE 7.1   The relationship among size, velocity, and duration

Chapter 18 for a more detailed description of release planning). Later in this chapter, I will explain why using a velocity range to do these calculations is more accurate than using an average velocity, but for illustrative purposes, I use average velocity here.

Though the basic relationship among size, velocity, and duration remains the same, some details can vary based on where you are in the development effort, what you're trying to measure, and how you intend to use the data. Let's look more closely at estimation and velocity to see how these factors change depending on what you are trying to do and when.

What and When We Estimate

In Figure 7.1 story points were used to express the PBI estimates for calculating the release duration. Throughout the development life of a product, however, we need to estimate at varying levels of granularity and, thus, will use different units to do so (see Figure 7.2).

Most organizations make estimates for planning purposes at three different levels of detail. These estimates manifest themselves in the portfolio backlog, product backlog, and sprint backlog. Let's briefly examine each.

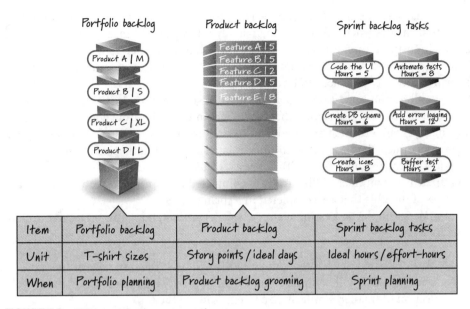

FIGURE 7.2   What and when we estimate

Portfolio Backlog Item Estimates

Although the portfolio backlog is not formally a part of Scrum, many organizations maintain one that contains a prioritized list of all of the products (or projects) that need to be built. To properly prioritize a portfolio backlog item we need to know the approximate cost of each item. As I discussed in Chapter 5, we typically won't have a complete, detailed set of requirements at the time when this cost number is initially requested, so we can't use the standard technique of estimating each individual, detailed requirement and then summing those estimates to get an aggregate estimate of the total cost.

Instead, to estimate portfolio backlog items, many organizations choose to use rough, relative size estimates like T-shirt sizes (such as small, medium, large, extra-large, and so on). I will discuss the use of T-shirt sizes for portfolio planning in Chapter 16.

Product Backlog Estimates

Once a product or project is approved and we start adding more detail to its product backlog items, however, we need to estimate differently. When PBIs have risen in priority and been groomed to include more detail, most teams prefer to put numeric size estimates on them, using either story points or ideal days. I will discuss both of these approaches later in the chapter.

Estimating PBIs is part of the overall product backlog grooming activity. Figure 6.9 illustrates when this grooming usually takes place. Typically, PBI estimation occurs in "estimation meetings," the first of which likely coincides with initial release planning. The product owner might also call additional estimation meetings during a sprint if any new PBIs need to be estimated.

Not all Scrum practitioners believe that PBI size estimation is a necessary activity. Their experience has shown that when Scrum teams become good enough, they are able to create PBIs that are small and of roughly the same size. Such practitioners have determined that it is wasteful to estimate small, similarly sized items. Instead, they just count the number of PBIs. They still use the concept of velocity, but it is measured as the number of PBIs that are completed in a sprint, instead of the sum of the sizes of the PBIs that are completed in a sprint.

I understand the "no-estimates-required" argument, but I still prefer to estimate PBIs for a few reasons:

- As I discussed in Chapter 5, not all PBIs will be at the same size at the same time, so there will be some larger PBIs in the backlog even if we do have a collection of smaller, similarly sized items toward the top.
- It can take some time for teams to acquire the skills to break down PBIs to be roughly the same size.
- Teams might have to split stories at unnatural points to achieve the same-size goal.
- Finally, and most importantly, one of the primary values of estimation is the learning that happens during the estimation conversations. Nothing promotes a healthy debate like asking people to put a number on something, which will immediately surface any disagreements and force assumptions to be exposed. If we were to do away with estimation, we would need to substitute an equally effective way of promoting these healthy discussions.

Task Estimates

At the most detailed level we have the tasks that reside in the sprint backlog. Most teams choose to size their tasks during sprint planning so that they can acquire confidence that the commitments they are considering are reasonable (see Chapter 19 for more details).

Tasks are sized in **ideal hours** (also referred to as effort-hours, man-hours, or person-hours). In Figure 7.2, the team estimates that the UI task will take five effort-hours to complete. That doesn't mean it will take five elapsed hours. It might take one person a couple of days to code the UI, or it could take a couple of people working together less than a day. The estimate simply states how much of the team's effort is expected to complete the task. I will describe the use of task estimates in more detail in Chapter 19 when I describe the details of sprint planning.

PBI Estimation Concepts

Though all three levels of detail are important, the remainder of this chapter focuses on product-backlog-level estimation. There are several important concepts that Scrum teams use when estimating PBIs (see Figure 7.3).

Let's examine each concept.

Estimate as a Team

In many traditional organizations the project manager, product manager, architect, or lead developer might do the initial size estimation. Other team members might get a chance to review and comment on those estimates at a later time. In Scrum, we follow a simple rule: The people who will do the work collectively provide the estimates.

To be clear, when I say people who will do the work, I mean the development team that will do the hands-on work to design, build, and test the PBIs. The product owner and ScrumMaster don't provide estimates. Both of these roles are present when the PBIs are being estimated, but they don't do any hands-on estimation (see Figure 7.4).

The product owner's role is to describe the PBIs and to answer clarifying questions that the team might ask. The product owner should not guide or "anchor" the team toward a desired estimate. The ScrumMaster's role is to help coach and facilitate the estimation activity.

The goal is for the development team to determine the size of each PBI from its collective perspective. Because everyone sees a story from a different point of view, depending on his area of expertise, it is important that all members of the development team participate during estimation.

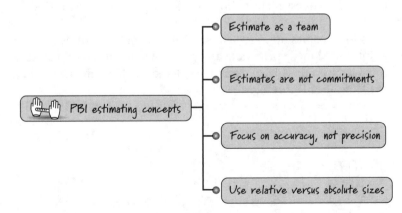

FIGURE 7.3   Product backlog item estimating concepts

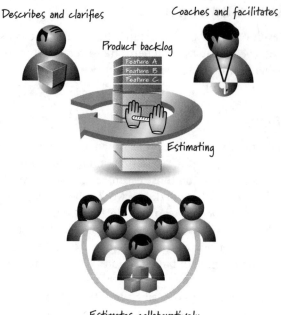

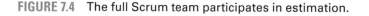

FIGURE 7.4   The full Scrum team participates in estimation.

Estimates Are Not Commitments

Estimates are not commitments, and it is important that we not treat them as such. That statement typically concerns managers. "What do you mean we're not asking the team to commit to its estimates? How are we going to get precise estimates unless they do?"

When this topic comes up in my classes, I do a simple visual demonstration to make the point. I hold up a sticky note and say, "Imagine that I ask you to size this story and you tell me it's this big." I then use my hands to illustrate the size of story, as shown on the left side of Figure 7.5.

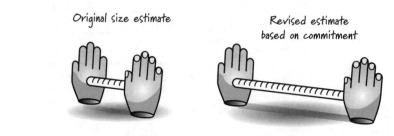

FIGURE 7.5   Effect of committing on estimates

Next, I say something like "Oh, I forgot to mention, your entire bonus next year depends on your estimate being correct. I give you the opportunity to reestimate now." At that point I start separating my hands to show progressively larger and larger estimates (see the right side of Figure 7.5). Then I usually say something like "Hey, tell me when to stop; my arms only go so far. I'm not a basketball player!"

The point is clear. If I ask people to estimate a story's size, I expect to get a realistic estimate. If I then tell them their bonuses will be based on the estimate being correct, everyone, including me, will give a much larger estimate than the one we originally thought was correct.

The estimates ought to be a realistic measure of how big something is. We don't want them artificially inflated due to external influences. That behavior only results in bloated schedules and a back-and-forth game of estimate inflation by team members and reduction by management. When all is said and done, we have no real understanding of the numbers because they have been manipulated so many times by different people.

Accuracy versus Precision

Our estimates should be accurate without being overly precise. We have all been involved with products where the estimates were at a ridiculous level of **precision**. You know, the one where the estimate was 10,275 man-hours or the other one where the projected cost was $132,865.87.

Generating these wrong, overly precise estimates is wasteful. First, there is the wasted effort of coming up with the estimate, which can be considerable. Second, there is the waste that occurs when we deceive ourselves by thinking we understand something that we don't, and then make important, wrong, and costly business decisions based on this deception.

We should invest enough effort to get a good-enough, roughly right estimate (see Figure 7.6).

When estimating, there will always be a point of diminishing returns, beyond which for every additional unit of effort we invest we don't get a corresponding increase in the **accuracy** of the estimate. Beyond that point we are just wasting our time and probably starting to negatively affect the estimate's accuracy by considering an increasing amount of lower-value data.

Relative Size Estimation

We should estimate PBIs using relative sizes, not absolute sizes. We compare items to determine how large an item is relative to the others (see Figure 7.7).

As shown in Figure 7.7, while it's pretty easy to discuss how big one glass is relative to another, I might not have a good feel for the absolute quantity of liquid each glass might hold.

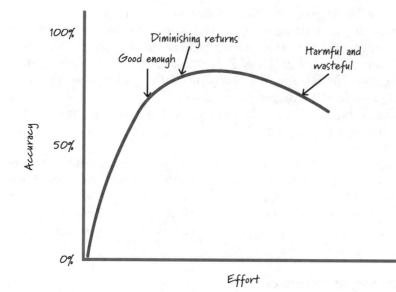

FIGURE 7.6   Effort versus accuracy when estimating

1X   4X   9X

FIGURE 7.7   Relative size estimation

My personal observations have convinced me that people are much better at relative size estimation than absolute size estimation. Here is an example I use in my classes to illustrate the point (see Figure 7.8).

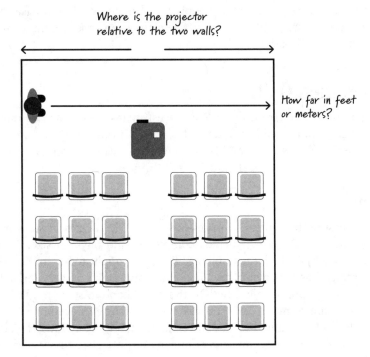

FIGURE 7.8   Absolute versus relative size estimation

I begin by going to one side of the classroom and facing the wall on the opposite side of the room. I first ask everyone in the room to write down how far away they think I am from the opposite wall in absolute size units, for example, feet or meters. (I tell the people who look up to count ceiling tiles to stop cheating!)

In many classrooms there is typically a ceiling-mounted LCD projector that is about midway across the room. So, I then ask everyone to write down a second estimate indicating where the projector is relative to the far wall and me.

I almost always get the same results. In a typical class of 30 people, when I ask, "How far in absolute distance am I from the other wall?" I usually get 27 different answers. When I then ask, "Relative to me and the other wall, where is the projector?" 29 out of the 30 people say "about halfway"; the 30th person is just messing with me and will say something like "5/11 of the way!"

Yes, this is not a rigorous scientific experiment, but most people seem to quickly agree with the idea that they are actually better at judging relative sizes than absolute sizes. For reference, there are times when the projector is one-third of the way or two-thirds of the way across the room from me, and in those cases the results are almost always the same: most people write down the same relative size distance.

Bottom line, if we're going to ask people to estimate, we should base the technique on what people are good at (relative size estimation) and not on what they're bad at (absolute size estimation).

PBI Estimation Units

Although there is no standard unit for PBI size estimates, by far the two most common units are story points and ideal days. There isn't a right or wrong choice when deciding between these two. I'd say 70% of the organizations I work with use story points and the other 30% use ideal days. Let's examine each.

Story Points

Story points measure the bigness or magnitude of a PBI. We expect story points to be influenced by several factors, such as complexity and physical size. Something doesn't have to be physically large to be big. The story might represent the development of a complex business algorithm. The end result won't be very large, but the effort required to develop it might be. On the other hand, a story might be physically quite big but not complex. Let's say we have to update every cell in a 60,000-cell spreadsheet. None of the individual updates is difficult, but the updates can't be automated. How much of this work can we get done in a sprint? Though not complex, this would be a large story.

Story points combine factors like complexity and physical size into one relative size measure. The goal is to be able to compare stories and say things like "Well, if the create-a-ticket story is a 2, then the search-for-a-ticket story is an 8," implying that the searching story is roughly four times the size of the creation story.

In the example at the beginning of this chapter, the approach was to estimate the PBI sizes and then derive the duration by dividing the sum of the sizes by the average velocity. Because size measures like story points are ultimately used to calculate time (duration), story points must reflect the effort associated with the story from the development team's perspective.

Ideal Days

An alternative approach for estimating PBIs is to use ideal days. Ideal days are a familiar unit—they represent the number of effort-days or person-days needed to complete a story. Ideal time is not the same thing as elapsed time. Ideally the American football game has four quarters that are each 15 minutes long (so the game is played in one ideal hour). However, it takes more like three to three and a half hours to actually play the game.

I stated earlier that there isn't a right or wrong answer when choosing between story points and ideal days. However, an important factor against ideal time is the risk of misinterpretation.

For example, it's currently early afternoon on Tuesday and I show you a PBI and ask, "How big is this PBI?" You say, "Two days." I say, "OK, so you'll be done Thursday early in the afternoon." You say, "No, I'm finishing up a two-day activity this afternoon and tomorrow [Wednesday]. I need the entire day just to get caught up, so I can probably start the PBI on Thursday. But since I don't have any full days to dedicate to the PBI, I'm thinking I should be done sometime next Monday." I then say, "I don't understand; you told me it was a two-day PBI, so you should be done on Thursday." You say, "I said two ideal days, not two calendar days. Please don't map my ideal days onto a calendar; it doesn't work that way."

For the 30% of the organizations that I work with that use ideal time successfully, their comment would be "Yeah, but we don't have that misinterpretation problem. We can tell people two days and they know it's not two calendar days."

If there is a low risk of misinterpretation in your organization, ideal time will likely work just fine. If you believe people will misinterpret ideal time, you're better off using story points.

There are other differences between story points and ideal time, but misinterpretation is one of the bigger issues. A student in one of my classes summed up her preference between the two when she said to her colleagues, "Look, we've been using ideal time for the past 15 years that I've been here and it has never worked. Honestly, I'd just like to try something different."

Planning Poker

Planning Poker is a technique for sizing PBIs that was first described by James Grenning (Grenning 2002) and then popularized by Mike Cohn (Cohn 2006). Planning Poker is based on a few important concepts (see Figure 7.9).

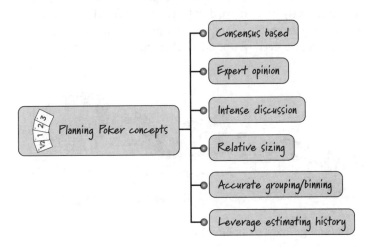

FIGURE 7.9   Planning Poker concepts

Planning Poker is a consensus-based technique for estimating effort. Knowledgeable people (the experts) slated to work on a PBI engage in an intense discussion to expose assumptions, acquire a shared understanding, and size the PBI. Planning Poker yields relative size estimates by accurately grouping or binning together items of similar size. The team leverages its established PBI estimation history to more easily estimate the next set of PBIs.

Estimation Scale

To perform Planning Poker, the team must decide which scale or sequence of numbers it will use for assigning estimates. Because our goal is to be accurate and not overly precise, we prefer to not use all of the numbers. Instead, we favor a scale of sizes with more numbers at the small end of the range and fewer, more widely spaced numbers at the large end of the range.

The most frequently used scale is the one proposed by Mike Cohn, based in part on a modified Fibonacci sequence: 1, 2, 3, 5, 8, 13, 20, 40, and 100. An alternative scale that some teams use is based on powers of 2: 1, 2, 4, 8, 16, 32, ...

When using this type of scale, we group or bin together like-size PBIs and assign them the same number on the scale. To illustrate this concept, let's say we work at the post office and we need to group packages of similar size together in the same bin (see Figure 7.10).

When we receive a package, we need to decide which bin to place the package in. Now, not all packages in the same bin are or will be identically the same physical shape, size, or weight, so we need to examine the packages that are currently in the bins so that we can find the best-fit bin for the package we are estimating. Once we find the closest matching bin, we put the package in the bin and move on to the next package. Obviously, the more packages we put into the bins, the easier it should be to size and bin future packages because we'll have more points of comparison.

To avoid being overly precise, we don't have a "4 bin" (if we're using a scale based on the Fibonacci sequence). So, when we get a package that we feel is larger than a 2 but smaller than an 8, we need to put it in either the "3 bin" or the "5 bin."

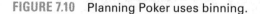

FIGURE 7.10   Planning Poker uses binning.

How to Play

The full Scrum team participates when performing Planning Poker. During the session, the product owner presents, describes, and clarifies PBIs. The ScrumMaster coaches the team to help it better apply Planning Poker. The ScrumMaster is also constantly looking for people who, by their body language or by their silence, seem to disagree and helping them engage. And the development team is collaboratively generating the estimates.

Each development team member is provided with a set of Planning Poker cards (see Figure 7.11).

A common interpretation of these cards is described in Table 7.1.

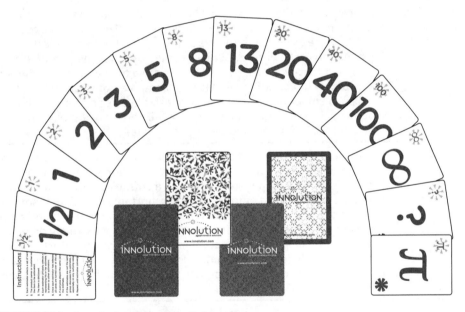

FIGURE 7.11   Innolution Planning Poker cards

TABLE 7.1   Common Interpretation of Planning Poker Cards

Card	Interpretation
0	Not shown in Figure 7.11 but included in some decks to indicate that the item is already completed or it is so small that it doesn't make sense to even give it a size number.
1/2	Used to size tiny items.
1, 2, 3	Used to size small items.

continues

TABLE 7.1   Common Interpretation of Planning Poker Cards (*Continued*)

Card	Interpretation
5, 8, 13	Used to size medium items. For many teams, an item of size 13 would be the largest they would schedule into a sprint. They would break any item larger than 13 into a set of smaller items.
20, 40	Used to size large items (for example, feature- or theme-level stories).
100	Either a very large feature or an epic.
∞ (infinity)	Used to indicate that the item is so large it doesn't even make sense to put a number on it.
? (question mark)	Indicates that a team member doesn't understand the item and is asking the product owner to provide additional clarification. Some team members also use the question mark as a way of recusing themselves from the estimation of the current item—typically because the person is so far removed from the item he has no idea how to estimate it. Although it is acceptable not to estimate, it is unacceptable not to participate! So, just because someone doesn't feel comfortable offering up an estimate, that doesn't allow him to disengage from the conversation or responsibility of helping the team find a consensus estimate.
π (pi)	In this context, π doesn't mean 3.1415926! Instead, the pi card is used when a team member wants to say, "I'm tired and hungry and I want to get some pie!" Some Planning Poker decks use a coffee cup image instead of pi. In either case, this card emphasizes an important point. The team members can engage in an intense estimation discussion for only a limited period of time (perhaps an hour or two). At that point, they really do need a break or the enthusiasm for the discussion will turn into an effort to figure out how to quickly get the estimates done, regardless of their accuracy or the learning that takes place. If people are playing the pi card, the team needs to take a break.

The rules of Planning Poker are as follows:

1. The product owner selects a PBI to be estimated and reads the item to the team.
2. Development team members discuss the item and ask clarifying questions to the product owner, who answers the questions.
3. Each estimator privately selects a card representing his estimate.
4. Once each estimator has made a private selection, all private estimates are simultaneously exposed to all estimators.
5. If everyone selects the same card, we have consensus, and that consensus number becomes the PBI estimate.

6. If the estimates are not the same, the team members engage in a focused discussion to expose assumptions and misunderstandings. Typically we start by asking the high and low estimators to explain or justify their estimates.

7. After the discussion, we return to step 3 and repeat until consensus is reached.

In Planning Poker we don't take averages or use any number not on the scale/cards. The goal is not to compromise, but instead for the development team to reach a consensus about the estimate of the story's overall size (effort) from the team perspective. Usually this consensus can be achieved within two or three rounds of voting, during which the team members' focused discussion helps obtain a shared understanding of the story.

Benefits

Planning Poker brings together the diverse team of people who will do the work and allows them to reach consensus on an accurate estimate that is frequently much better than any one individual could produce.

As I mentioned earlier, there are some in the agile community who believe that estimating PBIs is not worthwhile. The intense discussion of the PBIs fostered by Planning Poker, however, is incredibly valuable. In my experience, you really motivate people to think about the details of the PBIs and expose any assumptions when you ask them to put a size number on them.

The majority of the value associated with Planning Poker is the discussion and better understanding that team members will share about the PBIs. I hope they also get size estimates on the PBIs; however, I am more concerned that they learn about the PBIs. If they do, they have gotten a good return on the team's investment.

What Is Velocity?

Velocity is the amount of work completed each sprint. It is measured by adding the sizes of the PBIs that are completed by the end of the sprint. A PBI is either done or it's not done. The product owner doesn't get any value from undone items, so velocity does not include the size numbers of partially completed PBIs.

Velocity measures output (the size of what was delivered), not outcome (the value of what was delivered). We assume that if the product owner has agreed that the team should work on a PBI, it must have some value to him. However, completing a PBI of size 8 doesn't necessarily deliver more business value than completing a PBI of size 3. Perhaps the PBI of size 3 is high value and therefore we work on it early (because it is high value and low cost), and we work on the PBI of size 8 later (because it is lower value and higher cost).

Velocity is used for two important purposes. First, it is an essential concept for Scrum planning. For release-level planning, as shown in Figure 7.1, we divide the size of the release by the team's average velocity to calculate the number of sprints necessary to complete the release. Additionally, at sprint planning, a team's velocity is used as one input to help determine its capacity to commit to work during the upcoming sprint (see Chapter 19 for more details).

Velocity is also a diagnostic metric that the team can use to evaluate and improve its use of Scrum to deliver customer value. By observing its own velocity over time, the team can gain insight into how specific process changes affect the delivery of measurable customer value.

Calculate a Velocity Range

For planning purposes, velocity is most useful when expressed as a range, such as "The team is typically able to complete between 25 and 30 points each sprint." Using a range allows us to be accurate without being overly precise.

With a velocity range we can more accurately provide answers to questions like "When will we be done?" "How many items can we complete?" or "How much will all this cost?" Because most of these questions get asked early on in a product development effort, when we have the least information about the product, it's impossible to give a very precise answer. By using a range, we can communicate our uncertainty (see Figure 7.12).

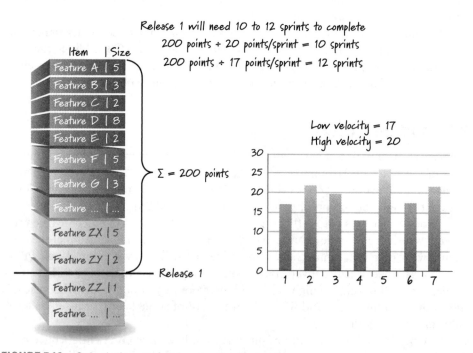

FIGURE 7.12 Calculating and using a velocity range

In this example (a revision of Figure 7.1), rather than declaring the precise sprint by which all of the items in the release will be completed (which would likely be a guess on our part), we instead provide a range as an answer to the question. To calculate this range we need two velocities for our team. If we divide the release size by the team's faster velocity, we get the fewest number of sprints required. And if we divide the release size by the team's slower velocity, we get the greatest number of sprints.

Using some simple math (like high and low averages, 90% confidence intervals, and so on), we can easily get two velocity numbers from our team's historical velocity data (17 and 20 in the example here). In Chapter 18 I will provide more detail on performing these calculations to answer questions about when, how many, and how much.

Forecasting Velocity

In the previous examples I assumed that the team had historical velocity data that we could use to predict future velocity. Certainly one of the benefits of having long-lived teams is that they will acquire such useful historical data (see Chapter 11 for a more detailed discussion of the benefits of long-lived teams). But how do we handle the situation where we have a new team whose members haven't worked together and therefore have no historical data? We'll have to forecast it.

One common way to forecast a team's velocity is to have the team perform sprint planning to determine what PBIs it could commit to delivering during a single sprint. If the commitment seems reasonable, we would simply add the sizes of the committed PBIs and use that as the team's forecasted velocity.

Because what we really want is a velocity *range*, we could have the team plan two sprints and use one estimated velocity number as the high and the other as the low (the two estimates would likely be different). Alternatively, we could make some intuitive adjustments to one estimated velocity based on historical data for other teams, thereby converting the one estimate into a two-estimate range.

As soon as the team has performed a sprint and we have an actual velocity measurement, we should discard the forecast and use the actual. And as the team builds up a history of actual velocities, we should compute averages or apply other statistics to the data to extract a velocity range. (See Cohn 2009 for more examples.)

Affecting Velocity

Do you believe that a team's velocity should constantly increase over time? An executive once said to me, "Last year my team's velocity averaged 30 points per sprint. This year I'm expecting the team to achieve 35 points per sprint." This executive believes that the team's velocity should correspond to trend 1 in Figure 7.13.

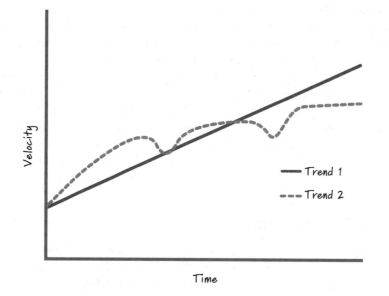

FIGURE 7.13 A team's velocity over time

His reasoning was that if the team is constantly inspecting and adapting (continuously improving), its velocity should keep getting better and better.

I would expect a team that is aggressively trying to improve itself and is focused on delivering features in accordance with a robust definition of done and low technical debt (see Chapter 8) to see an increase in velocity. Well, at least an increase up to a certain point, at which time its velocity will likely plateau (more like trend 2 in Figure 7.13).

Just because a team's velocity has leveled out doesn't mean there is no more upward potential. There are a number of ways that the Scrum team and managers can help get velocity to the next plateau. For example, introducing new tools or increasing training can have a positive effect on velocity. Or managers can strategically change team composition with the hope that the change will eventually lead to a greater overall velocity. Of course, managers should be careful because haphazardly moving people on and off teams can and probably will cause velocity to decline.

Although introducing new tools, getting training, or changing team composition can have a positive effect on velocity, these actions usually cause a dip in velocity while the team absorbs and processes the change (see Figure 7.13, trend 2). After this decline, there will probably be an increase to the point where the team establishes a new plateau until some other change causes yet another plateau to be achievable.

Of course, there is one obvious thing we could do to try to improve velocity: work longer hours. Working a lot of consecutive overtime might initially cause velocity to increase (see "Overtime" in Figure 7.14).

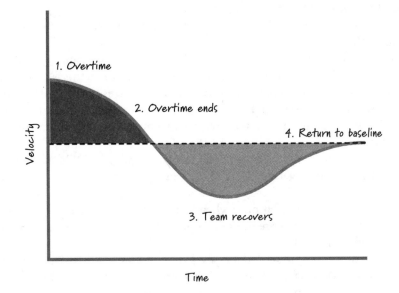

That increase will almost certainly be followed by an aggressive decline in velocity along with a simultaneous decline in quality. Even after the overtime period ends, the team will need some amount of time to recover before returning to its reasonable baseline velocity. I have seen examples of where the trough (decreased velocity area) during the recovery period is larger than the crest (increased velocity area) during the overtime period.

The end result is that lots of overtime may provide some short-term benefits, but these are frequently far outweighed by the long-term consequences.

Misusing Velocity

Velocity is used as a planning tool and as a team diagnostic metric. It should not be used as a performance metric in an attempt to judge team productivity. When misused in this way, velocity can motivate wasteful and dangerous behavior.

For example, say I have decided to give the largest bonus to the team that has the highest velocity. Superficially this idea might seem sensible; the team with the highest velocity must be getting the most work done each sprint, right? So, why not reward that behavior?

Well, if I'm comparing teams that aren't sizing their PBIs using a common baseline (which is very likely true), comparing the numbers would make no sense. Let's say that team A assigns a value of 5 to a PBI, whereas team B assigns a value of 50 to the same PBI. Team A doesn't really want me to compare its velocity against team B's velocity. Team B's velocity will be ten times that of team A, even if both teams actually get about the same quantity of work completed each sprint.

Once team A sees the problem, its members will start to game the system to ensure that their velocity numbers are higher. The easy way to do this is to just change the scale the team uses to estimate PBIs. So, team A now sizes the same item (the one it originally sized a 5) to be a 500. I call this behavior **point inflation,** and it serves no purpose other than to align a team's behavior with a misguided measurement system. Don't do this.

Even if teams are using the same units to consistently size PBIs, if I set up the reward system to favor bigger numbers, that's exactly what I'll get—bigger numbers (point inflation).

Even worse than point inflation is when teams cut corners to get more "done" in an effort to achieve higher, more desirable velocities. Doing so leads to increasingly greater levels of technical debt.

At the end of the day, we should judge velocity on how well it assists us with performing accurate planning and how well it helps a team to internally improve itself. Any other uses will likely promote the wrong behavior.

Closing

In this chapter I discussed how sizes are estimated, velocity is measured, and duration is calculated. I illustrated how estimation applies to portfolio-level items, product backlog items, and tasks. I then focused specifically on PBIs by discussing important concepts related to PBI estimation, including story points and ideal days. Next I described a technique known as Planning Poker that is commonly used to estimate PBIs.

I moved from estimation to a discussion of velocity and how it should be used. I reinforced that velocity is most helpful when expressed as a range instead of a single number. I briefly mentioned ways that we might forecast the velocity for a new team. I concluded by discussing how velocity can be and frequently is misused. In the next chapter, I will focus on the concept of technical debt and how we deal with it when using Scrum.

Chapter 8

TECHNICAL DEBT

In this chapter I discuss the concept of technical debt. I begin by defining technical debt, which encompasses naive debt, unavoidable debt, and strategic debt. Next I examine some common causes of technical debt and the consequences of accruing high levels of debt. I then describe three activities associated with technical debt: managing the accrual of technical debt, making technical debt visible, and servicing technical debt. I specifically emphasize how to apply these activities when using Scrum.

Overview

Ward Cunningham was the first to write about the concept of **technical debt** (Cunningham 1992). He defined it as follows:

> *Shipping first time code is like going into debt. A little debt speeds development so long as it is paid back promptly with a rewrite. . . . The danger occurs when the debt is not repaid. Every minute spent on not-quite-right code counts as interest on that debt. Entire engineering organizations can be brought to a stand-still under the debt load of an unconsolidated implementation. . . .*

Cunningham used the technical debt metaphor to explain to his business team why creating software fast to get feedback was a good thing. In doing so, however, he emphasized two key points: The team and organization need to be vigilant about repayment of the debt as their understanding of the business domain improves, and the design and implementation of the system need to evolve to better embrace that understanding.

Since the introduction of the term in the early 1990s, the software industry has taken some liberties with Cunningham's definition. Nowadays, technical debt refers both to the shortcuts we purposely take and also to the many bad things that plague software systems. These include

- Unfit (bad) design—a design that once made sense but no longer does, given important changes to the business or technologies we now use
- Defects—known problems in the software that we haven't yet invested time in removing
- Insufficient test coverage—areas where we know we should do more testing but don't
- Excessive manual testing—testing by hand when we really should have automated tests

- Poor integration and release management—performing these activities in a manner that is time-consuming and error-prone
- Lack of platform experience—for example, we have mainframe applications written in COBOL but we don't have many experienced COBOL programmers around anymore
- And many more, because the term *technical debt* today is really used as a placeholder for a multidimensional problem

Cunningham didn't intend for technical debt to refer to team member or business immaturity or process deficiencies that lead to sloppy design, poor engineering practices, and a lack of testing. This kind of debt can be eliminated through proper training, a good understanding of how to apply technical practices, and sound business decision making. Because of the irresponsible and frequently accidental nature of how this type of debt is generated, I refer to it as **naive technical debt**. It is also known by other names: *reckless debt* (Fowler 2009), *unintentional debt* (McConnell 2007), and *mess* (Martin 2008).

In addition, there is **unavoidable technical debt**, which is usually unpredictable and unpreventable. For example, our understanding of what makes for a good design emerges from doing the design work and building user-valuable features on it. We can't perfectly predict up front how our product and its design will need to evolve over time. So, design and implementation decisions we made early on might need to change as we close important learning loops and acquire validated learning. The changes required in the affected areas are unavoidable technical debt.

As another example, say we licensed a third-party component for use in our product and the interfaces to that component evolve over time. Our product that once functioned well with the third-party component accrues technical debt through no fault of our own. Although this debt might be predictable (it's not unreasonable to assume that the vendor will change its component interfaces over time), it's not preventable because we can't foresee how the component developers might evolve the component in the future.

The final type of technical debt is **strategic technical debt**. This kind of debt is a tool that can be used to help organizations better quantify and leverage the economics of important, often time-sensitive, decisions. For example, an organization might deliberately make a strategic decision to take shortcuts during product development to achieve an important short-term goal, such as getting a time-sensitive product into the marketplace. Also, for a capital-strapped organization that is at risk of running out of money before it can complete its product, getting a product with technical debt to market at a reduced initial development cost and then generating revenue to self-fund ongoing development may be the only way for the organization to avoid death before deployment.

Regardless of how the debt was accrued, technical debt is a powerful metaphor because it raises awareness of and provides visibility into an important issue. The metaphor resonates well with business people who tend to be well versed in financial debt. When they hear *technical debt*, they can quickly appreciate the insightful parallels, the most important being that just like financial debt, technical debt requires interest payments, which come in the form of extra future development effort. We can choose to continue paying the interest (by working around the problems), or we can pay down the debt principal (for example, by **refactoring** the code to make it cleaner and easier to modify).

Consequences of Technical Debt

As the level of technical debt rises, so does the severity of the consequences. Let's discuss a few of the more notable consequences of high levels of technical debt (summarized in Figure 8.1).

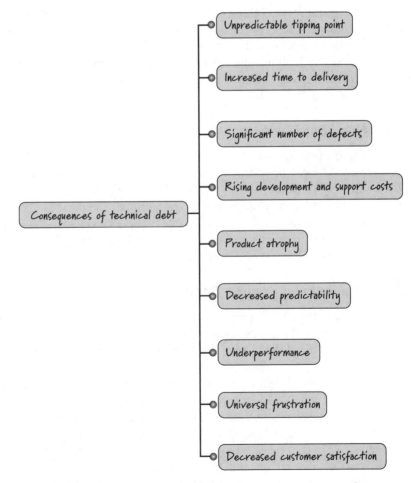

FIGURE 8.1   Consequences of technical debt

Unpredictable Tipping Point

An important attribute of technical debt is that it grows in an unpredictable, nonlinear fashion. Each bit of technical debt, when added to the pool of existing technical debt, might do significantly more harm than the size of that new debt might imply. At some point, technical debt achieves a sort of "critical mass," where the product reaches a tipping point and becomes unmanageable or chaotic. At the tipping point, even small changes to the product become major occasions of uncertainty. This nonlinear characteristic is a significant business risk; we don't know when the next piece of straw is going to break the camel's back, but when it does, all consequences are amplified.

Increased Time to Delivery

Taking on technical debt means taking a loan today against the time required to do future work. The greater the debt today, the slower the velocity tomorrow. When velocity slows, it takes longer to deliver new features and product fixes to customers. So, in the presence of high technical debt, the time between deliverables actually increases rather than decreases. In ever-competitive marketplaces, technical debt is actively working against our best interests.

Significant Number of Defects

Products with significant technical debt become more complex, making it harder to do things correctly. The compounding defects can cause critical product failures to happen with alarming frequency. These failures become a major disruption to the normal flow of value-added development work. In addition, the overhead of having to manage lots of defects eats into the time available to produce value-added features. At some point, we begin to drown but are so busy treading defect-filled waters we can't see how to pull ourselves out of the mess we are in.

Rising Development and Support Costs

As technical debt increases, development and support costs start rising. What used to be simple and cheap to do is now complicated and expensive. In the presence of increasing levels of technical debt, even small changes become very expensive (see Figure 8.2).

When the high technical debt curve in Figure 8.2 starts its aggressive climb, we reach a critical mass of technical debt and are at the tipping point.

Additionally, rising costs can change the economics of whether to proceed with a feature or defect repair. A feature that could be built (or a defect that could be repaired) at a low cost in the presence of low technical debt might become too expensive in the presence of high technical debt. As a result of rising costs, our products become less adaptive to the evolving environment in which they must exist.

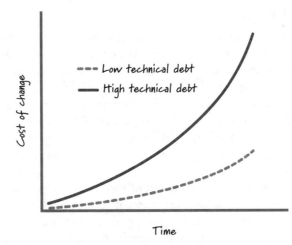

FIGURE 8.2   Cost-of-change curve affected by technical debt

Product Atrophy

As we stop adding new features or fixing defects that could rejuvenate our aging product, the product becomes less and less appealing to current and potential customers. As a result, the product starts to atrophy and simply ceases to be a viable option for most customers. Those who stay with the product are typically stuck with it for the time being. But as soon as the first opportunity to switch to another product appears, they'll probably take it!

Decreased Predictability

For a product with high levels of technical debt, making any sort of prediction is nearly impossible. For example, estimates become bad estimates even for the most experienced team members. There is simply too much uncertainty surrounding how long something might take when dealing with a debt-ridden product. Consequently, our ability to make commitments and have a reasonable expectation of meeting them is seriously impaired. The business stops trusting anything development has to say, and customers stop trusting anything the business has to say!

Underperformance

Sadly, as technical debt increases, people come to expect increasingly lower development performance and therefore reduce their expectations of what is possible. Of course, the lowered expectations start to propagate through the value chain, resulting in lower overall performance on an organization-wide basis.

Universal Frustration

The unfortunate human consequence of high technical debt is that everyone in the value chain becomes frustrated. The accumulation of all of those small but annoying shortcuts makes work on the product painful. Eventually the joy in development disappears and is replaced with the day-to-day grind of fighting issues that no one wants to (or should have to) deal with. People burn out. Knowledgeable members of the development team begin to leave to pursue more gratifying opportunities; and, as they are the ones in the best position to actually do something about the debt problem, their leaving makes things even worse for those who remain. Morale spirals downward with increasing intensity.

Technical debt doesn't suck the joy out of just technical people; it has the same effect on business people. How long do we want to keep making business commitments that can't be met? And what about our poor customers, who are trying to run their businesses on top of our debt-ridden product? They, too, quickly grow tired of the repeated product failures and our inability to fulfill any promises that we make. The trust that once existed through the value chain is replaced with frustration and resentment.

Decreased Customer Satisfaction

Customer satisfaction will decrease as customer frustration increases. So the extent of the damage caused by technical debt is not just isolated to the development team or even to the development organization as a whole. Even worse, the consequences of technical debt can substantially affect our customers and their perception of us.

Causes of Technical Debt

Recall that technical debt comes in three main forms, each of which has a different root cause. Unavoidable technical debt accrues regardless of the preventive measures we adopt. Naive technical debt results from team member, organizational, and/or process immaturity. Strategic debt is something we might choose to take on when the benefits of accruing the debt substantially exceed the cost of the debt.

Pressure to Meet a Deadline

Both strategic and naive technical debt, however, are often driven by business pressure to meet an important looming deadline (see Figure 8.3, based on Mar 2006).

The vertical dimension represents the amount of work we want to accomplish by a desired release date (shown on the horizontal dimension). The line between the amount of work and the desired release date represents the constant projected velocity at which work must be completed to meet the desired release date. By working at the projected velocity, we aim to complete high-quality features in a timely way while minimizing the accrual of technical debt.

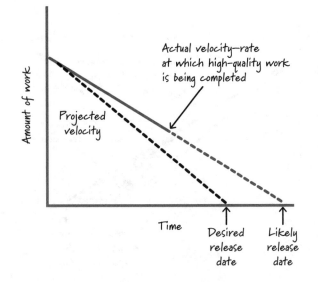

FIGURE 8.3   Pressure to meet a deadline can lead to technical debt.

However, as we start doing the work, the actual velocity needed to produce high-quality results is slower than the projected velocity. If we continue producing results at the actual velocity, we'll miss the desired release date and finish instead on the likely release date.

Attempting to Falsely Accelerate Velocity

At this point we need to make a business decision. Do we want to cut scope to meet the desired release date, or do we wish to add more time to the schedule to accommodate a delivery on the likely release date? Unfortunately, in many circumstances the business rejects both of those options and decrees that the team must meet the desired release date with all of the features. In this situation, the team doing the work is being told to accelerate its velocity to meet the desired release date (see Figure 8.4).

By working at this accelerated velocity, the team will have to make deliberate decisions to take on technical debt (meaning they will have to cut corners to work fast enough to meet the desired release date). Perhaps the design won't be as good as it should be, or specific types of testing (perhaps load testing) will be deferred. As a result, we will accrue technical debt as shown in the triangular region of Figure 8.4. This region represents all of the work we should have done but didn't have time to do.

Myth: Less Testing Can Accelerate Velocity

A prevalent myth is that testing is additional overhead, and by reducing it, we can accelerate velocity (see Figure 8.5).

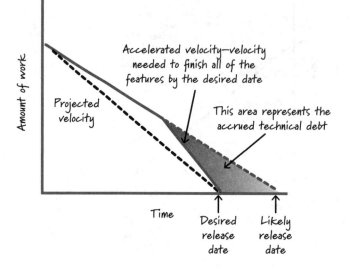

FIGURE 8.4 Accruing technical debt to meet unreasonable fixed scope and date

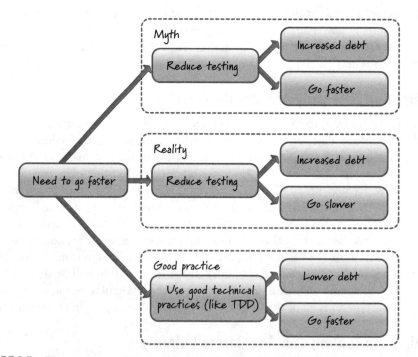

FIGURE 8.5 The myth, reality, and good practice of how testing affects velocity

The reality is that reducing testing will both increase debt and cause us to go slower, because problems will go undetected until later when it is much more time-consuming to fix them. Experienced teams deliver good-quality results faster and with less technical debt when testing is fundamentally integrated into the development process. These teams use good technical practices such as **test-driven development** (**TDD**)—where the developer writes and automates a small unit test before writing the small piece of code that will make the test pass (Crispin and Gregory 2009).

Debt Builds on Debt

Future technical debt builds quickly on top of existing technical debt. And, as the technical debt begins to build, economically harmful consequences start to appear. Figure 8.6 illustrates the consequences of building Release 2 on top of the technical debt from Release 1.

In Figure 8.6, the actual velocity during Release 2 is slower than it was in Release 1. It is clear that at this velocity we once again will miss the targeted release date. And, once again, the business insists that the team meet the desired release date with all of the features. As a result, we accrue even more technical debt.

If this pattern continues, eventually the velocity line might become horizontal. This would be a state where the technical debt in the system is so high that our effective velocity is zero. The result is the kind of product in which we are terrified to make any changes, because a small change in one area could cause 18 other things to break in what appear to be totally unrelated areas of the product. Worse yet, there is no way we can predict that those specific 18 things would break. And, of course, we

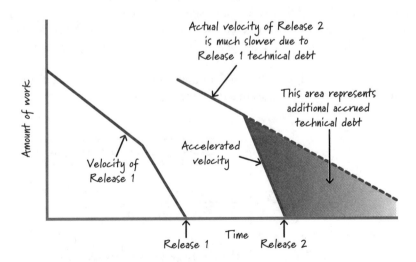

FIGURE 8.6   As technical debt increases, velocity decreases.

don't have any appreciable test framework to help us determine when they break—but, not to worry, our customers are sure to let us know!

Once we find ourselves in a situation with high technical debt, all choices become bad choices:

- Do nothing, and the problem gets worse.
- Make ever-larger investments in technical debt reduction that can consume more and more of our valuable product development resources.
- Declare technical bankruptcy, retire the technical debt, and replace the debt-ridden product with a new product at the full cost and risk of developing a new product.

With choices like these looming on the horizon, it is critical that we properly manage our technical debt before it spirals out of control.

Technical Debt Must Be Managed

Technical debt, like financial debt, has to be managed. It is important to realize that no product will be debt free, so I'm not suggesting that you try to achieve a debt-free status. Even if it were possible, the economics of being debt free simply might not be justified. We should, however, keep technical debt low enough that it doesn't significantly affect future product development.

Technical debt management requires a balanced technical and business discussion that must involve technical and business people. That is one reason why each Scrum team has a product owner. Having the product owner as part of the Scrum team allows for a balanced discussion of business and technical perspectives to make good economic trade-offs. As I will describe in Chapter 9, it is therefore essential that we choose a product owner with the proper business acumen to participate in these discussions.

There are three principal technical debt management activities (see Figure 8.7). I will address each of these activities in the following sections.

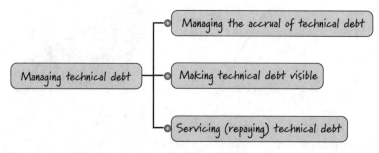

FIGURE 8.7 Activities for managing technical debt

Managing the Accrual of Technical Debt

A critical dimension of managing technical debt is to manage the debt accrual process. As I discussed earlier, there is only so much technical debt we can take on before we reach a critical mass. By analogy, continuously accruing technical debt is equivalent to continuously borrowing money against our house. At some point we just need to stop and say, "No more!" because the consequences become too severe.

First, we need to stop adding naive debt to our products (stop being reckless and creating messes). We also need to realize that there is only so much strategic debt or unavoidable debt we can accrue without repayment before we reach the tipping point. I will discuss approaches to addressing each of these. I won't discuss how to manage the accrual of unavoidable debt, because by its nature it is unpreventable (but we can make it visible and service it once we discover it).

Use Good Technical Practices

The first approach to managing the accrual of technical debt is to stop adding naive debt to our products. Using good technical practices is an excellent starting point. Although Scrum does not formally define **technical practices**, every successful Scrum team that I have seen employs practices such as simple design, test-driven development, **continuous integration**, automated testing, refactoring, and so on (see Chapter 20 for additional discussion). Understanding and proactively using these practices will help teams stop adding many forms of naive debt to their products.

In the case of accrued technical debt, code refactoring is an important tool for paying it down. Refactoring is a disciplined technique for restructuring an existing body of code, altering its internal structure without changing its external behavior (Fowler et al. 1999). In other words, we clean up under the hood, but from the customer's perspective the product still works the same. By refactoring, we strive to reduce complexity while improving maintainability and extensibility. The result of refactoring is making the work at hand easier (the equivalent of reducing interest payments).

Cunningham (2011) explains the benefits of refactoring by example:

> ... *customer is willing to pay for a new feature; feature doesn't fit in; reorganize the code so that it does fit in; now the feature is easy to implement. This could be called just-in-time refactoring. I would explain this to management as follows: we hope to have a place in our software for every new request. But sometimes we don't have a place for a feature so we have to make the place first, then implement the feature. ...*

Use a Strong Definition of Done

Work that we should have performed when a feature was built, but ended up deferring until a later time, is an important cause of technical debt. Using Scrum, we want a strong definition of done (see Chapter 4) to help guide the team to a low- or no-debt solution at the end of each sprint.

The more technically encompassing we make our definition-of-done checklist, the less likely we are to accrue technical debt. And, as I discussed in Chapter 2, many times the cost of paying back technical debt that slips past a weak definition of done is substantially greater than addressing it during the sprint. Operating without a strong definition of done is like granting a license to accrue technical debt.

Properly Understand Technical Debt Economics

To use technical debt strategically and advantageously, we must properly understand how it affects the economics of our decisions. Sadly, most organizations don't understand the implications of technical debt well enough to correctly quantify the economics of taking it on. Let me illustrate by example (see Figure 8.8).

In this example, assume the following:

- Each month of development costs $100K.
- We cannot reasonably meet the target delivery date (at ten months) with all of the requested, must-have features.
- Dropping features is just not an option.

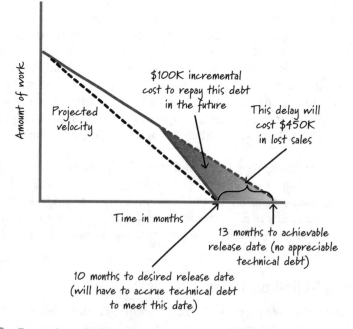

FIGURE 8.8   Example technical debt economic analysis

Let's consider two possible alternatives. First, delay the delivery date of the product by three months so that we can reasonably and professionally complete the work on the must-have feature set with minimum technical debt at 13 months. The total development cost would then be $1.3M. In discussions with sales and marketing, we also project that a three-month cost of delay equates to $450K in lost sales.

Second, accelerate development by taking shortcuts in order to meet the original target delivery date at ten months. To correctly quantify the economics of this option, we need to know the cost of taking on the technical debt.

This is where things get difficult. Imagine that we ask the development team, "So, if you have to make some design and implementation compromises today to get the must-have features done by the original desired date, how much additional money will it take to repay the debt after we do the first release?"

Let's say the team discusses the question and believes it will need four months to get the system cleaned up. This means the team will need one additional month over and above the three months it "saved" by originally cutting corners. The net result is that the team will spend an incremental $100K on development ($1.4M on development instead of the $1.3M in the first option). That's $100K the organization would not have to spend if we took the time to do the work the right way and did not put the technical debt into the product in the first place.

On the surface, the correct economic decision seems clear. Should we take on a technical debt of $100K to generate incremental revenue of $450K? Sure, who wouldn't do that? And that might be the correct answer if we believe that we have considered all (or even most) of the important cost factors associated with the technical debt.

However, here are just two of what could be many factors that we didn't consider:

- What about the delay cost of having to repay the technical debt? The $100K covers the expense of the team to do technical debt reduction work in the future. However, what about the cost of the time to do the debt reduction? Time spent repaying the principal on the debt is a delay cost on some other product or the next release of the same product. What is the cost of that delay? So, if it takes the team one extra month to repay the debt, some other product's release is likely delayed by one month. That lost opportunity cost has a real economic impact that must be considered.
- Most organizations are not good about repaying their technical debt. When push comes to shove, business people frequently favor developing new features versus reworking features that already exist. So, the reality is that we may not actually end up repaying any or all of the debt, which means we will likely have to pay interest on the debt for the useful life of the system. This also must be considered.

Table 8.1 summarizes the numbers of this example.

TABLE 8.1   Example Economics of Avoiding versus Taking on Technical Debt

	Avoid Debt	Take on Debt
Monthly development cost	$100K	$100K
Total development months	13	10
Total development cost	$1.3M	$1M
Delay in months (to release product)	3	0
Delay cost per month	$150K	$150K
Total delay cost	$450K	0
Debt-servicing months	0	4
Debt-servicing cost	$0	$400K
Total cost in lifecycle profits	$1.75M	$1.4M
Delay cost of incremental time to repay debt	$0	X
Lifetime interest payments on technical debt	$0	Y
Other debt-related costs	$0	Z
Real cost in lifecycle profits	$1.75M	$1.4M + X + Y + Z

Clearly, technical debt has tentacles that reach out and affect many different aspects of the overall economic calculation. Failing to consider at least the most important of these factors will ensure that we won't correctly quantify the economics of assuming technical debt.

Of course, if the economics in favor of taking on the debt are overwhelming and compelling—for example, we will go out of business if we don't take on that debt and get the product into the marketplace with all of the must-have features, or we will miss being first to market and lose the lion's share of the marketplace revenue—we don't need to spend time considering less important factors because we already know it's economically sensible to take on the debt.

More often, however, the decision isn't so clear-cut. The choice of whether or not to assume the debt usually requires detailed analysis to discern which is the better option. When deciding, err on the side of not taking on the debt. In my experience, most organizations substantially underestimate the true cost of assuming technical debt and aren't nearly as diligent as they think they will be at repaying it.

Making Technical Debt Visible

One of the principal benefits of the technical debt metaphor is that it enables the development team and the business people to have a necessary conversation using a shared context. To have that conversation, both need visibility into the product's technical debt position in a way that each can understand.

Make Technical Debt Visible at the Business Level

The problem in many organizations is that whereas the development team has at least some reasonable visibility into the product's technical debt position, the business people typically do not. Ask any technical person who has knowledge of a product where the greatest concentration of technical debt in the product is, and chances are she can answer that question. Ask the same question of a business person and she will typically have no appreciable understanding of how much, or what type of, technical debt exists.

The same would not be true for financial debt. Ask a business person about the organization's financial debt position and she will be able to give you a very accurate answer.

So it is essential to provide business people with visibility into the product's technical debt position. If I could quantify technical debt numerically—and there is significant current research work in the area of how to quantify technical debt (SEI 2011)—I might consider entering short-term and long-term technical debt line items on the organization's balance sheet right next to financial debt (see Table 8.2).

I can't actually point to any organizations that have short-term and long-term technical debt items on their balance sheets (although I think it is a good idea). I am

TABLE 8.2   Technical Debt Shown on the Organization's Balance Sheet

Assets		Liabilities	
Cash	$600K	Current Liabilities	
Accounts Receivable	$450K	Notes Payable	$100K
		Accounts Payable	$75K
		Short-Term Technical Debt	**$90K**
Tools and Equipment	$250K	Long-Term Liabilities	
		Notes Payable	$300K
		Long-Term Technical Debt	**$650K**
. . .	. . .	. . .	. . .

simply using this as an example to illustrate that each organization needs to find a way to communicate the magnitude of a product's technical debt in a way that the business people can understand. Otherwise, the business doesn't have the proper visibility into the true condition of the product to make informed economic decisions.

A way that some organizations do make visible the business consequences of technical debt is by tracking velocity over time. Figure 8.6 illustrated how an increase in technical debt results in a decrease in velocity. This decrease can be described in financial terms. For example, assume we have a Scrum team with a fixed cost per sprint of $20K and a historical velocity of 20 points per sprint. Using these numbers, we can compute that the team has a cost per point of $1K. If the accrual of technical debt causes the team's velocity to decrease to 10 points per sprint, the cost per point will rise to $2K. In aggregate, if the team has roughly 200 points of work to complete and velocity declines by one-half, what would have cost $200K to complete will now cost $400K. So, using velocity, we can clearly see the financial cost of the interest payments on the accrued technical debt.

Make Technical Debt Visible at the Technical Level

Technical people often have **tacit knowledge** of where at least the most egregious technical debt is located in the product. However, that understanding may not be visible in a way that it can be analyzed, discussed, and acted upon. Figure 8.9 illustrates three ways of making technical debt visible at the technical level.

First, technical debt could be logged like defects into an existing defect-tracking system (left side of Figure 8.9). This has the advantage of putting the debt in a familiar place using known tools and techniques. If the debt information is colocated with defect information, it is important to tag the debt in a way that it can easily be found,

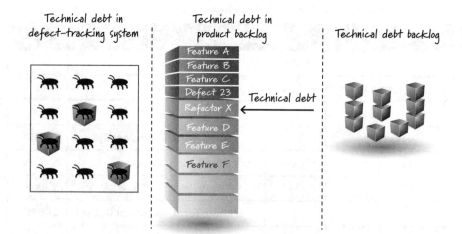

FIGURE 8.9   Ways to make technical debt visible at the technical level

because the team may choose to service the debt differently from the way it services defects (as I will discuss shortly).

Another approach to making technical debt visible is to create product backlog items that represent technical debt (middle of Figure 8.9). Doing so will give important technical debt visibility on a par with that of new features in the product backlog. Teams typically use this approach when the cost of servicing the technical debt is quite high and the product owner needs to be involved in deciding how that work should be ordered relative to value-added new features in the product backlog.

A third approach to making technical debt visible is to create a special technical debt backlog that makes individual technical debt items visible (right side of Figure 8.9). Whenever new technical debt is discovered or introduced into the product, a development team member can create a new technical debt item and add it to the technical debt backlog. By making the technical debt items visible, the development team can not only see its technical debt position but also can proactively determine when it wants to service each piece of technical debt.

For colocated teams, a simple approach to visualizing the technical debt backlog is to create a technical debt board on the wall and use sticky notes or cards to represent specific technical debt items. Usually the technical debt board would be placed right next to the sprint backlog so that during sprint planning the team has visibility into the technical debt that it can consider servicing in the upcoming sprint (I will discuss this approach in the next section).

Most teams treat the technical debt backlog in a low-ceremony way by just placing technical debt cards on the wall. However, others might choose to groom the technical debt backlog a bit more by investing a little time to order the cards or to give a rough idea of the effort required to address the debt described on the card.

Servicing the Technical Debt

The last activity in managing technical debt is to service or repay the debt. When discussing debt servicing, I find it helpful to use the following status categories:

- **Happened-upon technical debt**—debt that the development team was unaware existed until it was exposed during the normal course of performing work on the product. For example, the team is adding a new feature to the product and in doing so it realizes that a work-around had been built into the code years before by someone who has long since departed.
- **Known technical debt**—debt that is known to the development team and has been made visible using one of the previously discussed approaches.
- **Targeted technical debt**—debt that is known and has been targeted for servicing by the development team.

Based on these categories, I generally apply the following algorithm when servicing technical debt:

1. Determine if the known technical debt should be serviced (as I will discuss, not all debt should be serviced). If it should be serviced, go to step 2.
2. If you are in the code doing work and you discover happened-upon technical debt, clean it up. If the amount of happened-upon technical debt exceeds some reasonable threshold, clean it up until you reach that threshold. Then classify the nonserviced, happened-upon technical debt as known technical debt (for example, by creating entries in the technical debt backlog).
3. Every sprint, consider designating some amount of known technical debt as targeted technical debt to be serviced during the sprint. Favor servicing known technical debt with a high interest rate that is aligned with customer-valuable work.

The approaches shown in Figure 8.10 expand on this algorithm for servicing technical debt.

I will describe each of these approaches and how they specifically apply when using Scrum.

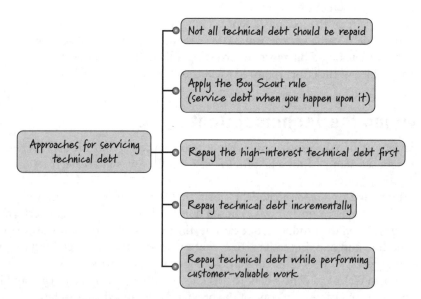

FIGURE 8.10   Approaches for servicing technical debt

Not All Technical Debt Should Be Repaid

Sometimes technical debt should not be repaid. This is one area where the analogy with financial debt gets stretched. Typically the expectation is that all financial debt eventually will be repaid—although we know that isn't always true!

There are a number of scenarios under which technical debt should not be repaid. I will discuss three: product nearing end of life, throwaway prototype, and product built for a short life.

Product Nearing End of Life

If a product has accrued significant technical debt and it is approaching end of life, investing in any substantial debt repayment would be fiscally irresponsible. If the product is low value, we would likely retire the product (and therefore the debt) and devote our resources to higher-value products. If we have a high-value, high-technical-debt product that is nearing end of life, it might make more sense to take on the high risk and high cost of developing a new product than to repay the technical debt in the old product.

Throwaway Prototype

There are times when deliberately taking on technical debt with absolutely no plan to ever repay it might be the most economically sensible thing to do. A common example would be the development of a throwaway prototype that is created for knowledge-acquisition purposes (Goldberg and Rubin 1995). The value of the prototype is not the code but rather the validated learning we get (Ries 2011). Because the prototype is not engineered for a life in the marketplace, it likely has some or a lot of technical debt. However, because it is a throwaway prototype, there is no reason to repay the debt. Of course, if we create a throwaway prototype and then decide not to throw it away, but instead treat it like an evolutionary prototype and evolve it into the product, we will almost certainly be starting with a foundation that is mired in significant technical debt.

Product Built for a Short Life

If we build a product for a very short production life, the economics might dictate that technical debt should not be repaid. I illustrate this scenario with an interesting example that I encountered in the late 1980s. At the time I was working for ParcPlace Systems, the early market leader in object-oriented development environments. Back in those days I was helping several high-profile Wall Street banks adopt Smalltalk as a development platform. In one particular case I was brought in to coach a team to help its members better understand object-oriented technology and to more effectively use the Smalltalk development environment. This team had just produced one of the first-of-its-kind derivative trading systems. When I arrived, one of my first requests to the group VP was to review the design and implementation of the product the team had just built—the product had not yet gone live but was scheduled to do so soon.

After a day of reviewing the architecture and code I met with the VP and told him that his system might just be the nastiest-looking Smalltalk implementation I had ever seen. I pointed out that the implementation had enormous problems that had to be addressed immediately or their system (and business) was in for a world of hurt.

At that point the VP told me (word for word), "Son, if you spend one nickel to clean up that system, I will personally take you out back and shoot you." I was, to say the least, dumbfounded by his remark. I responded, "You need to trust me on this one. That system is poorly designed and horribly implemented and you will have long-term problems with it." He retorted, "You don't understand my business. In my marketplace, when we come out with a new financial instrument, we make the lion's share of our profit in the first three months. That's about how long it takes for my competitors to rush in with their 'me-too' products. At that point, I am better off exiting that market and developing a new product. I only need that new system to last three months. I don't care if you hold it together with chewing gum and baling wire. Just don't delay my revenue generation and give my competitors an opportunity to beat me to market. We're turning it on."

That's exactly what they did. In the first *hour* the system was in operation, the traders using it generated $14M in revenue. I personally thought they took a large risk by turning the system on in its fragile state, but from a revenue perspective I was wrong.

Usually organizations don't build products with an expected life of three months. Typically we are interested in engineering a product for an extended life in the marketplace.

Apply the Boy Scout Rule (Service Debt When You Happen Upon It)

There is a **Boy Scout rule**: "Always leave the campground cleaner than you found it." If you find a mess on the ground, you clean it up regardless of who might have made the mess. You intentionally improve the environment for the next group of campers. Bob Martin (and others) has nicely explained why this rule applies to product development and technical debt (Martin 2008).

Following this rule, we try to always make our product design and implementation a little better, not a little worse, every time we touch it. When a development team member is working in an area of the product and sees a problem (happened-upon technical debt), she cleans up the problem. She doesn't do this just because it is good for her, though it almost certainly is, but also because it is good for the whole development team and the organization.

The algorithm provided earlier stated that we service the happened-upon debt up to a reasonable threshold. We can't just blatantly say that the team should service the entire happened-upon technical debt when it is discovered. The servicing of that debt might require significant effort, and the team is in the middle of a sprint in which it has other work to complete. If the team tries to service the entire debt, it may not be able to meet its original sprint goal.

To address this issue, the team might budget a percentage of time to allow for servicing happened-upon debt when it is discovered. One way to set this budget is to increase the estimated size of individual PBIs to allow for the additional debt servicing that typically occurs. Alternatively, the team might choose to budget a percentage of its capacity during sprint planning to service happened-upon debt. Examples I have seen in the past range from 5% up to 33% of the sprint capacity. You should let your particular circumstances guide your capacity allocation if you choose to use this approach.

As for any happened-upon debt that is not serviced when discovered, it should be classified as known debt and made visible using whatever technique the team has decided to use for visualizing technical debt.

Repay Technical Debt Incrementally

In some products the accrued technical debt level might be quite high. Teams working on such products frequently end up making large balloon payments as a means of servicing their debt load. They would be far better off if they made many, timely, incremental payments against known technical debt instead of large late payments. Smaller, more frequent payments are akin to making monthly payments against a home mortgage. Doing so allows some of the debt to be serviced each month, avoiding a large balloon payment at the end of the loan.

I get concerned when I hear teams discussing their "technical debt sprints" or "refactoring sprints." These are sprints whose only goal is to perform technical debt reduction work. These sound like balloon payments to me. In fact, these sprints give the appearance that the debt level was allowed to grow without attention to reduction. Now it has become such a problem that instead of developing customer-valuable features in the next sprint, the team is going to deliver no customer value but instead dedicate itself to dealing with a problem that it should have been dealing with a little bit each sprint. There are times when the technical debt is so high and attention to it so low that a sprint dedicated to raising awareness and making a concerted, full-team-focused effort on repayment is helpful. However, as a rule, such sprints are to be avoided whenever possible; repayment should occur incrementally.

Using this approach, we take some amount of known technical debt and designate it as targeted technical debt to be serviced during the next sprint. The decision as to how much targeted technical debt to take on each sprint can be made by the Scrum team during sprint planning.

Repay the High-Interest Technical Debt First

Although it is convenient to lump all types of shortcuts or deficiencies under one label of technical debt, it is important to realize that not all types of technical debt are of equal importance. An example of an important form of debt is a frequently modified module that a lot of other code depends on and is in real need of refactoring because it's becoming increasingly difficult to change. We pay interest on that debt all of the time, and the magnitude of the interest continues to increase as we make more and more changes.

On the other hand, we could have technical debt (known design or implementation issues) in a part of the product that is rarely used and almost never modified. On a day-to-day basis we are not paying any, or at least not much, interest on this debt. This is not a form of debt that requires a lot of attention, unless there is a not-so-insignificant risk that this part of the product could fail and that the failure would have major repercussions.

When servicing technical debt, therefore, we should target and service the high-interest technical debt first. Any reasonable business person would do the same with financial debt. For example, unless there is a compelling reason, as a rule we would pay off the financial debt with an 18% interest rate before we repay the debt with a 6% interest rate.

Some organizations have accrued such high levels of technical debt that they can become a bit paralyzed because they don't know how to get started. For them, the high-interest debt might be obvious but daunting in size. To prime the pump of debt reduction, they may choose to repay a small debt to get accustomed to the process of debt repayment. I am in favor of taking whatever actions might be culturally necessary to give organizations the jolt they need to start managing their debt. As I will describe next, if we repay technical debt while performing customer-valuable work, we can incrementally focus on a small amount of debt that is worth repaying.

Repay Technical Debt While Performing Customer-Valuable Work

An excellent way to repay known technical debt incrementally, while focusing on high-interest technical debt and aligning technical debt servicing with the Scrum value-centric approach, is to make debt payments while performing customer-valuable work. So, whenever possible, avoid scheduling a full sprint of debt reduction work, or for that matter defining individual product backlog items that are specific to debt reduction. Instead, we should service known technical debt coincident with the development of customer-valuable features in the product backlog.

Let's assume that for every customer-valuable product backlog item we work on, we also do several things. First, we commit to doing high-quality work so that we don't add new naive technical debt when we create the customer feature. Second, we apply the Boy Scout rule and clean up whatever happened-upon technical debt that we reasonably can when we are in the area doing work related to our feature. And third (the core attribute of this approach), we specifically repay targeted technical debt in the area in which we will be working.

Using this approach has several advantages:

- It aligns debt reduction work with customer-valuable work that the product owner can properly prioritize.
- It makes it clear to all development team members that technical debt reduction is a shared responsibility and not something to defer and delegate to someone or some other team to clean up.
- It reinforces technical debt prevention and removal skills because everyone gets to practice them all the time.
- It helps us identify the high-interest areas where we should focus our technical debt servicing. At the very least we know that the code (or other development artifact) we are touching is still important because we are using it to create the new feature.
- It avoids the waste of repaying technical debt in areas where we really don't have to.

Earlier I mentioned an approach that I have seen several Scrum teams use to help manage the alignment of known technical debt reduction activities with product backlog items (shown in Figure 8.11).

Using this approach, known technical debt items are entered into a technical debt backlog that is placed on the wall next to the sprint backlog during sprint planning (or inside a tool to achieve the equivalent effect).

During sprint planning, as the team members are working with the product owner to select customer-valuable items from the product backlog to work on in the next sprint, they consider the cards on the technical debt board to see if the work they are planning to do on the new product backlog item would naturally intersect an area of the product associated with a technical debt card. If so, someone takes the card from the technical debt board and places it in the sprint backlog as work for this sprint. Then, when performing the work necessary to complete the product backlog

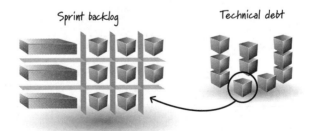

Sprint backlog   Technical debt

FIGURE 8.11   A technique for managing technical debt when using Scrum

item, the team members would also address the technical debt tasks they pulled into the sprint.

This approach is a very simple and elegant way of aligning technical debt servicing with the creation of user value.

Closing

In this chapter I discussed the concept of technical debt, which accrues when we take shortcuts today at tomorrow's expense. I distinguished among naive, unavoidable, and strategic technical debt. I went on to explain the consequences of poorly managed levels of technical debt. I then discussed the three activities associated with controlling technical debt: managing the accrual of technical debt, making technical debt visible, and servicing technical debt.

This chapter concludes Part I. In the next chapter, I will transition and begin the discussion of the various roles on a Scrum development effort, beginning with the product owner role.

Part II
Roles

Chapter 9
PRODUCT OWNER

In this chapter I expand the description of the product owner role. I begin by explaining the purpose of this role relative to other Scrum roles. Then I detail the principal responsibilities and characteristics of a product owner. Next I present a "day in the life" of a product owner over the course of multiple weeks. I then discuss who should be a product owner for different types of product development. I conclude by describing how the product owner role can be combined with other roles and how it can be scaled up into a product owner team.

Overview

The product owner is the empowered central point of product leadership. It is one of the three collaborating roles that constitute every Scrum team (the others being the ScrumMaster and the development team).

The product owner needs to look in at least two directions simultaneously (see Figure 9.1).

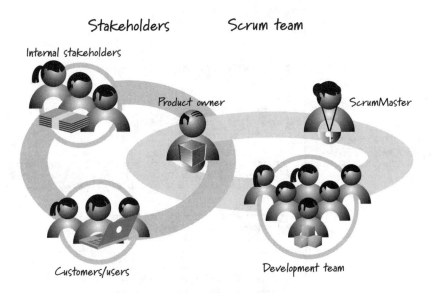

FIGURE 9.1 The product owner faces two directions simultaneously.

On one hand, the product owner must understand the needs and priorities of the organizational stakeholders, the customers, and the users well enough to act as their voice. In this respect the product owner acts as a product manager, ensuring that the right solution is developed.

On the other hand, the product owner must communicate to the development team what to build and the order in which to build it. The product owner must also ensure that the criteria for accepting features are specified and the tests that verify those criteria are later run to determine whether the features are complete. The product owner doesn't write detail-level tests but ensures that the high-level ones are written so that the team can determine when the product owner will consider the feature complete. In these respects the product owner is part business analyst and part tester.

Principal Responsibilities

Figure 9.2 illustrates the principal product owner responsibilities.

This is clearly a full-time role with significant responsibilities. As a matter of fact, when you read the description that follows, you might start to think that it is not practical for one person to handle all of these responsibilities or to have all of the attributes necessary to be successful in the role. In most cases a single person can and should fill the product owner role; however, under certain circumstances, product owner teams or product owner proxies might be practical. Both concepts will be covered later in the chapter.

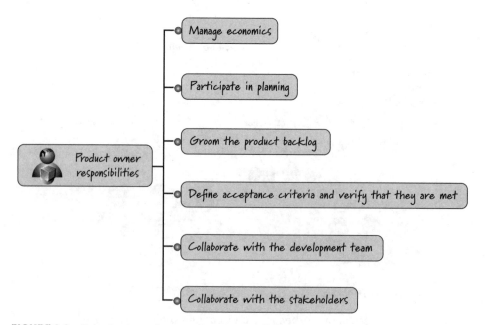

FIGURE 9.2   Principal product owner responsibilities

Manage Economics

The product owner is responsible for ensuring that good economic decisions are continuously being made at the release, sprint, and product backlog levels (see Figure 9.3).

Release-Level Economics

At the release level the product owner continuously makes trade-offs in scope, date, budget, and quality as a stream of economically important information arrives during product development. Trade-offs made at the beginning of a release might no longer be appropriate in the presence of new information that arrives during the release.

For example, what if several weeks into a six-month, fixed-date development effort we recognize an opportunity to increase revenue by 50% if we take one extra week (4% schedule slip) to add a newly identified feature to the release? Should we trade one week's time and the additional cost for the extra revenue? The product owner oversees this decision. In many cases he can unilaterally make the decision. Other times the product owner might recommend a decision but still work with others to secure their input (and at times approval) to execute the decision.

Also, at the end of every sprint the product owner oversees a decision as to whether or not to fund the next sprint. If good progress is being made toward the release goal or the next sprint is otherwise economically justified, the next sprint will be funded. If poor progress is being made or the economics don't support additional expenditures, the effort might be canceled.

A satisfied product owner might also oversee a decision to stop funding further development at the end of a sprint if the product is ready to ship and additional expenditures simply aren't justified. For example, let's say we planned for a ten-sprint release. After sprint 7, the product owner reviews the remaining product backlog items and concludes that the cost to create those items is greater than the value they deliver. The product owner might conclude that shipping the product early instead of

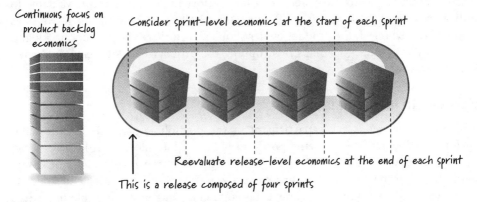

FIGURE 9.3   The product owner manages economics.

continuing with the original ten-sprint plan is economically more sensible. This flexibility to deliver early is enabled by ensuring that the higher-value items at the top of the product backlog are worked on first and the team is completing work each sprint in accordance with a strong definition of done.

And, of course, the product owner might also conclude that we should stop funding at the end of a sprint because core economic properties have changed. For example, what if we are creating a country-specific product and a regulatory agency in that country revises its laws, making it unprofitable or perhaps even illegal for us to sell the product? In cases like these, a product owner might oversee canceling the development effort even if things are otherwise going well.

Sprint-Level Economics

In addition to release-level economics, the product owner also manages sprint-level economics, ensuring that a good return on investment (ROI) is delivered from each sprint. Good product owners treat their organization's money as if it were their own money. In most cases the product owner knows the cost of the next sprint (the duration and team composition of the sprint are known). With this knowledge the product owner should ask himself at sprint planning, "Would I write a check out of my own bank account equal to the cost of this sprint to get the features that we're planning to build in this sprint?" If the answer is no, a good product owner wouldn't spend the organization's money either.

Product Backlog Economics

As I discussed in Chapter 6, the product owner is responsible for prioritizing the product backlog. When economic conditions change, the priorities in the product backlog will likely change as well.

For example, let's say that at the start of a release the product owner believes a feature is valuable to a large percentage of the target users and the team believes that only a modest effort is required to create it. After a few sprints, however, the team discovers that the feature will require a large effort to complete and is valuable to only a fraction of the target users. Because the cost/benefit ratio of this feature has dramatically changed, the product owner should reprioritize the product backlog to reflect this knowledge—perhaps by dropping the product backlog items associated with the feature.

Participate in Planning

The product owner is a key participant in the portfolio-, product-, release-, and sprint-planning activities. During portfolio planning (see Chapter 16), the product owner works with internal stakeholders (perhaps an approval committee or governance board) to position the product correctly in the portfolio backlog and to determine when to start and end product development. During product planning (see

Chapter 17), the product owner works with the stakeholders to envision the product. During release planning (see Chapter 18), the product owner works with the stakeholders and the team to define the content of the next release. During sprint planning (see Chapter 19), the product owner works with the development team to define a sprint goal. He also provides valuable input that enables the development team to select a set of product backlog items that the team can realistically deliver by the end of the sprint.

Groom the Product Backlog

The product owner oversees the grooming of the product backlog, which includes creating and refining, estimating, and prioritizing product backlog items (see Chapter 6). The product owner doesn't personally perform all of the grooming work. For example, he might not write all of the product backlog items; others might contribute them. The product owner also doesn't estimate the items (the development team does that) but is available for questions and clarification during estimation. The product owner is, however, ultimately responsible for making sure that the grooming activities take place in a way that promotes the smooth flow of delivered value.

Define Acceptance Criteria and Verify That They Are Met

The product owner is responsible for defining the acceptance criteria for each product backlog item. These are the conditions under which the product owner would be satisfied that the functional and nonfunctional requirements have been met. The product owner may also write acceptance tests corresponding to the acceptance criteria, or he could enlist the assistance of subject matter experts (SMEs) or development team members. In either case, the product owner should ensure that these acceptance criteria (and frequently specific acceptance tests) are created before an item is considered at a sprint-planning meeting. Without them, the team would have an incomplete understanding of the item and would not be ready to include it in a sprint. For this reason, many Scrum teams include the existence of clear acceptance criteria as an item on their definition-of-ready checklist (see Chapter 6).

The product owner is ultimately responsible for confirming that the acceptance criteria are met. Once again, the product owner may choose to run acceptance tests himself or may enlist the assistance of expert users to help confirm that the product backlog item meets the conditions of satisfaction. The team might help create a testing infrastructure that enables the product owner or the feature SMEs to run these tests more efficiently, but the product owner should be the final judge of whether an item meets expectations.

It is important for the product owner to verify acceptance criteria during sprint execution rather than waiting until the sprint review. By doing some testing as the features are completed, the product owner can identify mistakes and misunderstandings that the team can fix before the sprint review. Also, because the team is allowed to demonstrate only completed features at the review, the product owner must ensure that acceptance tests are run prior to the review so that the team knows which features actually meet the definition of done.

Collaborate with the Development Team

The product owner must closely collaborate with the development team on a frequent basis. The product owner is an engaged, committed, everyday role. Many organizations just starting to adopt Scrum fail to foster adequate product owner engagement with the development team, delaying essential feedback and substantially reducing the value of that feedback when it does occur.

This failure to engage can also occur when people new to the product owner role assume that their level of involvement when using Scrum should resemble their involvement during phase-based development. Figure 9.4 compares the typical level of customer- or business-side engagement during a traditional sequential development effort with that expected of a product owner when using Scrum.

Using traditional, phase-based development, the pattern of engagement resembles a U-shaped or bathtub-shaped curve. Initially the customers have considerable up-front involvement to help define the complete set of requirements. Once the effort transitions into more technical phases (such as design, coding, and certain types of testing), the customers are "no longer needed." As such, their level of engagement is quite low or nonexistent during a majority of the effort. In fact, during traditional development, the customers don't reenter the process until near the very end, when they are required to perform user acceptance testing on what was built. What customers typically discover at this point is that what has been built isn't exactly what they

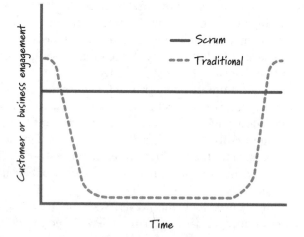

FIGURE 9.4   Comparison of customer or business engagement over time

wanted. To make matters worse, it's usually too late or too costly for them to make changes—at least in this release. Customers who come in expecting to be delighted instead leave surprised, frustrated, and disappointed. This is when the finger-pointing moves into high gear. The customer claims, "If you guys had read my requirements document more carefully, you would have built what I really wanted," and the development team retorts, "Well, if you had written your document more clearly, we would have built something different. We built what you asked for!"

Using Scrum, we build a feature at a time, not a phase at a time. This means that we perform all activities to create a particular feature (design, code, integrate, test) during one sprint. Therefore, a constant high level of engagement by the product owner is essential. With such close interaction on short, timeboxed iterations there is far less chance for the product owner and the development team to become disconnected. A secondary benefit is that there is no finger-pointing when doing Scrum well!

Collaborate with the Stakeholders

The product owner is the single voice of the entire stakeholder community, internal and external. **Internal stakeholders** can include business systems owners, executive management, program management, marketing, and sales. **External stakeholders** can include customers, users, partners, regulatory bodies, and others. The product owner must work closely with the entire stakeholder community to gather input and synthesize a coherent vision to guide product development.

If the product owner becomes overwhelmed and spreads himself too thin, it will be difficult for him to collaborate with both the development team and the stakeholders at the required level. In some circumstances the workload may be more than one person can reasonably perform, in which case the product owner may enlist the assistance of others to help fulfill the responsibilities of the role. I will address this later when I discuss the concept of a product owner team.

Characteristics/Skills

Figure 9.5 illustrates important characteristics of the product owner role.

Although there are numerous characteristics that I look for in a good product owner, they can be grouped into four categories: domain skills, people skills, decision making, and accountability.

Domain Skills

The product owner is a visionary who can synthesize a product vision and lead the team to achieve that vision. Having a vision doesn't mean that every detail of the vision or the path to achieving the vision is perfectly clear. A good product owner knows that not everything can be anticipated up front and is willing to adapt when change is warranted.

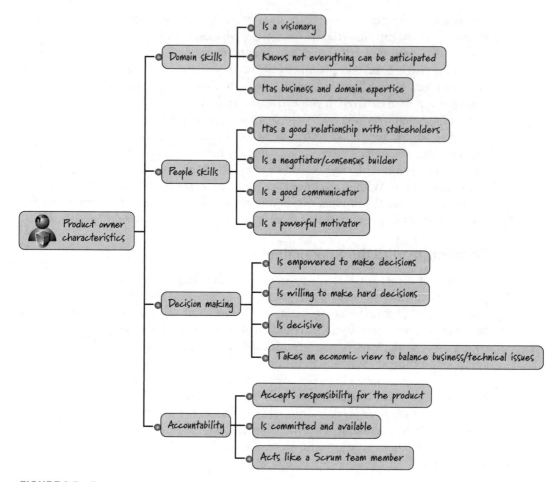

FIGURE 9.5   Product owner characteristics

To be effective at vision creation and execution, a product owner must have appropriate business and domain knowledge. It's difficult to be an effective product owner if you're new to the product domain. How can you set priorities among competing features if you don't know the subject matter?

People Skills

A product owner must also be the "voice of the customer," which requires a good relationship with stakeholders. Because there are frequently multiple stakeholders who could have conflicting needs, the product owner must also be a good negotiator and consensus builder.

The product owner is the linchpin between the stakeholder community and the rest of the Scrum team. In this position, the product owner needs good communication skills to work with both constituencies and to convey information to each group in the appropriate language. A good communicator also exhibits the following qualities: is willing to speak up even if doing so goes against the status quo; confident in his ideas; knowledgeable of the subject matter; able to communicate in a simple, concise, and easily understood way; and credible.

A product owner is also a powerful motivator. When the going gets tough, the product owner can remind people of why they are investing the effort and help people maintain an enthusiastic outlook by reinforcing the business proposition.

Decision Making

The product owner must be empowered to make decisions. A frequent impediment to organizations new to Scrum is that the person selected to be the product owner is not empowered to make any significant decisions. Such a person is not the product owner.

The product owner must also be willing to make the hard decisions—usually by trading off constraints like scope, date, and budget. These decisions must be made in a timely manner and should not be reversed without good reason. In other words, the product owner should be a decisive decision maker.

In making these decisions, a product owner must maintain the proper balance between business needs and technical realities. Although the Scrum team as a whole is responsible when systems accrue unacceptable levels of technical debt, naive product owner decisions and ones that fail to consider system-level effects can frequently be a significant contributing factor.

Accountability

The product owner is held accountable for delivering good business results. This accountability doesn't absolve other Scrum team members from their own accountability to participate in generating a good return on investment. However, the product owner is on the hook for making sure the resources are being used in an economically sensible way and must accept responsibility if they are not. After all, the product owner has many opportunities along the way to change the product backlog, readjust priorities, or even oversee canceling the development effort entirely.

The product owner must be committed and available to both the stakeholders and the rest of the Scrum team. Being a product owner is a full-time job; to try to do it part-time is a recipe for failure.

Finally, the product owner is a member of the Scrum team and therefore realizes that good economic results are impossible without the collaborative efforts of the full Scrum team. So, the product owner treats the development team and Scrum-Master with respect and trusts that they are partners in delivering the desired results. Together, all Scrum team members should share a Musketeer attitude (I will describe this concept further in Chapter 11). There is no us-versus-them attitude. The product owner, ScrumMaster, and development team are one unit working together toward the same goal.

A Day in the Life

To better appreciate the scope of product owner responsibilities, let's look at a "day in the life" of a product owner across part of a product development effort (see Figure 9.6).

During weeks 1 and 2 the product owner is engaged in both portfolio planning (see Chapter 16) and product planning (see Chapter 17). As part of portfolio planning, the product owner might work with the portfolio manager or the governance

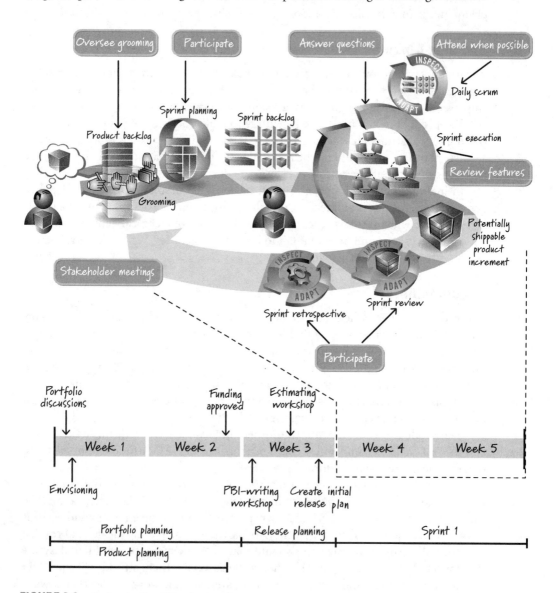

FIGURE 9.6   A day in the life of a product owner

board to discuss portfolio expectations that could influence the new-product planning. Those discussions provide input to **product planning**, where the product owner, working with appropriate stakeholders and others, will perform the envisioning of the new product.

At the completion of product planning, the proposed product will be submitted to portfolio planning, where it is subjected to the organization's **economic filter** to determine if development will be funded and when work can begin. Figure 9.6 shows all of this occurring immediately after product planning is complete; in many organizations there would likely be a delay between the end of envisioning and when the approval committee or governance board would review and approve funding and work would begin.

In week 3 the product owner is engaged in initial release planning (see Chapter 18). This typically involves a PBI-writing (story-writing) workshop (see Chapter 5 for more details) that includes internal stakeholders, the development team members, and possibly external stakeholders to generate a high-level product backlog that can be used during release planning. The development team members should be available to participate because funding has already been approved. If necessary, a surrogate team can be used if the development team is not yet formed.

Following the PBI-writing workshop, the product owner participates in an estimating workshop (probably a series of meetings over a day or two) during which development team members (or a surrogate team if the actual team has not yet been assigned) estimate the size of high-value product backlog items.

Next, the product owner facilitates an initial release-planning session (longer-term planning). Because some number of product backlog items have already been estimated, the focus of this release-planning activity is on prioritizing the product backlog and balancing the constraints of scope, schedule, and budget (see Chapter 18). The stakeholders are the principal co-participants in this activity; however, some or all of the development team members will need to be involved at some point to identify technical dependencies that could affect the order of the product backlog items.

The goal is to do a sufficient amount of release planning to have an acceptable level of clarity of the overall release, and to provide initial answers to business questions such as what will be delivered and when. For most products this activity should take no more than a day or two to complete. As I will discuss in Chapter 18, release planning is an ongoing activity, so we shouldn't overinvest at this point by trying to be very precise; we'll update the release plan as better information becomes available.

Following release planning, the Scrum team performs the first sprint (Figure 9.6 shows a two-week sprint during weeks 4 and 5). At the start of the sprint the product owner oversees the sprint-planning activity (see Chapter 19). During sprint execution (see Chapter 20), the product owner tries to attend the team's daily scrums; this may not always be possible, but it is a good practice. During the daily scrum, the product owner listens to better understand how the current sprint is progressing and to identify opportunities to assist the development team. Perhaps a team member mentions he is a little fuzzy on the specifics of a product backlog item and needs some clarification before he can complete his current task. If it is a quick clarification, the product owner might offer it up during the daily scrum. If the answer requires anything other than a few-second response, the product owner should say, "I'd be happy to stick around after the daily scrum and discuss it with you."

The product owner must also be available (typically every day) to answer questions and to test features as they become reviewable. If the product owner knows he can't be available every day to perform these responsibilities, he must delegate them to an appropriate person so that the development team will not be blocked. I will discuss this idea further later in this chapter.

Also during sprint execution the product owner meets with both the internal and external stakeholders to ensure that priorities for the upcoming sprint are correct and to secure valuable user input that will affect the features chosen for future sprints.

The product owner also performs frequent product backlog grooming, which includes writing new product backlog items and refining existing items, then working with the team to get them estimated, and the stakeholders and team to get them prioritized.

At the end of the sprint, the product owner participates in the two end-of-sprint inspect-and-adapt activities: the sprint review (see Chapter 21) and the sprint retrospective (see Chapter 22). After these are completed, the sprint cycle repeats and the product owner participates in the next sprint-planning activity.

Who Should Be a Product Owner?

Most non-Scrum organizations probably won't have an existing role labeled "product owner." So, who within the organization should fill the product owner role?

As I mentioned earlier in this chapter, the product owner needs to face two directions simultaneously: toward the internal and external stakeholders and toward the development team. Thus, the product owner role is a melding of authority and responsibilities that have historically been found in several traditional roles. In its most encompassing expression, a product owner incorporates elements of the roles of product manager, product marketer, project manager (discussed further in Chapter 13), business analyst, and acceptance tester.

Exactly who should be the product owner depends on the type of development effort and the specific organization. Table 9.1 suggests good candidates for the product owner role for different types of development.

Internal Development

On an internal development effort, an empowered person from the group that will benefit from the development should be the product owner. For example, if an internal IT group develops a system for the marketing group, an empowered person from the marketing team should be the product owner (see Figure 9.7).

TABLE 9.1 Product Owners for Different Types of Product Development

Development Type	Candidate Product Owner
Internal development	Representative/customer from the business area benefiting from the solution
Commercial development	Internal proxy for the actual customers and users (typically a product manager, product marketer, or project manager)
Outsourced development	Representative/customer from the company paying for the solution and receiving the benefits
Component team (architectural development)	Typically a technical person who can best prioritize the backlog of technical items

FIGURE 9.7 Example of a product owner on internal development

Some organizations (typically those that haven't yet learned the importance of having a business person as the day-to-day engaged product owner) might ask an IT person to handle the day-to-day product owner responsibilities. I will review the issues with this approach when I discuss the concept of a product owner team later in this chapter.

Commercial Development

On a commercial development effort—for example, a company building a product for sale to external customers—the product owner should be an organization employee who acts as the voice of the actual customers. Frequently this person comes from the ranks of product management or product marketing (see Figure 9.8).

External customers

Product management
Product marketing
Project management

Development department

Customer product

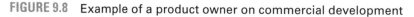

FIGURE 9.8   Example of a product owner on commercial development

Scrum practitioners have hotly debated whether or not the product owner role is really just the Scrum (and agile) renaming of the product *manager* role. Some believe the two roles are synonymous. Others advocate that the product owner role is larger than the product manager role. And, of course, still others argue that the product manager role is larger. Here's how I view it.

The areas of product management and product marketing are quite expansive. Pragmatic Marketing, Inc., a well-known and respected company in the product management/marketing field, has created a highly regarded framework that defines the roles and responsibilities for technology product management and product marketing teams (see Figure 9.9).

To cover all of these activities, Pragmatic Marketing suggests that multiple roles are needed, including product strategy champions, technical product managers, and marketing product managers. Most people would agree that if a commercial organization needs to perform all of these activities for a larger product, a team of people is likely necessary.

Is the product owner expected to perform all of these activities? Those who believe the product owner role is a subset of the traditional product manager role argue that a product owner is really just the "technical product manager" and therefore would focus primarily on the small number of activities shown inside the dashed line in Figure 9.9. They believe that because the product owner has to be available to the team on a day-to-day basis, he would not have time to focus on the other activities.

Certainly the product owner is responsible for performing the activities within the dashed line, but I believe that the product owner role is also responsible for more

FIGURE 9.9 Pragmatic Marketing framework

activities. In fact, I believe that the product owner *role* should be responsible for performing as many of the activities shown in Figure 9.9 as are necessary and practical for the product owner to perform. The extent of that responsibility would depend on the organization, the specific product, and the skills of the person selected to be the product owner. For example, an organization that is producing a simple unit-conversion application for sale in a mobile device app store will not require as many activities as an organization creating the next major release of its enterprise Business Intelligence product. Therefore, it isn't practical to universally define the extent of the product owner's responsibility relative to the Pragmatic Marketing framework.

As I will discuss shortly, there are times when the scope of the product owner activities may be too large for any one person to adequately perform. In such cases, we might have a product owner team that includes people who focus on strategy and marketing. However, there will always be a single individual who functions in the product owner role for a Scrum team.

Outsourced Development Project

On an outsourced development effort—for example, company A contracting with company B to build a solution—a representative from company A should be the product owner. Company B may assign an internal person to closely liaise with the product owner, but the product owner should be from the company that is paying for the solution and receiving the benefits (see Figure 9.10).

The product owner role gets complicated if company A and company B enter into a traditional fixed-price development contract. In that case company B will almost certainly feel that it should be fulfilling most of the product owner responsibilities because it has assumed the risk of a fixed-price contract. In reality, though, company A, as the actual customer, should fill the product owner role. A more appropriate contract would have company A leasing the high-performance development team and ScrumMaster from company B and company A providing the product owner.

Component Development

Last, some organizations might use component teams (see Chapter 12) that build parts of customer solutions but not full customer solutions. These teams tend to create components or other assets that are then reused by other teams to assemble customer-valuable solutions. Because these teams focus at a technical component level, their product owners are typically technically oriented people who are capable of defining and prioritizing the technical features in their backlogs (see Figure 9.11).

In the figure, there are three business-oriented feature teams that create features that are valuable to the end users. Each feature team has its own product owner

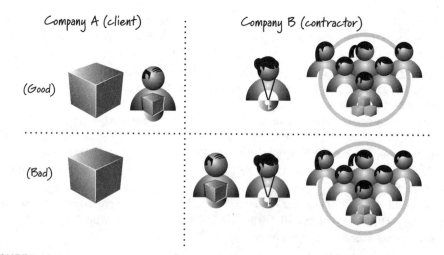

FIGURE 9.10   Example of a product owner on outsourced development

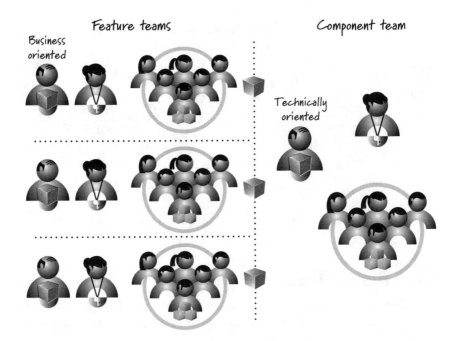

FIGURE 9.11   Example of a product owner on component development

focused on that team's features. Each of these feature teams also leverages the work of a component team that provides them with an asset necessary to complete their features. The component team needs a product owner who can prioritize and oversee the development of the various component-level requests being made by the feature teams. The component team's product owner is likely to be more technically oriented than the product owners of the feature teams.

Product Owner Combined with Other Roles

If capacity permits, the same person may act as the product owner for more than one Scrum team (see Figure 9.12).

Usually it is easier for this person to be the product owner of multiple teams on the same development effort, because the work of these teams will most likely be highly interrelated.

Although there are times when the same individual may be the product owner and a member of the development team, it is considered a bad idea for the same person to be both the product owner and the ScrumMaster on the same Scrum team. These two roles counterbalance each other; having one person play both roles creates a conflict of interest that we should try to avoid.

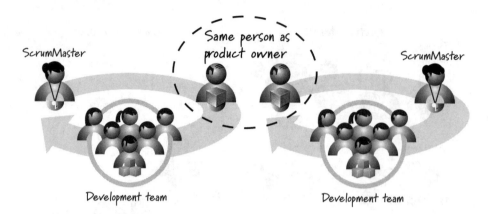

FIGURE 9.12 Same person as product owner of more than one Scrum team

Product Owner Team

Every Scrum team must have a single person who is identified as the product owner and is the only person empowered and accountable for fulfilling the product owner responsibilities for that Scrum team.

Should we allow a team of people to perform the product owner role? If by team we mean a group of people with shared decision making and accountability, definitely not. To properly apply Scrum, we need one individual to be *the* product owner, making decisions and acting as the single voice of the stakeholder communities to the Scrum team.

That being said, some organizations might form what they call a "product owner team" because they recognize that, in their circumstances, the product owner cannot do the job without a select group of people to provide input and guidance. In other companies, the workload of being a product owner might be greater than any one full-time person can reasonably perform. In those cases, the product owner delegates some product owner responsibilities to other people. Forming a product owner team in either of these circumstances is acceptable as long as there is one person on the team who is the ultimate decision maker and as long as having a product owner team does not degrade into design by committee, with every decision needing approval from eight other people.

Be careful when creating product owner teams. Product owners who are not properly skilled to be the empowered central point of product leadership don't need a committee—they need a different role. Similarly, product owners who are too busy to fulfill their responsibilities might not need a team. Perhaps the real problem is that the organization has chosen to start too many development efforts at one time, or there are just too few product owners to cover the necessary products.

Alternatively, perhaps the product we are building is just too large and should be broken into a series of smaller pieces with more frequent releases. With small pieces a single person might more easily fill the product owner role. Also, if we have structured our teams poorly (see Chapter 12), or poorly conceived the product backlog structures (see Chapter 6), a single product owner might find it difficult to do his job. Be sure that your product owner teams are truly necessary and not just masking an underlying problem; otherwise, the situation will become more complicated and jeopardize your overall outcome.

Product Owner Proxy

As I mentioned earlier, some companies doing internal development ask an IT person (for example, a business analyst or development manager) to be the product owner because the business unit person is too busy with other work. Because everyone knows that the IT person is really not empowered to make important final decisions (one of the key responsibilities of any product owner), organizations that do this have filled the product owner role ineffectively and confusingly. A better solution is to free up enough of the business unit person's time to be the true product owner but have the IT person act as the product owner proxy in certain interactions with the team.

A **product owner proxy** is a person enlisted by the product owner to act on his behalf in particular situations. Everyone on the Scrum team knows that the proxy is not the actual product owner, but everyone also knows that the product owner has empowered the proxy to make at least some tactical decisions on his behalf. A common example is when the product owner spends a great deal of time meeting with customers and users to make sure he has his fingers on the pulse of the marketplace. This person is reliably unavailable to the development team on a day-to-day basis. In this case, the product owner might enlist the support of a proxy to handle the day-to-day interaction with the development team regarding product backlog items.

For this approach to work, it is essential that the product owner actually empower the proxy to make decisions and not unreasonably overrule those decisions in a way that would undermine the proxy's credibility with the team. Remember, even though the product owner can empower others to assist him, he cannot delegate the ultimate responsibility for ensuring that the work gets done—he is still on the hook for that.

Chief Product Owner

Another situation where a product owner team is frequently created is on very large products. Earlier I noted that a single person might be the product owner for a couple of Scrum teams, but what about scenarios that involve many teams? For example, I trained and coached an organization that had a development effort that involved upward of 2,500 people. With an average team size of fewer than 10 people, the organization had more than 250 teams on the effort. One person can't be the product owner for 250 teams. In fact, one person can't be the engaged, day-to-day product

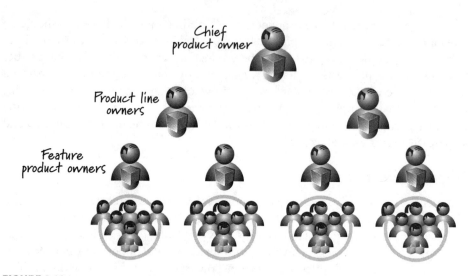

FIGURE 9.13   Hierarchical product owner role

owner for more than a few teams. In cases like these, the product owner role needs to scale hierarchically as shown in Figure 9.13.

Ultimately in Figure 9.13 the person labeled **chief product owner** is *the* product owner for the whole product. However, the chief product owner has a team of product owners to ensure that the product owner role is filled correctly at each lower level in the hierarchy. If you choose to use this approach, ensure that the individual team product owners remain empowered to make the vast majority of the decisions at their levels, rather than having to pass such decisions up the hierarchy to be made at higher levels.

Closing

In this chapter I expanded the description of the product owner role. I emphasized this role as the empowered central point of product leadership and described important responsibilities and characteristics of the role. I then described what the product owner does during the various Scrum activities on a project. I went on to discuss what type of person should fill the role for different project types. Then I described how a single person might be the product owner for more than one Scrum team, and how on occasion a single person might be both a product owner and a team member on the same Scrum team. I ended by discussing the idea of a product owner team with a focus on product owner proxies and chief product owners. In the next chapter I will discuss the ScrumMaster role.

Chapter 10

SCRUMMASTER

In this chapter I describe the ScrumMaster role. I begin by describing the purpose of the role relative to the other Scrum roles. Then I define the principal responsibilities and characteristics of a ScrumMaster. Next I illustrate a "day in the life" of the ScrumMaster, which leads to a discussion of whether or not the ScrumMaster role is full-time. I end by describing the kind of person who typically fulfills the Scrum-Master role.

Overview

The ScrumMaster is one of the three roles that constitute every Scrum team (the others being the product owner and the development team). While the product owner is focused on building the right product and the development team is focused on building the product right, the ScrumMaster is focused on helping everyone understand and embrace the Scrum values, principles, and practices. The ScrumMaster acts as a coach to both the development team and the product owner. A ScrumMaster also provides process leadership, helping the Scrum team and the rest of the organization develop their own high-performance, organization-specific Scrum approach.

Principal Responsibilities

Figure 10.1 illustrates the principal ScrumMaster responsibilities.

Coach

The ScrumMaster is the agile coach for the Scrum team—both the development team and the product owner (see Adkins 2010 for a comprehensive description of an agile coach). By coaching both roles, the ScrumMaster can remove barriers between the roles and enable the product owner to directly drive development.

Analogous to the coach of a sports team, the ScrumMaster observes how the team is using Scrum and does anything possible to help it get to the next level of performance. When problems arise that the team can and should be able to solve, the ScrumMaster's attitude, like that of any good coach, is "I'm not here to solve your problems for you; instead, I'm here to help you solve your own problems." If the problem is an impediment that the team can't resolve, the ScrumMaster takes ownership of getting it resolved.

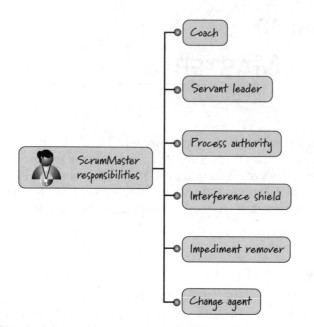

FIGURE 10.1 Principal ScrumMaster responsibilities

The ScrumMaster coaches a new product owner by helping him understand and perform his product owner responsibilities. Once the ScrumMaster helps the product owner get established in his role, she provides him with ongoing assistance for activities such as grooming the product backlog. Furthermore, in keeping with the sports team analogy, the ScrumMaster's relationship with the product owner is very much like a sports team coach's main role with the team's owner: help the owner maximize business outcomes using Scrum, manage expectations, make sure the owner is providing the team with what it needs, and listen to the owner's complaints and requests for change and translate those into actionable improvements for the team.

Servant Leader

The ScrumMaster is often described as a **servant leader** of the Scrum team. Even when acting as the team's coach, the ScrumMaster is first and foremost a servant to the Scrum team, ensuring that its highest-priority needs are being met. A servant leader would never ask, "So, what are you going to do for me today?" Instead, a servant leader asks, "So, what can I do today to help you and the team be more effective?"

Process Authority

The ScrumMaster is the Scrum team's process authority. In this capacity, the Scrum-Master is empowered to ensure that the Scrum team enacts and adheres to the Scrum values, principles, and practices along with the Scrum team's specific approaches. The ScrumMaster continuously helps the Scrum team improve the process, whenever possible, to maximize delivered business value.

Authority in this context is not the same type of authority that a functional manager or project manager would have. For example, the ScrumMaster doesn't hire and fire and cannot dictate to the team what tasks it should do or how to do them. The ScrumMaster also is not responsible for making sure the work gets done. Instead, the ScrumMaster helps the team define and adhere to its own process for making sure the work gets done.

Interference Shield

The ScrumMaster protects the development team from outside interference so that it can remain focused on delivering business value every sprint. Interference can come from any number of sources, from managers who want to redirect team members in the middle of a sprint, to issues originating from other teams. No matter what the source of the interference, the ScrumMaster acts as an interceptor (fielding inquiries, addressing management, and arbitrating disputes) so that the team can focus on delivering value.

Impediment Remover

The ScrumMaster also takes responsibility for removing impediments that inhibit the team's productivity (when the team members themselves cannot reasonably remove them). For example, I observed a Scrum team that was consistently unable to meet its sprint goals. The impediment was unstable production servers that the team used during testing (as part of its definition of done). The team itself had no control over these servers—that was the responsibility of the VP of Operations. Because the team itself could not remove the impediment, the ScrumMaster took ownership of improving the server stability by working with the VP of Operations and others who could actually do something about the stability issue.

Change Agent

The ScrumMaster must help change more than faulty servers and similar impediments. A good ScrumMaster must help change minds as well. Scrum can be very disruptive to the status quo; the change that is required to be successful with Scrum can be difficult. The ScrumMaster helps others understand the need for change, the impacts of Scrum outside of the Scrum team, and the broad-reaching benefits Scrum can help achieve. The ScrumMaster also ensures that effective change is occurring at all levels of the organization, enabling not only short-term success but, more importantly, the long-term benefits from using Scrum. In large organizations, the Scrum-Masters might band together to become a more effective force for change.

Characteristics/Skills

Figure 10.2 illustrates important ScrumMaster characteristics.

Knowledgeable

To be an effective process coach, the ScrumMaster must be very knowledgeable about Scrum. The ScrumMaster should also understand the technical issues the team needs to address and technologies the team will use to create solutions. A ScrumMaster doesn't need to have tech-lead- or dev-lead-level knowledge, but reasonable technical knowledge is an asset. The ScrumMaster also doesn't need to be an expert in the business domain (the product owner does), but again, working knowledge of the business domain is very helpful.

Questioning

ScrumMasters use their coaching skills in conjunction with their process, technical, and business knowledge to ask great questions. They engage in intentional inquiry, asking the kinds of questions that make people stop and say, "Hmm. I never thought about that. Now that you ask that question, it makes me think there might be another way to go." Great ScrumMasters almost never directly answer a question but instead reflexively answer with their own question—not an annoying question, or a question

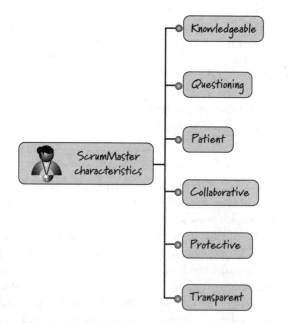

FIGURE 10.2   ScrumMaster characteristics

for the sake of asking a question, but rather a thoughtful, deep, probing question—thereby helping people realize that they have the insight to find their own answers (a form of Socratic questioning).

Patient

Because ScrumMasters prefer not to give out answers, they need to be patient, giving teams time to arrive at appropriate answers on their own. At times it is hard for me to be a ScrumMaster because I see the issue the team is dealing with and I "know" the answer. Well, at least I *think* I know the answer! It is arrogant for me (or any ScrumMaster) to believe that I am smarter than the collective intelligence of the team. So, at times I just have to bite my tongue and be patient, letting the team work out the solution, periodically asking probing questions to help guide things along.

Collaborative

The ScrumMaster must have excellent collaboration skills to work with the product owner, development team, and all the other parties, even those who might not be directly involved with Scrum. Also, as the process coach, the ScrumMaster is always looking for opportunities to help the Scrum team members achieve an enviable level of intra-team collaboration. A ScrumMaster can assist in this effort by personally exhibiting effective collaboration skills.

Protective

The ScrumMaster should be very protective of the team. The common analogy is that the ScrumMaster acts like a sheepdog, guarding the flock from wolves that might try to attack. In our context wolves could be organizational impediments or people with differing agendas. The ScrumMaster is adept at ensuring the protection of the team within the greater context of making economically sound business decisions. With acute sensitivity toward both team protection and business needs, the ScrumMaster helps the Scrum team achieve a healthy balance.

The ScrumMaster also helps team members who begin to wander away from the flock. When things get difficult, it is easy for people to fall back on familiar, non-agile approaches. In this case it is the ScrumMaster's job to help shepherd straying team members, helping them overcome their difficulties by reinforcing how to use Scrum more effectively.

Transparent

Finally, the ScrumMaster is transparent in all forms of communication. When working with team members, there is no room for hidden agendas; what you see and hear from the ScrumMaster must be what you get. People expect nothing less of a servant leader. The ScrumMaster also promotes transparent communication outside of the

Scrum team. Without transparent access to information it is difficult for the organization to inspect and adapt to achieve its desired business results from using Scrum.

A Day in the Life

What exactly is life like for a ScrumMaster during a sprint? Figure 10.3 is indicative (not a precise statement) of how much time the ScrumMaster of a newly formed team might spend doing each of the activities throughout a sprint. The percentage allocations would be different for a ScrumMaster of a high-performing Scrum team that has been working together for several years.

As illustrated in the figure, the ScrumMaster spends time each day organizing and facilitating the Scrum activities, including sprint planning, sprint execution, sprint reviews, sprint retrospectives, and daily scrums. This includes setting up the activities, overseeing their execution, and enabling the rest of the Scrum team to perform at a level where high-value results are achieved.

The ScrumMaster also spends time each day coaching the team members to help them improve their use of Scrum and technical practices. The ScrumMaster might also perform refresher training—for example, reminding a new team about the rules of Planning Poker when estimating product backlog items. Also, some amount of each day is dedicated to communicating (for example, updating sprint and release burndown or burnup charts, or discussions with non-Scrum-team members).

Throughout the sprint, the ScrumMaster spends some time working with the product owner on product backlog grooming activities (for example, writing and prioritizing new product backlog items). The ScrumMaster also works with the product owner to ensure that economically viable trade-offs are being made regarding important variables such as feature, date, budget, and quality.

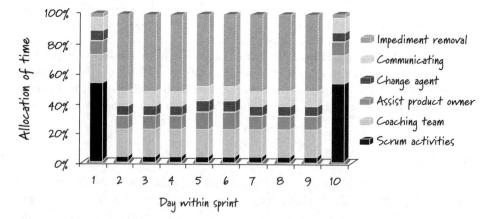

FIGURE 10.3   A day in the life of a ScrumMaster

The ScrumMaster also spends time acting as a change agent to help the organization better embrace Scrum throughout the value chain (from sales, marketing, HR, subcontracting, and so on).

The ScrumMaster spends a variable amount of time each day removing impediments. She might budget a fixed amount of time each day specifically for impediment removal. Of course, impediments can appear at any time, and they might be large and time-sensitive, so the ScrumMaster might need to dynamically reallocate time from other activities to address them.

Most teams and organizations that are new to Scrum will have many impediments when starting out and tend to focus on the ones that are obvious and somewhat easy to remove. That doesn't mean, however, that all impediments will be easily dispatched. In fact, the next level of impediments is often much more difficult and time-consuming to address. Impediment removal is a big variable in the ScrumMaster's day; it could easily change the allocations of time shown in Figure 10.3.

Fulfilling the Role

When considering the ScrumMaster role, we need to decide who is best suited for it, whether the role is a full-time job, and whether it can be combined with other Scrum and non-Scrum roles. Let's consider each of these.

Who Should Be a ScrumMaster?

Organizations new to Scrum won't have people in a role called ScrumMaster. So where do we find the ScrumMasters? I've seen great ScrumMasters come from many different existing roles. Some ScrumMasters were previously project managers or product managers (although product managers are more likely to transition into the role of product owner). Other ScrumMasters come from a development, testing, or other technical background. As long as an individual has the characteristics that I mentioned earlier and is willing to take on the responsibilities of the role, she can be an effective ScrumMaster.

Some organizations feel that the tech lead or dev lead should be the ScrumMaster. These people in fact might make great ScrumMasters, but they also might *not* be the best choice for the role. People who are in a technical leadership position are there for a reason—they are technically very good at what they do. The ScrumMaster role is not one where that level of technical excellence is exploited to its full potential. Any time technical leaders are doing ScrumMaster work, they are necessarily providing less technical leadership. Making them ScrumMasters, therefore, might adversely affect the technical outcome. I will address later in this chapter whether a development team member can simultaneously fill the ScrumMaster role.

Functional area managers or resource managers can also be successful Scrum-Masters if they have the skills to do the job. It would be best if such managers no longer retained people management responsibility, at least not for members of their Scrum teams. Because a ScrumMaster has no managerial authority, team members might be confused about whether the person is wearing her ScrumMaster or manager hat in a particular instance. I prefer to avoid this situation and not have team members report to the ScrumMaster. In certain organizations, however, it might be unavoidable, so we learn to deal with any potential conflict of interest as best we can.

Is ScrumMaster a Full-Time Job?

Every Scrum team has a ScrumMaster, but is the ScrumMaster a full-time role? Possibly not. A Scrum team that has been working together for an extended period of time and has become highly proficient with Scrum might require less coaching than a new team made up of people who have never worked together and are new to Scrum.

Although the ScrumMaster might need to spend less time with the team day to day as the team matures, the ScrumMaster role remains critical to the success of Scrum within the organization. Usually as the Scrum team's need for a ScrumMaster decreases, the need for the ScrumMaster to focus on broader organizational impediments and to be a change agent throughout the organization value chain increases.

In most cases, the ScrumMaster role remains a significant commitment of time. In those cases where it's not a full-time commitment, some combination of roles may take place.

ScrumMaster Combined with Other Roles

If capacity permits and a single person is both a talented ScrumMaster and development team member, that person may act in both roles. However, this combination could suffer from a conflict of interest when the person tries to wear both hats. For example, what if the person in the combined roles has important ScrumMaster activities (like removing impediments) to perform and also has critical task-level work to do? Because both are important, compromising either will reduce the Scrum team's effectiveness. Complicating the trade-off is the fact that impediments can occur unpredictably and be very time-consuming to address. This makes it even harder to predict how much time a ScrumMaster as team member will actually have available to do task-level work.

There is, however, a different approach that is often better. If a ScrumMaster truly has available capacity, in many cases my preference is to have that person be the ScrumMaster for more than one Scrum team (see Figure 10.4).

Becoming a good ScrumMaster requires acquiring a valuable, not-so-common set of skills. I prefer that a person who has those skills share them with multiple teams rather than spend time performing non-ScrumMaster activities. However, that is just a personal preference. I have seen successful Scrum teams use either of these approaches. There is no generic right or wrong answer, although there might be a right or wrong answer in a specific organizational context.

FIGURE 10.4   Same person as ScrumMaster of more than one team

As I mentioned in Chapter 9, one combination of roles that is highly discouraged is having the same person serve as both ScrumMaster and product owner. The ScrumMaster is the coach of the Scrum team, which means the ScrumMaster is the Scrum coach for the product owner. It is hard to be your own coach. In addition, the product owner has real product authority and can make demands on the team. The ScrumMaster frequently acts as the balancing agent between the demands of the product owner and the needs and abilities of the development team. Having the product owner and the ScrumMaster be the same person would add confusion where it could be easily avoided.

Closing

In this chapter I described the ScrumMaster role. I emphasized the ScrumMaster responsibilities as coach, servant leader, process authority, interference shield, impediment remover, and change agent. I then discussed how the ScrumMaster should be knowledgeable about Scrum, ask great questions, patiently wait for the team to solve its problems, collaborate with everyone, protect the team from undue interference, and communicate in a visible and transparent way. Next I described how the Scrum-Master's time is allocated across a sprint to provide a deeper appreciation for this critical role. I concluded by discussing who within the organization should be the ScrumMaster, whether or not the role is full-time, and how the ScrumMaster role might be combined with other Scrum roles.

In the next chapter I will explore the role that the development team plays in Scrum.

Chapter 11

DEVELOPMENT TEAM

In this chapter I describe the development team role. I begin by discussing five principal responsibilities of this role and conclude by describing ten characteristics that a development team should exhibit.

Overview

Traditional software development approaches define various job types, such as architect, programmer, tester, database administrator, UI designer, and so on. Scrum defines the role of development team, which is simply a cross-functional collection of these types of people. In particular, the development team is one of the three roles on every Scrum team. The development team's members, collectively, have the skills required to deliver the business value requested by the product owner.

The term *development team* may appear to be the wrong label to apply to a team that is composed of more than just developers. Other labels have been used, such as *delivery team*, *design-build-test team*, and just *team*. It's not apparent that any of these labels is more appropriate, less ambiguous, or easier to use than *development team*. For now, the Scrum community has converged on the use of the term *development team*, and I will use that term in this book.

Role-Specific Teams

Many organizations are accustomed to intentionally splitting different job roles into specialized, role-specific teams. These organizations might have one team of designers, one of developers, and another of testers. These teams hand off work to one another when it is complete and more or less function independently of each other.

In Scrum, the development team must do all of the work to produce one or more vertical slices of working product functionality each sprint, including the design, development, integration, and testing of that functionality. Thus, we need a team that is skilled at all of those tasks.

Some organizations try to maintain a separate testing or QA team while doing Scrum. Now, I admit there are times when having a separate team that focuses specifically on testing might be necessary—for example, a regulatory requirement might be that a separate team perform a particular type of testing. However, most of the time there is no such need. Testing should be fully interwoven into the work that takes place during every sprint. Therefore, the development team doing the work during that sprint should do the testing.

Whenever you can, you should create cross-functional teams. Parceling the work out to different role-specific teams is suspect and is likely a serious impediment to the successful use of Scrum. Make sure you have a real need (besides habit) for keeping any role-specific teams.

Principal Responsibilities

Figure 11.1 illustrates the Scrum activities, annotated with the principal development team responsibilities.

I will describe each of these responsibilities.

Perform Sprint Execution

During sprint execution, development team members perform the hands-on, creative work of designing, building, integrating, and testing product backlog items into increments of potentially shippable functionality. To do this, they self-organize

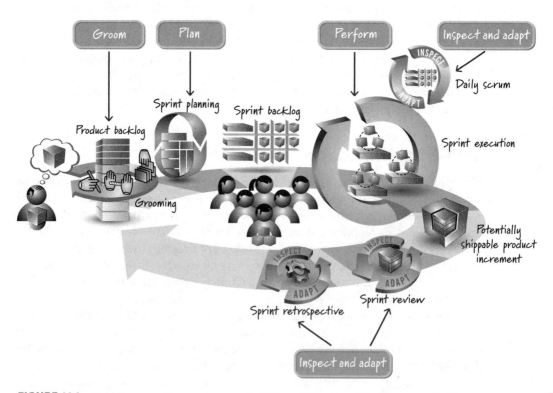

FIGURE 11.1 Development team responsibilities with respect to Scrum activities

and collectively decide how to plan, manage, carry out, and communicate work (see Chapter 20 for details). The development team spends a majority of its time performing sprint execution.

Inspect and Adapt Each Day

Each development team member is expected to participate in each daily scrum, during which the team members collectively inspect progress toward the sprint goal and adapt the plan for the current day's work. If some team members do not participate, the team can miss pieces of the big picture and may fail to achieve its sprint goal.

Groom the Product Backlog

Part of each sprint must be spent preparing for the next. A large part of that work focuses on product backlog grooming, which includes creating and refining, estimating, and prioritizing product backlog items (see Chapter 6 for details). The development team should allocate up to 10% of its available capacity every sprint to assist the product owner with these activities.

Plan the Sprint

At the beginning of each sprint, the development team participates in sprint planning. In collaboration with the product owner and with facilitation from the Scrum-Master, the development team helps to establish the goal for the next sprint. The team then determines which high-priority subset of product backlog items to build to achieve that goal (see Chapter 19). For a two-week sprint, sprint planning typically takes about half a day. A four-week sprint might need up to a full day for sprint planning.

Notice that planning happens iteratively. Rather than focusing on a very large, uncertain, and overly detailed plan at the start of a development effort, the team makes a series of smaller, more certain, and more detailed plans just in time at the beginning of each sprint.

Inspect and Adapt the Product and Process

At the end of each sprint, the development team participates in the two inspect-and-adapt activities: sprint review and sprint retrospective. The sprint review is where the development team, product owner, ScrumMaster, stakeholders, sponsors, customers, and interested members of other teams review the just-completed features of the current sprint and discuss how to best move forward (see Chapter 21). The sprint retrospective is where the Scrum team inspects and adapts its Scrum process and technical practices to improve how it uses Scrum to deliver business value (see Chapter 22).

Characteristics/Skills

Figure 11.2 illustrates important characteristics of the development team.

Self-Organizing

Team members self-organize to determine the best way to accomplish the sprint goal. There is no project manager or other manager who tells the team how to do its work (and a ScrumMaster should never presume to). **Self-organization** is a bottom-up, emergent property of the system—there is no external dominating force applying traditional top-down, command-and-control management.

Let me illustrate with an example. Where I live in Colorado, there is a pond at the entrance of my subdivision. Over the winter a flock of Canada geese comes and roosts there. So each year we have a couple of hundred geese that simultaneously make a big mess and are pretty to look at. Now, I also have two dogs named Letti and Toast. Normally they stay inside the fenced backyard. Occasionally we let them roam free outside the fence, and if they see the geese by the pond, they run down to greet them. I don't think they would hurt the geese, but when they see Letti and Toast coming, the geese decide to cede the pond to them for a while, so they take off en masse.

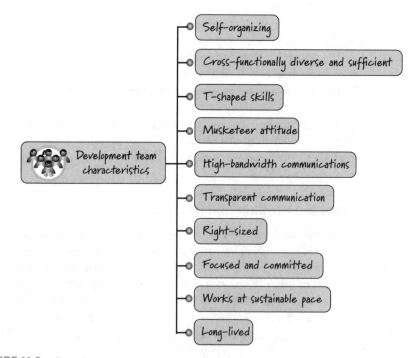

FIGURE 11.2 Development team characteristics

Did you ever wonder when birds take off how it is that they know to form their characteristic V pattern (flocking pattern)? Do you think there is a "manager bird," with a flipchart, down at my pond that calls a meeting to instruct the birds on how to flock (see Figure 11.3)?

I've lived by the pond for many years, and I don't ever recall seeing that meeting. (Although years ago my son Jonah declared, "Dad, you've never seen it because they do that meeting at night!" Hmm. Maybe he's on to something.)

No, unless my son is right and the birds are much craftier than I think, the geese flock through self-organization, a bottom-up emergent property of a **complex adaptive system**. In such systems, many entities interact with each other in various ways, and these interactions are governed by simple, localized rules operating in a context of constant feedback (see Figure 11.4).

These types of systems exhibit interesting characteristics, such as being remarkably robust and producing amazing novelty.

Like the flocking birds, a development team has no top-down command-and-control authority that tells the team how to do its work. Instead, a cross-functionally diverse team of people organize themselves in the most appropriate way to get work done. In effect, what emerges is the team's own equivalent of the V pattern.

FIGURE 11.3   Flocking isn't the result of top-down planning.

FIGURE 11.4   Flocking: simple rules and frequent feedback

Managers, however, do have a vital role in Scrum. They create (and re-create) the environment for the self-organizing team. We'll talk more about the role of managers in Chapter 13.

Cross-Functionally Diverse and Sufficient

Development team members should be cross-functionally diverse; collectively they should possess the necessary and sufficient set of skills to get the job done. A well-formed team can take an item off of the product backlog and produce a good-quality, working feature that meets the Scrum team's definition of done.

Teams composed solely of people with the same skills (traditional silo teams) can at most do part of the job. As a result, silo teams end up handing off work products to other silo teams. For example, the development team hands the code off to the testing team, or the UI team hands off screen designs to the business logic team. Handoffs represent an excellent opportunity for miscommunication and costly mistakes. Having diverse teams minimizes the number of handoffs. And creating diverse teams doesn't prevent us from having multiple team members who might be highly skilled in the same discipline such as Java or C++ development or testing.

Cross-functionally diverse teams also bring multiple perspectives, leading to better outcomes (see Figure 11.5).

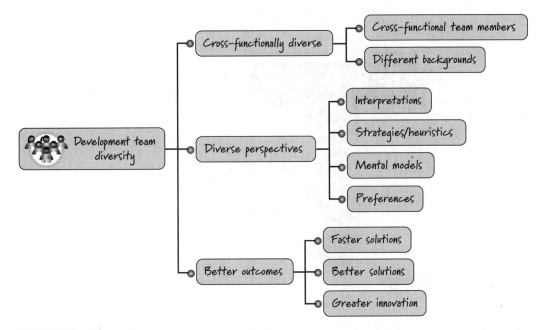

FIGURE 11.5 Team diversity

A cross-functionally diverse team has members from different backgrounds. Each team member brings a set of cognitive tools for problem solving; these tools can involve different interpretations (of the same data), different strategies (or heuristics) for solving problems, different mental models of how things work, and different preferences for both approaches and solutions. This kind of diversity typically leads to better outcomes in terms of faster solutions, higher-quality deliverables, and greater innovation, all of which translate into greater economic value (Page 2007).

We should also strive for team diversity by having a good mix of senior- and junior-level personnel on the same team. Too many senior-level people might cause unnecessary turbulence, similar to having too many cooks in the kitchen. Too many junior people, however, and the team might not be sufficiently skilled to get the job done. A good mix promotes a healthy, collaborative learning environment.

T-Shaped Skills

Flexible development teams are composed of members with T-shaped skills (see Figure 11.6).

T-shaped skills mean that a team member (say, Sue) has deep skills in her preferred functional area, discipline, or specialty. For example, Sue is a great user-experience (UX) designer—that is her specialty and where she prefers to do work. Sue,

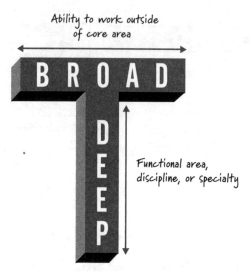

Ability to work outside of core area

BROAD

DEEP

Functional area, discipline, or specialty

FIGURE 11.6   T-shaped skills

however, can also work outside of her core specialty area, doing some testing and some documentation. She isn't as good a tester or documenter as those who specialize in those areas, but she can help out with testing or documentation if that's where the team is experiencing a bottleneck and needs to swarm people to get the job done. In this respect Sue has broad skills that allow her to work outside her core area.

It's unrealistic to believe that every person on a team could work on every task. That's a lofty goal to have. For example, in domains with intense specialization, like video game development, where a team could have an artist, animator, audio engineer, artificial intelligence (AI) programmer, and tester, it's unreasonable to assume that everyone can do every job. If I were on a team developing a video game, I could work on the AI and do some testing, but I couldn't work on the art design (and you wouldn't want me to!). However, I might be able to help the artists with nonartistic design work such as using Photoshop to convert file formats or create scripts to apply operations on multiple files.

Managers should focus on forming teams that have the best set of T-shaped skills that are possible with available personnel. However, it might not be possible to get exactly the desired team skill set from the get-go, so the desired skill set could evolve over time as the needs of the product development effort evolve. Therefore, it is critical to have an environment where people are constantly learning and adding to their skill sets, whether those include domain knowledge, technical knowledge, thinking skills, or other capabilities. Management needs to support team members with time to learn and experiment (see Chapter 13).

Is it OK to have pure specialists on the team? Let's take our earlier example of Sue and assume she is a great UX designer, but that's all she can do. And, because we have so few UX designers, we really don't want her doing anything but critical UX design work. We need her skills on the team, but we'll be able to fill only about 10% of her time with team-related work. In these cases, an obvious solution is to divide Sue's time among multiple teams.

However, we must be practical. Sue would be far too fractured if she divided her time in 10% increments to many teams at the same time. She would soon become a bottleneck (see the "Focused and Committed" section later in this chapter). Recall from Chapter 3 that our goal shouldn't be to keep people like Sue 100% utilized. Instead, we should be more concerned about the idle work (the baton sitting on the ground) that occurs when we rely too much on an overutilized resource. So, we might allocate Sue as a specialist to a reasonable number of products, but not so many that she is the cause of baton dropping.

Alternatively, because our goal is to achieve good flow with team members who have broad T-shaped skills, we should encourage Sue to help other team members acquire reasonable UX design knowledge so that we no longer need to rely so heavily on specialists.

To summarize, then, our goal is to form a team with members who have the proper skills to cover the core specialty areas and in aggregate have some overlap in skills to provide additional flexibility. To meet this goal, many team members should have T-shaped skills, but we still might have some specialists in the mix.

Musketeer Attitude

Members of the development team (and the Scrum team as a whole!) need to have the same attitude as the Three Musketeers—"All for one and one for all." This **Musketeer attitude** reinforces the point that the team members collectively own the responsibility of getting the job done. They win as a team or they fail as a team.

In a well-functioning Scrum team, I would never expect anyone to say, "I got my part done. You didn't get your part done. Therefore we failed." This attitude misses the point that team members are all in the same boat together (see Figure 11.7).

Team members must appreciate that they must work together to meet their commitments, because if they fail, it's going to be everybody's problem in the end. Having team members with a Musketeer attitude is critical to achieving shared success.

Having team members with T-shaped skills encourages this attitude and makes it practical because people are capable of working on more than one type of task. On these teams I don't expect to hear a person who is capable of doing the work say, "That's not my job."

However, because it is not always possible for a person to do every job, I might hear someone say, "I'm not capable of doing that job." In this case the team might choose to have the person without the skills apprentice with a person who has the skills so that in the future the team will have greater aggregate capabilities.

Even if skills limitations prevent people from working cross-functionally, team members can still organize their work to ensure a good flow through the sprint so

FIGURE 11.7   Team members must act as if they are all in the same boat.

that no one team member is overburdened. For example, holding all of the testing work until the end of the sprint so that the "tester" can do the work is most certainly a prescription for failure. See Chapter 20 for a deeper discussion of how the team should manage flow during sprint execution.

So, with a Musketeer attitude, no one is just "along for the ride." Each team member is responsible for making sure she is fully engaged at all times. Frequently this will mean speaking up and engaging in activities outside one's specialty to add to the diversity of the discussion. For example, although a team member's specialty might be testing, if she thinks there is a problem in the design the team is coming up with for a given feature, it's her duty to speak up, rather than shrug and say, "Not my job; they know better than I do anyway."

High-Bandwidth Communications

Development team members need to communicate with one another, as well as with the product owner and ScrumMaster, in a high-bandwidth manner, where valuable information is exchanged quickly and efficiently with minimal overhead.

High-bandwidth communications increase both the frequency and quality of information sharing. As a result, the Scrum team has more frequent opportunities to inspect and adapt, leading to better and faster decision making. Because the economic value of information is time-sensitive, accelerating the rate of information sharing allows the team to maximize its value. By quickly exploiting emergent opportunities and recognizing wasteful situations, the team can avoid expending more resources by going down the wrong path.

There are a number of ways that a team can achieve high-bandwidth communications. The Agile Manifesto (Beck et al. 2001) states that face-to-face communication is a preferred approach. Certainly, team members who are physically separated or primarily use noninteractive communication (such as documents) are at a disadvantage to colocated team members engaged in real-time, face-to-face collaboration.

Whenever possible, I prefer my team members to be colocated. However, many organizations, for various business reasons, have created distributed teams, so colocation may not always be possible or practical. I have worked with many distributed teams that have achieved the benefits of high-bandwidth communications, so being face-to-face isn't the only way to achieve the goal—but it's a great place to start if business conditions permit.

For distributed teams, a certain level of technology support can help improve communication bandwidth. I have worked with organizations where team members were widely distributed. Through the use of some rather impressive teleconferencing equipment, I participated in discussions that felt like everyone was colocated. Was it as good as being colocated? No. But the technology went a long way to improving the communication bandwidth among the team members.

Having teams composed of cross-functional team members is a critical step toward achieving high-bandwidth communications. Such teams have more streamlined communication channels simply because they have easy access to the people needed to get the job done. Also, such cross-functionally diverse teams are far less likely to have formal handoffs (which usually take the form of written documents) from one team to another. With everyone on the same team, the frequency and formality of handoffs are reduced, which improves communication speed.

We should also reduce time spent on ceremonies where team members perform a process that adds little or no value. For example, if team members have to go through three levels of indirection before they can speak with an actual customer or user, the ceremony of "talking to a customer" is probably a serious impediment to high-bandwidth communications. Having to create low- or no-value documents or requiring lengthy and potentially unnecessary approval and sign-off procedures reduces bandwidth. We need to identify and eliminate these impediments to improve overall team communication performance.

Finally, having small teams also improves bandwidth. Communication channels within a team do not scale linearly with the number of team members but instead increase by the square of the number of people on the team according to the formula $N(N-1)/2$. So, if there are 5 people on the team, there are 10 channels of communication. If there are 10 people on the team, there are 45 channels of communications. More people means more communication overhead and therefore lower bandwidth.

Transparent Communication

In addition to being high bandwidth (fast and efficient with minimal overhead), communication within the team should be transparent. Transparent communication provides a clear understanding of what is actually happening to avoid surprises and help build trust among the team members. I have always felt that teams should communicate in a way that aligns with the spirit of the **principle of least astonishment**. Simply put, people should communicate in a way that is least likely to surprise one another. For example, I recall that on one Scrum team I coached, a particular individual would consistently choose his words during the daily scrums to occlude what he had accomplished and what he was planning to do. People were frequently surprised ("astonished") to later learn that his communications were intentionally opaque and designed to mislead. This resulted in other team members not trusting this individual, which in turn impeded the team's ability to self-organize and meet its sprint goals.

Right-Sized

Scrum favors small teams. The general rule is that having five to nine people on the team is best. There is published research that backs up the claim that small teams tend to be the most efficient (Putnam 1996; Putnam and Myers 1998). My experience over the past 25 years is that teams of five to seven are the sweet spot for rapidly delivering business value.

Mike Cohn lists a handful of reasons to keep teams small, which include the following (Cohn 2009):

- There is less social loafing—people exerting less effort because they believe that others will pick up the slack.
- Constructive interaction is more likely to occur on a small team.
- Less time is spent coordinating efforts.
- No one can fade into the background.
- Small teams are more satisfying to their members.
- Harmful overspecialization is less likely to occur.

It is possible to have too small a team. For example, a team is too small if it doesn't have the necessary people to get the job done, or if it has too few people to operate efficiently.

Just because Scrum favors small teams doesn't mean we can't use Scrum on larger development efforts. Scrum is frequently used to build products that require more than 9 people. However, rather than having one large Scrum team with, say, 36 development team members, we would instead have four or more Scrum teams, each with a development team of 9 or fewer people.

A Scrum project scales not by having a larger development team but by having multiple Scrum teams. Multiple Scrum teams can coordinate with each other in a variety of ways. One common approach is known as the **scrum of scrums**, where members of each Scrum team come together to perform a higher-level equivalent of the daily scrum (see Chapter 12 for details).

Focused and Committed

Team members need to be focused and committed to the team's goal. Focused means that each team member is engaged, concentrating on and devoting her attention to the team's goal. Committed means that during both good times and bad, each team member is dedicated to meeting the team's collective goal.

If a person is working on only one product, it is far easier for that person to be focused and committed. When asked to work on multiple concurrent product development efforts, a person must split her time across those products, reducing her focus and commitment on all products.

Ask any person who works on multiple products about her focus and commitment and you will likely be told something like "I have so much to do that I just try to do the best job that I can on each product and then hop to the next product. I don't ever feel like I have time to focus on any one product and do it well. If there is an emergency situation on several products, I simply won't be able to help out on all of them."

It is harder for a team member to do a good-quality job when she is hopping from product to product. It's even harder to be truly committed to multiple products simultaneously. Instead of being in one boat with her team members, the multitasking team member is moving from boat to boat. If many of the boats spring a leak at the same time, how does this person choose which boat's crew to help? If a person isn't there to bail water, that team member is not *committed* to that team. At best she is *involved* with that team. To be fair to the other team members the involved team member should make it perfectly clear that she is only involved and therefore might not be available at critical times.

There is considerable data to support the widely held belief that being on multiple products (or projects) or multiple teams reduces productivity. Figure 11.8 shows a graph of such data (Wheelwright and Clark 1992).

This data indicates that nobody is 100% productive—there is overhead just to be a good corporate citizen. Productivity actually seems better with two projects than with one. This occurs because it is possible to get blocked on one project, so having a second one to switch to allows a person to be incrementally more productive.

Based on this data, working on three or more concurrent projects is a bad economic choice because more time is spent on coordinating, remembering, and tracking down information and less time is spent doing value-adding work. So, how many projects/products (and probably different teams) should a person be on simultaneously? Probably not more than two. I have a strong preference for one, because in today's highly connected, information-rich world with email, instant messaging, Twitter, Facebook, and other technologies, being a good corporate citizen is probably the equivalent of being on one project!

Now what about those specialists who might need to be concurrently allocated to several products? Earlier I used the example of Sue (the UX designer), who was allocated 10% to a team (with the rest of her time going to other teams). As much as we

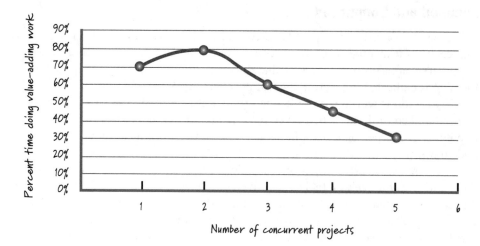

FIGURE 11.8   The cost of multitasking

would like Sue to be on one or two products, what if we need her part-time on five? As a practical approach, let the specialist decide how many products she can commit to and focus on simultaneously. If she says she can't commit to any more, don't assign her to that next product or team. If from a business perspective we are uncomfortable with her decision to not take on another product (let's say Sue is comfortable with only three concurrent products), perhaps we should seek an alternative solution to this problem.

Here are a few. First, do fewer projects concurrently. This is frequently the correct solution because many organizations have chosen to start too many projects at once (see Chapter 16 for a more detailed discussion). Another solution is to hire more specialists to share the burden. The third solution is to help other people broaden their skill sets to include the specialty skill. And, of course, the fourth solution is some combination of the first three solutions. In the end, forcing people to work on too many projects/teams concurrently will reduce their focus and commitment and jeopardize business outcomes.

Working at a Sustainable Pace

One of Scrum's guiding principles is that team members must work at a sustainable pace. (No more death marches!) In doing so, they deliver world-class products and maintain a healthy and fun environment.

Using sequential development, we defer important activities like integration and testing until near the end, when there typically is a crushing workload of issues to deal with as we approach the delivery date. The result is a steep increase in intensity in the latter phases (see Figure 11.9).

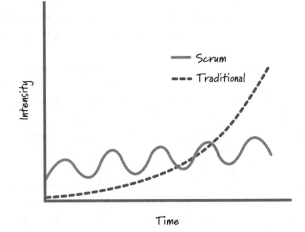

FIGURE 11.9   Sustainable pace over time

This incredibly intense time is symbolized by the superheroes pulling all-nighters and working weekends trying to get out the release. Some people thrive on this type of work, love the attention, and want to be rewarded for their extraordinary effort. The stress on everyone else is overwhelming. As an organization we should be asking, "Why did we have to work nights and weekends, and what should we change?"

Compare that with the typical intensity profile when using Scrum, where we've been continuously developing, testing, and integrating working features every sprint. During each sprint the team members should be using good technical practices such as refactoring, continuous integration, and automated tests to ensure that they can deliver value at frequent, regular intervals without killing themselves.

So, within a given sprint we'll likely see intensity increase a bit near the end of the sprint as we ensure that all work associated with our strong definition of done has been met. However, the overall intensity of work during each sprint should closely resemble the intensity of the previous sprint, reinforcing the team's working at a sustainable pace.

The aggregate result is a leveling of the work; it doesn't come in huge chunks or intense bursts, especially late when it is most harmful. This leveling means that Scrum teams will likely work fewer overtime hours and therefore be less likely to burn out.

Long-Lived

Effective use of Scrum requires teams, not groups. A **team** is made up of a diverse, cross-functional collection of collaborating people who are aligned to a common vision and work together to achieve that vision. A **group** is a collection of people with a common label. Other than sharing the group name, group members don't share much else and won't effectively fulfill the responsibilities I described for the development team role.

As a rule, teams should be long-lived. I keep my teams together as long as it is economically sensible to do so. And the economics are very favorable for long-lived teams. Research by Katz has shown that long-lived teams are more productive than newly formed groups (Katz 1982). Furthermore, research by Staats demonstrates that team familiarity (team members' prior shared work experience) can positively impact the efficiency and quality of team output (Staats 2011). Improved productivity, efficiency, and quality lead to improved business results.

If we start out with a group of people who have never worked together, we have to spend time and money to get these people to gel into a real team. Most groups need to transition through phases, such as forming, storming, norming, and performing, to become highly functional teams (Tuckman 1965). Once we have a well-functioning team, we have a real business asset. Its members know how to work together, and they have earned each other's trust. In addition, the team has amassed important historical information, such as the team's velocity and shared estimating history (see Chapter 7). If we disband the team or significantly change its composition, this valuable, team-specific historical information no longer has a context for direct use.

Far too often I see organizations failing to appreciate the asset value of teams. Most organizations have developed skills and processes for moving people around to dynamically form "teams" (really groups). In my opinion such practices miss a critical aspect of Scrum—the value is in the team. The *currency of agile* is the team. In fact, one of the core values of the Agile Manifesto is "Individuals and Interactions." In other words, the team is the valuable asset.

Moving people around from team to team destroys the integrity of the team. I doubt that the New York City police SWAT (special weapons and tactics) team is recomposed with any frequency. Their team members have learned how to work together, and in a hot situation they have each other's backs. Moving people on and off that team would likely harm trust, integrity, and operational efficiency (a drop in velocity in our case, and in the specific case of the SWAT team, safety).

Most organizations would be far better off if they adopted a policy of keeping at least the core of their teams together as long as they can and moving teams from product to product. The economics of moving well-formed teams is almost always superior to the economics of moving people.

I'm not saying that you should always and can always keep your teams together for extended periods of time. For example, if we have a team that really hasn't gelled the way we had hoped, or is otherwise dysfunctional, it is often less disruptive and economically more sensible to disband the team.

In another case, I coached an organization where we knowingly broke up a high-performance Scrum team as part of a split-and-seed strategy for broadening the adoption of Scrum within the organization. We didn't split the team because it completed its work and it was time to reassign people to new teams for the next development effort. Instead, we split it because we believed it was more valuable to form six new Scrum teams, each with a person experienced with Scrum, than to keep the original team together.

Finally, because teams are the assets, they are the unit of capacity that we should use to help establish the proper WIP limit on how many and which types of product development efforts we should pursue simultaneously. I will discuss this concept further in Chapter 16.

Closing

In this chapter I described the team role. I emphasized how the team is responsible for turning product backlog items into potentially shippable product increments. I also discussed the responsibilities of the team during each sprint. I then listed ten characteristics we want from our teams. In particular, we want team members who self-organize and are functionally diverse and sufficiently skilled to get the job done. Given the work the team must do, we want a good combination of T-shaped skills to enable effective swarming behavior. If people don't yet have the necessary breadth in their skills, we want people who are interested in acquiring that breadth.

We also want team members with an all-in-it-together Musketeer attitude. Teams should be created so that high-bandwidth communication is practical and encouraged. And we favor smaller rather than larger teams. To remain focused and committed, we prefer that team members work on only one or two development efforts at a time. Looking longer-term, we prefer to select team members who can stay together for an extended period of time on long-lived teams.

In the next chapter I will focus on the various Scrum team structures that you can use when scaling up your use of Scrum.

Chapter 12

SCRUM TEAM STRUCTURES

Scrum teams are essential assets of a Scrum organization. How they are structured and related to one another can significantly affect an organization's success with Scrum. In this chapter I discuss different ways to structure Scrum teams. I begin by discussing the distinction between a feature team and a component team. I then focus on the issue of coordinating multiple, collaborating Scrum teams.

Overview

If you have one small product, you don't need to worry much about the content of this chapter. Just create one cross-functional development team using the characteristics I described in Chapter 11, and make sure to properly fill the ScrumMaster and product owner roles. From a Scrum team perspective, you're all set to go!

Let's say, however, that your one, cross-functional Scrum team becomes a high-performance engine for delivering business value and your organization starts to grow. Or, you are already a larger organization and after developing your first product with Scrum, your use of Scrum begins to spread. In both instances you might soon find yourself needing to coordinate the work of multiple Scrum teams whose combined effort is required to deliver increasingly greater business value.

How should you structure these teams so that they are high performing and well coordinated? I address this question by considering whether you should create feature or component teams and what approaches can be used for coordinating multi-team activities.

Feature Teams versus Component Teams

A **feature team** is a cross-functional and cross-component team that can pull end-customer features from the product backlog and complete them. A component team, on the other hand, focuses on the development of a component or subsystem that can be used to create only part of an end-customer feature.

In Chapter 6 I discussed how a GPS manufacturer might create a routing component team to manage the sophisticated code associated with determining a route from an origin to a destination. Any time there is a request for new GPS features that involves routing, the routing-specific pieces of those features would be assigned to the routing component team for development.

Component teams are sometimes referred to as asset or subsystem teams. Often a community of practice made up of people with a similar specialty skill (see Figure 13.4) also functions like a component team. On these teams, all members likely report to the same functional manager and might operate as a shared, centralized resource to other teams. One example might be the centralized UX department that creates UI designs for other teams.

Scrum favors feature teams. Unfortunately, many organizations prefer component teams, often because they believe that a team of experts who are trusted to make safe and effective changes to a particular area of code should own that area of the code. Their thinking is that people unfamiliar with the code could inadvertently break it in unpredictable ways. They prefer having a component team responsible for developing that code and making changes on behalf of others.

Let's say we are developing a product whose features frequently cut across three component areas (see Figure 12.1).

In this example, there is no feature team that works on a complete product backlog item. Instead, a feature is selected from the top of the product backlog and is split into its component-level pieces (the three pieces shown inside the dashed rectangle of Figure 12.1). This splitting is done either collectively by the members of the component Scrum teams, or perhaps by an architect.

The individual pieces of the feature are then placed into the respective product backlogs of component teams (for example, the first piece is put into the component area 1 product backlog—"CA 1 PB" in the figure). Each component team performs

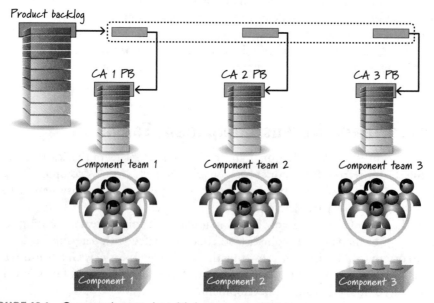

FIGURE 12.1 One product and multiple component teams

Scrum against its own component-area-specific backlog, completing component-specific pieces of end-customer features but not the full feature. Using a technique like scrum of scrums, which I will discuss shortly, the component teams integrate their individual component-level pieces back together and deliver the full end-customer feature.

If there is only one product channeling requests to the component teams, this approach will probably work. However, most organizations frequently form component teams around component areas that they intend to reuse on multiple products. Figure 12.2 shows how the work might flow if there were two products channeling requests to the same component teams.

Each feature-level product backlog contains end-customer-valuable items that can span the multiple component areas. So, in Figure 12.2, there are now two products that need component teams to work on their specific component-level pieces.

Imagine you are the product owner of one of the component teams. You now have to prioritize competing requests from two products, while at the same time coordinating with the other component-level teams to make sure the various pieces get integrated together at the appropriate time.

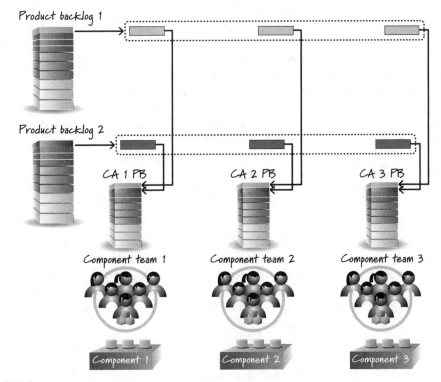

FIGURE 12.2 Two products and multiple component teams

With two products the logistics of this problem are probably still manageable. However, what if the organization works on 10 or 15 products at the same time, and each of those products is dropping component-level pieces into the component team backlogs? At this scale the logistics of figuring out the proper order to work on the individual pieces within a particular component team backlog, while at the same time coordinating and integrating with all of the other component teams, become unmanageable.

In my experience, most organizations using component teams recognize that there's a problem when things begin to fall on the floor (the baton drops, causing a break in value-delivery flow). It usually goes something like this. A senior manager asks a feature-level product owner, "How come the customer feature isn't ready?" The response: "Well, all but one of the component teams finished the pieces we assigned to them. Because that last team didn't finish, the feature isn't done." The manager might then say, "Why didn't that team finish the piece you gave them?" The response might be "I asked, and I was told that they had 15 other competing requests for changes in their component area, and for technical reasons they felt it made more sense to work on the requests from other products before ours. But they still promise to finish our piece—perhaps in the next sprint."

This is no way to operate a business. We can never be certain when (or even if) we can deliver a feature—because the responsibility for delivery has been distributed among two or more component teams, each of which might have very different priorities. Using component teams this way multiplicatively increases the probability that a feature won't get finished, because there are now multiple points of failure (each component team) instead of one (a single feature team).

Is there a solution to this problem? Well, a very good solution would be to create cross-functional feature teams that have all of the skills necessary to work on multiple end-customer features and get them done—without having to farm out pieces to component teams. But what about the principal reason that most organizations create component teams—having a single trusted team to work in a component area? Won't feature teams lead to chaotic development and maintenance of reusable components with large amounts of technical debt? Not if we have well-formed feature teams that, over time, share code ownership and collectively become trusted custodians of the code.

A transitory approach en route to this multi-feature-team model with full shared code ownership is to organize the teams as shown in Figure 12.3.

In this approach, the concept of a feature team has been reintroduced. There is now a single feature team that can pull an end-customer-valuable feature off of the product backlog. This feature team has complete responsibility for doing the work and managing the logistics of getting the feature done.

Trusted component teams also remain in this model to help maintain the integrity of the individual component areas. These component teams still have a product backlog that typically contains technically oriented work that needs to take place within the component area (perhaps technical debt repayment work).

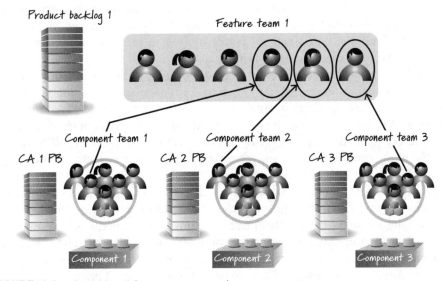

FIGURE 12.3   Combined feature team and component teams

Also, as illustrated in Figure 12.3, a member of a component team can be assigned to be a member of a feature team. This person has the dual responsibility of being both a pollinator and a harvester (Goldberg and Rubin 1995).

In the role of pollinator, the component team members pollinate feature teams with knowledge of the component areas to help better promote shared code ownership within the feature teams. In the role of harvester, component team members collect changes that the feature teams need to make within component areas and discuss those changes with their colleagues on the component teams, each of whom might also be collecting changes to the same component areas. In these discussions, the component team members can better ensure that the component-area changes needed to satisfy the requests of multiple feature teams can be coordinated. Additionally, the people making the component-area changes can do so in a coherent, non-conflicting fashion, thus better ensuring the conceptual integrity of the component areas. The component team members can also keep each other apprised of potential reuse opportunities because everyone has a shared understanding of the changes being harvested in the component areas.

Like the pure component team approach, this approach also can break at large scale—but for different reasons, ones that we can actually address. For example, when I introduced this approach to people at one large company, they remarked, "But our features can cut across up to 50 different systems [components]. We can't move 50 people up to be on one feature team." Although a feature may indeed cut across 50 components, it is rare that all 50 of the components need to directly interact with one another. As a result, we don't need one team of 50 people, but instead we can create several "feature teams" that form around smaller clusters of components that do have a high degree of interaction (see Chapter 13, Figure 13.5 and Figure 13.6, for examples) and then coordinate the efforts of these teams with the multiple-team techniques that I will describe later in this chapter.

Another way the approach in Figure 12.3 can break is if the organization is working on 40 different products and has only four team members in a component area. It doesn't make sense to assign people out to ten different feature teams at the same time. However, this problem can be solved by reducing the number of products being developed concurrently (see Chapter 16), training (or hiring) more people who have expertise in the component area, and, preferably, better promoting shared code ownership (which is the long-term vision).

In my experience there is no one-size-fits-all solution to the issue of feature versus component teams. Most large and successful Scrum organizations tend to have a blended model composed mostly of feature teams with the occasional component team—when the economics of having the component team as a centralized resource make sense. Sadly, many organizations favor the reverse—mostly component teams with the occasional feature team. These organizations pay a great price in the form of delays from frequently disrupted flow.

Multiple-Team Coordination

Scrum scales not by having increasingly larger development teams, but instead by having multiple right-sized Scrum teams. When there is more than one Scrum team, however, we have the issue of how to coordinate those teams. Two techniques for multiteam coordination are the scrum of scrums and the more comprehensive form of multiteam coordination known as a release train.

Scrum of Scrums

In Chapter 2 I noted that each day during sprint execution the development team performs a daily scrum. Each team's daily scrum includes only the members of that Scrum team.

A common approach to coordinating work among multiple teams is the scrum of scrums or SoS (see Figure 12.4).

This practice allows multiple teams to coordinate their inter-team work. The team that performs the SoS is composed of individual members of the various development teams. Each development team determines which member to send to the scrum of scrums based on who can best speak to the inter-team dependency issues. Although I prefer to have consistency of representation, the person representing a team at the SoS can change over time based on who is best able to represent the team and speak to the issues at that point in time.

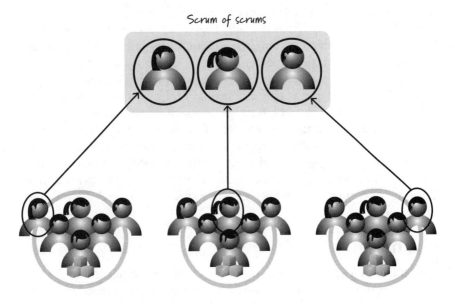

Scrum of scrums

FIGURE 12.4   Scrum of scrums

Some teams send both a development team member and their ScrumMaster (who might be shared among two or several Scrum teams) to the SoS—collectively being cautious of not allowing the overall number of participants to become too large. It might even make sense to have a ScrumMaster at the level of the scrum of scrums. If such a role exists, it could be filled by one of the individual team ScrumMasters or by a ScrumMaster not working directly with any of those teams.

There are multiple approaches to conducting a scrum of scrums, and the participants should decide which approach works best for them. Typical of all approaches, the SoS is not held every day but instead a few times a week as needed. Participants at the scrum of scrums answer similar questions to the ones answered at the daily scrum:

- What has my team done since we last met that could affect other teams?
- What will my team do before we meet again that could affect other teams?
- What problems is my team having that it could use help from other teams to resolve?

Some teams timebox their scrum of scrums to be no more than 15 minutes, just like an individual Scrum team's daily scrum. And they defer problem solving to occur after the scrum of scrums has completed so that only those participants whose involvement is necessary for problem resolution need attend.

An alternative approach is to extend the scrum of scrums beyond the 15-minute timebox. Although the participants might begin each SoS with a 15-minute timebox for answering the three questions, the SoS continues past that 15-minute activity, providing the participants the opportunity to problem-solve issues that came up.

In theory, the scrum of scrums can be scaled to multiple levels. Let's say there is a product being developed with many teams. Typically these teams would group together into feature-area clusters. Within a given cluster of teams a traditional SoS can be used to help coordinate the work of a feature area. It would also make sense to have a higher-level SoS, called a scrum of scrum of scrums (more easily thought of and pronounced as a "program-level scrum"!) that would help coordinate the work among the clusters. Although this approach can work, there are other techniques for coordinating large numbers of teams. One in particular is the release train, which I will discuss next.

Release Train

A **release train** is an approach to aligning the vision, planning, and interdependencies of many teams by providing cross-team **synchronization** based on a common cadence. A release train focuses on fast, flexible flow at the level of a larger product.

The train metaphor is used to imply that there is a published schedule of when features will "leave the station." All of the teams participating in the development of the product need to get their cargo onto the train at the appointed time. As in any country with reliable trains, the release train always departs on time and waits for no one. Likewise, if a team misses the train, it need not fret because there will be another train departing at a known time in the future.

Leffingwell defines the rules of a release train as follows (Leffingwell 2011):

- Frequent, periodic planning and release (or potentially shippable increment—PSI) dates for the solution are fixed (dates are fixed, quality is fixed, scope is variable).
- Teams apply common iteration lengths.
- Intermediate, global, objective milestones are established.
- Continuous system integration is implemented at the top, or system, level, as well as at the feature and component levels.
- Release increments (PSIs) are available at regular (typically 60- to 120-day) intervals for customer preview, internal review, and system-level QA.
- System-level hardening iterations are (or may be) used to reduce technical debt and to provide time for specialty release-level validation and testing.
- For teams to build on top of similar constructs, certain infrastructure components—interfaces, system development kits, common installs and licensing utilities, user-experience frameworks, data and web services, and the like—must typically track ahead.

Figure 12.5 shows a partial release train picture based on Leffingwell's definition.

The release train is a rich concept with multiple levels of detail, including portfolio and release levels. As I mentioned in Chapter 6, the release train is based on an enterprise backlog model that contains three levels of backlogs: portfolio backlog (with epics owned by portfolio management), program backlog (with features owned by program management), and the team backlogs (with sprintable user stories owned by product owners). Figure 12.5 illustrates only the team level. Details of portfolio-level planning and release-level planning will be discussed in Chapter 16 and Chapter 18 respectively.

The team-level train in Figure 12.5 shows a total of nine teams clustered into three feature areas. Each team within a feature area performs its own sprint, drawing work from its associated feature-area backlog. Using a technique like scrum of scrums, all the teams within a feature area coordinate and integrate their work each sprint.

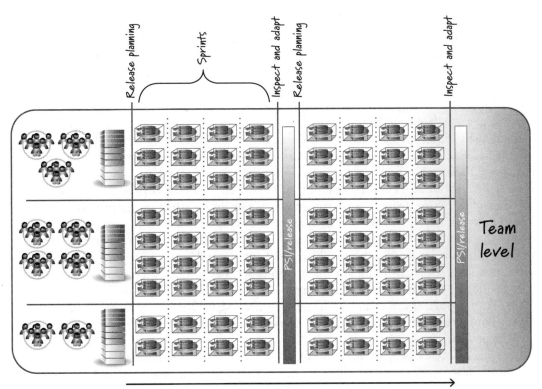

FIGURE 12.5   Release train structure

Also, as often as is practical, there should be system-wide integration and testing across the feature areas. Some teams reserve the last sprint before the train departs to be a time for *hardening* what has been developed in the previous sprints and integrating and testing the results across the various feature areas (for example, sprint 4 in Figure 12.5 might be a hardening sprint). As team skills mature, the need for a hardening sprint should diminish.

The durations of all sprints for teams participating in the release train are identical, and all sprints are aligned. The result is that sprints of every team start and end on the same dates. Doing this enables **synchronization** to take place not only within a given feature area but across all teams working on the product.

Finally, a PSI (release increment) is available after a fixed number of sprints, which in the case of Figure 12.5 is four sprints. Knowing that release points will occur at reliable times allows the organization to synchronize its other activities to known future dates. At these release points, the organization can choose to deploy a PSI to its customers (if that is the business-appropriate thing to do) or use it instead to confirm that the work performed within the individual feature areas has been integrated and tested across the feature areas, and to solicit internal review.

Each release train begins with a release-planning meeting that spans all of the teams working on the PSI (see Figure 12.5). That means that potentially hundreds of people are simultaneously participating in a joint planning event. I have to admit it is fascinating to see this happen. Here is an overview of planning at this scale.

First, you will need a big room! The chief product owner (see Figure 9.13) leads this activity and typically kicks things off. Individual Scrum team members colocate at the same table or area of the room (preferably near open wall space where they can hang up their artifacts). Scrum teams in the same feature area cluster nearby. Once the chief product owner provides the big picture for the PSI, teams gather with other feature-area teams. Feature-area product owners then provide the big-picture overview of their feature areas for the upcoming release train.

Individual Scrum teams then begin mapping out their sprints by slotting features into specific sprints. This activity is referred to as sprint mapping, which I will discuss in Chapter 18. Because Scrum teams are actually working on the creation of a larger, multiteam deliverable, there will be inter-team dependencies. To help manage these dependencies, at any point a member of one Scrum team can get up and walk over to another Scrum team (perhaps carrying a note card or Post-It) and ask the other Scrum team if it can complete the piece of work identified on the card during the upcoming release train. If it can, the team making the request can then commit to the dependent feature.

During all of this, people with multiteam responsibilities, such as the chief product owner, feature-area product owners, and shared architects, can circulate from table to table to help ensure that the big picture is understood and that a coherent overall plan for the upcoming release train makes sense. Of course, a Scrum team can always request that one of these shared individuals come over to assist.

Once the release train sprints are completed and we arrive at a PSI release point (train departure), we then perform release-train-level inspect-and-adapt activities. The first is a PSI review of the full set of cargo that was placed on the release train. The second is a retrospective at the release train level that is focused on how to make future release trains more efficient. Then we are off to the release planning for the next release train.

Closing

In this chapter I discussed different ways to structure Scrum teams. I began by describing feature teams that are cross-functionally diverse and sufficient to pull an end-customer feature from a product backlog and get it done. I then compared feature teams with component teams that work in specific component, asset, or architectural areas, which represent only parts of what needs to be integrated into end-customer features. I went on to show a blended model of feature and component teams and how it could be used to help an organization transition to a point where it has mostly feature teams, each with excellent shared code ownership.

I then discussed how to coordinate multiple Scrum teams, starting first with a traditional Scrum practice called the scrum of scrums and then describing a concept called a release train, which can be used to coordinate the activities of a large number of Scrum teams. In the next chapter I will depart from the traditional Scrum team roles and discuss the role of managers in a Scrum organization.

Chapter 13
MANAGERS

In a world where teams self-organize, is there a place for managers? Absolutely. Even though the Scrum framework doesn't specifically mention the manager role, managers still play an important part in an agile organization. After all, plenty of non-Scrum roles exist within organizations that are nonetheless crucial to the company's operations. (Accountant isn't a Scrum role, but I haven't met a Scrum team member yet who doesn't want to get paid!)

In this chapter I discuss the responsibilities of functional-area managers (also called resource managers), such as development managers, QA managers, and art directors, within a Scrum organization. I conclude by discussing the project manager role within a Scrum organization.

This chapter is more immediately relevant to organizations that have functional-area managers and project managers. If your organization is small and relatively light on managers, you can skip this chapter. However, you will probably still find it valuable to read as it will provide insight that will be necessary later on as your organization grows.

Overview

According to a 2011 industry agile survey, the number-one impediment to adopting Scrum is the feeling of a loss of management control (see Figure 13.1, from Version-One 2011).

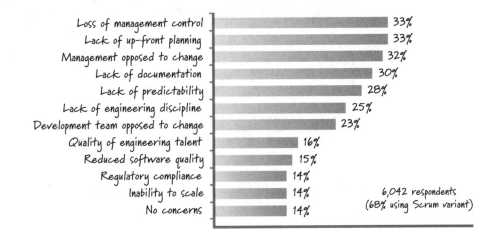

FIGURE 13.1   Greatest concerns about adopting agile

Fear that the manager role will become less relevant is unwarranted. Within a Scrum organization, the managers continue to have important responsibilities (see Figure 13.2).

In particular, functional managers in a Scrum organization are responsible for fashioning teams, nurturing teams, aligning and adapting the environment, and managing the value-creation flow.

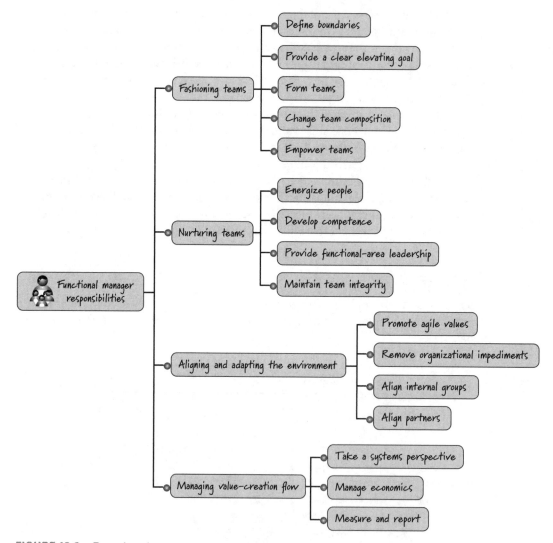

FIGURE 13.2 Functional manager responsibilities in a Scrum organization

Fashioning Teams

Managers fashion teams, the process of which includes defining boundaries, providing a clear elevating goal, forming teams, changing team composition, and empowering teams.

Define Boundaries

In Chapter 11 I described how a self-organizing team manages its response to the environment in which it is placed. The environment, however, is under the influence of managers (see Figure 13.3).

It is rare that a self-organizing team gets to decide what products or projects it will pursue. For example, if the organization builds accounting software, the team can't just decide it would like to build traffic-light control software. Managers almost always make these decisions—managers get to define the sandboxes or boundaries within which a team is permitted to self-organize.

As an example, if the teams are creating sand castles, management is deciding how many sand castles to create (how many sandboxes) and the boundaries of each sandbox, in which a specific team may self-organize and create its sand castle. Or, to use a more IT-specific example, managers in an organization that builds accounting software can decide which accounting applications to build and can set boundaries by deciding if the development teams will hand off to deployment teams for later deployment or if the development teams must deploy as part of each sprint.

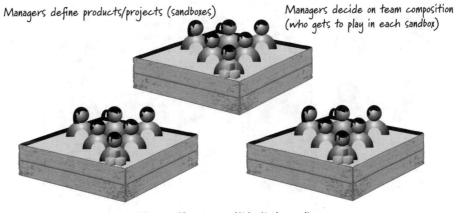

Managers define products/projects (sandboxes)

Managers decide on team composition (who gets to play in each sandbox)

Teams self-manage within their sandboxes

FIGURE 13.3 Managers define the boundaries.

Provide a Clear Elevating Goal

Managers also provide a clear elevating goal to each team. This goal gives purpose and direction to the team. Following the sandbox analogy, managers can decide that they want a sand castle that will win best of show at this weekend's sand castle competition, and the product owner working on the Scrum team might then further define the goal to be "Create a medieval castle, complete with turrets and a surrounding moat."

Form Teams

Teams do not typically form themselves (team members do not self-select who will be on the team). Managers compose teams. Returning to our sandbox analogy, this means that managers almost always decide who gets to play in each sandbox, not the individual team members themselves. Certainly team members can and should provide input into the team formation process—for example, by requesting to be on a particular team or by interviewing new candidates for an existing team. However, in most organizations managers make the final decision to ensure that team formation properly balances business needs and constraints.

In a Scrum environment, functional managers representing different disciplines or communities of practice work with one another to select members of cross-functional Scrum teams (see Figure 13.4).

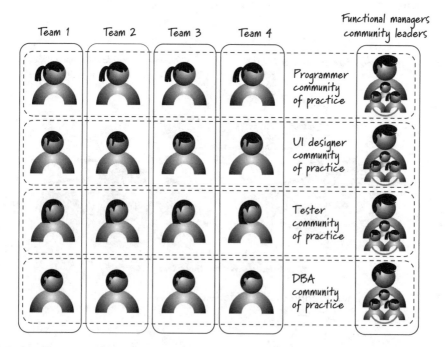

FIGURE 13.4   Functional managers collectively create Scrum teams.

In this figure each horizontal band represents a functional area or community of practice composed of people with similar specialty skills (for example, a community of developers, UI designers, testers, or DBAs). Each functional area has a functional manager.

The functional managers are collectively responsible for selecting the proper people from each functional area to form Scrum teams, which are shown vertically in the figure. Managers strive to form teams that are cross-functionally diverse and sufficient, where the team members have a good complement of T-shaped skills (see Chapter 11).

Change Team Composition

Managers also have the obligation to change a team's composition if they believe that doing so will improve the overall health and performance of the team and the organization as a whole.

Let's say, for instance, that Fred is a low-performing person on the development team. Fred also has a bad attitude and is negatively affecting the team's ability to perform. How should Fred's situation be handled?

First, I would expect Fred's teammates to discuss the situation with him with the goal of trying to help him and the team. If they are unsuccessful, the ScrumMaster, as Scrum team coach, would work with Fred to help him be a more effective team member. If coaching doesn't work, Fred's situation would most likely escalate out of the Scrum team to his resource manager (the person to whom Fred reports within the organization), because the ScrumMaster does not have hiring and firing authority.

At this point Fred's resource manager (perhaps in conjunction with someone from human resources) would handle his performance issues in a humane and appropriate manner. The resource manager would certainly want to consult the ScrumMaster and development team members to deepen his understanding of the situation. At that point the resource manager might decide to immediately remove Fred from the Scrum team and assign him to another team where he might be a better fit. Alternatively, he could put Fred on a performance improvement plan (either on his current team or on a new team), and if Fred doesn't improve per the plan, he might be let go.

While managers have "firing" authority and team members and ScrumMasters do not, team members certainly are involved in the process of ensuring that the team is well fashioned.

Managers may also have to alter team composition when doing so better optimizes the organization's ability to deliver across its portfolio of products. For example, even though we prefer our teams to be long-lived, it may be necessary from time to time to move a person who has a special set of skills off of one team and onto another team that has an immediate, high-value need for those skills. Managers need to make such changes with care because both teams will be affected by the change in team member composition.

Empower Teams

For teams to self-organize they must be empowered, which requires authorization and trust from managers. One principal way of empowering teams is for managers to delegate responsibilities to them with the primary goal of allowing self-organizing teams to manage themselves better. That being said, teams don't get to make all of the "management" decisions (as we discussed earlier, Fred's team members cannot fire him for being a poor performer). However, teams can be empowered to take on typical management activities.

For each activity type or specific decision the manager might consider delegating, he picks the proper level of authority for empowering the team. Appelo defines seven levels of authority as shown in Table 13.1, each with an example (Appelo 2011).

These levels range from one extreme, *tell*, where the manager makes the decision and informs the team, to the other extreme, *delegate*, where the team has full authority to make the decision.

When managers delegate tasks, they must trust that the teams will carry out their responsibilities as expected. And the teams must trust that their managers will not take actions that are in contradiction to delegated authority. For example, managers should not delegate authority for a decision to the team and then go off and make the decision.

TABLE 13.1   Appelo's Seven Levels of Authority, with Examples

Level	Name	Description	Example
1	Tell	Manager makes the decision and tells the team	Relocate to a new office building
2	Sell	Manager convinces the team about the decision	Decision to use Scrum
3	Consult	Manager gets input from the team before making the decision	Select new team members
4	Agree	Manager and team make the decision together	Choose logo for business unit
5	Advise	Manager advises to influence the decision made by the team	Select architecture or component
6	Inquire	Manager inquires after the team has made the decision	Sprint length
7	Delegate	Manager fully delegates the decision to the team	Coding guidelines

Managers should also help the team members trust each other. They can do this by defining the proper boundary for the environment in which the team operates, which will help intra-team trust to form by setting limits on how far trust must be extended. Managers should also help team members understand the importance on a self-organizing team of meeting personal commitments, because there is no manager within the team to pressure people to get work done. And managers should reinforce a Musketeer attitude among team members, so that they can trust that everyone truly is committed to working together to meet team goals.

Nurturing Teams

Once Scrum teams have been fashioned, managers then must nurture them. By nurture I don't mean that managers should *manage* the teams. Instead, managers should energize people, focus on competence development, provide functional-area leadership, and maintain team integrity.

Energize People

Providing a clear elevating goal creates a foundation upon which to energize team members. By energize I mean that managers should constantly seek ways to motivate people to intrinsically want to do great work. We all want to work in a fun, creative, value-delivering environment, and managers are responsible for nurturing that environment. Through proper management, managers can positively influence the intrinsic motivation and energy of team members.

Conversely, managers can take actions that have the opposite affect—that sap energy from the environment and lead to demotivated people. For example, historically, functional managers are accustomed to assigning task-level work to people in their area. Doing so in a Scrum environment would deenergize people by undermining the foundation of team self-organization and compromising the ability of the team to deliver value.

Develop Competence

Within Scrum organizations, each team member still reports to a functional or resource manager who is typically not the ScrumMaster or the product owner. And, just as in non-Scrum environments, these managers take an active role in coaching and assisting their direct reports with their career goals by promoting opportunities for competency development and providing frequent, actionable feedback on performance.

Managers need to foster an environment where people are constantly learning and adding to their skill sets. They need to make it clear that learning is not only encouraged but is in fact a priority at the individual, team, and organizational levels.

Actions such as providing team members with time for training or attending conferences will speak louder than words. Within this supportive learning environment, managers coach team members to advance their domain knowledge, technical knowledge, thinking skills, and so on.

Managers must also provide frequent feedback to teams and individuals. In many non-Scrum organizations, performance feedback comes in the form of the annual performance review. In organizations using Scrum that choose to perform these reviews, the functional managers would be expected to continue the process. However, organizations that have internalized core Scrum values and principles soon realize that providing performance feedback to individuals once (or twice) a year is out of sync with the cadence of Scrum teams that are performing and learning in short-duration sprints. These annual performance reviews can also foster low-trust competition in the team rather than self-organization with a Musketeer attitude. Individual performance measures can also interfere with superior team performance by driving independent behavior—people optimize how they are personally being measured at the expense of the team. Successful Scrum organizations soon begin to question the value of even doing these annual performance reviews, realizing they may indeed cause more harm than good.

That doesn't mean individual performance isn't assessed in Scrum organizations. Managers should just align the frequency of their feedback to individuals to better match that of the learning loops of the team of which their direct reports are members. One such approach would be for managers to provide feedback every sprint. Individual feedback should also be well positioned in the context of how individual performance is supportive (or not) of team performance.

Provide Functional-Area Leadership

As in non-Scrum organizations, functional managers in Scrum organizations continue to provide leadership specific to their functional area.

Functional managers usually have good working knowledge of their functional area and can provide thought leadership within the area. This type of leadership does not involve a functional manager assigning tasks to his direct reports or telling them how to do their jobs. Such actions would be debilitating to a self-organizing team. This type of leadership does, however, support an important need for consistency, coherence, and coaching within the functional area.

For example, in game development companies, the artists report to the art director, who himself is a highly skilled artist. The art director provides art leadership to the artists by helping to set art standards for the game and then reviewing the work of individual artists to ensure holistic consistency. We don't want to have an artist on one Scrum team doing gothic art and an artist on another team doing cartoon art. The art director provides overall leadership within the area to help better ensure high-value, coherent results.

Functional managers also provide leadership by establishing area-relevant standards and by encouraging initiatives specific to their functional area. For example, let's say the QA director wants to select new test automation tools that can be used across multiple development efforts. To accomplish this, the QA director may ask the QA-centric people who report to him, but who are all members of different Scrum teams (as illustrated in Figure 13.4), to collaborate on the selection.

Maintain Team Integrity

In Chapter 11 I stated that the currency of agile is the team. Because the team replaces the individual as the unit of capacity, managers should work proactively to maintain team integrity. That means not pulling people off of teams mid-sprint to work on pet projects or unnecessarily assigning people to work on multiple teams.

Because the economics of long-lived teams are compelling, managers should also try to keep teams together as long as the economics justify doing so. At the end of a development effort, managers should first try to assign the team as a whole to the next development effort. They should do this before they impair a high-value asset by breaking it into pieces and losing the value-added cohesion of the team.

Aligning and Adapting the Environment

Getting a single team, or even the IT or development departments, to use Scrum is a good start. However, to realize the extraordinary benefits of Scrum, the entire value chain from suppliers to customers needs to embrace agile. Managers are responsible for aligning and adapting the environment (the value chain) by promoting agile values, removing organizational impediments, aligning internal groups, and aligning partners.

Promote Agile Values

Managers must embrace agile values and principles. They need to understand and truly believe them, live them, and encourage others to do the same. Far too often when I teach classes or coach Scrum teams I hear, "Yes, all of this makes sense to us, but we need to get our management to buy in or we won't be able to really do Scrum. I wish they were in the room to hear this." These teams are correct. They will eventually need management support if they are to be successful over the long term.

Once I was engaged in a lunchtime discussion with the management team of an organization that was just starting to adopt Scrum. During our discussion I remarked that managers should avoid pulling someone off an in-flight team to temporarily work on some other project because of the disruption it would create. Timidly, but with true sincerity, a manager in the room said, "OK, but I do that all the time and didn't think it was a bad thing. What are the other things I should know as a manager in an emerging agile organization so that I can better align my behavior and the environment to promote agility?"

In response to her question I began a discussion of core agile values and principles (similar to Chapter 3) to give her and her colleagues awareness of how a manager can help reinforce agile principles instead of unknowingly working in contradiction to them. Of course, only through their day-to-day behaviors can managers truly promote agile values.

Remove Organizational Impediments

Managers also work hand in hand with ScrumMasters to remove impediments. Though the ScrumMaster is the person pushing to remove organizational impediments, many impediments, especially those that are environmental in nature, require intervention from managers to actually be removed.

Align Internal Groups

The engineering or IT group is often the first to adopt Scrum. Let's say that after a reasonable period of time the first-adopter group becomes very skilled at creating customer-valuable features each sprint. However, until those features are actually made available to customers, no real value has been delivered. What if the deployment group does not operate in an agile way, and if pushing features into production every few weeks just isn't something that group can or is willing to do? Can the organization really claim to be a high-performance Scrum organization if it can't get the value into customers' hands in a timely way?

What if there is the same sort of misalignment upstream of development? Perhaps sales and marketing are operating on a different set of principles. What if their attitude is "You guys in development can use whatever process you want to build things. You just need to be able to answer all of my up-front, very detailed questions and meet the date we already provided to the customers." Or perhaps the folks in HR are still recruiting people for old job descriptions rather than targeting people who have T-shaped skills and a desire to work in self-organizing teams.

We can't realize the full, long-term potential benefits of Scrum in such environments. Managers (including executives) have the obligation to fashion the environment in order to achieve good internal alignment among the various groups, such as governance, finance, sales, marketing, deployment, and support. Managers must see the whole and align the whole with agile principles.

Align Partners

Why stop at internal alignment? Managers must also help the organization embrace a more agile approach to supplier management and outsourcing. If the way we engage our external partners follows a traditional arms-length, contract-heavy, negotiation-style approach, the organization will fail to achieve its full potential with Scrum.

Instead, managers should promote the use of agile principles when engaging partners. For example, the simplest form of outsourcing agreement is to lease the Scrum team of a third party. Instead of doing all of the difficult work of creating a high-performance team, managers buy access to a high-performance team that others have already created. At that point, the organization uses Scrum as described in this book, but the development team (and perhaps the ScrumMaster) is "owned" by a third party and not the organization.

To achieve this level of agile-partner alignment, managers should consider alternatives to writing fixed-priced contracts with outsourcers. Such contracts put the organization and its contractors immediately at odds with one another. (The contractor wants to deliver as little as possible to meet the contract so it can maximize its gross margins, and the organization wants to get as much as possible for the fixed price.) This is hardly an agile way of operating. Managers should change this style of engagement.

Managing Value-Creation Flow

Overall, managers in a Scrum environment are responsible for setting strategic direction and for ensuring that organizational resources are being marshaled in an economically sensible way to achieve strategic goals. Managers manage the value-creation flow by taking a systems perspective, managing economics, and measuring and reporting.

Take a Systems Perspective

To effectively manage the flow of value creation, managers must take a systems perspective. One of the larger impediments I have seen to successful Scrum adoption is when managers refuse to think systemically and instead focus only on their own areas or fiefdoms. I often hear, "Yes, but doing what you propose would require a change in the reporting structure or in key job descriptions." When people say this, what I hear is "I can't imagine that we would actually do those things, so I can't [or won't] make the change in my area to better align what we do with Scrum values and principles and the rest of the agile organization."

Such localized thinking makes it difficult to achieve any sort of sensible internal agile alignment and can lead to different parts of the organization quite literally working against the greater good of the system. Managers in a Scrum organization must be willing to take a see-the-whole perspective if they are to realize long-term, high-performance Scrum benefits.

Manage Economics

Organizations expect managers to be trusted stewards of the financial resources that are made available to them. Higher-level managers in a Scrum organization therefore still manage economics (such as profit and loss) for their areas. Functional managers or resource managers may not have direct profit responsibility but are still held accountable for how the financial resources entrusted to them are being spent.

Managers (perhaps at the executive level) are also expected to oversee economics at the higher level of the organization. This frequently occurs through their involvement in portfolio management and corporate governance. Through portfolio management, they determine which development efforts to fund, to what degree, and the order in which they should be done. And, once an effort is under way, managers review and react to the continuous stream of real-time feedback based on iterative and incremental development and, when appropriate, terminate an effort whose economics no longer justify additional expenditures (see Chapter 16).

Monitor Measures and Reports

Many measures and reports are collected and generated at the request of managers, so there is a real opportunity for managers to ensure that only those measures that add to the value-creation flow are captured and reported. This goal can be achieved by ensuring that measures and reporting align well with core Scrum values and principles.

In Chapter 3 I described several Scrum principles that can guide how managers approach measuring and reporting. The following are a few examples:

- Focus on idle work, not idle workers. To accomplish this, measure when and how often the flow of work is being impeded rather than how good you are at keeping people busy. A measure such as cycle time will expose the length of time between when work starts and when it finishes. If cycle time is increasing, you need to investigate why.
- Measure progress by working, validated assets. Does it really matter if you deliver on time and on budget if you don't deliver a product that people want? Focus on measuring the value delivered (working and validated assets), but don't lose sight of the variables (date, scope, budget, and quality) needed to deliver value.
- Organize flow for fast feedback. Align your measures to determine how quickly the learning cycle is completed (assume, build, feedback, inspect, and adapt).

This last measure is at the heart of **innovation accounting**, which is effective in any organization that creates a product or service under conditions of extreme uncertainty (Ries 2011). Innovation accounting uses actionable metrics to evaluate how fast we are learning as a critical measure of our progress toward converging on a business-valuable result. Innovation accounting is based on three steps:

1. Create a minimum viable product (MVP) to establish actual baseline values of the actionable metrics on where the organization or product is today.
2. Using a series of incremental improvements to the product, try to improve the actionable measures from the baseline toward the ideal or desired values.
3. If actionable measures show that the product is making demonstrable progress toward the desired target, persevere on the current path; otherwise **pivot** to a new strategy and begin the process again.

I will discuss the concepts of pivot and persevere in more detail in Chapter 14, Chapter 16, and Chapter 17.

Project Managers

So far we have been discussing the role of functional manager or resource manager. What about the project manager role? Is there such a role in a Scrum organization?

Project Management Responsibilities on a Scrum Team

A common misperception is that the ScrumMaster is really just the "agile project manager" or a project manager with a different title. On the surface there are some similarities between a ScrumMaster and a project manager—for example, both do impediment removal. However, being a servant leader significantly differentiates this role from a more command-and-control-focused project manager.

To answer the question "Where is the project manager?" let's look at the core project management responsibilities as defined by the Project Management Institute (PMI 2008) and summarized in Table 13.2.

TABLE 13.2   Traditional Project Management Responsibilities

Project Management Activity	Description
Integration	Identify, define, combine, unify, and coordinate the various processes and project management activities.
Scope	Define and control what is and is not included in the project, ensuring that the project includes all of the work required.

continues

TABLE 13.2   Traditional Project Management Responsibilities (*Continued*)

Project Management Activity	Description
Time	Manage timely completion of the project by defining what to do, when to do it, and what resources are necessary.
Cost	Estimate, budget, and control costs to meet an approved budget.
Quality	Define quality requirements and/or standards, perform quality assurance, and monitor and record results of quality-focused activities.
Team (human resource)	Organize, manage, and lead the project team.
Communications	Generate, collect, distribute, store, retrieve, and dispose of project information.
Risk	Plan, identify, analyze, respond, monitor, and control project risks.
Procurement	Acquire products, services, or results needed from outside the project team.

Certainly these responsibilities remain important and need to be addressed. So, if there is no project manager, who oversees these activities?

Table 13.3 shows that these traditional project manager responsibilities are distributed among the various Scrum team roles and possibly other managers.

TABLE 13.3   Mapping of Project Management Responsibilities in a Scrum Organization

Project Management Activity	Product Owner	ScrumMaster	Development Team	Other Manager
Integration	✔			✔
Scope	Macro level		Sprint level	
Time	Macro level	Helps Scrum team use time effectively	Sprint level	
Cost	✔		Story/task estimating	

TABLE 13.3   Mapping of Project Management Responsibilities in a Scrum Organization (*Continued*)

Project Management Activity	Product Owner	ScrumMaster	Development Team	Other Manager
Quality	✔	✔	✔	✔
Team (human resource)			✔	Formation
Communications	✔	✔	✔	✔
Risk	✔	✔	✔	✔
Procurement	✔			✔

Based on Table 13.3, a person who was a project manager might assume any of the three Scrum roles, depending on that person's skills and desire. Many project managers make excellent ScrumMasters, if they can forgo any command-and-control management tendencies.

However, as you can see from Table 13.3, the product owner assumes at least as many project management responsibilities as the ScrumMaster. So, project managers can also make a transition into the role of product owner, if they have the proper domain knowledge and other skills to execute the product owner role. Or, less frequently, a project manager with a technical background might choose to become a member of the development team.

Retaining a Separate Project Manager Role

It would seem that project managers might become ScrumMasters, product owners, or team members. That is not, however, always the case. Companies that have large and complex development efforts sometimes decide to retain a separate project manager when logistics and coordination tasks are so overwhelming that the teams cannot be expected to keep up with them.

As a rule, I want the Scrum teams on a development effort to handle their own logistics and coordination. Scrum teams should not expect that someone external to the teams is responsible for coordinating things on their behalf. That expectation leads to team members thinking, "If someone else is responsible for coordinating, then we aren't."

The logistics and dependencies of smaller development efforts with only a few Scrum teams are easily handled via day-to-day inter-team coordination (using a technique like the scrum of scrums, see Chapter 12). However, what if we have a development effort with tens or hundreds of Scrum teams and hundreds or maybe a thousand developers?

Much like the one-product-one-backlog rule in Chapter 6, the teams-should-handle-their-own-coordination rule is the correct starting place. However, just as the issue of scale might cause us to relax the one-product-one-backlog rule, so might it cause us to retain one or more project or program managers to help coordinate all of the moving parts.

Before we rush down the path of retaining a coordination-specific role just because we have a lot of teams, we should step back and look at the inter-team communication channels. My experience with these situations is that rarely are the communication channels fully connected among all teams (see Figure 13.5).

More likely the teams cluster (or should cluster) together into feature areas or some equivalent, where the communication channels are more intense within a given cluster and more lightly coupled across clusters (see Figure 13.6).

In such cases, the Scrum teams can easily manage their own inter-team coordination. But who owns the cross-cluster coordination? The default answer is the teams themselves. In many cases this approach works just fine. The collaboration can be

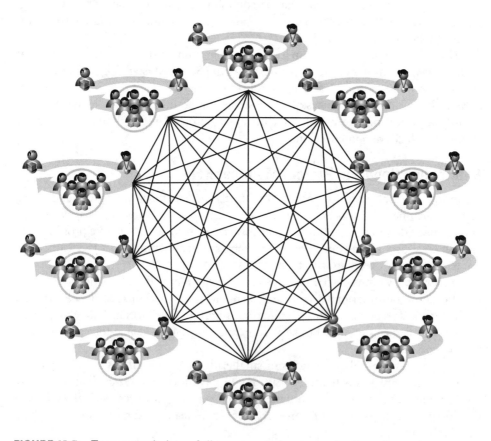

FIGURE 13.5   Teams rarely have fully connected communication channels.

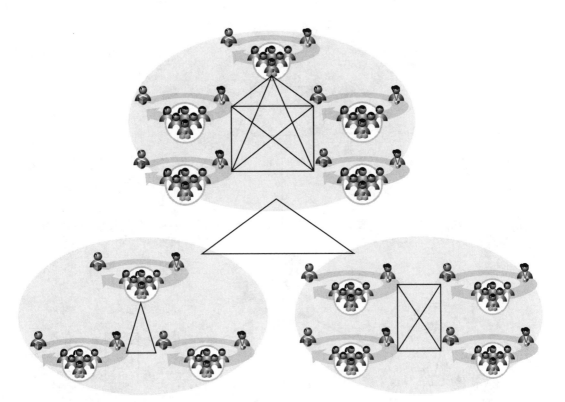

FIGURE 13.6 Teams frequently form collaboration clusters.

handled like a scrum of scrums where a representative of each cluster meets with representatives of the other clusters to discuss dependency coordination.

However, in the presence of many different clusters, even this scrum-of-scrum type of coordination among the teams might prove difficult. In such cases I have seen organizations funnel the coordination effort through a project or program manager (see Figure 13.7).

I would prefer not to have a project manager at the center of the coordination. Such an approach runs the risk of the individual Scrum teams handing off responsibility for coordination to a third party.

However, at a sufficiently large scale I do recognize that having a person or people who focus full-time on overseeing logistics and coordination can provide a level of perceived comfort that the baton won't get dropped. To clarify that the individual teams cannot delegate their inter-cluster coordination responsibilities to someone else, I prefer to think of the project manager as an assistant (like a servant leader) to the Scrum teams. In this role, the project manager is expected to have the whole-system perspective and to work diligently with each of the clusters or individual teams to ensure that everyone has the appropriate understanding of what cross-team coordination is required—but the teams still own the coordination.

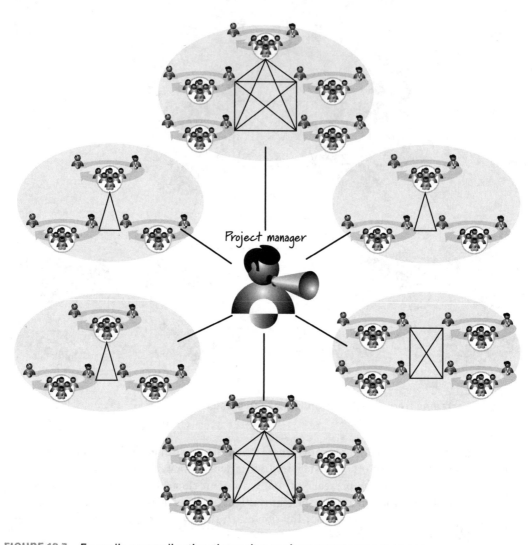

FIGURE 13.7 Funneling coordination through a project or program manager

This same use of a project manager can also be helpful on development efforts where using Scrum represents just one small part of a much greater product or services development. For example, there might be subcontractors, internal non-Scrum teams, and other internal organizations associated with delivering the product. In particular, the logistics of dealing with subcontractors or suppliers can be quite involved and time-consuming. With so many moving parts, it is helpful to have someone focused solely on the logistics (see Figure 13.8).

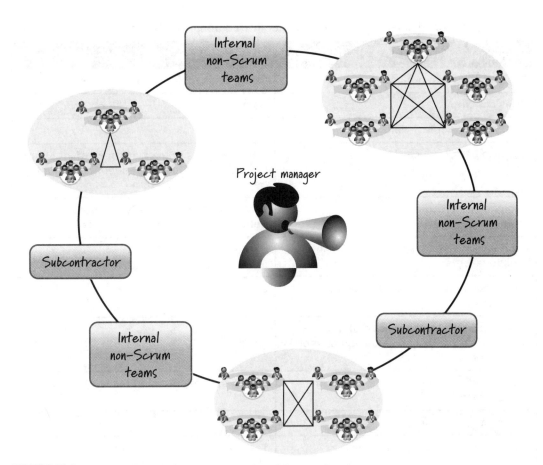

FIGURE 13.8   Project manager on complex, multiparty development

Once again, the goal isn't for the project manager to be in charge. Rather, the project manager is the person who is concerned with making sure that dependencies across the various areas are understood and communicated in a way so that the teams can most effectively coordinate their work with the other teams.

Closing

In this chapter I described the role of functional managers within a Scrum organization. I grouped managerial responsibilities into the categories of fashioning teams, nurturing teams, aligning and adapting the environment, and managing the value-creation flow.

Table 13.4 summarizes the responsibilities of functional managers in a traditional organization and those of functional managers in a Scrum organization.

TABLE 13.4   Comparison of Functional Manager in Traditional and Scrum Environments

Traditional	Scrum
Assigns people to projects	Collectively fashions great teams
Hires and fires	Same
Focuses on people development	Same
Reviews performance	Still involved but the frequency of feedback is significantly higher and feedback must be tied back to the team
Assigns tasks to team members (sometimes)	Lets team members self-organize and define and select their own tasks
Establishes cross-project standards in functional area	Same
Encourages functional-area-specific initiatives	Same
Has good working knowledge of the functional area and can lend a hand when necessary	Same
Is skilled at moving direct reports from team to team	Focuses on maintaining team integrity
Removes impediments	Same
Focuses on own functional area	Takes a see-the-whole perspective for alignment and value creation
Manages economics (P&L)	Same
Monitors measures and reports	Aligns measures and reports with agile principles to focus on value-creation flow

Although the majority of this chapter was focused on the role of functional manager, I ended with a discussion of the role of project manager. I focused on both how the traditional responsibilities of this role are shared among the three Scrum team roles and how on complex development efforts some organizations find it helpful to have one or more project managers in addition to the three Scrum roles.

This chapter concludes Part II. In the next chapter I will begin the discussion of planning by describing important Scrum planning principles.

PART III
PLANNING

Chapter 14
SCRUM PLANNING PRINCIPLES

An old myth states that development with Scrum takes off with no planning. We just start the first sprint and figure out the details in flight. This isn't true. We do real planning in Scrum. In fact, we plan at multiple levels of detail and at many points in time. To some it may seem like Scrum deemphasizes planning because a majority of the planning occurs just in time instead of substantially up front. In my experience, however, teams often spend more time planning with Scrum than with traditional development; it just might feel a bit different.

In this chapter I expand upon several of the Scrum principles described in Chapter 3, with a focus on how they apply to planning. In doing so, I set the foundation for the discussion in Chapter 15 of the multiple levels at which Scrum planning takes place. In subsequent chapters I will explore in greater detail portfolio planning, product planning, release planning, and sprint planning.

Overview

Chapter 3 described key Scrum principles, a number of which are fundamental to how we approach planning when using Scrum. This chapter emphasizes the principles shown in Figure 14.1.

FIGURE 14.1   Scrum planning principles

Additional Scrum principles (such as work in short timescales, leverage cadence, and others) will be emphasized in subsequent planning chapters.

Don't Assume We Can Get the Plans Right Up Front

The traditional, predictive approach to planning is to create a detailed plan up front before development work begins. The goal is to get it right so that the rest of the work can proceed in an orderly fashion. Some people argue that without this plan we won't know where we are going and cannot coordinate the people and their activities, especially on larger development efforts with multiple teams. There is truth in that argument.

The Scrum approach to planning is true to its empirical roots of inspection and adaptation. When developing using Scrum, we don't believe we can get it right up front, so we don't try to produce *all* of the planning artifacts up front. We do, however, produce *some* of the planning artifacts early on in order to achieve a good balance between up-front and just-in-time planning.

Up-Front Planning Should Be Helpful without Being Excessive

Let's look at an example that illustrates the principle that *up-front planning should be helpful without being excessive.*

I live in Colorado where the skiing is world-class. Occasionally I do some recreational skiing, but I'm no expert. A friend of mine, John, is an extreme skier. Honestly, there are times I wish I were one as well, but I'm not that skilled or that crazy; John is. Once John was sharing pictures of his adventures on a particularly insane mountain. Out of curiosity I asked him a simple question: "When you are positioned at the top of the mountain preparing to start your run, do you plan your entire route down?"

After he finished chuckling, he remarked, "No, if I did that I would just get myself killed." He went on to say, "I pick a spot some distance down the mountain. My first goal is to ski to that spot. Maybe I plan the first two or three turns. Realistically, planning any further would be impossible and dangerous."

"Why?" I asked.

"The terrain isn't what it appears to be from the top because the lighting and other factors play tricks on you. Also, there are probably some trees down there somewhere, but from up top I can't see them—if I decide while standing at the top to turn right at some point, and actually follow through on it, I might fly right into those trees. Plus there's no predicting the 15-year-old on a snowboard who will fly over my head yelling, 'Watch out, dude!' You never know when you'll have to change course, or why."

After he finished his explanation, I remembered thinking, "Wow, that sounds like every interesting product development effort I've worked on." You never can predict with great certainty when you'll have to change course, or why. On the products where I was asked to create a detailed up-front plan, I did create one. But I can't recall a single time this approach worked out. After we finished, I can't recall ever looking back at the original plan and saying, "Got it perfect!" In a sense, trying to do too much up-front planning is like trying to plan every turn while standing on top of the mountain. Planning at this level of detail is wasteful; believing the plan is correct to the point of ignoring real-time data is downright dangerous.

Most of us have been involved in developing products where the level of detail associated with up-front predictive planning was just absurd. Does that mean we should do no up-front planning? No, that would be negligent and foolhardy. John certainly does some up-front planning—he studies major features of the terrain to give himself confidence before he starts his run. Equally foolhardy, however, is to plan to the point where it is difficult or costly to react to reality. Like John, we must find the proper balance between up-front prediction and just-in-time adaptation.

Keep Planning Options Open Until the Last Responsible Moment

To achieve a good balance between up-front and just-in-time planning, we are guided by the principle that we should keep important options open until the last responsible moment. This means we save the planning that is best performed in a just-in-time fashion for a time when we have much better information. Why make an early planning decision based on poor information? In addition to being very costly, premature decision making can also be dangerous, as John pointed out.

Focus More on Adapting and Replanning Than on Conforming to a Plan

One of the issues on many product development efforts is that too much emphasis is placed on the up-front plan and not enough on continuous planning. If we spend significant time up front developing a highly predictive plan, and we believe we got it right, there will be significant inertia to conform to the plan instead of updating it to respond to change. If we believe instead, as we do with Scrum, that you can't get the plans right up front and you can't eliminate change, we will value responding to change and replanning over following the up-front plan.

In the 1980s I spent time either helping develop large plans or working as a consultant to companies that had developed such plans. You know the type of plans I'm talking about—the ones yielding a large Gantt chart that we print (across multiple pages), tape together, and hang on the wall (see Figure 14.2).

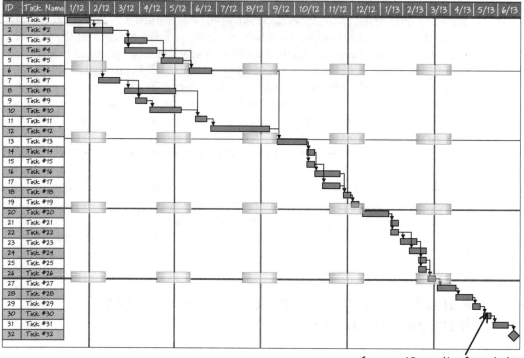

FIGURE 14.2   Big up-front Gantt chart

On several of these development efforts we spent up to six weeks developing highly predictive up-front plans. Once we produced these plans, they became the maps for the projects. Much as a legal system might assume "innocent until proven guilty," these plans were "assumed correct until proven wrong." A bit of wisdom often attributed to the Swiss Army, but more likely derived from the *SAS Survival Guide* (Wiseman 2010), seems appropriate here: "When lost in the woods, if the map doesn't agree with the terrain, in all cases believe the terrain." (See Figure 14.3.)

On any given product, our misguided faith in the map leads us to conclude that progress can and should be measured as conformance to or variation from the plan. When plan deviations occur, our desire for plan conformance blinds us to the fact that the map itself could be wrong. If the map becomes more important than the terrain, we have lost touch with the reality in which we must navigate.

When using Scrum, we view the up-front plan as helpful, but we believe that reading and adapting to the terrain are necessities. This is a reasonable belief when you consider that any up-front plan is put together when we have the least possible knowledge that we will ever have about our product. As such, up-front plans very accurately encode our early ignorance.

FIGURE 14.3   When the map and the terrain don't agree, believe the terrain.

In Scrum, we favor frequent replanning as we validate our assumptions. We use our validated learning to continuously produce better, more useful plans. We don't worry about our plans being wrong, because we know we will soon replace them with more accurate plans. Because we work in short sprints of a few weeks to no more than a month, even if we're wrong, we won't spend too long going down the wrong path before adjusting course.

Although most Scrum teams I have seen don't employ a Gantt chart, they do plan and do value having some form of longer-term planning. In fact, as I will discuss in Chapter 15, Scrum teams plan at multiple levels of detail. What we don't want is to get so wedded to our plans that we aren't willing to replan when things change or when we learn important information to which we must react.

Correctly Manage the Planning Inventory

In Chapter 3 I discussed a key Scrum principle of managing inventory (also referred to as work in process or WIP). When determining the proper balance between up-front and just-in-time planning, a key insight is to realize that creating a large inventory of predictive, not-yet-validated planning artifacts is potentially very wasteful.

Correctly managing our inventory of planning artifacts is the economically sensible thing to do.

Take the previous example of the large Gantt chart produced up front. As the development effort unfolds and we validate our assumptions by acquiring knowledge about what we're doing, we'll learn where our original plan was wrong. Unfortunately, by that time we're saddled with the waste of having to unwind and redo the future plans that have been invalidated by what we just learned.

This generates at least three forms of waste. First, there is the wasted effort to produce the parts of the plan that now have to be discarded. Second, there is the potentially significant waste of having to update the plan. And third, there is the wasted opportunity of not having invested our time in more valuable activities (like delivering high-value, working software) instead of doing up-front work that then requires future work to fix.

I always try to balance how much planning I do at a given time against the probability that what I'm doing will amount to waste if there is a change. For example, in the Gantt chart in Figure 14.2, I could have George's name next to a task that is going to start 18 months from today. What do you think the chances are that George will work on that specific task 18 months from today? Probably close to zero percent!

So, if there is such a high probability of the plan being wrong that far into the future, why plan that far out? Usually because we are trying to answer questions like "When will we be done?" or "How many people will we need for this development effort?" Unless we predict all of the work, how can we answer these questions with any certainty?

When a product will ship and which features we can get into a product by a predetermined date are valid questions that need to be addressed. However, we can't deceive ourselves into thinking we have the right answer just because we did long-term, low-certainty guessing. I will address these planning questions in the next several chapters.

Favor Smaller and More Frequent Releases

Scrum favors smaller, more frequent releases because they provide faster feedback and improve a product's return on investment (ROI). We can almost always improve the lifecycle profits of our product by leveraging incremental development and multiple releases of smaller marketable subsets of features.

Consider the economics of a single-release product, as shown in Figure 14.4 (from Denne and Cleland-Huang 2003). At the beginning of development we are spending money (starting the investment period) without any return. The release of the product occurs on the downward slope of the curve during the investment period. Eventually we achieve self-funding, when the product's revenue equals the

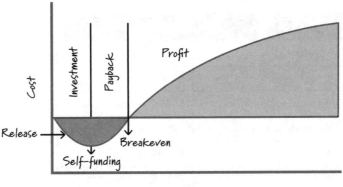

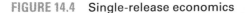

FIGURE 14.4   Single-release economics

cost of development. Once revenues exceed costs, we enter the payback period, where we start to recoup our investment. When total revenue equals total costs, we have achieved the breakeven point. From that point forward we are finally profitable!

To illustrate the benefits of smaller, more frequent releases, assume we release twice instead of once (see Figure 14.5). In this case we reach self-funding, breakeven, and profitability sooner, thus improving the overall ROI for the product.

As a specific example (adapted from Patton 2008), look at the ROI improvement of a model with the assumptions shown in Table 14.1.

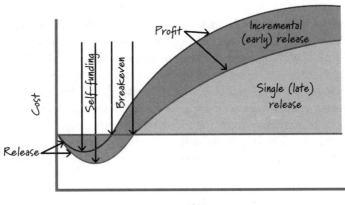

FIGURE 14.5   Multi-release economics

TABLE 14.1   ROI Model Assumptions

Variable	Value
Revenue (all features)	$300K/month
Revenue (1/2 features)	$200K/month
Revenue (1/3 features)	$150K/month
Delay from delivery to revenue	1 month
Development cost	$100K/month
Release cost	$100K per release

TABLE 14.2   ROI of Different Release Cycles

	Single Release (12 months)	Semiannual Releases	Quarterly Releases
Total cost	$1.3M	$1.4M	$1.6M
Total two-year return	$3.6M	$4.8M	$5.25M
Net two-year return	$2.3M	$3.4M	$3.65M
Cash investment	$1.3M	$0.7M	$0.45M
Internal rate of return (as a surrogate for ROI)	9.1%	15.7%	19.5%

The results, shown in Table 14.2, illustrate that, with a single release, after 12 months we have an ROI of 9.1%. If instead we do two semiannual releases, the ROI improves to 15.7%; with quarterly releases we achieve an ROI of 19.5%.

There are some limitations to this approach. First, for any product there is a minimum releasable or marketable set of features. Therefore, we can't just continue making the initial release smaller, because eventually it becomes so small as to not be marketable. Also, in some markets smaller and more frequent releases might not be an option. However, if your marketplace is open to receiving partial value sooner, delivering smaller and more frequent marketable releases is a very important principle to follow.

Plan to Learn Fast and Pivot When Necessary

There is no amount of up-front predicting or guessing that will replace doing something, learning fast, and then pivoting if necessary. By pivoting I mean changing directions while staying grounded in what we've learned. Ries defines pivoting to be "a structured course correction designed to test a new fundamental hypothesis about the product, strategy, and engine of growth" (Ries 2011). Just like John the skier, we need to be prepared to pivot quickly when we learn that our current plan is no longer valid.

As I discussed in Chapter 3, our goal is to move through the learning loop quickly and economically. So we should structure our plans with learning as a key goal. By getting fast feedback, we can determine whether our plans are taking us in a viable direction. If not, we can pivot or redirect ourselves.

Closing

In this chapter I discussed and provided an overview of several Scrum planning principles. These principles enable us to plan in an economically sensible fashion by doing a helpful amount of up-front planning, balanced with more detailed, just-in-time planning as we learn more about what we are building and how to build it. In the next five chapters I will illustrate with examples how to leverage these principles at a deeper level in the context of the multiple levels of Scrum planning.

Chapter 15
MULTILEVEL PLANNING

On Scrum projects, we plan at multiple levels of detail and at multiple times through-out product development. In this chapter I provide a high-level, top-down description of the various Scrum planning activities and how they are interrelated. In the next several chapters I will explore portfolio planning, product planning (envisioning), release planning, and sprint planning in greater detail.

Overview

When developing a product with Scrum, planning takes place at multiple levels (see Figure 15.1).

At the highest level is strategy planning, which although critical to an organization's success is outside the scope of this book. Formally Scrum defines only

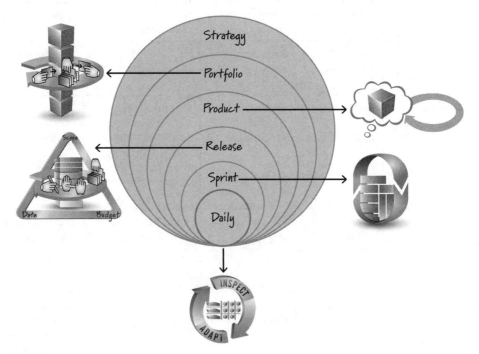

FIGURE 15.1   Different levels of planning

sprint planning and daily planning (via the daily scrum). However, most organizations will benefit from portfolio, product, and release planning, so I will summarize approaches for each of them in this chapter and then discuss each in detail in subsequent chapters.

Table 15.1 summarizes five types of planning, with an emphasis on the span of time typically covered by each type, who is involved, what the focus is, and what the deliverables are at each level.

To illustrate planning at each of these levels, I will use the redesign of the Scrum Alliance website (www.scrumalliance.org) as an example. The relevant context for this product is that in 2006 the Scrum Alliance, a nonprofit organization focused on the worldwide promotion of Scrum, had a dreadful website. It wasn't pretty, was hard to navigate, and was content poor. When I became the Managing Director of the Scrum Alliance at the end of 2006, one of the first things the board of directors asked for was a new and much better website. I was the product owner for this effort and will describe the hierarchy of planning we performed to realize a new website.

TABLE 15.1 Planning Level Details

Level	Horizon	Who	Focus	Deliverables
Portfolio	Possibly a year or more	Stakeholders and product owners	Managing a portfolio of products	Portfolio backlog and collection of in-process products
Product (envisioning)	Up to many months or longer	Product owner, stakeholders	Vision and product evolution over time	Product vision, roadmap, and high-level features
Release	Three (or fewer) to nine months	Entire Scrum team, stakeholders	Continuously balance customer value and overall quality against the constraints of scope, schedule, and budget	Release plan
Sprint	Every iteration (one week to one calendar month)	Entire Scrum team	What features to deliver in the next sprint	Sprint goal and sprint backlog
Daily	Every day	ScrumMaster, development team	How to complete committed features	Inspection of current progress and adaptation of how best to organize the upcoming day's work

Portfolio Planning

Portfolio planning (or portfolio management) is an activity for determining which products to work on, in what order, and for how long. Although portfolio planning is conceptually at a higher level than product planning (because it deals with a collection of products), one of its primary inputs is a newly envisioned product idea from product planning.

In 2006, the Scrum Alliance was a relatively new organization, and its portfolio contained only the ongoing development of its existing website. Once the initial envisioning of the new Scrum Alliance website was completed, the board of directors (the stakeholders of the Scrum Alliance portfolio backlog) approved the development of the first release of the new website.

Product Planning (Envisioning)

The goals of product-level planning (which I also refer to as **envisioning**) are to capture the essence of a potential product and to create a rough plan for the creation of that product. Envisioning begins with the creation of a vision, followed by the creation of a high-level product backlog and frequently a product roadmap.

Vision

The **product vision** provides a clear description of the areas in which the stakeholders, such as users and customers, get value. In our case, the users were the 10,000 worldwide members of the Scrum Alliance at the time (at the end of 2011 there were 150,000 worldwide members). The customer, who paid for the new product, was the Scrum Alliance board of directors on behalf of the members.

Our vision for the new Scrum Alliance website was as follows:

> For people worldwide who are interested in Scrum, the new Scrum Alliance website will be their trusted source of Scrum knowledge. It will be feature and content rich and will be their first stop on the Internet for learning more about Scrum or to collaborate on Scrum topics of interest.

High-Level Product Backlog

Once a product vision has been established, the next step is to generate an initial high-level version of the product backlog. In the case of the redesigned Scrum Alliance website, at the end of 2006 we already had a growing product backlog of features that the stakeholders and users wanted for the new and improved website.

Product backlog items included the following epic-level user stories:

As a Certified Scrum Trainer I want to be able to post my public Scrum class on the Scrum Alliance website so that the community will know the details surrounding where and when I am offering the class.

As a prospective student I want to be able to see details of all publicly available Scrum classes so that I can find one that meets my criteria for attendance.

If our product had been completely new, we would have had to do at least some minimal up-front requirements generation to populate our product backlog and estimate at least the highest-priority items. In our case we had some product backlog items that we used as a starting point for ideas to be included in our vision of the new website.

Product Roadmap

Once a product vision and high-level product backlog have been established, it is helpful to build a product roadmap (sometimes referred to as a release roadmap). A **product roadmap** communicates the incremental nature of how the product will be built and delivered over time, along with the important factors that drive each individual release.

Today many organizations are striving for **continuous deployment**, where they deploy working features into production as soon as they become available. If your organization is focused on this practice, you might not need to produce a product roadmap. However, even if you do intend to deploy continuously, a product roadmap might be a useful tool for helping your organization think about larger collections of features, constraints that might dictate which features should be done around the same time, and when certain features should be available.

Figure 15.2 shows a product roadmap in a format promoted by Luke Hohmann (Hohmann 2003).

Shown in the roadmap are two releases, one in each of the first two calendar quarters of 2007. The "0.5" release in Q1 2007 was the first release of the new website; we chose that number because we planned for this first release to have fewer than half of the features of the old Scrum Alliance website, but it would include new features that were better than those of the old website. The desired features centered on listing all publicly available Scrum classes anywhere in the world and basic support for Certified Scrum Trainers (CSTs). Release 0.5 was a **fixed-scope release** because we knew the specific features we wanted to have on the new website before we could retire the old site. What we didn't know was how long it would take to get those features ready for launch. In Chapter 18 I will discuss how to determine the ship date for a fixed-scope release.

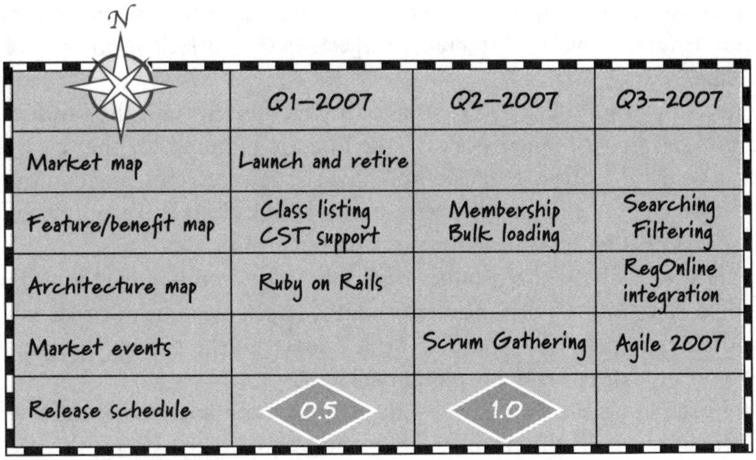

N	Q1–2007	Q2–2007	Q3–2007
Market map	Launch and retire		
Feature/benefit map	Class listing CST support	Membership Bulk loading	Searching Filtering
Architecture map	Ruby on Rails		RegOnline integration
Market events		Scrum Gathering	Agile 2007
Release schedule	0.5	1.0	

FIGURE 15.2   Scrum Alliance website product roadmap

Release 1.0 was a fixed-date release. We knew we wanted the release to coincide with a Scrum Alliance conference (called a Scrum Gathering) that began on May 7, 2007, in Portland, Oregon. Our goal was to have an exciting set of features available by the first day of that conference. What we didn't know was how many features we could get into that release. In Chapter 18 I will discuss how to determine the content of a fixed-date release.

To summarize, on the Scrum Alliance website initial product roadmap we identified both a fixed-scope release (0.5) and a fixed-date release (1.0).

No matter what product you are creating, by the end of product-level planning, you should have a product vision, a high-level product backlog populated with estimated user stories, and (optionally) a product roadmap. In addition, you might also produce other artifacts to provide decision makers with sufficient confidence to move forward to develop the product.

The outputs of product-level planning became inputs to portfolio planning, where the initial 0.5 release of the redesigned website was approved by the board of directors.

Release Planning

Release planning is about making scope, date, and budget trade-offs for incremental deliveries.

On most development efforts it is sensible and necessary to do initial release planning after envisioning (product planning) and before starting the first sprint associated with the release. At this point, you can create an initial **release plan** that balances how much you can develop in the release against when the release will be available.

To have some idea of what you can deliver by a fixed date or when you can deliver a fixed set of features, you need to create and estimate a sufficient number of product backlog items.

A simple way to visualize a release is to draw a line through the product backlog (see Figure 15.3). All of the items above the line are planned for the release, and all of the items below the line are not planned for the release. This line can move up or down in the product backlog as you gain better insight into the product. In Chapter 18 I will discuss how to determine the position of this line.

You can now easily tie the product roadmap to the product backlog to provide a more detailed elaboration of the contents of at least the near-term releases identified in the product roadmap (see Figure 15.4). A release on the product roadmap corresponds to a set of features in the product backlog.

The release plan must also have a time dimension associated with it, which can be expressed in terms of the number of sprints required to accomplish the release. Most releases are large and have more features than can be built in one sprint (see Figure 15.5).

During release planning you might go so far as to guess the features that will be delivered in the first couple of sprints. This can be helpful when multiple teams need to coordinate work or when a team needs to request additional hardware, tools, or assistance in advance. But guessing ahead more than a couple of sprints is almost always unnecessary and violates the principle of doing planning just in time and just enough.

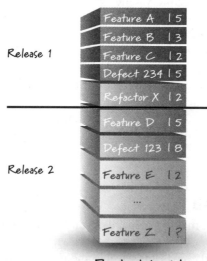

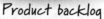

FIGURE 15.3   A release line in the product backlog

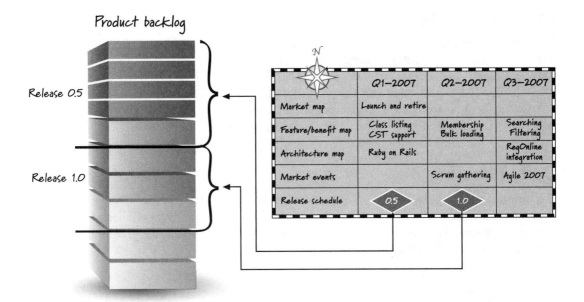

Product backlog

Release 0.5

Release 1.0

	Q1–2007	Q2–2007	Q3–2007
Market map	Launch and retire		
Feature/benefit map	Class listing CST support	Membership Bulk loading	Searching Filtering
Architecture map	Ruby on Rails		RegOnline integration
Market events		Scrum gathering	Agile 2007
Release schedule	0.5	1.0	

FIGURE 15.4   Product roadmap releases mapped to the product backlog

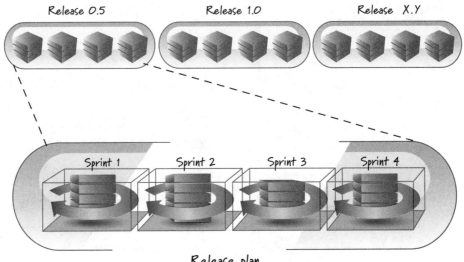

Release 0.5   Release 1.0   Release X.Y

Sprint 1   Sprint 2   Sprint 3   Sprint 4

Release plan

FIGURE 15.5   A release can encompass one or more sprints.

Sprint Planning

The specific product backlog items that the Scrum team will work on in the next sprint are agreed to at sprint planning, which occurs at the beginning of each sprint. During this activity, the team generates a sprint backlog: a description of the task-level work that has to be completed to get the product backlog items done (see Figure 15.6).

During sprint planning the team does the next level of just-in-time detailed planning. I will discuss the details of sprint planning in Chapter 19.

Daily Planning

The most detailed level of planning occurs during the team's daily scrum meeting. Recall that this is the activity where the team members get together and each person takes turns stating what she got done since the last daily scrum, what she is planning to work on today, and whether she has any impediments.

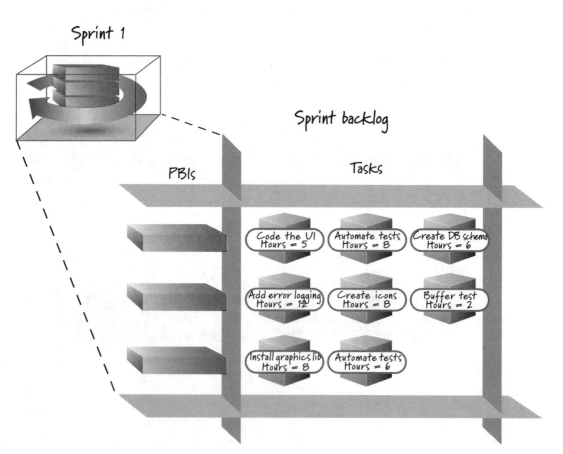

FIGURE 15.6   Each sprint has a sprint backlog.

During the daily scrum, team members collectively describe, in a highly visible manner, the big-picture plan for that day. This also allows the team to use resource alerts. For example, someone might say, "Today I am going to work on the stored procedure task, and I should have that done by lunch. Whoever is going to work on the business logic task, please keep in mind that the business logic task is on the critical path for getting our work done this sprint and you should be ready to work on it right after lunch." Such communications can quickly identify potential work blockages and enable a better flow through sprint execution.

Closing

This chapter illustrated how planning at multiple levels of detail happens on a development effort using Scrum. Figure 15.7 (shown on the next page) graphically summarizes the artifacts produced at these levels (except the portfolio and daily planning levels) and their interrelated nature.

In the next several chapters I will explore in greater depth the topics of portfolio planning, product planning, release planning, and sprint planning.

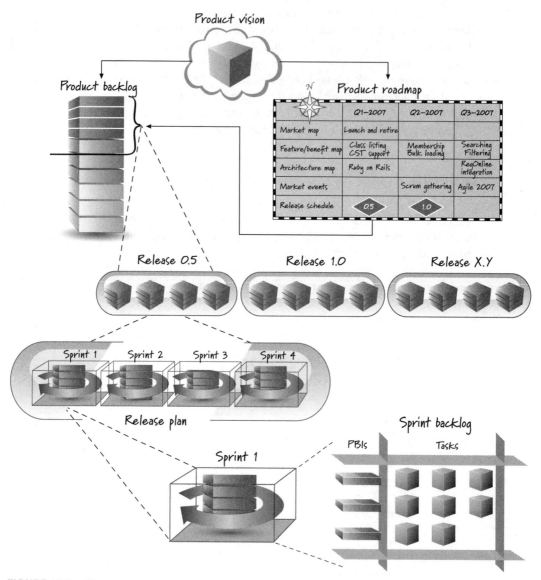

FIGURE 15.7 Hierarchical Scrum planning

Chapter 16

PORTFOLIO PLANNING

Most organizations want or need to produce more than one product at a time. These multiproduct organizations need a way to make economically sound choices regarding how to manage their product portfolios. They also need their portfolio management or governance processes to align well with core agile practices; otherwise, there will be a fundamental disconnect with the agile approach being used at the individual product level. This chapter lays out 11 strategies for portfolio planning, grouped by scheduling, product inflow, and product outflow. It ends with a discussion of how to determine whether or not more work should be invested in in-process products.

Overview

Portfolio planning (or portfolio management) is an activity for determining which portfolio backlog items to work on, in which order, and for how long. A portfolio backlog item can be a product, a product increment (one release of a product), or a project (if your organization prefers to plan work around projects). In this chapter I use the word *product* generically to mean all types of portfolio backlog items.

In my experience, most organizations (agile or otherwise) do a very poor job of portfolio-level planning. Many have portfolio-level planning processes that are fundamentally at odds with core agile principles. When this happens, decisions are made at the portfolio level that disrupt the fast, flexible flow of work. In this chapter I discuss how to avoid this disconnect by performing portfolio planning in a manner that is well aligned with core agile principles.

Timing

Portfolio planning is a never-ending activity. As long as we have products to develop or maintain, we have a portfolio to manage.

As shown in Figure 15.1, portfolio planning deals with a collection of products and is therefore larger in scope and higher level than individual product-level planning (envisioning). Being higher level, however, doesn't mean that portfolio planning precedes product planning. In fact, the output of planning or envisioning a new product is an important input to portfolio planning. Using data from envisioning, portfolio planning determines whether to fund the product and how to sequence it into the **portfolio backlog**. Portfolio planning isn't just for newly envisioned products, though. It also occurs at regularly scheduled intervals to review products that are already in process (under development, already live in production, or currently being sold).

Participants

Because portfolio planning focuses on both new products and **in-process products**, its participants include an appropriate set of internal stakeholders, the product owners of individual products, and optionally, but frequently, senior architects and technical leads.

The stakeholders must have a sufficiently broad business perspective to properly prioritize the portfolio backlog and make decisions regarding in-process products. In some organizations the stakeholders collectively form an approval committee, governance board, or some equivalent entity that oversees the portfolio-planning process.

Product owners also participate in portfolio planning as champions of their respective products and advocates for necessary resources.

Frequently the input of senior architects or technical leads is needed to ensure that important technical constraints are factored into portfolio-planning decisions.

Process

Figure 16.1 illustrates the portfolio-planning activity.

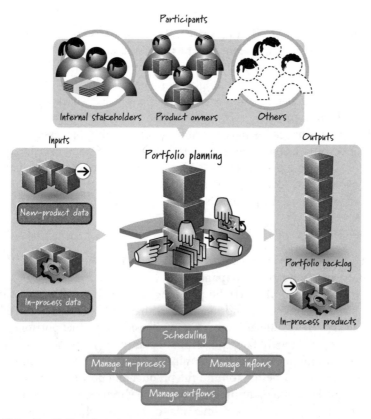

FIGURE 16.1   Portfolio-planning activity

As I stated earlier, inputs to portfolio planning include newly envisioned products (candidates for inclusion in the portfolio backlog) and in-process products. The new products come with data that was gathered during envisioning, such as cost, duration, value, risk, and so on. In-process products come with their own set of data, such as intermediate customer feedback, updated cost, schedule, and scope estimates, technical debt levels, and market-related data, which will help determine the path forward for these products.

Portfolio planning has two outputs. The first is the portfolio backlog, which is a prioritized list of future products, ones that have been approved but for which development has not yet begun. The second is a set of active products—new products that have been approved and are slated for immediate development, as well as products that are currently in process and have been approved to continue.

To arrive at these outputs, participants engage in four categories of activities: scheduling, managing inflows, managing outflows, and managing in-process products. Figure 16.2 summarizes the specific strategies associated with each of these categories.

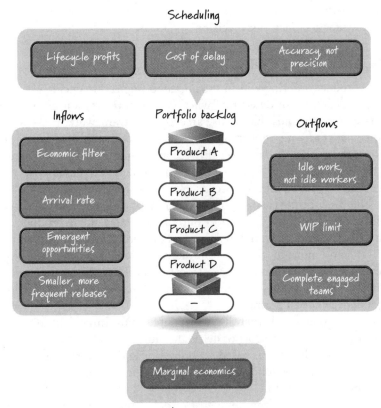

FIGURE 16.2 Portfolio-planning strategies

The scheduling strategies help determine the proper sequence of the products in the portfolio backlog. Inflow strategies guide participants in knowing when to insert items into the portfolio backlog. Outflow strategies inform participants about when to pull a product out of the portfolio backlog. The in-process-product strategy is used to decide when to preserve, pivot, deliver, or terminate a product that is currently in process.

The remainder of this chapter will discuss the 11 strategies that make up these four categories.

Scheduling Strategies

Portfolio planning must allocate an organization's limited amount of resources to products in an economically sensible way. Although there are many ways to decide the sequence of products, I focus on three strategies:

- Optimize for lifecycle profits.
- Calculate the cost of delay.
- Estimate for accuracy, not precision.

Optimize for Lifecycle Profits

To optimize product ordering within the portfolio we need to decide which variable to measure so that we can determine whether our optimization efforts are working. Reinertsen recommends that we use an economic framework where we consider all decisions and trade-offs in a standardized and useful unit of measure: **lifecycle profits** (Reinertsen 2009b). Based on this recommendation, our goal should be to sequence the items in the portfolio backlog to maximize overall lifecycle profits.

For a specific product, lifecycle profits are the total profit potential for the product over its lifetime. In the case of portfolio planning, we are interested in optimizing the lifecycle profits of the entire portfolio rather than a single product. Thus, we might have to suboptimize individual products in order to optimize the portfolio (Poppendieck and Poppendieck 2003). So the goal of the strategy of optimizing for lifecycle profits is to find the sequence of portfolio backlog items that provides the greatest lifecycle profits across the entire portfolio (see the next section on calculating the cost of delay for an example).

Reinertsen further asserts that the two variables most important to assessing the impact on lifecycle profits are cost of delay and duration (a good common proxy of which is effort or product size). Based on how similar these variables are (or aren't) across products in the portfolio, he suggests selecting one of the three scheduling approaches shown in Table 16.1.

When all products have the same cost of delay, the preferred scheduling strategy is to do the shortest job first. When products are the same size (have the same

TABLE 16.1   Different Portfolio Scheduling Principles

(If) Cost of Delay	(And) Duration/Size	(Then) Scheduling Approach
Same across all products	Varies across products	Shortest job first
Varies across products	Same across all products	High delay cost first
Varies across products	Varies across products	Weighted shortest job first

duration), the preferred scheduling strategy is to first work on the products with a high cost of delay. When both cost of delay and duration can vary (which is the normal case in product development), the economically optimal sequencing is achieved using **weighted shortest job first** (WSJF), which is calculated as cost of delay divided by duration (or effort to implement).

Next I will discuss both cost of delay and estimating the effort/cost of products in the portfolio.

Calculate Cost of Delay

When we sequence items in the portfolio backlog, we must necessarily work on some products before we work on others. Those that we don't work on immediately have a delayed start and therefore a delayed delivery date, for which there exists a quantifiable cost.

As I described in Chapter 3, the cost of delay provides essential information for making informed economic decisions. Yet most organizations aren't even in a position to answer a question as simple as "If we delay the product deployment by one month, what would be the cost of that delay in lifecycle profits?"

Being blind to the cost of delay, most organizations choose to sequence their portfolio using the simple (and frequently wrong) approach of "high profit first" (see Table 16.2).

In this example, project A has a 20% ROI and project B has a 15% ROI. Using the high-profit-first scheduling strategy, we would do project A before project B because it has the higher return on investment. Although this approach seems sensible, it fails to take into account the cost of delay of each product, which could substantially alter

TABLE 16.2   Example of Using Cost of Delay to Sequence the Portfolio

	Project A	Project B
Return on investment (ROI)	20%	15%
Cost of delay (1 month)	$5K	$75K

the lifecycle profit calculation. For example, what if project A has a $5K/month cost of delay and project B has a $75K/month cost of delay (as shown in Table 16.2)? In this case, delaying project B to work first on project A has a much greater impact on portfolio lifecycle profitability.

Cost of delay embodies the fact that time does or can affect most variables. In the previous example, the ROIs of project A and project B were computed using specific, time-dependent assumptions (for example, when development would start and end, what resources would be available at that time, how much the resources would costs, what prices people would be willing to pay to purchase the product over time, what technology and business risks would exist and what probabilities of occurrence and cost impacts they would have). Delay or accelerate development and the values of these variables can and frequently do change. So, cost of delay is not the only factor to consider when prioritizing items in the portfolio; instead, it is the time dimension that must be considered because it affects all other prioritization variables such as cost, benefit, knowledge, and risk.

The most frequent complaint I hear about cost of delay is that it is not clear how it should be calculated. Most of the time this concern is unfounded because running two different spreadsheet models that calculate profitability (one without a delay and one with a delay) should effectively calculate the cost of delay.

Leffingwell offers a model for calculating cost of delay that is the aggregation of three product attributes (Leffingwell 2011):

- User value—potential value in the eyes of the user
- Time value—how user value decays over time
- Risk reduction/opportunity enablement—the value in terms of mitigating a risk or exploiting an opportunity

To calculate the cost of a delay for a product, each of these three attributes is assigned its own individual cost-of-delay number using a scale of 1 (lowest) to 10 (highest). The total product cost of delay is the sum of the three individual delay costs.

An alternative, and frequently effective, approach for making informed scheduling decisions is to characterize the general profile of the delay cost (see Figure 16.3).

Table 16.3 describes each of these profiles in more detail.

If calculating a precise cost-of-delay number is very time-consuming or error-prone, consider selecting an appropriate delay profile (or creating a new one) and use that profile instead of a specific delay number when making scheduling decisions.

Does cost of delay apply in organizations that develop products in highly regulated industries like medical devices or health care where compliance and patient safety are critical? Such critical factors must be considered when determining product priorities; however, important properties of these factors can be accounted for using cost of delay expressed in terms of lifecycle profits.

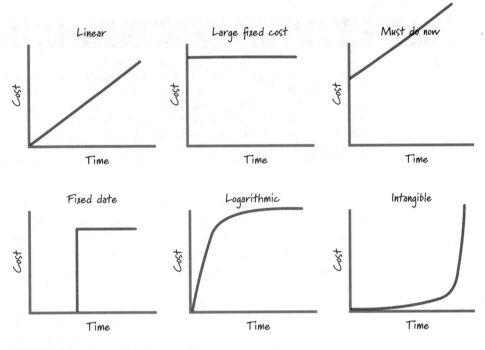

FIGURE 16.3   Cost-of-delay profiles

TABLE 16.3   Description of Cost-of-Delay Profiles

Profile Name	Description
Linear	A product with a cost of delay that increases at a constant rate.
Large fixed cost	A product that accrues a one-time cost if not acted on immediately; for example, we receive a substantial payment only after the product is delivered.
Must do now	A product that we "must do now" because we experience an immediate and aggressively increasing cost of delay; for example, a product without which we incur immediate lost revenue or cost savings that continue to grow over time.
Fixed date	A product that must be delivered by a fixed future date and therefore has a zero cost of delay until the fixed date occurs. After the fixed date passes, the full cost of at least the initial delay is accrued.
Logarithmic	A product that accrues most of the delay cost very early, with increasingly less incremental delay thereafter.

continues

TABLE 16.3 Description of Cost-of-Delay Profiles (*Continued*)

Profile Name	Description
Intangible	A product (or body of work) that has no "apparent" cost of delay for an extended period of time and then, suddenly, accrues a very high delay cost. An example would be how many organizations treat technical debt. Today there appears to be little or no cost of delay of not repaying the technical debt. However, as I described in Chapter 8, technical debt can reach a tipping point, at which time the cost of delaying other work is noticeable and very high.

For example, in the United States, organizations such as health plans and health-care providers must use certain codes to identify specific diagnoses and clinical procedures on claims, encounter forms, and other electronic transactions. The standard for these codes at the time this book was written is *International Classification of Diseases*, 9th revision (ICD-9-CM). However, a new standard, ICD-10-CM, will replace ICD-9-CM on October 1, 2013. At that time, organizations that are subject to U.S. HIPPA (Health Insurance Portability and Accountability Act of 1996) regulations must comply with ICD-10-CM. Many such organizations have a portfolio of products that need remediation—in a fashion strikingly similar to the Year 2000 (Y2K) problem at the turn of the millennium. Because all products in the remediation portfolio have a fixed-date cost-of-delay profile (as shown in Figure 16.3), to rationally sequence the remediation work, these organizations need to consider what the cost of the delay (in lifecycle profits) would be for each product if the remediation work on that product is *not* completed by October 1, 2013. For example, a critical product that is not in compliance could generate a loss of $100M/year, whereas another noncompliant product might generate a loss of $5M/year. So calculating cost of delay is a critical variable for sequencing the remediation portfolio in an economically sensible way.

Estimate for Accuracy, Not Precision

To properly schedule portfolio backlog items we also need to understand their effort/cost (because cost affects lifecycle profits). When estimating the size of portfolio backlog items, we are looking for accuracy, not precision, because of the very limited data we have at the time when a first estimate is required.

In Chapter 7 I discussed the fact that some organizations prefer to estimate portfolio backlog items using T-shirt sizes instead of overly precise numbers. Each T-shirt size corresponds to an associated cost range (see Table 16.4 for an example of one organization's mapping).

In this table, the rough cost range includes the labor cost (which typically represents the majority of a product's cost in this organization) as well as capital expenditures and any other costs deemed material to the product development effort.

TABLE 16.4   Example of T-Shirt Size Estimation

Size	Rough Cost Range
Extra-small (XS)	$10K to $25K
Small (S)	$25K to $50K
Medium (M)	$50K to $125K
Large (L)	$125K to $350K
Extra-large (XL)	>$350K

The benefit of T-shirt size estimation is that it's fast, usually accurate enough, and provides actionable information at a portfolio level.

How accurate is accurate enough? Let me give you an example. In the aforementioned organization, the engineering department had spent considerable time in the past trying to give very precise estimates. People weren't sure whether T-shirt sizes would be accurate enough, but everyone agreed to give them a try. Soon after, marketing came to engineering with an idea for a project; the engineering department discussed it and assigned it a size, Medium.

Marketing was then able to decide if the benefit of doing the project exceeded the cost of a medium-size project ($50K to $125K). This was just as helpful as it had been back when engineering spent a great deal of time to come up with a more precise-sounding, but inaccurate, guess of $72,381.27. This organization found that the ranges were accurate enough and eliminated waste, without raising expectations too high or providing a false sense of security.

Inflow Strategies

As I will discuss in Chapter 17, the envisioning process details the vision for a new product and collects a set of information that the decision makers need in order to make a go/no-go funding decision. Inflow strategies deal with how to apply the organization's economic filter to make a go/no-go decision. They also deal with how to balance the rate at which products are inserted into the portfolio backlog against the rate at which they are being pulled out, how to quickly embrace an emergent opportunity when it appears, and how to prevent portfolio bottlenecks by using smaller, more frequent releases.

Apply the Economic Filter

The output from envisioning is a product vision along with the information needed to clear the confidence threshold associated with the envisioning (product-planning) activity (see Chapter 17). This output is the new-product data that is an input to portfolio planning (see Figure 16.1). Based on this data, the organization needs to make a go/no-go decision for moving forward with development of the product. I refer to this activity as applying the economic filter to the new product to see if it meets the organization's funding requirements (see Figure 16.4).

Although each organization needs to define an economic filter that best matches its particular funding policies, a good economic filter should quickly indicate approval of any opportunity that delivers overwhelming value relative to its cost; most everything else (unless there are extenuating circumstances) should be rejected. If the resulting value of developing the product completely overwhelms the costs of developing it, it shouldn't be necessary to spend any significant time discussing it—just approve it and move on to sequencing it into the portfolio backlog. If we find ourselves squabbling over a small difference in cost or value before we can make a decision, we should reject the product because there is clearly not overwhelming economic support for developing it. In most organizations there are simply too many high-value product development opportunities to waste time discussing questionable opportunities.

Balance the Arrival Rate with the Departure Rate

In practice we want a steady stream of products moving into the portfolio backlog balanced against a steady stream of products being pulled from the portfolio backlog (see Figure 16.5).

What we don't want is to overload the portfolio backlog by inserting too many products into it at the same time. This has the effect of overwhelming the system.

To illustrate why, say you want to go to dinner at your favorite restaurant. You get in your car and you drive over. When you arrive, you notice that a large tour bus full of hungry senior citizens has just unloaded and gone into the restaurant.

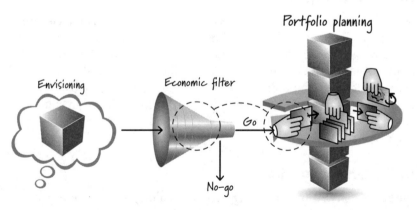

FIGURE 16.4 Applying the economic filter

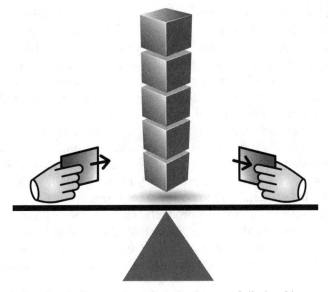

FIGURE 16.5   Balancing inflow and outflow in the portfolio backlog

What would you do? Are you going to enter the restaurant and attempt to dine there? If so, what do you think the consequences of all those hungry seniors descending on the restaurant at the same time will be? Chances are they will overwhelm the restaurant's capabilities. If you risk dining there, you will likely suffer a long and rather unsatisfying experience. Perhaps you should get back in your car and go to another restaurant!

Many organizations conduct an annual strategic-planning event, usually sometime during the third quarter of their fiscal year. Frequently one of the outcomes of strategic planning is a complete list of the products that the organization will work on during the next fiscal year. These products then get simultaneously inserted into the portfolio backlog, typically overwhelming the portfolio-planning process.

I am not suggesting that organizations shouldn't do strategic planning. They should define their strategic direction, but just not *all* of the specific details (at a product level) of how they will achieve that strategy. Deciding at a once-a-year meeting everything to work on over the next fiscal year or longer, and then inserting all of those items into the portfolio backlog at the same time, is a critical decision (and in some organizations an irreversible decision) made in the presence of great uncertainty and violates the principle of keeping planning options open until the last responsible moment (see Chapter 14).

Deciding the entire portfolio of products at one time also violates the principle of using economically sensible batch sizes (as discussed in Chapter 3). Processing a large batch of products to determine how to sequence them into the portfolio backlog is very expensive and potentially wasteful (because we are planning up to a year or more in advance). It is expensive not only because there are a lot of products to process, but also because a large number of items in the portfolio backlog complicate the scheduling I discussed earlier in this chapter. Determining a good sequencing is a much simpler problem when there are fewer items to sequence. In fact, in the presence of just a small number of portfolio backlog items, any sequencing that avoids an overtly dumb prioritization is typically good enough.

To combat overwhelming the portfolio backlog all at once, we can introduce products to the portfolio at more frequent intervals, for example, monthly (or at least quarterly) instead of annually. Doing so significantly reduces the effort (and cost) required to review and insert new products into the portfolio and provides more overall stability and predictability to portfolio planning.

We should also focus on smaller products (see the strategy on smaller, more frequent releases). This should result in a constant stream of products that are completed, thus freeing up capacity to pull new products from the portfolio backlog at a regular pace. This frequent pulling of products from the portfolio backlog will assist in balancing inflow with outflow.

Last, when the size of the portfolio backlog starts to increase, we can start to throttle the flow of products into the portfolio backlog. We can accomplish this by tweaking the economic filter to raise the product approval criteria so that only higher-value products are allowed to pass through the filter. This will reduce the insertion rate to help establish a better equilibrium with the departure rate.

Quickly Embrace Emergent Opportunities

Portfolio planning needs to embrace **emergent opportunities**. An emergent opportunity is one that was previously unknown, or was deemed sufficiently unlikely to occur and therefore not something worth spending money on today.

For example, one organization I worked with participates in the online betting marketplace. Its business is highly regulated by the jurisdictions in which it is permitted to offer its betting exchanges. Regulators around the world are somewhat unpredictable—especially when it comes to gambling—which makes it difficult to know if and when it will ever be possible to offer a product in a particular jurisdiction. Working in this environment, you need to be prepared for emergent opportunities because regulations can change along with a change in a country's governing party.

One such opportunity was the ability to provide an online betting exchange for horse racing in California. California has a significant number of racetracks, making it a very lucrative opportunity should its regulations change (which, by the way, they did—though illegal for years, online exchange betting is legal as of May 2012). If the organization were in the habit of doing strategic planning only once a year in October (before the laws changed), it would have missed the opportunity to exploit this emergent opportunity—unless it was willing to take on the risk of building an exchange for a marketplace that didn't exist and might never materialize.

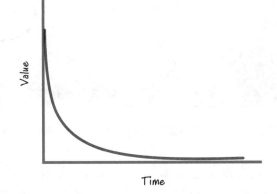

FIGURE 16.6   The value of many emergent opportunities decays rapidly.

Such an emergent opportunity needs to be exploited quickly. Being second to market with an online betting exchange in California would garner little to no market share. Figure 16.6 illustrates this common case where the economic value of an emergent opportunity decays rapidly over time.

By not acting swiftly, as soon as the opportunity becomes available, we immediately lose almost all of the economic value, making it a bad economic choice to pursue it sometime later (such as at the next annual strategic-planning session).

If an organization uses a regular and frequent schedule for evaluating opportunities, such as the once-a-month schedule, and has an efficient economic filter, while at the same time using smaller releases and a WIP limit, it will never have to wait long to consider an emergent opportunity.

Plan for Smaller, More Frequent Releases

As I discussed in Chapter 14, the economics of smaller, more frequent releases are compelling. Figures 14.4 and 14.5, along with Table 14.1, illustrate that we can almost always increase the lifecycle profits of a product if we split a product into a series of smaller, incremental releases.

In addition to this significant benefit, there is another reason we want to manage our portfolio with smaller, more frequent releases—to avoid a convoy effect (see Figure 16.7).

What happens if you are driving on a one-lane country road and you get trapped behind a large farm vehicle (like the one shown in Figure 16.7)? Chances are you and a convoy of smaller vehicles will be trapped behind the larger, slower vehicle for a long time. The cause of the convoy is obvious; the big farm vehicle is hogging the road (the shared resource).

FIGURE 16.7   Large products in the portfolio backlog create a convoy.

This same scenario will occur if we allow large products into the portfolio backlog. Large products require a lot of resources for a considerable amount of time. Those resources are now unavailable to many other smaller products that are caught in the queue behind the large product. And, while caught in the queue, each accrues a cost for being delayed. When we add up the delay costs of all of those small products and then factor in the compelling economics of doing smaller, incremental releases, it becomes clear that large products cause significant economic damage to lifecycle profits.

To combat this issue, some organizations institute a size policy during portfolio planning that specifically limits how large a product development effort may be. One example I encountered was that no product development effort could be larger than nine months. If a proposal was made for a larger product effort, it was summarily rejected and the advocates were told to come up with a way of delivering the product in smaller, more frequent releases.

I have also worked with organizations whose culture is "We can never assume there will be a second release of any product." This belief is completely at odds with doing smaller, more frequent releases. If we believe that we might never have a second release, the natural reaction is to load up the first release with everything we need, plus everything we think that one day we might need. In this case, not only do we generate larger product development efforts, but we are almost certainly delaying the high-value features of other products while working on the very low-value features of the larger product. This approach is economically damaging. Organizations need to make it clear that follow-on releases can and will be done based on their individual economic merit, and that planning under the assumption of a single release is highly discouraged.

Outflow Strategies

Strategies for managing outflow help organizations decide when to pull a product out of the portfolio backlog. I describe three strategies:

- Focus on idle work, not idle workers.
- Establish a WIP limit.
- Wait for a complete team.

Focus on Idle Work, Not Idle Workers

A key strategy for determining when to pull a product from the portfolio backlog is to remember the principle I discussed in Chapter 3—focus on idle work, not idle workers. This principle states that idle work is far more wasteful and economically damaging than idle workers. This is contrary to how many organizations manage their portfolio.

A common, but misguided, approach to releasing products for development is

1. Pull the top product from the portfolio backlog and assign people to work on it.
2. Are all the people 100% utilized (working at 100% capacity)? If not, repeat step 1.

This approach will keep everyone very busy. What it will also do is keep the work on every product slow and error-prone. A better strategy is to start working on a product only when we can ensure two things: a good flow of work on the new product and that the new product won't disrupt the flow on other in-process products. This strategy is used in close coordination with the next strategy: establish a WIP limit.

Establish a WIP Limit

Consider this scenario. Have you ever gone to a restaurant and seen available tables, yet the staff won't seat you? If you have, you know it's frustrating. Perhaps you think, "Why won't they seat me? They have available tables. Don't they want my business?"

Let's say that several waiters called in sick that day. In that case, a smart restaurateur shouldn't seat you. What happens if he does? Perhaps you have to wait 45 minutes before a server comes to your table. I don't know about you, but I would not be a happy patron if I had to sit for 45 minutes before someone came over to talk to me! I'd actually prefer that they tell me up front, "Sorry, sir, but four of our waiters called in sick today, so it will be 45 minutes before we can seat you." At least this information would give me the option of waiting or going somewhere else.

What would be worse is if they actually seated my party at an available table and then attempted to give us service. If they did that, the service for everyone else in the restaurant would suffer. Seating too many parties relative to the available server capacity would mean that all of the servers will be overworked and everyone will have a bad experience. That's why a smart restaurateur won't seat parties beyond his capacity.

If only we would follow the lead of the smart restaurateur during portfolio planning. We should never pull more products out of the portfolio backlog than we have capacity to complete. Doing so will cause reduced capacity to be available to each product (resulting in each being delayed), as well as cause the quality of work on all products to suffer. Getting work done slower and at lower quality is not a winning strategy.

So how do we determine the appropriate WIP limit? In Chapter 11, I discussed the idea that teams are the unit of capacity that we should use for establishing a WIP limit. Knowing how many Scrum teams and knowing what kinds of products they are capable of working on will guide us as to how many and which types of product development efforts we should pursue simultaneously (see Figure 16.8).

The left side of Figure 16.8 shows that we have three teams that are capable of working on type I products and two teams that can work on type II products. This information would be an excellent starting point for establishing the maximum number of each type of product that our organization can work on simultaneously. Imagine how much more difficult it would be to try to determine the proper number of concurrent development efforts using just the information regarding number of people with particular skill sets (right side of Figure 16.8).

Wait for a Complete Team

The final outflow strategy is to wait for a complete Scrum team to be available before starting to work on a product. Organizations that violate the "Focus on idle work, not idle workers" principle frequently start working on a product when only a couple of people are available. Their thinking might go like this: "Well, a couple of developers aren't at 100% capacity yet, so let's have them at least start making progress on that next product."

This is a flawed strategy because it will cause even more work to get blocked on other products, slowing down all product delivery and generating significant delay costs.

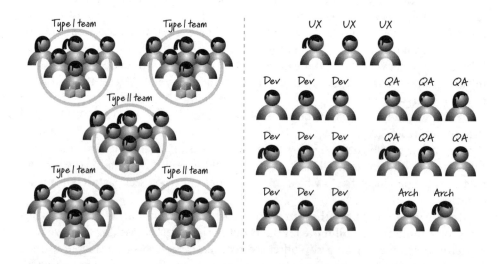

FIGURE 16.8   Teams are the unit of capacity for establishing the product WIP limit.

Because the unit of capacity in Scrum is the team, we shouldn't start working on a product if we don't have a complete Scrum team. Doing so makes no sense from a Scrum perspective. An incomplete Scrum team is insufficient for getting features to a done state.

One variation I would consider is on products that require multiple Scrum teams. Let's say we have a product that requires three Scrum teams. If one complete Scrum team is available and it makes sense to start development with just that one complete team, I would consider starting the product. I would then roll the other full Scrum teams on as they became available.

In-Process Strategies

Strategies for managing in-process products guide us as to whether it is appropriate to preserve, pivot, deliver, or terminate a product that is currently being worked on. We need to make these decisions at regular intervals (say, the end of each sprint) and occasionally at off-cycle times, when abnormal events occur that require us to revisit our in-process products.

There are many different strategies we could consider here, and the governance function of each organization is sure to have its own set of guidelines for dealing with in-process products. However, I will focus on just one strategy—marginal economics. This should be the overarching strategy that guides decision making, and it aligns well with the core Scrum and agile principles I describe in this book.

Use Marginal Economics

From an economic perspective, all work that has been performed on the product up to the decision point is a "sunk cost." We are interested only in the marginal economics of taking the next step. We should ask ourselves only if spending the next chunk of money is justified by the return that investment would generate. The hard part is making that decision without burdening ourselves with the money we have already spent.

Using marginal economics, we can decide what to do with products that are currently being developed. For each product we scrutinize under the lens of marginal economics, there are four principal options:

- Preserve—continue developing the product.
- Deliver—stop working on the product and ship it.
- Pivot—take what we have learned and change directions.
- Terminate—stop working on the product and kill it.

Figure 16.9 illustrates the decision flow associated with these four options.

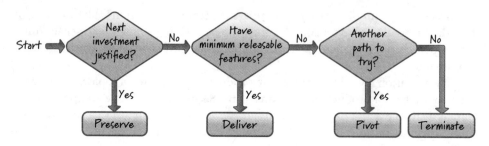

FIGURE 16.9   In-process product decision flow based on marginal economics

If the next investment in the current product is economically justified, *preserving* would be a likely choice. This is the scenario where we review an in-process product and conclude that we should continue spending money on its development.

If further investment in a product is not economically justified, we should decide whether to deliver, pivot, or terminate the product.

If the product we have created thus far contains the minimum releasable features (MRFs), we can consider *delivering* the product. If not, and we are going down the wrong path, and we think there is another path worth exploring, we could *pivot* and change to a new product path. This option would likely involve a return to envisioning to consider the new path (see Chapter 17).

And, if further investment is not justified and we are unhappy with where we are and our prospects for a successful pivot, *terminating* the product would be a viable option.

Foolish behavior can result when marginal economics are ignored. Here's a question to consider: "In your organization, if you spend the first dollar on developing a product, is there any circumstance under which you would terminate development?" I am surprised by the number of times people tell me that their organizations won't ever (or only very rarely) kill a product once the first dollar is spent—in for a penny, in for a pound seems to be their strategy.

At one organization, I was surprised at the explanation for why the company doesn't terminate products. I asked the IT executives, "Suppose you start working on a product that you believe is valuable to 100% of your customers and will cost $1M to develop. After you have spent $1M developing it, you learn it would be valuable to only 10% of your customers and will cost a total of $10M to develop. Would you spend the additional $9M to complete the product?" Their response: "Yes, we would." My response: "That makes no sense to me! The cost/benefit ratio of this product has changed by a factor of 100. Why would you do that?" Their response: "You don't understand how we do accounting. If we kill the product after we spend $1M and before the system goes into production, the IT department will suffer a $1M hit against its expense budget. If we spend the other $9M and put the system into production for one day, the full cost of the system moves to the business unit where it can capitalize the expenditure."

Clearly in this example, gaming the accounting system has trumped common sense.

Marginal economics is a powerful tool for doing the right thing and for exposing foolish and wasteful behavior. It should be your principal strategy when considering what to do with in-process development.

Closing

In this chapter I discussed 11 important strategies for portfolio planning (portfolio management). My intent was not to provide a cafeteria where you selectively pick and choose which strategies to use. All 11 strategies reinforce one another. You will derive the maximum benefit by doing all of them. That being said, if for some reason I were forced to use just one strategy from each category, I would focus on cost of delay, smaller and more frequent releases, WIP limit, and marginal economics.

In the next chapter I will discuss product planning (envisioning). The output of that process provides us with candidate products to consider during portfolio planning.

Chapter 17

ENVISIONING (PRODUCT PLANNING)

Before beginning the first customer-value-creation sprint, we need an initial product backlog. And to generate an initial product backlog we need a product vision. Many organizations also find it useful to create a preliminary product roadmap, which defines a potential series of incremental releases. Your organization might have other front-end artifacts that it prefers to create as well. I refer to the activity of creating these artifacts as envisioning, or product-level planning.

In this chapter I describe an envisioning approach that is well aligned with Scrum principles. It is also very useful for organizations that are trying to develop products using Scrum but must still integrate with a front-end approval process that is not agile.

Overview

Let's say you have an intriguing idea for a new product or the next version of an existing product. The goal of envisioning is to expound upon that idea, describing the essence of the potential product and creating a rough plan for how to approach its creation. At the end of envisioning, you should have sufficient confidence to subject the idea to portfolio planning (see Chapter 16), where you can decide whether you want to fund the next level of more detailed development.

Envisioning a product in Scrum should not be confused with heavier-weight, ceremonial, plan-intensive project chartering. With Scrum, we don't believe that we can (or should try to) know all the details about a product before we start. We do, however, understand that product funding usually can't move forward without first having a vision; enough details to understand the customers, features, and high-level solution; and an idea of how much the product might cost.

We don't spend too much time or effort envisioning because we want to quickly advance past the guessing stage, where we *think* we know the needs of the customer and the potential solution, to the fast-feedback stage—the customer-value-creation sprints. After all, it's only when we actually start implementing the solution through a continuous cycle of interactions with our complex environment that we acquire validated learning based on the reality in which our product must exist and thrive.

Timing

Envisioning, which is concerned with product-level planning, is an ongoing activity, not a one-time event (see Figure 17.1).

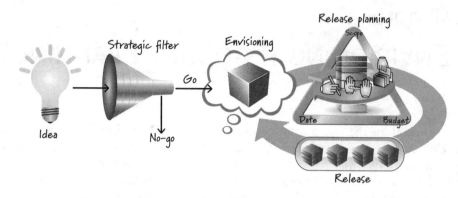

FIGURE 17.1   Envisioning is an ongoing activity.

Envisioning begins with an idea for a product that someone or some team has generated (a process often referred to as ideation). This idea is first passed through the organization's **strategic filter** to determine if it is consistent with the organization's strategic direction and therefore worthy of deeper investigation and investment.

Once the idea has cleared the strategic filter, we do initial envisioning. During this process, we generate enough understanding of the desired future product to define what the minimal first release should be. Doing so allows us to deliver high value quickly and at a low cost. It also puts something tangible in the hands of the actual users and customers as soon as possible, giving us actionable feedback to confirm or refute the assumptions we made about the target customers, the desired set of features, and our overall solution. This feedback might be in line with our expectations, reinforcing our desire to persevere with our current vision. On the other hand, it could just as easily be completely different from what we expected, which would cause us to pivot from our original solution, reenvision what we are doing, and modify the plan accordingly.

Participants

The product owner is the only required participant during initial envisioning. Normally, though, the product owner oversees an initial envisioning that includes one or more internal stakeholders, who collaborate with the product owner to perform the envisioning work. In addition, specialists in areas such as market research, business-case development, user-experience design, and systems architecture frequently participate in various envisioning tasks as well. Figure 17.2 illustrates the envisioning activity (optional participants and artifacts are indicated with dashed outlines).

Ideally, the ScrumMaster and the development team that will be performing the customer-value-creation sprints will also participate in initial envisioning, lending

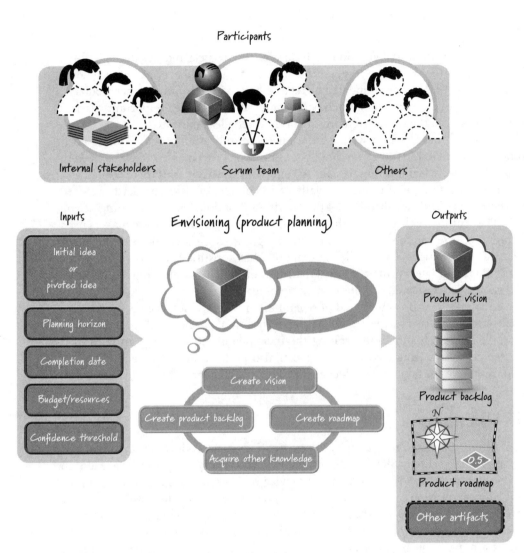

FIGURE 17.2   Envisioning (product-planning) activity

valuable feedback to the product vision and also eliminating the need to hand off the vision to another team to build the product. Often, however, the organization waits until initial envisioning is complete to fund the Scrum team, making it impossible to include it in initial envisioning activities. Once product development is under way and the full Scrum team has been allocated, however, the full Scrum team (product owner, ScrumMaster, and development team) should be included in any reenvisioning efforts.

Process

The main input for initial envisioning is an idea that has cleared the strategic filter. The main input for reenvisioning, on the other hand, would be a pivoted idea. Such an idea is one that has been updated or revised based on user or customer feedback, funding changes, unpredictable moves by competitors, or other important changes that occur within the complex environment in which ideas must exist.

We need other inputs as well. First, we need an indication of the planning horizon—how far into the future we should consider when we envision. We also need to know the expected completion date for the envisioning activities (if there is one), and the quantity and type of resources available to conduct envisioning. Last, we need to know the **confidence threshold**—the "definition of done" for envisioning, if you will. The confidence threshold is the set of information that the decision makers need in order to have enough confidence to make a go/no-go funding decision for more detailed development. I will talk more about what constitutes a reasonable confidence threshold later in the chapter. Finally, all of the envisioning inputs in Figure 17.2 should be considered simultaneously, not linearly.

Envisioning itself is composed of several different activities, each generating an important output such as the product vision or the initial product backlog. Frequently a simple product roadmap illustrating the incremental set of near-term releases is created as well. During envisioning, we can also perform any other activities that help us achieve the targeted confidence threshold in an economically sensible way.

SR4U Example

To illustrate the envisioning activity I use a fictitious new product idea called Smart-Review4You (or simply SR4U). The company, Review Everything, Inc., is a leader in online, consumer-supplied product and service reviews. Its core business is to provide a forum for people to exchange product and service reviews. Review Everything's revenues have been growing at a modest pace for the past several years and it is profitable. However, the company has many competitors that release innovative features with alarming frequency. Review Everything really needs a new, innovative service offering to leapfrog the competition.

Review Everything has a dedicated marketing team that constantly monitors the social media space to see how customers perceive its current services. In doing so, the team has learned that many users report spending too much time on the Review Everything site separating "authentic" reviews from "suspicious" reviews. Additionally, many users say that there are so many reviews available for certain products (for example, a DVD player) or services (for example, the Chinese restaurant on Main Street) that they find it difficult to wade through them to get an accurate overall picture.

This market intelligence leads to the idea for SR4U, a revolutionary way to identify, filter, and display online reviews that includes a trainable search agent. Marketing believes this idea could be the innovative service offering that Review Everything has been seeking. Marketing writes a one-page description of SR4U that includes its high-level target features, target customers, and key advantages. The team then sends this description to the New Product Approval Committee, which reviews it at its regularly scheduled Idea Review Meeting (held the second Wednesday of every month).

Senior management (which makes up the New Product Approval Committee) agrees that SR4U represents a significant opportunity to differentiate Review Everything, Inc., in the marketplace. The committee then designates Roger, a business representative from strategic marketing, as the product owner for SR4U.

Management has authorized two weeks to complete envisioning, at which time members of the approval committee will review the envisioning results and make a go/no-go decision to fund the initial development of SR4U. In addition to Roger, management has authorized two filtering subject matter experts (SMEs), a market researcher, and a number of stakeholders to participate in the envisioning. However, they have not authorized the larger expenditure of the full Scrum team during envisioning.

Roger is being asked to use the resources available to him to produce the following:

- Initial product vision, product backlog, and product roadmap
- Validation of the primary assumption that users significantly prefer SR4U-filtered results to unfiltered results (Later in the chapter I will describe how Roger and his colleagues will provide this validated learning.)
- A description of the other important assumptions (hypotheses) about the potential users and feature set that the first product release is supposed to test
- The few key, actionable measures used to test the other assumptions and to learn whether the initial release of SR4U is meeting expectations
- List of questions (known unknowns) that need to be addressed

Without this information, senior management would not have sufficient confidence to make an informed decision as to whether or not to move forward with the initial development.

Visioning

The first thing Roger and the stakeholders do is to create a shared, compelling vision for SR4U. In Scrum, a vision is not an elaborate, several-hundred-page document. If we need this much space to describe our vision, we probably don't understand it. Visions, even of complex products, should be simple to state and should provide a coherent direction to the people who are asked to realize them. Take, for example, President Kennedy's vision to go to the moon: "I believe that this nation should commit itself to achieving the goal, before this decade is out, of landing a man on the

Moon and returning him safely to the Earth" (Kennedy 1961). In 31 words Kennedy was able to express an aggressive, unambiguous vision that, to be realized, would eventually require the efforts of thousands of collaborating people building many complex systems with hundreds of thousands of interrelated components.

When developing products or services, the vision is frequently expressed in terms of how the stakeholders get value. Examples might include one or more areas of value from the categories shown in Figure 17.3.

The format of the vision itself can be anything from a Kennedy-esque statement to a fictitious magazine review. Examples of some popular product or service vision formats are described in Table 17.1 (based in part on Highsmith 2009). You should choose whatever format best suits your organization, envisioning group, and idea.

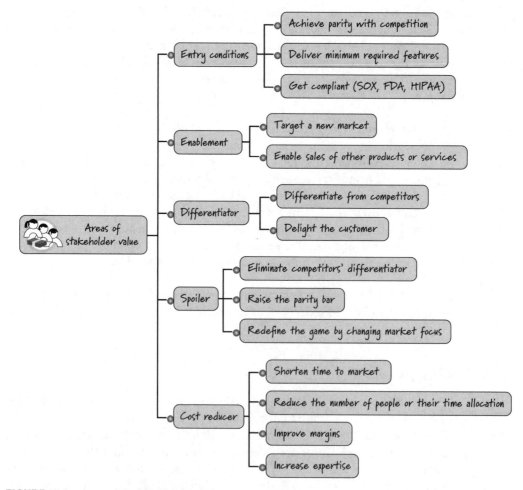

FIGURE 17.3   Areas of stakeholder value

TABLE 17.1   Popular Vision Formats

Format	Description
Elevator statement	Write a 30-second to one-minute quick pitch of the product vision. Imagine you have stepped into an elevator with a venture capitalist and you have to pitch him on your product vision. Could you do it in a short elevator ride?
Product datasheet	Write the product datasheet on the first day. Try to fit it on the front side of a one-page marketing piece.
Product vision box	Draw the box in which you want to put the product when it ships. Can you come up with three or four salient points to illustrate on the box? (Drafting 15 points is easier than drafting three or four.)
User conference slides	Create the two or three presentation slides that you would use to introduce the product at your user conference (or equivalent). Try to avoid any bullet points on your slides.
Press release	Write the press release you want to issue when the product becomes available. Good press releases clearly communicate what is newsworthy in one page or less.
Magazine review	Draft a fictitious magazine review bylined by the solution reviewer in your industry's most popular trade magazine.

At Review Everything, Roger and the stakeholders choose to use the press release format to describe SR4U. They begin by identifying several areas of **stakeholder value** (from Figure 17.3) that SR4U should deliver. The relevant areas are described in Table 17.2.

TABLE 17.2   SmartReview4You Potential Areas of Stakeholder Value

Area	Description
Cost reducer/time savings	SR4U must save its users considerable time when searching for reviews.
Differentiator/delight the customer	SR4U must provide a "wow" experience for its users. Users must feel that the service performed an impressive task for them, helping them make an informed purchase.
Spoiler/raise the parity bar	SR4U should create substantial chaos for its competitors. Their current solutions should immediately look antiquated by comparison. SR4U will establish a new baseline for online review services that others will have to scramble to meet.

Based on these areas of stakeholder value, Roger and the stakeholders craft the following press release (vision statement):

> Review Everything, Inc., announced today the successful launch of its new SmartReview4You service. This service provides all online users with their own trainable agent to scour the Internet and identify unbiased, relevant product or service review information.
>
> Remarked Doris Johnson, an avid user of online reviews, "I now have my very own personal assistant that mimics how I find and filter online reviews. It's amazing—I teach it what I like and don't like about reviews, then SmartReview4U tears across the Internet finding product or service reviews and automatically weeds out the biased or bogus ones. It does at lightning speed what used to take me forever. This service is a huge timesaver!"
>
> C. J. Rollins, CEO of Review Everything, Inc., said, "We are pleased to offer the world's first truly smart review service. Since the inception of the Internet people have leveraged the wisdom of the online crowd. However, the crowd can get very noisy at times and it is hard to separate the wheat from the chaff. Our super-smart service does the laborious work of sifting through the huge volume of online review information, eliminating suspicious reviews and returning only relevant ones. You read only the reviews you'd choose to consider if you spent hours searching on your own."
>
> The new SmartReview4You is available free of charge at the following website: www.smartreview4you.com.

High-Level Product Backlog Creation

Once we have a vision, we are ready to create high-level product backlog items. Although there are many ways to represent product backlog items, I like to use user stories (discussed in detail in Chapter 5). In the terminology of user stories, during envisioning I want to create epics—really large user stories that are consistent with the product level of planning. These epic-level stories align with the vision and provide the next level of product detail for senior management and the Scrum team.

The people who write these stories are usually the same people who created the vision—the product owner, stakeholders, and preferably the ScrumMaster and development team. As a general rule, I want all of my Scrum team members involved in writing these stories. However, as I mentioned previously, if the product development hasn't yet been approved/funded, the full Scrum team might not be available during envisioning. In those cases, the product owner might want to call in a favor and ask a few technical people with an interest in the product area to help out with story writing.

At Review Everything, SR4U has not yet been approved, so a development team has not been assigned. Therefore, Roger and the stakeholders ask Yvette, an experienced architect, to join them in their story brainstorming session. During the session they create a set of initial epics, including the following:

As a typical user I want to teach SR4U what types of reviews to discard so that SR4U will know what characteristics to use when discarding reviews on my behalf.

As a typical user I want a simple, Google-like interface for requesting a review search so that I don't have to spend much time describing what I want.

As a typical user I want to have SR4U monitor the Internet for new reviews on products or services of interest and automatically filter and report them to me so that I don't have to keep asking SR4U to do it for me.

As a sophisticated user I want to tell SR4U which sources to use when searching on my behalf so that I don't get back reviews from sites I don't like or trust.

As a product vendor I want to be able to show an SR4U-branded review summary for my product on my website so that people can immediately see what the marketplace thinks of my product as determined by a trusted source like SR4U.

Product Roadmap Definition

Once we have the initial vision and a high-level product backlog, we can define our initial product roadmap, a series of releases for achieving some or all of our product vision. When using Scrum, we always develop incrementally. We also try to deploy incrementally when that approach is sensible, meaning we focus on smaller, more frequent releases where we deliver some of the solution before we deliver all of the solution. A product roadmap is an initial overview of these incremental deployments. Of course, if we are planning only a single small release, we don't need a product roadmap.

Releasing frequently doesn't mean we set overly aggressive deadlines; such deadlines frequently result in missed dates. Instead, we focus each release on a small set of **minimum releasable features** (MRFs) around which the stakeholder community shares a strong group consensus. MRFs represent the smallest set of "must-have" features—the features that simply have to be in the release if we are to meet customer value and quality expectations. Some people refer to this set of features as the **minimum viable product** (MVP) or **minimum marketable features** (MMFs). While we might choose to deliver more than the MRFs in a given release, customers would not perceive enough value if we delivered any fewer. Therefore, it is always important to define the minimum set.

To complement the MRFs, some organizations use the strategy of fixed, periodic releases—for example, a release every quarter—to simplify the product roadmap (see Figure 17.4).

This approach has several advantages. First, it is easy to understand and provides everyone involved (internally and externally) with predictable releases. It also establishes a rhythm, or cadence, to releasing that helps marshal resources in a predictable way and allows for disparate groups to synchronize their plans.

If we use this strategy, we still determine the MRFs for each release. If the MRFs require less time to develop than the fixed time for the release, some additional high-value features will be created. Fixed, periodic releases might not always be applicable if external events (like a conference or a fixed launch date of a co-branded product) are driving the releases, but its benefits make it worth considering.

Each release on the roadmap should have a clearly defined **release goal** that communicates the purpose and desired outcome of the release. A release goal is created by considering many factors, including the target customers, high-level architectural issues, significant marketplace events, and so on.

When creating a product roadmap, we should consider the customers and how they might be segmented into different markets. The roadmap should express how and when to address these different customer segments. In the case of SR4U, the initial customer market is the individual consumer interested in reading helpful reviews before buying a product or service. The SR4U envisioning team further subdivides this market segment into "typical user" and "sophisticated user," those who want fine-grained control over how SR4U works. The team decides that the initial target will be the typical user.

The SR4U envisioning team can also foresee a future customer base of product and service vendors who would use SR4U to provide an unbiased Internet-wide review history of their offerings on their own websites. However, before vendors will see enough value to pay for the service and the brand, Review Everything, Inc., will first need to establish SR4U as a trusted brand for review aggregation and filtering.

When making a product roadmap, we also should consider high-level architectural or technology issues. For example, on SR4U the principal technology issue is to determine which forms of service access to provide. The team decides to initially provide access via a web browser. However, longer term, it can also envision mobile-device-specific applications for the iOS devices, Android devices, and potentially

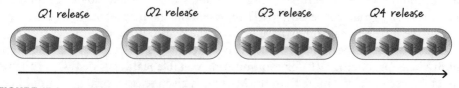

FIGURE 17.4   Fixed, periodic releases

other devices that are tailored to access the SR4U service. Even further down the road, the team also intends to provide an open API that SR4U's partners can access.

When defining a product roadmap, we also might need to allow for any significant market events that could influence the timing of our feature deliveries. Review Everything, for example, always attends the annual Social Media Expo conference. Roger and the stakeholders agree that having a release available by this year's conference (about three months away) would be a great place to get feedback on the service.

Our goal when creating the product roadmap is to consider any factors we deem relevant to help us define a target set of releases for our solution. Remember, though, that this roadmap is simply a rough first approximation of one or a few near-term releases. We must have the right to update the roadmap as better information becomes available.

We must also consider how far into the future our product roadmap will extend. Although our vision might be large and bold enough to require many years to fully realize, it is unlikely that we would attempt to produce a detailed roadmap that would extend completely across such a vision. When using Scrum, we produce the product roadmap as far into the future as is reasonable and desirable. How far into the future your roadmap should extend will depend on your particular circumstances. At a minimum, your roadmap will probably need to cover at least the span of time you are asking people to fund.

Roger and the SR4U stakeholders believe their vision will probably take several years to fully realize, but Roger decides that it would not be practical to try to extend the roadmap out that far given their low level of validated learning and how quickly things change in the online reviews marketplace. Roger and the stakeholders settle on a simple nine-month product roadmap, as shown in Figure 17.5.

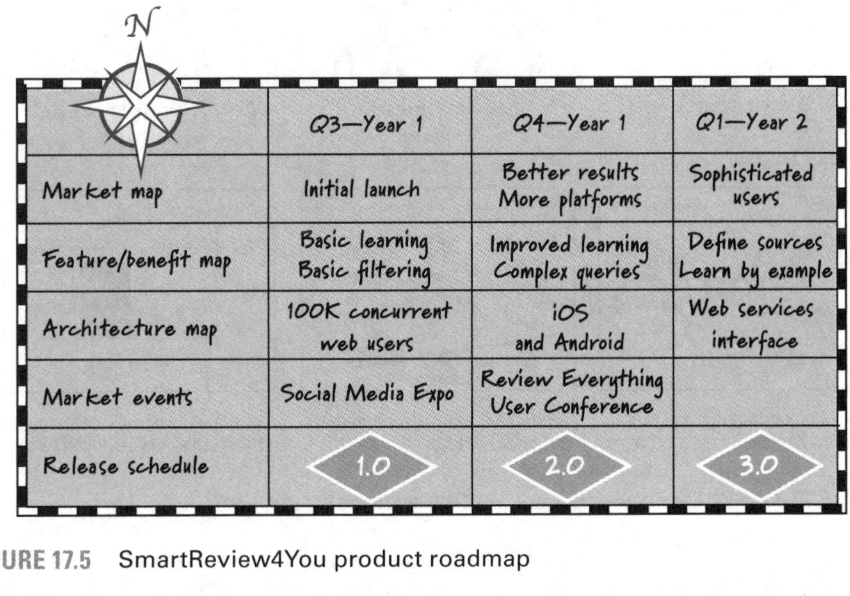

	Q3—Year 1	Q4—Year 1	Q1—Year 2
Market map	Initial launch	Better results More platforms	Sophisticated users
Feature/benefit map	Basic learning Basic filtering	Improved learning Complex queries	Define sources Learn by example
Architecture map	100K concurrent web users	iOS and Android	Web services interface
Market events	Social Media Expo	Review Everything User Conference	
Release schedule	1.0	2.0	3.0

FIGURE 17.5   SmartReview4You product roadmap

Other Activities

Envisioning can include any other type of work that those involved agree is relevant to achieving the target confidence threshold. Perhaps we want to do minimal market research into the target customers or users. Or maybe we want to do a quick competitive analysis of the proposed product against other offerings in the marketplace. Or perhaps we want to create a rough business model to help us decide whether the product passes the organization's "economic filter."

Some organizations might even decide to organize the envisioning work into one or more sprints. In these cases the assigned team (the envisioning Scrum team if you will) maintains a backlog of envisioning-related work that is prioritized and worked on in short-duration sprint cycles (perhaps one-week sprints). Some of these sprints might involve knowledge-acquisition work, as described in Chapter 5. Examples of knowledge-acquisition sprints might include creating a prototype or proof of concept of the product look and feel, or a critical architectural feature.

For SR4U, Roger and his team (including the SMEs) decide to perform one knowledge-acquisition sprint during envisioning. Before investing in the development of an automated system, Roger first wants to run a simple comparison test to confirm the core assumption that SR4U-filtered reviews are really much more helpful to users than unfiltered reviews (see Figure 17.6).

FIGURE 17.6   SR4U knowledge-acquisition sprint storyboard

During the envisioning sprint, the team will mock up one web page (an HTML, Google-simple search page for SR4U) where a small, sample group of users can submit a query for a product or service of their choosing and get back two sets of results. The first set will be the unfiltered reviews that would normally be returned to the query. The second set will be filtered to remove "suspect reviews." The users will not be told which reviews are filtered and which are not.

The sample users are told ahead of time that their query results will be ready the next day (via email) because, unbeknownst to them, Roger has no intention at this time of developing the technology necessary to automate the generation of their filtered query results. Instead, he asks a couple of SMEs to manually do the filtering and provide the users with both the filtered and unfiltered results. Roger and his team will then interview all members of the sample user group to see which results they prefer and why.

The goal behind this early test is to get basic validation of the core value proposition underlying SR4U—that users will be delighted by the SR4U-filtered set of reviews. If the SMEs can't manually generate compelling filtered results, Review Everything's ability to create an expert-system-type product that will deliver value in the marketplace is put in serious doubt.

Senior management also asks Roger to describe the other core assumptions/hypotheses that are not yet validated about the potential users and feature set along with key measures for testing these assumptions. He will collaborate with product marketing people and others to complete this work. Instead of doing an extensive, time-consuming market research study, Roger is planning to use the development of the first release as an experimental tool for discovering what people actually think of SR4U and what they really want in terms of features.

Economically Sensible Envisioning

Envisioning needs to be carried out in an economically sensible way. It should be viewed as an investment in acquiring the information necessary for management to make an informed decision about whether to fund the work required for developing a product based on the idea. If we do too little envisioning, we might find ourselves unprepared to do the first customer-value-creation sprint. On the other hand, doing too much envisioning will create a large inventory of product-planning artifacts that may have to be reworked or discarded when we start to acquire validated learning.

In many organizations, envisioning-type work goes by the name of **project chartering**, **project inception**, or **project initiation**. In some organizations the chartering process is part of a comprehensive stage-gate governance model. Frequently, in this context, chartering is a heavyweight, ceremonial, plan-intensive process based on a set of predicted data. This detailed but not-yet-validated data forms uncertain plans that provide only the illusion of certainty when making a go/no-go funding decision.

In addition, a heavyweight upstream approach is poorly aligned with the agile downstream Scrum development process. This impedance mismatch is like saying, "You can develop using Scrum, but before we approve development we will still need the same artifacts we always require: extensive up-front requirements, a full budget, and a precise schedule." With this type of misalignment, it will be difficult for an organization to achieve the long-term, high-value benefits from using Scrum.

In Scrum, we keep envisioning as simple as possible. We do just enough up-front predictive planning and knowledge-acquisition work based on the product's nature, size, and risk level. We allow the details of some other artifacts to be created in a just-in-time fashion. Our goal is to make the best decision we can today using reasonable information obtained in a financially and time-sensitive manner. We acknowledge that what we think we know about the product can and will change once we actually build something and start to subject it to customer and user scrutiny.

I have found several guidelines to be helpful for envisioning in an economically sensible way (see Figure 17.7).

Target a Realistic Confidence Threshold

The confidence threshold defines the minimum level and type of information that is being requested by decision makers to give them enough confidence to make the next-level go/no-go funding decision. Think of the confidence threshold as the bar that must be cleared before we can exit envisioning and subject the product to the scrutiny of portfolio planning—where we apply the economic filter to the product to determine if it meets the organization's funding criteria. And, if it does, we can get on to the business of validating key assumptions and building the product.

The height of that bar has real economic consequences (see Figure 17.8).

The higher the bar, the more time we need to clear it. Additional time spent during envisioning will likely delay when the product will ship, and that delay has a

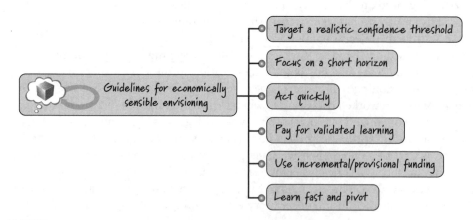

FIGURE 17.7   Guidelines for economically sensible envisioning

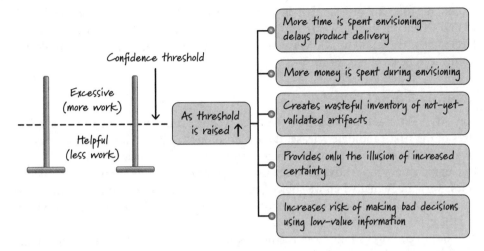

FIGURE 17.8   Consequences of setting the confidence threshold bar too high

cost (see Chapter 3). Envisioning time also has to be paid for, so the higher the bar, the greater the cost of clearing it. More predictive work also creates additional WIP (inventory) that might easily be wasted when things change. And most of that WIP is not yet validated (for example, planning artifacts that predict what might occur in the future), so additional increases to the bar height don't add any certainty to our efforts. Finally, more work can actually increase our risk of making a bad decision to proceed because of the illusion of certainty established by the ever-increasing set of planning artifacts that get produced. More planning artifacts do not imply more certainty or a better funding decision.

As I mentioned in Chapter 14, up-front planning should be helpful without being excessive, so we need to set the threshold to the helpful level, not to the excessive level. What exactly constitutes a helpful level versus an excessive level is organization and product specific. Some organizations are comfortable making decisions under very uncertain conditions while others require a high degree of certainty before proceeding. As the need for certainty increases, so does the effort required to collect data and generate validated learning. There is a practical limit to how much validated learning we can create until we get into development, start building something, and actually validate it with our users. So be realistic about how high the threshold is set.

Also, the threshold for envisioning the next release of a long-lived, core system will likely be less than the threshold for envisioning a new, highly innovative, and potentially expensive product.

Review Everything, Inc., has moved away from heavyweight up-front product-level planning. The approval committee has agreed that the confidence threshold should be set "good enough" or "barely sufficient" to proceed to initial development, where the company can validate assumptions with users. The approval committee is not looking for a full project plan down to the level of the tasks each person will work on and when. Instead, it wants good clarity on what the goal is for the next set of development work and how Roger plans to measure the results so that he can decide on the next, best course of action.

Focus on a Short Horizon

Don't try to envision too much at one time. Focus primarily on the must-have features of the first candidate release. If we plan on a very broad horizon, chances are we are wasting our time planning for things that might never happen. Plus, if we are developing a new, innovative product, most of our assumptions are not yet validated, so it is very likely that when we subject our product to the uncertain customer environment, we will learn something important that will motivate us to adapt our vision and the plans of what we are building.

For SR4U, Roger's high-level roadmap goes out nine months, but it is really the first release that is the focus. Everyone involved knows that until they actually have a review service that customers can use and comment on, they are all just guessing about the proper feature set. So trying to envision too far into the future will require them to base assumptions upon yet more assumptions, violating the principle of having fewer, short-lived important assumptions.

Act Quickly

Envisioning should not be a long, drawn-out process. It should be fast and efficient. The more quickly we finish, the sooner we get to building something tangible that we can use to validate whether our understandings and assumptions are correct or not.

Time spent envisioning should be included in the calculation of the time required to deliver a solution. The market clock starts ticking the moment the business opportunity becomes known (when the idea is generated) and doesn't stop ticking until we deliver the product. An unnecessarily long envisioning activity will delay product delivery, and that delay cost might be quite expensive. The economics of acting quickly during envisioning are compelling—as Smith and Reinertsen remark, it is the "bargain basement" of cycle-time reduction opportunities (Smith and Reinertsen 1998).

Acting quickly also promotes a sense of urgency to make a product decision. This urgency helps ensure that the proper resources are identified and committed to complete the envisioning work in a timely way.

One way to promote quick movement is to provide an expected completion date to the envisioning team (one of the inputs to envisioning). Not every idea will require the same amount of time to envision. As I mentioned earlier, a new, innovative product idea might require more time to envision than an enhancement or update to a long-existing product. In either case, however, we still want to place reasonable boundaries on the envisioning work so that we can quickly get to the point of validating our assumptions through real feedback.

In the case of SR4U, Roger and the others have two weeks to complete the visioning work. Roger will need to be dedicated full-time to meet this deadline. The filtering SMEs will need to be dedicated half-time during the second week, when they perform the knowledge-acquisition sprint. The market research person will be needed for two days during the first week.

Pay for Validated Learning

Evaluate envisioning activities from an economic perspective based on how they contribute to the acquisition of validated learning regarding the target customer, the target set of features, or the solution. Be wary about performing predictive activities that generate information with a high degree of uncertainty—information that is believed to be valid but has not yet truly been validated with customers or users. These activities purchase low-value information and are not only a bad return on investment; they are also potentially quite wasteful if once we get validated learning we end up discarding or reworking highly uncertain information that is wrong.

Also, generating a lot of low-value, highly uncertain information can clutter our judgment and cause us to believe we understand our situation better than we really do. As a result, we make important decisions under the illusion of certainty (see Figure 17.9).

In the case of SR4U, the content of the product backlog and the product roadmap represents uncertain information. Roger believes that what he has produced

FIGURE 17.9 Decision making under the illusion of certainty

represents a good guess as to what users will want and roughly when they will get it. However, the contents of both are subject to change as the team acquires validated learning during development, so he wants to be careful about how much detail he generates at this time.

During SR4U envisioning, senior management is willing to pay for validated learning regarding the core assumption that users prefer filtered versus unfiltered results. They believe it is economically sensible to buy this information during envisioning before they invest substantially more assets to acquire this same information later. It would be far less sensible to spend considerable money to build the first version of SR4U and then find out that users have no strong preference for filtered versus unfiltered results.

Use Incremental/Provisional Funding

Always consider an incremental or provisional approach to funding product development (see Figure 17.10).

Funding decisions are (or at least should be) constantly being made and remade as better information becomes available. On our first pass through envisioning we shouldn't try to generate enough information to approve and fund all future development of the product, but instead enough information to fund sufficient development to acquire the next important, critical real-world knowledge or feedback regarding our customers, features, or solution approach.

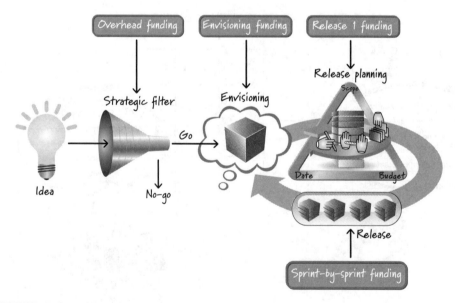

FIGURE 17.10   Incremental/provisional funding

Using **incremental funding**, we would fund just that first small part of the development effort and revisit the funding decision after we have the critical validated learning we paid to get. When we fund incrementally, we can reduce the scope of envisioning and the time it takes to complete it.

Also, remember that the fact that we allocate the funding doesn't necessarily mean we're going to spend the money. As we start getting feedback on a sprint-by-sprint basis, we could choose to pivot to a new vision or simply terminate the product development effort (see Chapter 16 for more details).

In the case of SR4U, Review Everything's policy is that funding is fluid and never given in large chunks but rather in sufficient quantity to validate the next important assumption. Based on feedback and learning, senior management might well continue to spend money that has already been allocated, allocate additional money, or stop funding any future development.

Learn Fast and Pivot (aka Fail Fast)

Envisioning is part of a learn-fast-and-pivot cycle. This approach is sometimes referred to by the catchy alliteration **fail fast**. Simply put, we responsibly and efficiently manage our resources to quickly and cheaply perform envisioning. Then we quickly and cheaply validate our customer, feature, and solution knowledge and assumptions to see whether our vision and product plans meet our business expectations. If we learn that they don't, we pivot quickly and reenvision a more appropriate version of the product, or we simply kill the product and halt any further expenditure.

We can substantially reduce our financial exposure if we are willing to make an informed decision based on reasonable information and then either change directions or terminate the product if we determine that our product vision is incorrect. It is usually far less expensive to start fast and learn fast that we were wrong than to spend a substantial amount of time and money up front to ensure that we make the "right" decision, only to find out eventually that we were wrong. This failing-fast approach is possible only if we are willing to kill a product once we have started spending money to develop it (see the discussion of marginal economics in Chapter 16).

In the case of SR4U, the goal is to very quickly (and cost-effectively) get feedback by getting an initial version of the review learning and filtering capabilities up and running so that people can start using the service. If the team learns after early feedback that the filtered results are not considered by the target user base to be substantially better than the unfiltered results, the company might invest more time in trying to improve the filtering algorithm. However, if after reasonable assets have been invested the company still isn't able to obtain a measurably better set of filtered results, it might be time to pivot and either terminate this product or consider a different direction in which to proceed that leverages the learning to date.

Closing

In this chapter I provided a detailed description of envisioning (product-level planning). I illustrated an approach to envisioning by showing how a fictitious company might create a product vision, high-level product backlog, and product roadmap for its SmartReview4You service. I also illustrated how a knowledge-acquisition sprint during envisioning can be useful in achieving the confidence threshold for completing envisioning. Then I provided guidance on how to perform economically sensible envisioning so that we can better align the up-front product-planning work with the Scrum customer-value-creation work that will follow.

In Chapter 18 I will discuss how we take the outputs of envisioning and use them during release planning.

Chapter 18

RELEASE PLANNING (LONGER-TERM PLANNING)

Release planning is longer-term planning that enables us to answer questions like "When will we be done?" or "Which features can I get by the end of the year?" or "How much will this cost?" Release planning must balance customer value and overall quality against the constraints of scope, schedule, and budget. In this chapter I discuss how release planning fits into the Scrum framework and how to perform release planning on both fixed-date and fixed-scope releases.

Overview

Every organization must determine the proper cadence for releasing features to its customers (see Figure 18.1).

Though the output of a sprint is potentially shippable, many organizations choose not to release new features after every sprint. Instead, they combine the results of multiple sprints into one release.

Other organizations match the release cadence to the sprint cadence. In such cases the organization releases the potentially shippable product increment created during that sprint at the end of each sprint.

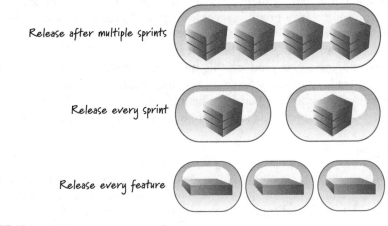

Release after multiple sprints

Release every sprint

Release every feature

FIGURE 18.1　Different release cadences

Some organizations don't even wait for the sprint to end; they release each feature as it is completed, a practice often referred to as **continuous deployment** (or **continuous delivery**). Such organizations release a feature or a change to a feature to some or all of their customers as soon as the feature is available, which might be as often as several times a day.

Whether the organization intends to deploy every sprint, every few sprints, or continuously, most organizations find some amount of longer-term, higher-level planning to be useful. I refer to this type of planning as release planning. If the term *release planning* seems inappropriate to your context, replace the term with one that is better suited. Synonyms I have heard different organizations use include

- Longer-term planning—connoting that the goal is to look at a horizon that is greater than a single sprint
- Milestone-driven planning—because releases tend to align with significant milestones, such as an important user conference or the completion of a minimum set of features for a viable, marketable release

Whatever you choose to call it, release planning targets a future state when important variables such as date, scope, and budget need to be balanced.

Timing

Release planning is not a one-time event but rather a frequent, every-sprint activity (see Figure 18.2). Initial release planning logically follows envisioning/product-level planning.

The purpose of product planning is to envision what the product should be; the aim of release planning is to determine the next logical step toward achieving the product goal.

Before starting a release, many organizations that use Scrum conduct initial release planning to create a preliminary release plan. Normally this activity lasts a day or two, but the duration varies based on the size and risk of the release and the participants' familiarity with what is being created.

When developing a new product, this initial release plan won't be complete or too precise. Instead, as validated learning becomes available during the release, we update the release plan. Release plans can be revised as part of each sprint review or in the normal course of preparing for and conducting each subsequent sprint.

Participants

Release planning involves collaboration between the stakeholders and the full Scrum team. At some point all of these people have to be involved because they'll need to make business and technical trade-offs to achieve a good balance of value and quality. Each person's exact involvement over time may vary.

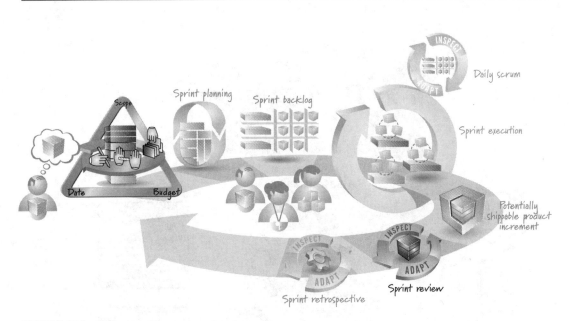

Daily scrum

Sprint planning

Sprint backlog

Sprint execution

Scope

Date   Budget

Potentially
shippable product
increment

Sprint retrospective

Sprint review

FIGURE 18.2   When release planning happens

Process

Figure 18.3 illustrates the release-planning activity.

The inputs to release planning include outputs from product planning, such as the product vision, high-level product backlog, and product roadmap. We also need the velocity of the team or teams that will work on the release. For an existing team, we use the team's known velocity; otherwise, we forecast the team's velocity during release planning (as described in Chapter 7).

One activity that recurs in release planning is to confirm the release constraints of scope, date, and budget and to review them to see if any changes should be made, given the passage of time and what we now know about the product and this release.

Another activity of release planning is product backlog grooming, which includes creating, estimating, and prioritizing more detailed product backlog items from high-level product backlog items. These activities could occur at multiple points in time:

- After product planning but before initial release planning
- As part of the initial release-planning activity
- During each sprint as necessary (see Chapter 6 for more details on product backlog grooming)

Each release should have a well-defined set of minimum releasable features (MRFs). The initial MRFs for a release might have been defined during envisioning.

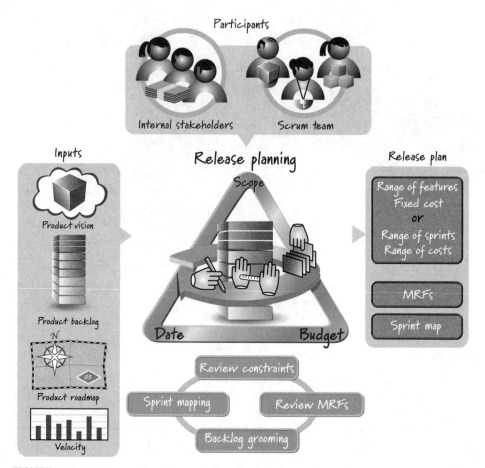

FIGURE 18.3 Release-planning activity

Even so, during release planning we always review the MRFs to ensure that they truly do represent the minimum viable product from the customers' perspective.

During release planning many organizations also produce a sprint map, indicating in which sprint some or many of the product backlog items might be created. A sprint map isn't intended to project too far into the future. Instead, a sprint map is useful for visualizing the near-term future to help us better manage our team's own dependencies and resource constraints, as well as coordinate the efforts of multiple collaborating teams.

The outputs of release planning are collectively referred to as the release plan. The release plan communicates, to the level of accuracy that is reasonable given where we are in the development effort, when we will finish, what features we will get, and what the cost will be. This plan also communicates a clear understanding of the desired MRFs for the release. Finally, it frequently will show how some of the product backlog items map to sprints within the release.

Release Constraints

The goal of release planning is to determine what constitutes the most valuable next release and what the desired level of quality is. The constraints of scope, date, and budget are important variables that affect how we will achieve our goal.

Based on product planning, one or more of these constraints will probably be established. Chapter 17 introduced the fictional company Review Everything, Inc. In that chapter, we followed Review Everything through envisioning a new product, SR4U, a trainable search agent for online reviews. In the product roadmap for SR4U, Roger and his team determined that it would be advantageous to release the first version of SR4U at an upcoming conference, the Social Media Expo. Thus, SR4U Release 1.0 has a fixed-date constraint—the release must be ready by a certain date: the Social Media Expo. The other constraints (scope and budget) are flexible.

Table 18.1 illustrates different combinations where these constraints are either fixed or flexible.

Let's review the different combinations in light of how they can affect release planning.

Fixed Everything

As I described in Chapter 3, traditional, plan-driven, predictive development approaches assume that the requirements are known or can be predicted up front and that the scope won't change. Based on these beliefs, we can create a complete plan and then estimate the cost and schedule. In Table 18.1 this approach is called "fixed everything."

In Scrum, we don't believe it's possible to get it all right up front; consequently, we also contend that a fixed-everything approach probably won't work. When doing

TABLE 18.1 Development Constraint Combinations

Project Type	Scope	Date	Budget
Fixed everything (not recommended)	Fixed	Fixed	Fixed
Fixed scope and date (not recommended)	Fixed	Fixed	Flexible
Fixed scope	Fixed	Flexible	Fixed (not really)
Fixed date	Flexible	Fixed	Fixed

release planning for product development with Scrum, we require at least one of these variables to be flexible.

Fixed Scope and Date

One approach is to fix both the scope and the date and let the budget be flexible. This approach suffers from a number of issues. First, in many organizations, increasing a budget once development has begun isn't very easy or likely. Second, in my experience, this approach locks down two variables that are very difficult to predefine. And, in practice, even if we start off believing we have a fixed-scope-and-date release, one of them will give.

Take the Y2K issue as an example. Many organizations working on mitigating the Y2K issues had a fixed set of applications that needed to be updated no later than December 31, 1999. Many fixed time and scope; the budget was their variable. In the end, however, they knew that no matter how much they increased their budget, they still weren't going to complete all the work by the hard deadline of December 31. The date wasn't moving, so the scope did. In a sense, the variables of date and scope are constantly playing a game of chicken with each other! (See Figure 18.4.)

At some point when time starts running out, either the scope or the date needs to give way. If neither does, the resulting crash will likely generate large technical debt.

Fixing scope and date and allowing the budget to be flexible assumes that applying more resources to a problem will increase the amount of work we accomplish and/or reduce the amount of time it takes to perform the work. There are certainly instances during product development when this is true. For example, we might choose to spend extra money to expedite when a piece of work is done (perhaps pay a subcontractor more money to do our work before someone else's work). In this case we spend money to buy time.

However, buying time or scope will go only so far. Frequently the work in product development is incompressible—meaning adding more resources or spending more money won't help and might even hurt. This is exemplified cleverly by Fred Brooks: "Nine women don't make a baby in a month" (Brooks 1995).

FIGURE 18.4   Fixed date and fixed scope playing a game of chicken

During product development, "flexible budget" frequently translates into "add more people." However, as Brooks warns and as many of us have experienced, "adding manpower to a late software project makes it later" (Brooks 1995). There are times when adding people with the proper skills early in the release might help. Throwing bodies at the problem late, however, will rarely help a fixed-scope-and-date release succeed.

The reality in many organizations is that a flexible budget rarely means adding more people. Usually it means the same people working more hours, especially if these people are salaried employees. Extensive overtime to meet fixed-scope and fixed-date constraints will burn out our staff and violate the Scrum principle of sustainable pace.

If we do find ourselves working on a release that is initially defined as fixed scope and fixed date, Scrum's iterative and incremental approach allows us to understand sooner when we're in trouble, providing more time to rebalance the constraints of scope, date, and budget to achieve a successful outcome.

So far, I've discussed the idea that fixed-everything and fixed-scope-and-date releases are overconstraining for product development. That leaves us two other realistic options: a fixed-scope or a fixed-date release.

Fixed Scope

A fixed-scope model is appropriate where the scope truly is more important than the date. In this model, when we run out of time and we haven't completed all of the features, we extend the date to ensure that we get everything required to meet the MRFs criteria. I don't refer to this model as fixed scope and fixed budget because the budget can't really be fixed; if we give the team more time to finish, people expect to be paid! In other words, if we provide more time to complete the fixed scope, we also have to provide more budget to pay people during that extra time.

Frequently, a fixed-scope scenario exists because the overall scope is too large. A better solution might be to consider smaller, more frequent fixed-date releases. Also, in organizations where multiple groups (such as development, marketing, and support) must coordinate activities, moving the date can be very disruptive to the other groups' plans. Even so, I discuss later in this chapter how to plan a fixed-scope release using Scrum in case you find yourself in a situation where the scope is more important than the date.

Fixed Date

Fixed date is the final approach shown in Table 18.1. Many people, myself included, consider this to be the approach most closely aligned with Scrum principles. Simply put, we can fix both the date and the budget, but the scope must be flexible.

The Scrum principle of creating the highest-priority features first should lessen any perceived pain of having to drop features. When we run out of time on a fixed-date release, whatever hasn't yet been built should be of lower value than what has already been built. It is much easier to make a decision to ship if the features that are missing are low value. If we are missing high-value features, we'll most likely extend the date if we can.

This works only when the high-priority features are truly done, per our agreed-upon definition of done. We don't want a scenario where the high-value, must-have features are really only 75% to 90% done and then we then have to drop one or two of them from the release in order to get the others to the 100% done level.

A fixed-date model becomes even easier to use if we can define a set of minimum releasable features that truly is small. If we can comfortably deliver the MRFs by the fixed date, we are in good shape, because any other features, by definition, are only nice-to-have features.

Fixed-date releases also dovetail nicely with the Scrum emphasis on timeboxing. By establishing a fixed amount of time for the release, we constrain the amount of work we can do and force people to make the difficult prioritization decisions that have to be made.

Variable Quality

If we overly constrain scope, date, and budget, quality becomes "flexible." This can lead us to deliver a solution that fails to meet customer expectations. Or, as I discussed in Chapter 8, flexible quality can result in the accrual of technical debt, which makes it more difficult in the future to add to or adapt our product.

Updating Constraints

An important part of ongoing release planning is to take our current knowledge and revisit these constraints to see if they should be rebalanced. For example, what should Roger and his team at Review Everything do if they approach the SR4U Release 1.0 deadline and it's clear that they won't complete the minimum releasable features? Because this is a fixed-date release, a good first strategy is to drop lower-value features. Let's assume, though, that in this case they would have to drop must-have features that are part of the MRFs in order to meet the date constraint.

Perhaps the right solution is to define a smaller set of features that are included in the MRFs. For example, the initial version of SR4U might focus on filtering restaurant reviews from only a small number of fixed sources. Roger and his team need to assess whether narrowing the scope degrades perceived customer value to an unacceptable level. And, if it is decided that Review Everything can't drop features without substantially damaging value, the company might consider adding more people (change the budget) or giving up on the hope of launching the service at the Social Media Expo (change the date).

These are the decisions that we must continuously make, revisit, and then make again during any development effort.

Grooming the Product Backlog

A fundamental activity of release planning is grooming the product backlog to meet our value and quality objectives. During envisioning (product planning) we create a high-level product backlog (perhaps with epic-level stories) and then use it to define a set of minimum releasable features for each release. Many of these backlog items are too large to be useful during release planning.

For example, during SR4U envisioning Roger provided a rough idea of which high-level features would be available by the Social Media Expo. Let's imagine that his roadmap indicates that Release 1.0 will focus on "basic learning" and "basic filtering" features corresponding to the following backlog items:

> As a typical user I want to teach SR4U what types of reviews to discard so that SR4U will know what characteristics to use when discarding reviews on my behalf.

> As a typical user I want a simple, Google-like interface for requesting a review search so that I don't have to spend much time describing what I want.

At release planning, these items will be too large to work with. To refine them Roger and his team would conduct a user-story-writing workshop (see Chapter 5) as part of the release-planning meeting or perhaps a separate story-writing workshop before the release-planning meeting. The results of this workshop would be many more detailed product backlog items, such as these:

> As a typical user I want to tell SR4U to ignore reviews that contain specific keywords that I feel show bias in a review so that I don't see any reviews containing those keywords.

> As a typical user I want to select a category of product or service so that I can help SR4U focus only on relevant reviews.

Once the stories are small enough, the team would estimate them (see Chapter 7) to communicate a rough idea of the cost. (Some amount of estimation is necessary for initial release planning. And as new stories emerge during the release, they too will need to be estimated for ongoing release-planning activities.) The release-planning participants would then prioritize the estimated stories based on the release goal and constraints. As the product backlog is reprioritized, the participants should be vigilant to ensure that the minimum releasable feature set is always identified and agreed upon.

Refine Minimum Releasable Features (MRFs)

As I described in Chapter 17, the minimum releasable features represent the smallest set of "must-have" features, the ones that simply have to be in the release if we are to meet customer value and quality expectations. An important part of release planning is to diligently reevaluate and refine what are truly the MRFs for the release. As we obtain fast feedback from our sprints and acquire validated learning, we are constantly adjusting the MRFs.

A problem I frequently see in organizations is an inability to agree on what constitutes the MRFs. Multiple competing stakeholders simply might not agree. Having poorly defined MRFs or MRFs that people only passive-aggressively agree with interferes with clear decision making during release planning. For example, we're running out of time; which feature should we drop? Lack of clarity regarding the MRFs might complicate this decision.

In Scrum, the product owner is ultimately responsible for defining the MRFs. Of course, he can and will do this in close collaboration with the proper stakeholders and the Scrum team.

For some, the MRFs concept may feel counterintuitive—why not try to deliver the largest set of features in a release instead of the smallest? The simple answer is that the largest set of features probably costs the most money, takes the most time, and has the most risk. Conversely, the smallest possible feature set should cost the least money, take the least time, and have the least risk. Thinking minimally better aligns us with the principle of delivering smaller and more frequent releases, as described in Chapter 14.

The MRFs should be defined with knowledge of the feature sizes, as determined during product backlog grooming. Not everyone agrees. Some believe that the MRFs should be defined independently of cost—meaning the MRFs are the minimum releasable features that will meet the users' value threshold for this release (and this determination is made independently of cost data). Initial MRFs can be envisioned without cost data, but because all of our release-planning decisions need to be made within a sensible economic framework, knowing feature costs provides a critical check on the economic viability of the MRFs. If we determine that the MRFs are not economically viable, perhaps it is time to pivot.

Sprint Mapping (PBI Slotting)

In each sprint the team works on a set of product backlog items. The team and product owner don't decide which specific product backlog items to work on in a given sprint until sprint planning. Does that mean we should give no consideration to mapping product backlog items to sprints before sprint-planning meetings?

Absolutely not! Some teams believe that a quick, early mapping (or slotting) of near-term product backlog items into sprints is helpful. For example, mapping out a few sprints in a multiteam environment might help the teams better coordinate their work.

To do this mapping we need an appropriately detailed, estimated, and prioritized product backlog. Using our team's velocity, we can approximate a set of product backlog items for each sprint by grouping together items whose aggregate size roughly equals the team's average velocity. The result might look like the left side of Figure 18.5. Some people prefer to show the sprint map horizontally (right side of Figure 18.5) to more closely resemble a timeline. I have seen some teams place the horizontally oriented sprint map of a Scrum team above a standard project plan (a Gantt chart, for example) that describes the work of non-Scrum teams to better visualize the alignment and touch points between the Scrum development work and the non-Scrum work.

When developing with one Scrum team we might do this mapping during initial release planning to get a rough idea of when certain features within the release will be created. This mapping activity might also cause us to reorganize the product backlog to group items in ways that are more natural or efficient. We also might choose to

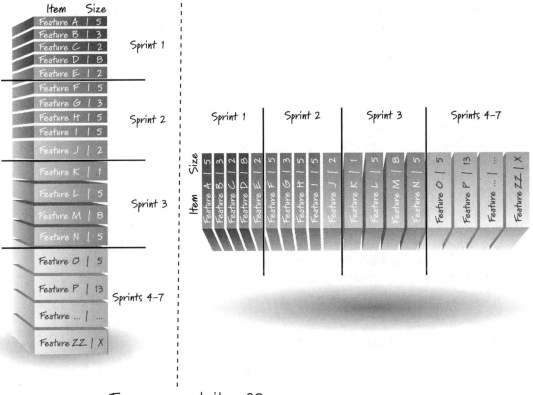

FIGURE 18.5 Mapping product backlog items to sprints

reorganize the work to ensure that the results at the end of a sprint are sufficient for us to get validated learning and actionable feedback.

When developing with multiple teams, we may want to do some forward-looking mapping of items to sprints to help manage inter-team dependencies. One approach is to use a form of rolling look-ahead planning (Cohn 2006), where each team considers the needed backlog items not only for the upcoming sprint but for at least two (and sometimes more) future sprints. This way, when more than one Scrum team is involved, the teams can know what team is going to work on which items and roughly when.

For example, assume that SR4U will have three Scrum teams. Team 1 focuses on the end-to-end processing of user requests. This team enables users to specify a review query, run the query, and get review results. Team 2 focuses on the AI engine, which has the logic for how to analyze and discriminate among reviews. Team 3 focuses on connecting to different Internet data sources for retrieving candidate reviews.

These three teams must coordinate their efforts to make sure that the minimum releasable features are produced and available in time for the Social Media Expo. It makes sense for all three teams to participate in joint release planning.

During an initial release-planning meeting each of the teams provides an idea of when it will work on its product backlog items. In the ensuing discussion, team 1 might say, "We think we'll be ready to create the *ignore reviews with specific keywords* feature in sprint 2. However, we will need team 3 to be able to retrieve data from at least one Internet source either before that sprint begins or very early during sprint 2." Members of team 3 can then examine their sprint map to see if they are currently planning to have at least one source available by sprint 2. If not, the two teams can discuss the dependency and see what modifications one or both of the teams need to make.

If we choose to do some early mapping, we must realize that this mapping can and will evolve during the creation of the release. Ultimately the decision as to which features each team will work on in a given sprint is made at the last responsible moment—the sprint planning for that sprint.

Alternatively, a preference of many organizations (especially those doing product development using only one team) is to perform little or no early mapping of product backlog items to sprints. Teams in such companies believe that the effort to produce the mapping is not justified by the value that it delivers. For these teams, the initial release-planning meeting would not involve the mapping step, at least not in any significant way.

Fixed-Date Release Planning

As I mentioned earlier, many organizations that use Scrum prefer to use fixed-date releases. Table 18.2 summarizes the steps for performing fixed-date release planning.

Let's use SR4U as an example. Release 1.0 is tied to the start of the Social Media Expo, which starts on Monday, September 26. The company decides that having an

TABLE 18.2 Steps for Performing Fixed-Date Release Planning

Step	Description	Comments
1	Determine how many sprints are in this release.	If all sprint lengths are equal, this is simple calendar math because you know when the first sprint will start and you know the delivery date.
2	Groom the product backlog to a sufficient depth by creating, estimating the size of, and prioritizing product backlog items.	Because we are trying to determine which PBIs we can get by a fixed date, we need enough of them to plan out to that date.
3	Measure or estimate the team's velocity as a range.	Determine an average faster and an average slower velocity for the team (see Chapter 7).
4	Multiply the slower velocity by the number of sprints. Count down that number of points into the product backlog and draw a line.	This is the "will-have" line.
5	Multiply the faster velocity by the number of sprints. Count down that number of points into the product backlog and draw a second line.	This is the "might-have" line.

initial version to demonstrate at this conference is an excellent first milestone on the path to realizing the product vision.

Although we just imagined SR4U with three teams, for this example, let's go back to the initial assumption that just one team would develop the product. Because Roger and the team want to begin sprint 1 the first week in July and finish by September 23 (the Friday before the Expo starts), they can easily calculate how many sprints they will need to perform in this release. Assuming that the length of each sprint is the same throughout this release, which is the normal case with Scrum, SR4U Release 1.0 has six, two-week (ten-day) sprints. Figure 18.6 maps these sprints onto the calendar.

FIGURE 18.6 Sprint calendar for SR4U Release 1.0

Next they determine how much work the team can get done in six sprints. Using the approach I discussed in Chapter 7, let's say they calculate the velocity of the team to be between 18 and 22 story points per sprint. Therefore, Roger and the team should be able to complete between 108 and 132 story points of work during this release.

Now they need to determine what features this range of story points represents. At the end of product planning, Roger and the team had a high-level product backlog with some epic- and theme-level user stories. As I discussed earlier, the SR4U team then conducted a user-story-writing workshop to create more detailed product backlog items. The team then estimated them, and the product owner, with input from the development team and stakeholders, prioritized them.

As part of this process, Roger and the team had to determine the set of must-have features that make up the MRFs. As a rule of thumb, on a fixed-date release I like the MRFs to require less than 100% of the time allocated to the release. I prefer somewhere closer to 60% to 70% for at least two reasons:

- If we run out of time for the release and all of the features targeted for the release are must-have items, which feature should we drop? By definition, if the features are all must-haves, we wouldn't be able to drop any. If we define the release to have about 60% to 70% must-have features, with the remaining scope being nice-to-have features, we can drop nice-to-have features if we have to drop scope.
- If we allocate 100% must-have features to the release, what happens during the release when an emergent must-have feature appears? In other words, a feature we didn't know about earlier presents itself and it absolutely must be included to have a viable release. How would we accommodate it? If we defined the release to include some nice-to-have features, we could drop one or more of them to include the new, emergent must-have feature.

The end result is a product backlog that structurally looks like Figure 18.7. This figure shows the total product backlog as Roger and the team understand it today, including themes and epics that are not planned for this release.

Roger and the team can then apply the results from the earlier velocity calculation, where the team estimated it would be able to complete between 108 and 132 points' worth of work over six sprints. The team can visualize where in the backlog it can get to by counting down a total of 108 points from the top and then counting down to a total of 132 points (see Figure 18.8).

You'll notice that these two lines split the product backlog into three sections (will have, might have, won't have). This approach illustrates how we can give a range answer to the question "What will I get by the release date?" Early in the release it is difficult to give a very precise answer to this question. The range answer is accurate and also communicates the uncertainty we have in the answer—the broader the range, the less certain we are.

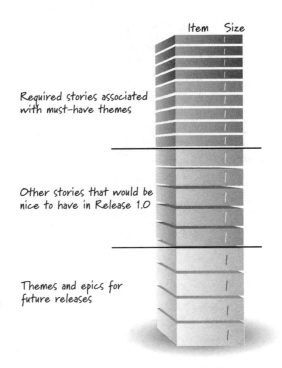

Item   Size

Required stories associated
with must-have themes

Other stories that would be
nice to have in Release 1.0

Themes and epics for
future releases

FIGURE 18.7   Product backlog ready for release planning

To understand whether they are in good shape with this release plan, Roger and the team need only to overlay the must-have line (from Figure 18.7) onto the product backlog (from Figure 18.8). Some possible results are shown in Figure 18.9. Notice that the must-have line separates the minimum releasable features that are above the line from the rest of the product backlog.

The left-most product backlog of Figure 18.9 communicates a very positive situation. You can interpret it as "We will have our must-have features." We should proceed with the release.

The middle backlog of Figure 18.9 can be interpreted as "We will have most of our must-have features, but we might or might not have all of them." There is clearly more risk associated with this scenario than the previous scenario. One option is to accept the risk that we won't get all of the must-have items and move on. Because we are planning to learn fast, we might decide to start this release and complete a few sprints. At that point, we could reevaluate where we are and then make a decision to continue with the release or kill it (as I discussed in previous chapters). Also, feedback from the work already completed might indicate that some of the features originally included in the MRFs aren't really must-have items after all and we are actually in good shape.

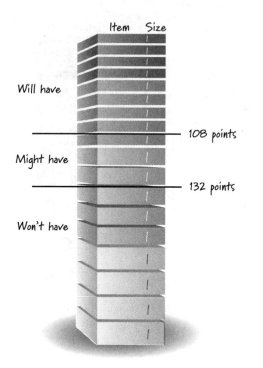

FIGURE 18.8   Determining the range of features on a fixed-date release

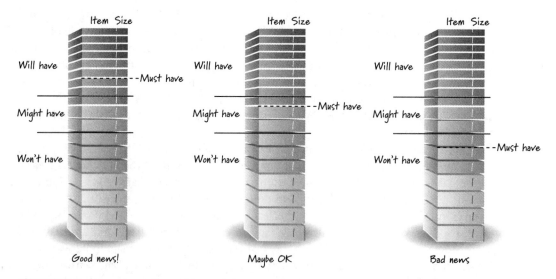

FIGURE 18.9   Location of must-have features relative to the range of deliverable features

Alternatively, we can consider setting a new, later release date that we could easily calculate, or we can suggest adding more people to the development effort to increase velocity (if we think that might help). At this point, some organizations might choose to accrue technical debt by having the team cut corners to ensure that all of the must-have features are delivered by the due date, albeit at a reduced quality level. However, if technical debt is taken on in the current release, it should be paid off in the next release, which will reduce the amount of value delivered then.

The right-most backlog in Figure 18.9 can be interpreted as "We won't have our must-have features." Perhaps we shouldn't proceed with this release, or maybe we should change the release date or consider adding more resources. If we choose to accrue technical debt in this scenario, it will probably be a lot of debt.

Of course, assuming that we proceed with the release, we must revisit our release plan every sprint to update it based on our current knowledge.

For example, at the end of each sprint we have an additional velocity data point, which for a new team without much historical velocity data, or a team doing radically different work from what it is used to, will cause us to recalculate the average points per sprint the team can get done. And, as you might expect, the items in the product backlog could change. New items could emerge and other items could be moved out of this release or deleted altogether as we learn that we don't need them now or ever. To visually communicate the revised release plan, we would redraw a picture similar to Figure 18.8.

Fixed-Scope Release Planning

Although fixed-date releases are very common with Scrum, what if for your product the scope truly is more important than the date? What if you have a large set of must-have features in your minimum releasable features set and you're willing to slip the delivery date to get them all?

If you're in this situation, have you truly winnowed down the must-have features to be the absolute bare minimum? I occasionally hear things like "But we're implementing a standard and you can't ship an implementation of half a standard." While this is perhaps true, in most standards there are still likely to be optional parts that we don't have to implement now (for example, think about web browser support for changing or emerging HTML or CSS standards). In other instances we might be able to go to market with less than the full implementation of the standard and let customers know which parts we support and which parts we don't.

My point is that if we think incrementally and aggressively target the true minimum releasable features, we can usually turn a fixed-scope release into a set of smaller fixed-date releases. When the set of minimum releasable features becomes small, another constraint (like time) typically becomes the dominant constraint.

Let's say that we have winnowed down the must-have features to the bare minimum and our principal release constraint is still focused on when we can we get those features. In this case we perform release planning as outlined in Table 18.3.

If we're doing a fixed-scope release, we must know what the features are at the start of the release. We might know these features if we are building a simple or familiar product. When developing innovative products, however, many features will emerge and evolve during the development effort. We certainly have some idea of the desired features up front, so we'll use them in our initial release planning. However, we must be prepared to continuously revise our release plan as our understanding of the required features changes.

If we perform a release-planning meeting at the start of the release, we must first groom the product backlog as we did during fixed-date planning. A difference is that during fixed-date planning we try to have fewer than 100% must-have items in the release to buffer against uncertainty. In fixed-scope planning we want the entire scope for the release to be must-have features. Our goal on fixed-scope releases is to get all of the must-have features completed in a timely way. If an emergent must-have feature appears, we will simply add it to the scope of the release and push out the release date.

During fixed-date planning, we know precisely how many sprints we will have. During fixed-scope planning, we need to calculate the number of sprints required to deliver the fixed set of features.

TABLE 18.3   Steps for Performing Fixed-Scope Release Planning

Step	Description	Comments
1	Groom the product backlog to include at least the PBIs we would like in this release by creating, estimating the size of, and prioritizing PBIs.	Because this is a fixed-scope release, we need to know which PBIs are in the fixed scope.
2	Determine the total size of the PBIs to be delivered in the release.	If we have a product backlog of estimated items, we simply sum the size estimates of all of the items we want in the release.
3	Measure or estimate the team's velocity as a range.	Determine an average faster and an average slower velocity for the team.
4	Divide the total size of the PBIs by the faster velocity and round up the answer to the next integer.	This will tell us the lowest number of sprints required to deliver the features.
5	Divide the total size of the PBIs by the slower velocity and round up the answer to the next integer.	This will tell us the highest number of sprints required to deliver the features.

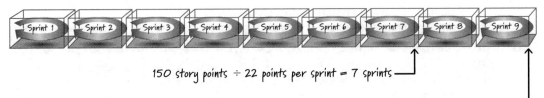

150 story points ÷ 22 points per sprint = 7 sprints

150 story points ÷ 18 points per sprint = 9 sprints

FIGURE 18.10   Results of fixed-scope planning

To perform the math we need the velocity range for our team (as we did with fixed-date planning). Let's say our team's velocity on two-week sprints ranges between 18 and 22 story points. To answer the question of when we will get the fixed set of features, we sum the sizes of all of those features and then divide by our team's higher and lower velocities. The result is a range of sprints within which delivery will take place.

Let's say we want 150 story points of features in the next release. If we divide 150 by 18 (our team's slower velocity) and round up, we get nine sprints. If we divide 150 by 22 (our team's faster velocity) and round up, we get seven sprints. We can visualize this as shown in Figure 18.10.

Notice that once again we give a range answer to the question we are being asked. In this case the question is "How many sprints will you need to complete a release with 150 points of work?" Our answer will be seven to nine sprints. Because these are two-week sprints, our answer also could be stated as 14 to 18 weeks.

Calculating Cost

Calculating costs on either a fixed-date or fixed-scope release is easy (see Table 18.4).

TABLE 18.4   Calculating the Cost of a Release

Step	Description	Comments
1	Determine who is on the team.	Assume that the team composition doesn't materially change either during a sprint or from sprint to sprint.
2	Determine the sprint length.	Assume that all sprints have the same length.
3	Based on team composition and sprint length, determine the personnel costs of running a sprint.	This is simple if previous assumptions are true, and only slightly more complicated if team composition or sprint length fluctuates.

continues

TABLE 18.4   Calculating the Cost of a Release (*Continued*)

Step	Description	Comments
4a	For a fixed-date release, multiply the number of sprints in the release by the cost per sprint.	The result is the fixed personnel cost for this release.
4b	For a fixed-scope release, multiply both the high and low number of sprints by the cost per sprint.	The results are the range of personnel costs associated with the release. One represents the lower amount the release should cost and the other the higher amount it should cost.

Let's assume that the composition of the team assigned to the development effort is reasonably stable. In other words, we aren't taking people off of the team or adding new people to the team. And, if we do, the changes are small and the people we move around get paid something reasonably similar.

Based on these assumptions, we can easily determine the cost per sprint, because we know who is on the team and the length of the sprints. If we remove other costs (like capital costs) from this discussion, which often is reasonable because the majority of software development costs are the cost of the people, personnel cost is a pretty good surrogate for the overall cost per sprint.

To finalize the calculation, we need to know the number of sprints within the release. On a fixed-date release we know exactly the number of sprints, so we multiply the number of sprints by the cost per sprint to determine the release cost.

On a fixed-scope release, we have a range of sprints. In our previous example we calculated a range of seven to nine sprints, so the cost for this release will range from seven to nine times the cost per sprint. Most organizations will budget at the high end of this range because the release may in fact take nine sprints to complete. If we budgeted for only seven sprints, we might have insufficient funds to complete the release.

Another approach to calculating cost can be used if you know your historic cost per story point. If you have data that indicates how many points of work were completed during a previous period of time (say, a year) and you divide that into the loaded labor cost of the team, you will know your cost per point. If it is reasonable to assume that the same cost per point would apply to the current release, you can roughly estimate the cost for a 150-point release (by multiplying 150 by the historic cost per point) even before doing initial release planning.

Communicating

An important aspect of release planning is communicating progress. Although any highly visible way of communicating progress can be used, most teams use some form of burndown and/or burnup chart as their principal information radiator of release status. Let's look at how to communicate release status on both fixed-scope and fixed-date releases.

Communicating Progress on a Fixed-Scope Release

On a fixed-scope release we have an idea of the total scope of work we wish to achieve. The goal is to communicate how we are progressing toward completing that work.

Fixed-Scope-Release Burndown Chart

A **burndown chart** for a fixed-scope release shows the total amount of unfinished work that remains each sprint to achieve the current release goal. In this type of chart, the vertical axis numbers are in the same units we use to size our product backlog items (typically story points or ideal days). The horizontal axis represents sprints (see Figure 18.11).

Using the example from earlier in the chapter, we have 150 story points at the start of development (at the end of initial release planning), which is the same as the start of sprint 1. At the end of each sprint we update this chart to show the total amount of work remaining within the release. The difference between the amount of work remaining at the beginning of a sprint and the work remaining at the end of the sprint represents the sprint velocity. This is plotted as the "Actual" line in Figure 18.11.

We can also show projected outcomes on the burndown chart. In Figure 18.11 there are three lines predicting when the release might be done, each corresponding to a predicted team velocity. If the team is able to work at its higher velocity of 22 points per sprint, the team would finish by the end of seven sprints. If the team

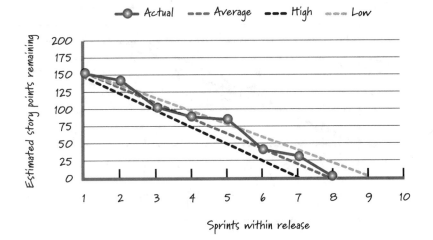

FIGURE 18.11   Fixed-scope-release burndown chart

operates at its lower velocity of 18, it might need a total of nine sprints. And, if the team operates at its average velocity of 20, it would need eight sprints.

There are several variations on the basic burndown chart; however, they are all similar in that they show each sprint the cumulative size of the work remaining to achieve the release goal.

Fixed-Scope-Release Burnup Chart

A **burnup chart** for a fixed-scope release shows the total amount of work in a release as a goal or target line and our progress each sprint toward achieving that goal (see Figure 18.12). The horizontal and vertical dimensions of the chart are identical to those of the release burndown chart.

In this chart, at the end of every sprint we increment the cumulative story points completed by the total story points completed in that sprint. The goal is to burn up to achieve the target number of story points in the release. And, like the release burndown chart, this chart shows the same three predictive lines indicating the likely number of sprints to achieve the target.

Some people prefer to use the burnup format because it can easily show a change in scope for the release. For example, if we add more scope in the current release (so the release really isn't fixed scope!), in the sprint where the new scope is added we simply move the target line up to indicate that a new, higher target exists from this point forward (see Figure 18.13).

It is also possible to show a change in scope on a release burndown chart (see Cohn 2006).

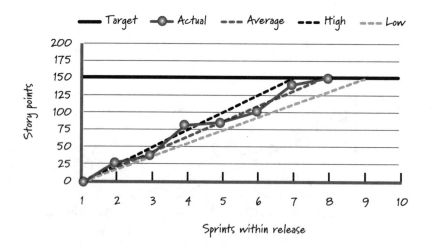

FIGURE 18.12   Fixed-scope-release burnup chart

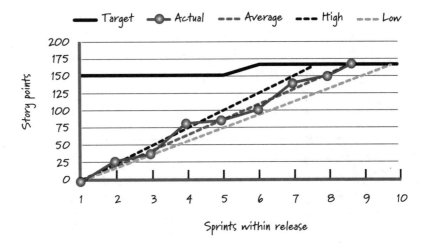

FIGURE 18.13   Variable-scope-release burnup chart

Communicating Progress on a Fixed-Date Release

With a fixed-date release we know the number of sprints in the release, so our goal is to communicate the range of features we expect to complete and our sprint-by-sprint progress toward the range. The traditional burndown and burnup charts aren't effective tools for fixed-date planning because they assume you know how much total scope you have to burn down or burn up. Remember this is fixed-date planning, so we are trying to calculate and communicate over time the narrowing range of scope that can be delivered by a fixed date.

Figure 18.9 shows how to visualize a range of features we expect to achieve in a fixed-date release. If we update the charts in Figure 18.9 at the end of each sprint, we have a very effective way of communicating the projected range of features we will complete by the fixed release date. We will also have an understanding of how likely we are to get the must-have features by the release date.

If we want to maintain one chart that shows our historical progress toward achieving the final scope, we can create a specialized burnup chart in the form of Figure 18.14.

This chart has all of the same elements as the charts in Figure 18.9. However, in Figure 18.14, the product backlog is inverted (intentionally positioned upside down) so that instead of the highest-priority item being physically positioned at the top, it is now at the bottom of the product backlog. Lower-priority items are now found higher up in the backlog. Inverting the backlog in this fashion eliminates the problem of having to know the scope of the product backlog items in the release (which traditional release burndown and burnup charts require).

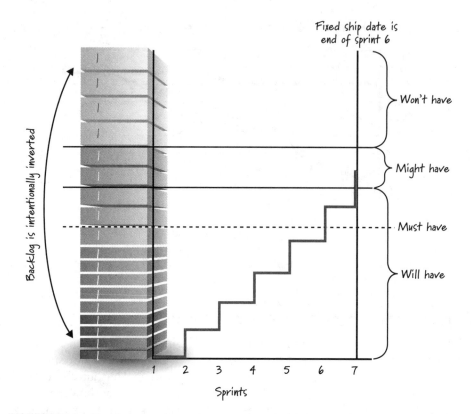

FIGURE 18.14   Fixed-date-release burnup chart (with inverted product backlog)

The chart shows the projected range of features that we expect to have by the end of sprint 6 (beginning of sprint 7). Each sprint we burn up the chart to show the features completed in that sprint. So at the end of sprint 1 (beginning of sprint 2) there is a vertical line whose length indicates how many features we completed in sprint 1. Using this approach allows us to see how we are progressing toward hitting our target range of features, as well as how we are progressing toward completing the must-have features. For simplicity, there are no trend lines on this graph, but they could easily be added to extrapolate from earlier sprints what scope we are likely to end up with.

Closing

In this chapter I expanded the description of release planning by discussing when release planning takes place, who is involved, what activities take place, and the elements of the resulting release plan. I also discussed the details of how to do both fixed-date and fixed-scope release planning and how to communicate progress during a release.

This chapter concludes Part III. In the next chapter I will discuss the next level of planning: sprint planning, which I include with Part IV to group together all of the chapters related to sprint-specific activities.

PART IV

SPRINTING

Chapter 19

SPRINT PLANNING

A release is typically composed of multiple sprints, each of which delivers customer or user value. Every sprint begins with sprint planning, a time when the Scrum team gathers to agree on a sprint goal and determine what it can deliver during the forthcoming sprint. In this chapter I discuss where sprint planning fits into the Scrum framework and how to perform it.

Overview

A product backlog may represent many weeks or months of work, which is much more than can be completed in a single, short sprint. To determine the most important subset of product backlog items to build in the next sprint, the Scrum team performs sprint planning. During sprint planning the Scrum team agrees on a goal for the sprint, and the development team determines the specific product backlog items that are aligned with that goal and that it can realistically deliver by the end of the sprint. To acquire confidence in what it can deliver, the development team creates a plan for how to complete the product backlog items. Together the product backlog items and the plan form the sprint backlog.

Timing

Sprint planning is a recurring, just-in-time activity that takes place at the beginning of each sprint, when we can leverage the best possible information to decide what to work on in the upcoming sprint (see Figure 19.1).

For a two-week to month-long sprint, sprint planning should take no longer than four to eight hours to complete.

Participants

The full Scrum team collaborates during sprint planning. The product owner shares the initial sprint goal, presents the prioritized product backlog, and answers any questions the team might have regarding the product backlog items. The development team works diligently to determine what it can deliver and then makes a realistic commitment at the end of sprint planning. The ScrumMaster, acting as the Scrum team coach, observes the planning activity, asks probing questions, and facilitates to help ensure a successful result. Because the ScrumMaster is not in charge of the

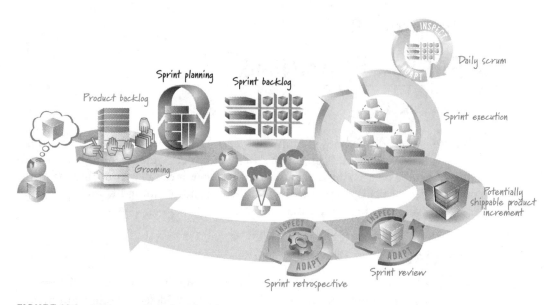

FIGURE 19.1   When sprint planning happens

development team, she cannot decide on behalf of the development team what commitment to make. The ScrumMaster can, however, challenge the team's commitment to ensure that it is realistic and appropriate.

Process

Figure 19.2 illustrates the sprint-planning activity.

Sprint planning relies on a set of inputs that guide the development team in determining what value it can realistically deliver by the end of the sprint. These inputs are described in Table 19.1.

The first and most crucial input to sprint planning is a product backlog that has been groomed prior to sprint planning so that the topmost items meet the Scrum team's definition of ready (see Chapter 6). Typically this means that the topmost items have well-defined acceptance criteria and are appropriately sized, estimated, and prioritized.

Engaged product owners also enter sprint planning having a good idea of what they want the team to deliver by the end of the sprint. They might have a specific set of high-priority product backlog items in mind—"I'd really like to get the top five product backlog items done this sprint"—or they might have a more general notion—"At the end of this sprint I want a typical user to be able to submit a simple keyword query." Knowing the sprint goal helps the team balance competing priorities. A product owner should communicate his initial sprint goal in a way that doesn't unduly influence the development team to commit to more than it realistically can deliver.

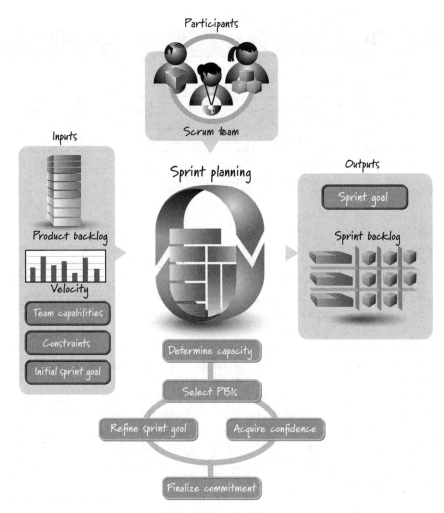

FIGURE 19.2 Sprint-planning activity

TABLE 19.1 Sprint-Planning Inputs

Input	Description
Product backlog	Prior to sprint planning, the topmost product backlog items have been groomed into a *ready* state.
Team velocity	The team's historical velocity is an indicator of how much work is practical for the team to complete in a sprint.

continues

TABLE 19.1 Sprint-Planning Inputs (*Continued*)

Input	Description
Constraints	Business or technical constraints that could materially affect what the team can deliver are identified.
Team capabilities	Capabilities take into account which people are on the team, what skills each team member has, and how available each person will be in the upcoming sprint.
Initial sprint goal	This is the business goal the product owner would like to see accomplished during the sprint.

The fact that the product owner knows what he wants, however, does not necessarily mean that the development team is capable of delivering it during that sprint. A realistic commitment is achieved only through collaboration (and at times negotiation) between the product owner and the development team members. The sprint-planning participants need to have the opportunity to review and discuss potential value-generating alternatives and decide what is practical given the team's capabilities, predicted velocity, and any known constraints.

To acquire confidence in what it can accomplish, the development team will create a plan for how it will achieve the sprint goal. Collectively the selected product backlog items and the plan form the sprint backlog (shown in Figure 19.2). Most teams break down each targeted product backlog item into a set of estimated tasks, which collectively form the plan. Teams that take this approach typically follow a helpful rule of breaking down tasks so that no one task is more than eight hours of effort, although some might be a bit larger. At this level of granularity the team has a good idea of what really needs to be done and whether it can accomplish those tasks in the time it has available.

At the end of sprint planning the development team's commitment is communicated through a finalized sprint goal and the sprint backlog.

Approaches to Sprint Planning

I will describe two approaches to sprint planning: two-part sprint planning and one-part sprint planning.

Two-Part Sprint Planning

One approach to sprint planning is to separate it into two parts (see Figure 19.3). During part 1 (the "what" part) the development team determines its capacity to complete work and then forecasts the product backlog items that it believes it can

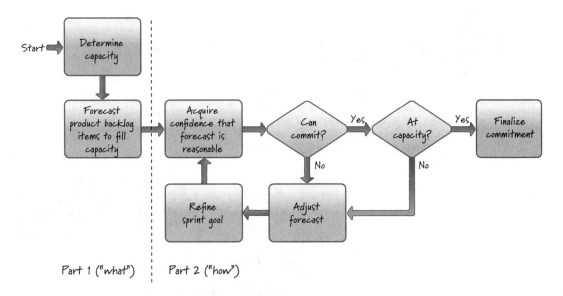

FIGURE 19.3   Two-part sprint-planning approach

deliver by the end of the sprint. So if the team believes it can accomplish 40 story points, it will select about 40 story points' worth of work.

During part 2 (the "how" part) the team acquires confidence in its ability to complete the items that it forecasted in part 1 by creating a plan. Most teams create this plan by breaking the product backlog items into a set of tasks and then estimating (in hours) the effort required to complete each task. The team then compares the estimate of task hours against its capacity, in terms of hours, to see if its initial commitment was realistic.

If the team finds it has selected too much or too little, or has selected items that can't realistically be developed together in the same sprint given one or more constraints, it can adjust its forecast and possibly refine the sprint goal to fit the available capacity and constraints. When the team's forecast is comfortably within its capacity range and constraints, it finalizes its commitment and sprint planning is over.

One-Part Sprint Planning

An alternative approach to sprint planning, and the one I see most frequently, is a one-part approach that interleaves selecting an item and acquiring confidence that it can be delivered. This approach is illustrated in Figure 19.4.

Using this approach, the development team begins by determining its capacity to complete work. Based on available capacity, the sprint goal may need to be refined. Next the team selects a product backlog item and then acquires confidence that the

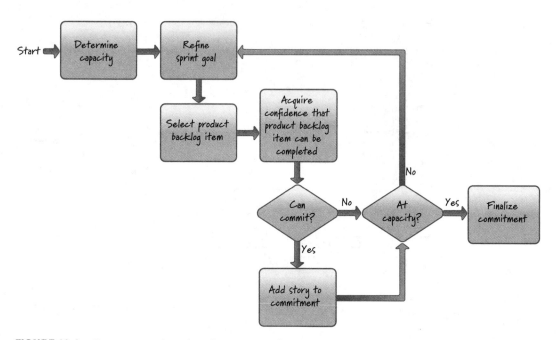

FIGURE 19.4   One-part sprint-planning approach

selected item will reasonably fit within the sprint, given other items already included in the team's evolving commitment. This cycle is then repeated until the team is out of capacity to do any more work. At that point the commitment is finalized and sprint planning is over.

Determining Capacity

An important first activity during sprint planning is determining the available capacity of the team to perform work during the sprint. Knowledge of capacity guides the Scrum team in determining what it can deliver.

What Is Capacity?

Figure 19.5 illustrates the various factors that influence a team's capacity to work on product backlog items during an upcoming sprint. These include the time needed for other Scrum activities, non-sprint-related commitments, personal time off, and the need for a buffer.

Let's say a team is doing a two-week (ten-day) sprint. Right away, we must accept that the team doesn't actually have ten days to dedicate to sprint execution. We know, for instance, that on a two-week sprint about a day of that time needs to be reserved

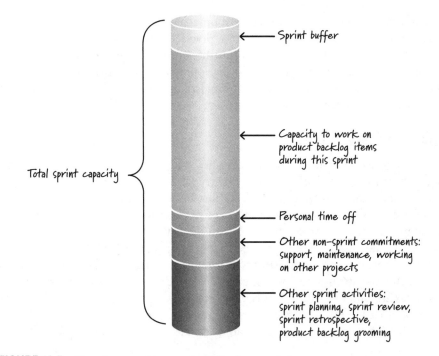

Sprint buffer

Capacity to work on
product backlog items
during this sprint

Total sprint capacity

Personal time off

Other non-sprint commitments:
support, maintenance, working
on other projects

Other sprint activities:
sprint planning, sprint review,
sprint retrospective,
product backlog grooming

FIGURE 19.5   Development team capacity in a sprint

collectively for sprint-planning, sprint review, and sprint retrospective activities. We also know that the team should reserve up to 10% of its time to assist the product owner with product backlog grooming (writing and refining, estimating, and prioritizing product backlog items) to help ensure that the items are ready.

The team must also determine how much time it should reserve for work outside the sprint, things like supporting the current product, maintaining another product, or other work unrelated to the current sprint. The team should also remember that in an eight-hour day, team members really don't have a full eight hours to work on product backlog items. There is some overhead required to be a good citizen of the organization—attending meetings, responding to emails, interruptions, and so on.

Next, the team needs to know if people have personal time off scheduled during a sprint because that also reduces overall team capacity.

After removing time dedicated to other Scrum activities, work outside the sprint, and personal time off, what remains is the capacity of the team to work on product backlog items for this sprint. However, from this total capacity we should reserve some buffer against things not going quite as planned. For example, any estimating we do won't be perfect, so items might turn out to be a bit larger than we thought. Or something can (and usually does) go wrong. Having a bit of buffer against unexpected problems is wise.

A team can use a number of different approaches to determine a practical buffer size (see Cohn 2006 for some examples). In practice, this buffer can be established empirically after a team performs several sprints and better understands how much buffer should be held in reserve to handle development uncertainty.

Once a buffer is defined, the team can finalize its available capacity for completing work during the sprint.

Capacity in Story Points

What unit of measure should we use for capacity? The two obvious answers are either the same units as the product backlog items (typically story points or ideal days) or the same units as the sprint backlog tasks (effort-hours).

A team's velocity is expressed in terms of product backlog item units (let's say story points). So, if we express capacity in story points, determining capacity is the same as predicting our team's target velocity for the upcoming sprint.

To make this determination, start with the team's long-term average velocity or the team's previous sprint velocity (sometimes referred to as the "yesterday's weather" approach) as an initial estimate of its capacity/velocity for the upcoming sprint. Then consider whether the upcoming sprint might differ from typical or previous sprints (it might not). The result is a reasonable adjusted capacity (predicted velocity) for the upcoming sprint.

For example, let's say our team's average velocity is 40 story points during a two-week sprint. The sprint we are planning, however, occurs during the last two weeks in December in the United States, which means many of our team members will be taking time off for the holidays. We would take on too much work if we used the average velocity of 40; we'd be better off assuming that a velocity closer to 20 (or thereabouts) is a more realistic capacity for the team during this sprint.

Capacity in Effort-Hours

An alternative way to express capacity is in effort-hours. Table 19.2 illustrates how to determine the team's effort-hour capacity to perform task-level work during a two-week or ten-day sprint.

The capacity calculation shown in Table 19.2 is derived as follows. First, the team members express how many days they have available to work on the upcoming sprint (the amount of unavailable time equates to the "personal time off" slice in Figure 19.5). Both Betty and Rajesh are planning to attend a two-day training class, so each of them has only eight days available in the sprint. Simon is planning a three-day weekend so he has nine available days.

Next, the team members determine how much time to reserve for other Scrum activities. They reserve a day of time for sprint planning, sprint review, and sprint retrospective activities. They also deduct the time needed to assist the product owner

TABLE 19.2   Determining Effort-Hour Capacity

Person	Days Available (Less Personal Time)	Days for Other Scrum Activities	Hours per Day	Available Effort-Hours
Jorge	10	2	4–7	32–56
Betty	8	2	5–6	30–36
Rajesh	8	2	4–6	24–36
Simon	9	2	2–3	14–21
Heidi	10	2	5–6	40–48
Total				140–197

with product backlog grooming activities. Together these represent two fewer days available per person to perform task-level work.

The team members then determine how many hours per day they could dedicate to work in this sprint. Each person gives a range that takes into account any overhead work not associated with items in the sprint backlog (the overhead equates to the "other non-sprint commitments" slice in Figure 19.5). For example, Simon is only half-time on this product, so he estimates only two to three hours a day to work on this product during the sprint.

After accounting for personal time off, other Scrum activities, and non-sprint commitments, the team in Table 19.2 estimates a capacity of 140 to 197 effort-hours to work on tasks in the sprint backlog.

I would caution this team against taking on 197 hours of work because it would leave no sprint buffer. A better strategy for this team would be to use a capacity that is probably greater than 140 hours but certainly less than 197 hours when committing to work during this sprint.

Selecting Product Backlog Items

Either approach to sprint planning requires that we select candidate product backlog items for inclusion in the commitment. Selection can be done in several ways. If we have a sprint goal, we would select product backlog items that align with that goal. If there is no formal sprint goal, our default is to select items from the top of the product backlog. We would start with the topmost item and then move to the next item and so forth. If the team were not able to commit to the next-highest-priority item (perhaps there is a skills capacity issue), it would select the next appropriate higher-priority backlog item that looks as if it can be completed within the constraints.

One of my rules when selecting product backlog items for a sprint is that we don't start what we can't finish. So if the next product backlog item is too big to complete in the sprint given the other items that we have already agreed to complete, we should either try to break down the next item into two or more smaller items, each of which would be valuable to our customers, or consider working on another item that we can complete. Also, having a good *definition of ready* will prevent product backlog items from being selected that are poorly defined or have unfulfilled resource or dependency constraints that would prevent our finishing them in a sprint.

The start-only-what-you-can-finish rule is based on the principles that we should limit WIP and that starting something and not finishing it generates a variety of forms of waste. I discussed both of these principles in Chapter 4 when I covered the rule of no goal-altering changes during a sprint. Also, letting incomplete items carry over from one sprint to the next doesn't achieve the goal of having a potentially shippable product increment at the end of each and every sprint.

Acquiring Confidence

One way to acquire confidence is to use predicted velocity to see if the commitment is realistic. If the predicted sprint velocity is 25 story points and our team has selected 45 story points' worth of work, the team should be concerned. At the very least we should start asking questions about why we think the commitment can be achieved. When used this way, velocity provides an excellent check and balance on the proposed commitment.

The risk of using velocity as the sole means of establishing confidence is that even though the numbers look right, the commitment might still be unachievable. For example, if the predicted sprint velocity is 25 story points and the team's commitment totals 21 story points, the commitment would seem reasonable. However, until we dig a little deeper to the task level, we don't really know if the set of product backlog items that total 21 story points can actually be completed—there could be dependency issues, skills capacity issues, as well as a host of other issues that make it impractical for the team to get them all done.

Most Scrum teams gain the necessary level of confidence by breaking the product backlog items down into the tasks that are required to complete them to the Scrum team's agreed-upon definition of done. These tasks can then be estimated (usually in effort-hours) and subtracted from the team's capacity. Breaking product backlog items into tasks is a form of design and just-in-time planning for how to get the items done.

The result is the sprint backlog. Figure 19.6 illustrates an example sprint backlog showing four product backlog items (totaling 21 points) that the team believes it can get done at the end of the sprint. The sprint backlog also shows a plan (in the form of tasks) for delivering the product backlog items to meet the sprint goal.

Is the team making a good commitment or not?

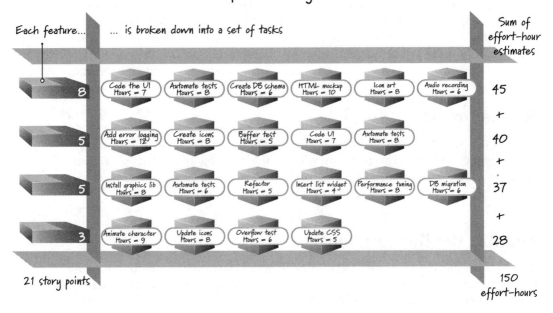

FIGURE 19.6   Sprint backlog showing PBIs and task plan

If the team's predicted velocity is 25 points, a commitment of 21 points seems reasonable. But let's use the task-level details to see if the commitment still looks good. The sum of the tasks for all four product backlog items is 150 effort-hours. Assume that the team for this sprint is the team identified in Table 19.2, which has a task-hour capacity of 140 to 197 effort-hours. A commitment of 150 effort-hours seems comfortably safe—there is likely still a reasonable sprint buffer for handling things that might go wrong.

However, just because the 150 hours are comfortably in the range of 140 to 197 hours doesn't guarantee that the commitment is good. Recall from Table 19.2 that Simon is available only two to three hours a day for nine of the ten days of the sprint. That means Simon has only between 14 and 21 effort-hours available for work on this sprint. What if Simon is the only person who can work on UI tasks? In this case the team might not be able to commit to the four product backlog items in Figure 19.6 because it might run out of "UI capacity" when it runs out of "Simon capacity."

Even though in Scrum we typically don't assign team members to tasks during sprint planning (notice that in Figure 19.6 there are no team member names on the tasks), we need to at least quickly consider our skills capacity or we could make a bad commitment. Just because our commitment is comfortably within the range of estimated aggregate capacity doesn't mean we won't run out of capacity in a particular skills area.

For this reason some teams choose to note on each task who is the person most likely to work on that task. Often this is an unnecessary and potentially wasteful step because unexpected events will occur during the sprint and tasks will need to be reassigned. Also, assigning tasks to individuals might be harmful if doing so reduces team ownership of the tasks. A better strategy (as I will discuss in Chapter 20) is to let team members select the work in an opportunistic, just-in-time fashion during the sprint.

Refine the Sprint Goal

The sprint goal summarizes the business purpose and value of the sprint. The product owner should come to sprint planning with an initial sprint goal. That initial goal, however, can be refined during the course of sprint planning as the sprint-planning participants work together to determine what can realistically be delivered.

Finalize the Commitment

At the completion of sprint planning the development team finalizes its commitment to the business value it will deliver by the end of the sprint. The sprint goal and the selected product backlog items embody that commitment.

As I mentioned in Chapter 2, some people prefer to use the term *forecast* to describe the business value that the development team believes it can produce by the end of the sprint. I prefer and use the term *commitment*. Regardless of which term you prefer, the approaches to sprint planning I describe in this chapter are the same.

The nuanced differences between these terms might affect only the scope of what the development team determines it can deliver and how the Scrum team deals with new information that arrives during sprint execution (see Chapter 4 for a discussion of changes during a sprint).

Closing

In this chapter I expanded the description of sprint planning by discussing when sprint planning takes place and who is involved. I discussed two different approaches to sprint planning. In the first approach the team selects a set of product backlog items and then acquires confidence that it can indeed deliver the full set. The second approach intermingles selecting a product backlog item with acquiring confidence that the item can be added to the incrementally growing commitment. I also explained two different ways to determine a development team's capacity to complete work. In the next chapter I will discuss details of how sprints are executed once they have been planned.

Chapter 20

SPRINT EXECUTION

Sprint execution is the work the Scrum team performs to meet the sprint goal. In this chapter I focus on the principles and techniques that guide how the Scrum team plans, manages, performs, and communicates during sprint execution.

Overview

Sprint execution is like a mini project unto itself—all of the work necessary to deliver a potentially shippable product increment is performed.

Timing

Sprint execution accounts for the majority of time during a sprint. It begins after sprint planning and ends when the sprint review starts (see Figure 20.1).

On a two-week-long sprint, sprint execution might account for about eight out of the ten days.

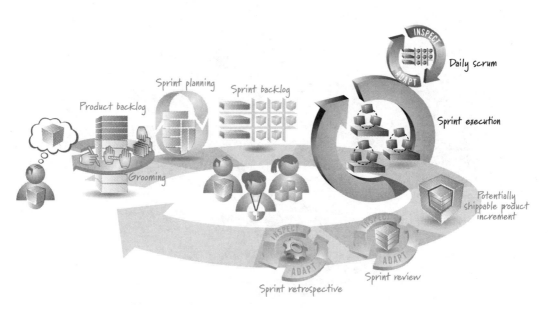

FIGURE 20.1   When sprint execution happens

Participants

During sprint execution the development team members self-organize and determine the best way to meet the goal established during sprint planning.

The ScrumMaster participates as the coach, facilitator, and impediment remover, doing whatever is possible to help the team be successful. The ScrumMaster doesn't assign work to the team or tell the team how to do the work. A self-organizing team figures these things out for itself.

The product owner must be available during sprint execution to answer clarifying questions, to review intermediate work and provide feedback to the team, to discuss adjustments to the sprint goal if conditions warrant, and to verify that the acceptance criteria of product backlog items have been met.

Process

Figure 20.2 illustrates the sprint execution activity.

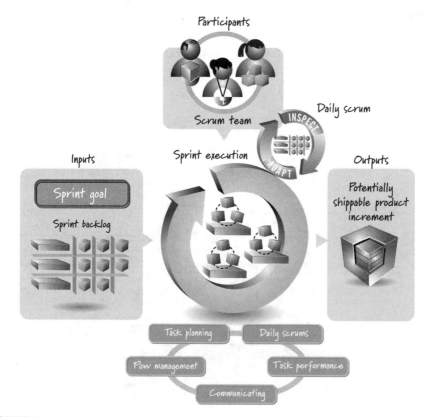

FIGURE 20.2   Sprint execution activity

The inputs to sprint execution are the sprint goal and the sprint backlog that were generated during sprint planning. The output from sprint execution is a potentially shippable product increment, which is a set of product backlog items completed to a high degree of confidence—where each item meets the Scrum team's agreed-upon definition of done (see Chapter 4). Sprint execution involves planning, managing, performing, and communicating the work necessary to create these working, tested features.

Sprint Execution Planning

During sprint planning the team produces a *plan* for how to achieve the sprint goal. Most teams create a sprint backlog, which typically lists product backlog items and their associated tasks and estimated effort-hours (see Figure 19.6). Although the team probably could create a full task-level sprint execution plan (the equivalent of a project plan for the sprint, perhaps in the format of a Gantt chart), the economics of doing so are hard to justify.

First, it's not clear that a team of five to nine people needs a Gantt chart to dictate who should do the work and when for the next short-duration sprint. Second, even if the team wanted to create a Gantt chart, it would be inaccurate soon after the team begins working. Sprint execution is where the rubber meets the road. A massive influx of learning comes from actually building and testing something. This learning will disrupt even the best-conceived early plan. As a result, the team wastes valuable time putting a plan together, only to waste even more time changing it to reflect the reality of sprint execution.

Of course, some up-front planning is helpful for exposing important task-level dependencies. For example, if we know that a feature we're creating during the sprint must be subjected to a special two-day-long stress test, it would be wise for the team to sequence the work so that this test starts at least two days before the end of sprint execution.

A good principle for sprint execution is to approach task-level planning opportunistically rather than trying to lay out up front a complete plan of how to do the work (Goldberg and Rubin 1995). Allow task planning to occur continuously during sprint execution as the team adapts to the evolving circumstances of the sprint.

Flow Management

It's the team's responsibility to manage the flow of work during sprint execution to meet the sprint goal. It must make decisions such as how much work the team should do in parallel, when work should begin on a specific item, how the task-level work should be organized, what work needs to be done, and who should do the work.

When answering these questions, teams should discard old behaviors, such as trying to keep everyone 100% busy (the consequences of which are described in Chapter 2), believing that work must be done sequentially, and having each person focus on just her part of the solution.

Parallel Work and Swarming

An important part of managing flow is determining how many product backlog items the team should work on in parallel to maximize the value delivered by the end of the sprint. Working on too many items at once contributes to team member multitasking, which in turn increases the time required to complete individual items and likely reduces their quality.

Figure 20.3 shows a simple example that I use in my training classes to illustrate the cost of multitasking.

The goal is to complete two identical tables by writing the letters *a* to *j*, the numbers 1 to 10, and Roman numerals i to x. One table is completed a row at a time, and the other is completed a column at a time. The row-at-time table represents multitasking (do the letter task, then do the number task, then do the Roman numeral task, and then repeat the sequence for the next letter, number, and Roman numeral). The column-at-a-time table represents single tasking.

The typical results shown in Figure 20.3 are that most people complete the column-at-a-time table in about half the time of the row-at-a-time table. Give it a try

Letters	Numbers	Roman numerals
a	1	i
b	2	ii
c	3	iii
d	4	iv
e	5	v
f	6	vi
g	7	vii
h	8	viii
i	9	ix
j	10	x

Row-at-a-time (multitasking)
Average time = 35 seconds

Letters	Numbers	Roman numerals
a	1	i
b	2	ii
c	3	iii
d	4	iv
e	5	v
f	6	vi
g	7	vii
h	8	viii
i	9	ix
j	10	x

Column-at-a-time (single tasking)
Average time = 16 seconds

FIGURE 20.3 Cost of multitasking

and time yourself, and you'll see! Also, if people make any errors, they make them when completing the row-at-a-time table. So, even for simple multitasking the overhead can be quite high. Imagine the waste involved when multitasking on complex project work.

Just as working on too many items at the same time is wasteful, working on too few items at a time is also wasteful. It leads to underutilization of team member skills and capacity, resulting in less work being completed and less value being delivered.

To find the proper balance, I recommend that teams work on the number of items that leverages, but does not overburden, the T-shaped skills (see Chapter 11) and available capacity (see Chapter 19) of the team members. The goal is to reduce the time required to complete individual items while maximizing the total value delivered during the sprint (typically the number of items completed during the sprint).

A term frequently used to describe this approach is **swarming**, where team members with available capacity gather to work on an item to finish what has already been started before moving ahead to start work on new items. Teams with a Musketeer attitude and some degree of T-shaped skills swarm. Teams that still think in terms of individual roles wind up with some members far ahead and others who are mired in unfinished work. A classic individual-role-focused thought is "The testers might still have 'their' work to finish up, but I'm finished coding this feature, so I'm off to start coding the next one." In a team that swarms, people would understand that it is typically better to stay focused and help get the testing done instead of running ahead to start working on new features.

Some people mistakenly believe that swarming is a strategy to ensure that team members are 100% busy. This is not the goal of swarming. If we wanted to ensure that people were 100% busy, we would just start working on all product backlog items at the same time! Why don't we do that? Because the extensive multitasking required to make that happen would ultimately slow the flow of completed items. Swarming, on the other hand, helps the team remain goal focused instead of task focused, which means it gets more things done, faster.

While swarming favors working on fewer items concurrently, it doesn't necessarily mean working on only one product backlog item at a time. One item at a time might be correct in a given context, but just saying that all team members should collectively focus on a single item at a time is potentially dangerous. A different number of items might be appropriate when we consider the actual work that needs to be done, the skills of the team members, and other conditions that exist at the time a decision to start or not start working on another item needs to be made.

Another dangerous approach would be to apply waterfall thinking at the sprint level and treat sprint execution like a mini waterfall project. Using this approach, we would start working on all product backlog items at the same time. First we would analyze all of the items to be worked on this sprint, then design them all, then code them all, and then, finally, test them all (see Figure 20.4).

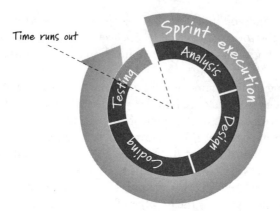

FIGURE 20.4 Mini waterfall during sprint execution—a bad idea

Although this approach may seem logical, it is very risky. What if the team runs out of time and doesn't finish all of the testing? Do we have a potentially shippable product increment? No; a reasonable definition of done would never allow untested features to be called done. By using a mini waterfall strategy, we could end up with 90% of each feature complete, but no feature 100% done. The product owner gets no economic value from partially done work.

Which Work to Start

Assuming that not all product backlog items are started simultaneously, at some point the team needs to determine which product backlog item to work on next.

The simplest way to select the next product backlog item is to choose the next-highest-priority item as specified by the product owner (via the item's position in the product backlog). This approach has the obvious advantage of ensuring that any items not completed during the sprint must be of lower priority than the ones that are completed.

Unfortunately, the simplest approach won't always work because technical dependencies or skills capacity constraints might dictate that items be selected in a different order. The development team needs the ability to opportunistically make this selection as it sees fit.

How to Organize Task Work

Once the development team decides to start working on a product backlog item, it must determine how to perform the task-level work on that item. If we apply waterfall thinking at the level of a single product backlog item, we would analyze the item, design it, code it, and then test it.

Believing there is a single, predetermined, logical ordering to the work (for example, you have to build it before you can do any testing) blinds the team to the opportunity to do things in a different and perhaps more efficient way. For example, I frequently hear new teams say something like "What will our testers be doing early in the sprint while they are waiting for features to be ready for testing?" Typically I respond by saying that for teams doing **test-first development**, where tests are written before the development is performed, the "testers" are the *first* to work on a feature (Crispin and Gregory 2009)!

Traditional role-based thinking plagues many teams. What we need instead is value-delivery-focused thinking, where the team members opportunistically organize the tasks and who will work on them. In doing so, they minimize the amount of time that work sits idle and reduce the size and frequency at which team members must "hand off" work to one another. This might mean, for example, that two people pair up on the first day of sprint execution and work in a highly interleaved fashion, with rapid cycles of test creation, code creation, test execution, and test and code refinement, and then repeat this cycle. This approach keeps work flowing (no blocked work), supports very fast feedback so that issues are identified and resolved quickly, and enables team members with T-shaped skills to swarm on an item to get it done.

What Work Needs to Be Done?

What task-level work does the team perform to complete a product backlog item? Ultimately the team decides. Product owners and managers must trust that the team members are responsible professionals who have a vested interest in doing great work. As such, they need to empower these individuals to do the necessary work to create innovative solutions in an economically sensible way.

Of course, product owners and managers do have influential input to what task-level work gets done. First, the product owner ensures that the scope of a feature and its acceptance criteria are defined (part of the definition of ready described in Chapter 6), both of which provide boundaries for the task-level work.

Product owners and managers also provide business-facing requirements for the definition of done. For example, if the business requires that the features developed in each sprint be released to the end customer at the conclusion of the sprint, that decision influences the task-level work the team will perform (there is more work involved with getting features live on production servers than there is in getting them built and tested).

Overall, the product owner must work with the team to ensure that technical decisions with important business consequences are made in an economically sensible way. Some of these decisions are embedded in the more technically oriented aspects of the definition of done. For example, the Scrum team may collectively decide that having automated regression tests (which have an economic cost and benefit) is important and in this way influence task-level work (to create and run automated tests).

Other decisions are feature specific. There is often a degree of flexibility regarding how much effort a team should exert on a feature. For example, enhancing or polishing a feature might be technically appealing but simply not worth the extra cost to the product owner at this time or ever. Conversely, cutting corners on a design or shortchanging where, how, or when we do testing also has economic consequences that must be considered (see the discussion of technical debt in Chapter 8). The team is expected to work with the product owner to discuss these trade-offs and make economically sensible choices.

Who Does the Work?

Who should work on each task? An obvious answer is the person best able to quickly and correctly get it done. What if that person is unavailable? Perhaps she is already working on another, more important task, or maybe she is out sick and the task needs to get done immediately.

There are a number of factors that can and should influence who will work on a task; it's the collective responsibility of the team members to consider those factors and make a good choice.

When team members have T-shaped skills, several people on the team have the ability to work on each task. When some skills overlap among team members, the team can swarm people to the tasks that are inhibiting the flow of a product backlog item through sprint execution, making the team more efficient.

Daily Scrum

The daily scrum is a critical, daily inspect-and-adapt activity to help the team achieve faster, more flexible flow toward the solution. As I discussed in Chapter 2, the daily scrum is a 15-minute, timeboxed activity that takes place once every 24 hours. The daily scrum serves as an inspection, synchronization, and daily adaptive planning activity that helps a self-organizing team do its job better.

The goal of the daily scrum is for people who are focused on meeting the sprint goal to get together and share the big picture of what is happening so that they can collectively understand how much to work on, which items to start working on, and how to best organize the work among the team members. The daily scrum also helps avoid waiting. If there is an issue that is blocking flow, the team would never have to wait more than a day to discuss it. Imagine if the team members got together only once a week—they would deny themselves the benefits of fast feedback (see Chapter 3). Overall the daily scrum is essential for flow management.

Task Performance—Technical Practices

Development team members are expected to be technically good at what they do. I'm not saying that you need a team of superstars to use Scrum. However, working in short, timeboxed iterations where there is an expectation of delivering potentially shippable product increments does exert pressure on teams to get the job done with good control over technical debt. If team members lack appropriate technical skills, they will likely fail to achieve the level of agility needed to deliver long-term, sustainable business value.

If you are using Scrum to develop software, team members need to be skilled in good technical practices for developing software. I'm not referring to esoteric skills but instead to skills that have been in use for decades and are essential to being successful with Scrum or arguably any software development approach—for example, continuous integration, automated testing, refactoring, test-driven development, and so on. Today the agile community refers to many of these technical practices as Extreme Programming (Beck and Andres 2004), but most are practices that predate that label (see Figure 20.5 for a subset of the Extreme Programming technical practices).

As an example, consider automated testing, which is necessary to support several of the practices in Figure 20.5. Development teams that don't focus on automating their tests will quickly start to slow down and take ever-increasing risks. At some point, it could take all of the sprint execution time just to manually rerun the regression tests for previously developed features. In such cases, the team might choose not

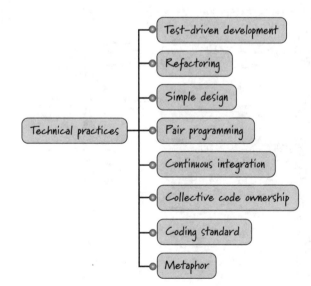

FIGURE 20.5   Subset of Extreme Programming technical practices

to rerun all of the manual tests each sprint, which could allow defects to propagate forward, adding to the system's technical debt (increased risk). You won't be agile for very long if you don't start automating your tests.

Similar arguments can be made for other core technical practices. Most teams achieve the long-term benefits of Scrum only if they also embrace strong technical practices when performing task-level work.

Communicating

One of the benefits of working in short timeboxes with small teams is that you don't need complex charts and reports to communicate progress! Although any highly visible way of communicating progress can be used, most teams use a combination of a task board and a burndown and/or burnup chart as their principal **information radiator**.

Task Board

The **task board** is a simple but powerful way to communicate sprint progress at a glance. Formally, the task board shows the evolving state of the sprint backlog over time (see Figure 20.6).

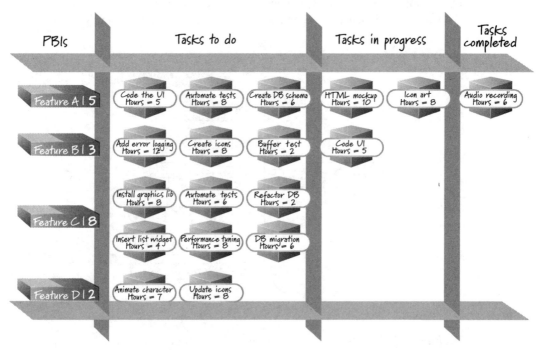

FIGURE 20.6   Example task board

On this task board each product backlog item planned to be worked on during the sprint is shown with the set of tasks necessary to get the item done. All tasks initially start off in the "to do" column. Once the team determines that it is appropriate to work on an item, team members start selecting tasks in the "to do" column for the item and move them into the "in progress" column to indicate that work on those tasks has begun. When a task is completed, it is moved to the "completed" column.

Of course, Figure 20.6 is just an example of how a task board might be structured. A team may choose to put other columns on its task board if it thinks that visualizing the flow of work through other states is helpful. In fact, an alternative agile approach called Kanban (Anderson 2010) uses just such a detailed board to visualize the flow of work through its various stages.

Sprint Burndown Chart

Each day during sprint execution team members update the estimate of how much effort remains for each uncompleted task. We could create a table to visualize this data. Table 20.1 shows an example of a 15-day sprint that initially has 30 tasks (not all of the days and tasks are shown in the table).

In Table 20.1 the number of hours remaining for each task follows the general trend of being smaller each day during the sprint—because tasks are being worked on and completed. If a task hasn't yet been started (it is still in the task board "to do" column), the size of the task might appear the same from day to day until the task is started. Of course, a task might turn out to be larger than expected, and if so, its size may actually increase day over day (see Table 20.1, task 4, days 4 and 5) or remain the same size even after the team has started working it (see Table 20.1 task 1, days 2 and 3)—either

TABLE 20.1 Sprint Backlog with Estimated Effort Remaining Each Day

Tasks	D1	D2	D3	D4	D5	D6	D7	D8	D9	...	D15
Task 1	8	4	4	2							
Task 2	12	8	16	14	9	6	2				
Task 3	5	5	3	3	1						
Task 4	7	7	7	5	10	6	3	1			
Task 5	3	3	3	3	3	3	3				
Task 6	14	14	14	14	14	14	14	8	4		
Task 7						8	6	4	2		
Tasks 8–30	151	139	143	134	118	99	89	101	84		0
Total	200	180	190	175	155	130	115	113	90		0

because no work took place on the task the previous day, or work did take place the previous day but the estimated effort remaining is the same.

New tasks related to the committed product backlog items can also be added to the sprint backlog at any time. For example, on day 6 in Table 20.1 the team discovered that task 7 was missing, so it added it. There is no reason to avoid adding a task to the sprint backlog. It represents real work that the team must do to complete a product backlog item that the team agreed to get done. Permitting unforeseen tasks to be added to the sprint backlog is not a loophole for introducing new work into the sprint. It simply acknowledges that during sprint planning we may not be able to fully define the complete set of tasks needed to design, build, integrate, and test the committed product backlog items. As our understanding of the work improves by doing it, we can and should adjust the sprint backlog.

If we plot the row labeled "Total" in Table 20.1, which is the sum of the remaining effort-hours across all uncompleted tasks on a given day, on a graph, we get another of the Scrum artifacts for communicating progress—the sprint burndown chart (see Figure 20.7).

In Chapter 18 I discussed release burndown charts, where the vertical axis numbers are either in story points or ideal days and the horizontal axis numbers are in sprints (see Figure 18.11). In sprint burndown charts the vertical axis numbers are the estimated effort-hours remaining, and the horizontal axis numbers are days within a sprint. Figure 20.7 shows that we have 200 estimated effort-hours remaining on the first day of the sprint and zero effort-hours remaining on day 15 (the last day of a three-week-long sprint). Each day we update this chart to show the total estimated effort remaining across all of the uncompleted tasks.

Like release burndown charts, sprint burndown charts are useful for tracking progress and can also be used as a leading indicator to predict when work will be

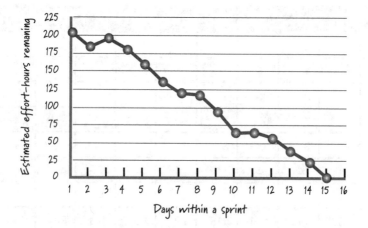

FIGURE 20.7   Sprint burndown chart

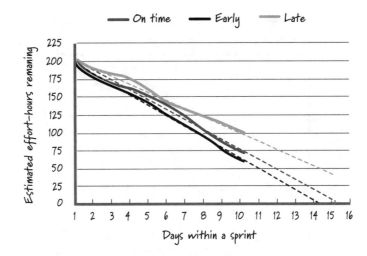

FIGURE 20.8   Sprint burndown chart with trend lines

completed. At any point in time we could compute a trend line based on historical data and use that trend line to see when we are likely to finish if the current pace and scope remain constant (see Figure 20.8).

In this figure, three different burndown lines are superimposed to illustrate distinct situations. When the trend line intersects the horizontal axis close to the end of the sprint duration, we can infer that we're in reasonable shape ("On time"). When it lands significantly to the left, we should probably take a look to see if we can safely take on additional work ("Early"). But when it lands significantly to the right ("Late"), that raises a flag that we're not proceeding at the expected pace or that we've taken on too much work (or both!). When that happens, we should dig deeper to see what's behind the data and what, if anything, needs to be done. By projecting the trend lines, we have another important set of data that adds to our knowledge of how we are managing flow within our sprint.

The sprint backlog and the sprint burndown charts always use estimated effort *remaining*. They do not capture actual effort expended. In Scrum there is no specific need to capture the *actuals*; however, your organization might choose to do so for non-Scrum reasons such as cost accounting or tax purposes.

Sprint Burnup Chart

Analogous to how a release burnup chart is an alternative way of visualizing progress through a release, a sprint burnup chart is an alternative way to visualize progress through a sprint. Both represent the amount of work completed toward achieving a goal, the release goal in one case and the sprint goal in the other.

Figure 20.9 shows an example sprint burnup chart.

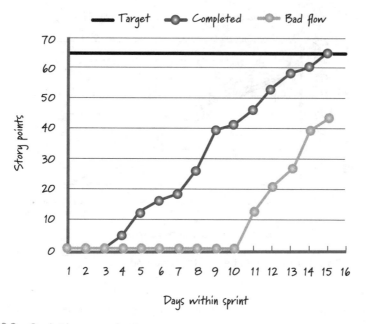

FIGURE 20.9   Sprint burnup chart

In sprint burnup charts the work can be represented in either effort-hours (as in the sprint burndown chart) or in story points (as shown in Figure 20.9). Many people prefer to use story points in their burnup charts, because at the end of the sprint the only thing that really matters to the Scrum team is business-valuable work that was completed during the sprint, and that is measured in story points (or ideal days), not task hours.

Also, if we measure story points of completed product backlog items, at a glance we can get a good feel for how the work is flowing and how the team is completing product backlog items through the sprint. To illustrate this point a third line (labeled "Bad flow") is included on the sprint burnup chart in Figure 20.9 (normally this line would not be on the chart; it is added in this example for comparison purposes). The "Bad flow" line illustrates what the burnup chart might look like if the team starts too many product backlog items at the same time, delays completion of items until later in the sprint, fails to meet the sprint target because of the reduced velocity of doing too much work in parallel, works on product backlog items that are large and therefore take a long time to finish, or takes other actions that result in bad flow.

Closing

In this chapter I discussed sprint execution, which accounts for the majority of the time during a sprint. I emphasized that sprint execution is not guided by a complete up-front plan that specifies what work will be done, when it will be done, and who will do it. Rather, sprint execution is performed opportunistically, leveraging the skills of the team, feedback from work already completed, and the evolving, unpredictable circumstances of the sprint. This doesn't mean that sprint execution is chaotic, but rather that it is guided by the application of good flow management principles, which determine how much work to do in parallel, which work to start, how to organize that work, who will do the work, and how much effort to invest in the work. In this context I discussed the value of the daily scrum meeting as an important activity in flow management. I also mentioned the importance of good technical practices in achieving high levels of agility. I concluded by discussing the various ways that the Scrum team can visually communicate sprint progress through the task board, sprint burndown chart, and sprint burnup chart. In the next chapter I will discuss the sprint review activity that naturally follows sprint execution.

Chapter 21

SPRINT REVIEW

Near the end of the sprint, the team conducts two important inspect-and-adapt activities: the sprint review and the sprint retrospective. The sprint review focuses on the product itself. The sprint retrospective, on the other hand, looks at the *process* the team is using to build the product.

In this chapter I describe the sprint review—its purpose, its participants, and the work required to make it happen. I conclude by addressing a few common sprint review issues.

Overview

During sprint planning we plan the work. During sprint execution we do the work. During sprint review we inspect (and adapt) the result of the work (the potentially shippable product increment). The sprint review occurs near the end of each sprint cycle, just after sprint execution and just before (or occasionally after) the sprint retrospective (see Figure 21.1).

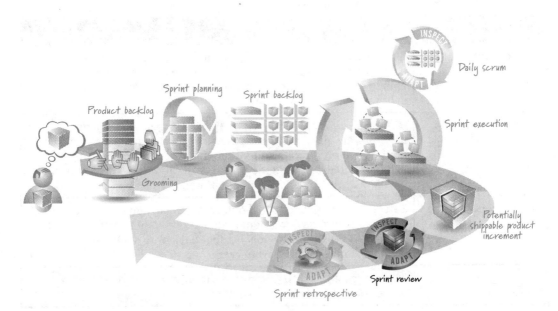

FIGURE 21.1   When the sprint review happens

The sprint review gives everyone with input to the product development effort an opportunity to inspect and adapt what has been built so far. The sprint review provides a transparent look at the current state of the product, including any inconvenient truths. It is the time to ask questions, make observations or suggestions, and have discussions about how to best move forward given current realities.

Because it helps ensure that the organization is creating a successful product, the sprint review is one of the most important learning loops in the Scrum framework. And, because sprints are short, this loop is a quick one, which allows for frequent course corrections to keep the product development moving in the right direction. If, instead, we were to defer this feedback until much later and assume that everything is going according to some baseline plan, we likely would get what many are accustomed to—surprise, disappointment, and frustration.

Participants

The sprint review provides an important opportunity for the Scrum team to get feedback from people who typically are not available on a daily basis during sprint execution. For these individuals, the sprint review is their first opportunity to see and discuss the work that was produced during the sprint. The sprint review, therefore, should be attended by all interested parties, who can come from a number of different sources, as summarized in Table 21.1.

TABLE 21.1   Sprint Review Attendee Sources

Source	Description
Scrum team	The product owner, ScrumMaster, and development team should all be present so that they can all hear the same feedback and be able to answer questions regarding the sprint and the product increment.
Internal stakeholders	Business owners, executives, and managers should see the progress firsthand so that they can suggest course corrections. For internal product development, internal users, subject matter experts, and the operations manager of the business function to which the product relates should attend.
Other internal teams	Sales, marketing, support, legal, compliance, and other Scrum and non-Scrum development teams might want to attend sprint reviews to provide area-specific feedback or to sync their own groups' work with the Scrum team.
External stakeholders	External customers, users, and partners can provide valuable feedback to the Scrum team and other attendees.

All Scrum team members (product owner, ScrumMaster, and development team) should be present at every sprint review so that they can describe what has been accomplished, answer questions, and enjoy the benefits of firsthand feedback.

Internal stakeholders, such as business-area owners (who may be paying for the system being built), executive management, and resource and other managers, should also attend. Their feedback is essential to ensuring that the team is progressing toward an economically sensible outcome. In addition, sprint reviews provide a convenient opportunity to learn the status of the product development effort. Also, for internal development efforts, the users will be internal to the organization; a representative sample of these users should attend along with subject matter experts who are an excellent source of feedback on what has been built.

Others in your organization might want to attend as well. Salespeople and marketing specialists frequently sit in. They can be an excellent source of feedback on whether the product is converging on a marketplace success. Other groups, such as support, legal, and compliance, might also come to sprint reviews to stay abreast of the team's progress, to provide timely input to the team, and to better gauge when to start their own related work.

Other internal development teams on related development efforts might send representatives so that they can ascertain where the product is headed and provide any relevant input on what they are doing and how it might impact the current development effort.

It's a good idea to at least periodically include external stakeholders, such as actual customers or users of what the team is building. With them in the room, the team can get direct feedback instead of indirect (or proxy) feedback via internal stakeholders. It may not make sense to have external stakeholders at every review, especially if we know that a particular review might involve some intense internal discussions that are best conducted with internal stakeholders only. If we do choose to include external stakeholders, unless there is just a single stakeholder, some consideration should be given to which of the potentially many customers or users we should invite. Common sense as well as sensitivity to the desires and personalities of specific people should be good guides on whom to invite.

Prework

Although the sprint review is an informal activity, the Scrum team has some minimal prework to complete (see Figure 21.2).

This prework includes determining whom to invite, scheduling the sprint review, confirming that the sprint work is done, preparing for the sprint review demonstration, and deciding who will lead the meeting and who will give the demo.

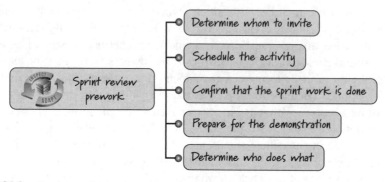

FIGURE 21.2   Sprint review prework

Determine Whom to Invite

The Scrum team first needs to determine who should attend the sprint review on a regular basis. The goal is to get the right set of people into the room to extract the highest possible value. Unless there is a good reason to not invite someone or some group, cast a broad net and let people vote with their feet—if they're interested, they'll walk to the room and attend the meeting.

Occasionally, the team might need to constrain attendance. For instance, the team might need to focus on a certain person or group whose input is essential to reviewing this sprint's work. Or the team might be building a feature for a specific client during this sprint and so cannot invite that client's competitors to the review meeting.

If you suspect these situations might arise, identify a core group that should be invited to every review and then issue a separate invitation to certain groups or clients on a sprint-by-sprint basis.

Schedule the Activity

The sprint review needs to be scheduled (when, where, and how long). Of the four required, recurring Scrum activities (sprint planning, daily scrum, sprint review, and sprint retrospective), the sprint review is the hardest to schedule because it includes many people who are outside of the Scrum team. The other three recurring activities involve only people on the Scrum team and therefore can be scheduled at its convenience alone.

To make scheduling easier, begin by determining when the key stakeholders (the core group I mentioned earlier) would prefer to hold the sprint review—say, Friday afternoons at 2:00 p.m.—and then schedule the rest of the sprint activities around this fixed time. If, as I discussed in Chapter 4, we use consistent-duration sprints (say, every two weeks), we can then schedule all, or at least most, of the sprint review meetings using a regular cadence (every second Friday at 2:00 p.m.). This has the dual benefit of reducing the administrative burden and costs while increasing attendance.

Sprint reviews vary in duration depending on several factors, including sprint length, team size, and whether multiple teams are participating in the same review. Typically, however, the sprint review does not exceed a four-hour timebox. Many teams have found the one-hour-per-sprint-week rule helpful. In other words, for a two-week sprint the review should take no more than two hours; for a four-week sprint it should take no more than four hours.

Confirm That the Sprint Work Is Done

At the sprint review, the team is allowed to present only completed work—work that meets the agreed-upon definition of done. (See Chapter 4 for more on this topic.) This implies, then, that sometime *before* the sprint review, someone has determined whether or not each backlog item is done; otherwise, how would the Scrum team know which items to present?

Ultimately it is the product owner's responsibility to determine if the work is done or not. As I mentioned in Chapter 9, the product owner should be performing just-in-time reviews of product backlog items as they become available during sprint execution. This way, by the time the sprint review happens, the team knows which items are complete.

Not everyone agrees that the product owner should review the work before the sprint review. Some practitioners contend that the product owner should review and formally accept the work only during the sprint review. They believe that if the product owner is allowed to review the work during the sprint, he might request changes that go beyond clarification—goal-altering changes that will disrupt sprint execution (see Chapter 4).

This is a potential risk, but the benefits of early product owner reviews (fast feedback) far outweigh any downside. Furthermore, if the product owner sees the team's work for the first time at the sprint review meeting, he has seen it too late. Here's why. The product owner must be available during sprint execution to answer questions and clarify product backlog items. While fulfilling these obligations, the product owner should also review the ongoing progress the team is making and provide critical, in-flight feedback that can be acted on in a timely, cost-effective manner. Deferring this feedback until the sprint review would create unnecessary work and likely frustrate the team ("Why didn't you mention that during the sprint, when we could have fixed it easily?"). It also could potentially irritate the stakeholders ("This feature would have been potentially shippable if you had just handled those things during the sprint!").

Beyond this, however, a product owner who rejects or questions work during the sprint review might not appear to be on the same page as the rest of the Scrum team. That disconnect could come across to the stakeholders as the old, adversarial, us-versus-them problem. The product owner and development team are on the same Scrum team and should come across as one unified team during the review meeting.

Prepare for the Demonstration

Beause all of the work the team presents at the sprint review is done (potentially shippable), it shouldn't take much preparatory work to demonstrate it. The goal is to provide transparency for inspecting and adapting the product, not to put on a glitzy Hollywood production or showcase to create excitement.

The sprint review is supposed to be an informal meeting with low ceremony and high value. Spending a lot of time to create a polished PowerPoint presentation hardly seems justified. Also, I would be concerned if I showed up at a sprint review to see working software and instead was given a PowerPoint presentation. I would be thinking, "Are these guys really done? Why won't they just show me what they created?"

Most teams have a rule of not spending more than 30 minutes to an hour per week of sprint duration to prepare for the sprint review. In addition, many also agree to show only those artifacts that were produced as a consequence of achieving the sprint goal.

Of course, there can be exceptions to the rule. I worked with an organization that developed systems under a U.S. Army contract. Most of the time, government employees (from the bureaucratic ranks) would attend the sprint reviews. Occasionally, however, the U.S. general in charge would be scheduled to attend a sprint review. In those cases, the team understandably invested a bit more time in prep and polish!

Determine Who Does What

Prior to the sprint review, the team needs to decide who on the Scrum team is going to facilitate the review and who will demonstrate the completed work. Typically the ScrumMaster facilitates, but the product owner might kick things off by welcoming members of the stakeholder community and providing a synopsis of the sprint results. As for demoing the completed work, I prefer that every member of the development team have an opportunity at some sprint review to go hands-on and demonstrate, rather than the same person always dominating the demo every sprint review. However, I try to not get too wrapped up in who is going to do these things. I let the Scrum team make that determination with a goal of maximizing the benefit of the review activity.

Approach

Figure 21.3 illustrates the sprint review activity.

The inputs to the sprint review are the sprint backlog and/or sprint goal and the potentially shippable product increment that the team actually produced.

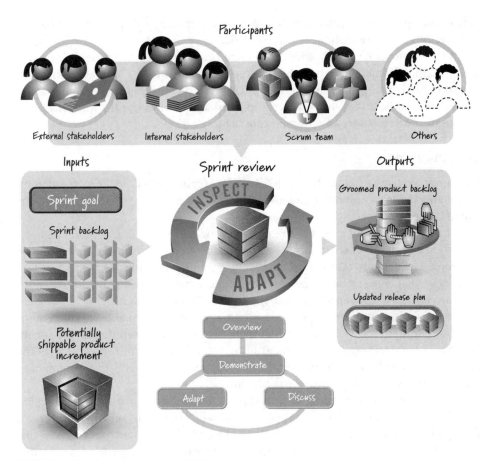

FIGURE 21.3   Sprint review activity

The outputs of the sprint review are a groomed product backlog and an updated release plan.

A common approach to conducting the sprint review includes providing a summary or synopsis of what has and has not been accomplished with regard to the sprint goal, demonstrating the potentially shippable product increment, discussing the current state of the product, and adapting the future product direction.

Summarize

The sprint review kicks off with a Scrum team member (frequently the product owner) presenting the sprint goal, the product backlog items associated with the sprint goal, and an overview of the product increment that was actually achieved during the sprint. This information provides a summary or synopsis of how the sprint results compare with the sprint goal.

If the results don't match, the Scrum team provides an explanation. It is important that the sprint review be a blame-free environment. If the goal wasn't met, everyone participating should refrain from trying to assess blame. The purpose of the review is to describe what was accomplished and then to use the information to determine the best course of action for moving forward.

Demonstrate

The sprint review is frequently mislabeled the "**sprint demo**" or just "the demo." Although a demonstration is quite helpful in the sprint review, the demo is not the aim of the sprint review.

The most important aspect of the sprint review is in-depth conversation and collaboration among the participants to enable productive adaptations to surface and be exploited. The demonstration of what actually got built is simply a very efficient way to energize that conversation around something concrete. Nothing provides focus to the conversation like being able to actually see how something works.

As determined in the prework, one or more Scrum team members will demonstrate all relevant aspects of the product increment that was built during the sprint. In certain organizations, such as game studios, it can be even more effective to let the stakeholders actually give themselves the demo, perhaps by playing the increment of the game that was developed during the sprint.

But what if there is nothing to demo? If the team didn't get anything done and there is truly nothing to show, the sprint review will likely focus on why nothing got done and how the future work will be affected by the lack of progress during this sprint. If, on the other hand, what was built can't easily be demoed, we have a different issue. Suppose, for instance, that the team did only architectural development work this sprint (built "glue code"). In that case, the development team might argue that demonstrating glue code doesn't make any sense or isn't practical. This statement, however, is almost never true. Here's why.

For the team to work exclusively on "glue code," it would have needed to convince the product owner to allow only technical product backlog items into the sprint. As I discussed in Chapter 5, if the product owner allows such items, he must understand the value of doing the work and also must know how to determine if the work is done. Also, most teams will include in their definition of ready that the Scrum team understands how to demonstrate the item at the sprint review.

At a minimum, the team must have some set of tests to demonstrate that the work is done to the satisfaction of the product owner. Those tests must have passed because the team can show only completed work at the sprint review. So, at the very least, the team can use those tests to demonstrate at the sprint review. Usually, though, if the team members give it some thought, they can do much better. The fact that something is hard to demo is not a valid excuse to exclude it from the demo.

Discuss

Demonstrating the product increment becomes the focal point for having an in-depth conversation. Observation, comments, and reasonable discussion regarding the product and direction are strongly encouraged among the participants. The sprint review, however, is not the place for deep problem solving; that type of work should be deferred to another meeting.

Vigorous discussion allows participants who aren't on the Scrum team to ask questions, understand the current state of the product, and help guide its direction. At the same time, the Scrum team members gain a deeper appreciation for the business and marketing side of their product by getting feedback on the convergence of the product toward delighted customers or users.

Adapt

Through demonstration and discussion, the team is able to ask and answer questions, including the following:

- Do the stakeholders like what they see?
- Do they want to see changes?
- Is what we're building still a good idea in the marketplace or to our internal customers?
- Are we missing an important feature?
- Are we overdeveloping/investing in a feature where we don't have to?

Asking and answering these questions provides input on how to adapt the product backlog and release plans.

I described in Chapter 6 how most teams naturally do some grooming as part of the sprint review. As everyone involved gains a better understanding of the current development effort and where it is going, new PBIs are often created or existing PBIs are reprioritized or deleted if they are no longer needed. This grooming might affect what the team will work on in the next sprint.

Also, as I described in Chapter 18, the grooming that happens during sprint review might also affect the larger-scope release plans. For example, based on the discussion and conclusions of the sprint review, we might decide to alter one of the key release-planning variables: scope, date, or budget. Perhaps, for instance, by reviewing the current product increment we decide to stop working on a major feature of the product (change the scope). This decision will necessarily affect the current release plan.

The sprint review gives us an opportunity to identify ways to adapt, to respond to change, when it is still affordable to do so—at the end of every single sprint.

Sprint Review Issues

Sprint reviews, however, are not without issues. Having worked with many organizations using Scrum, I have noticed several common sprint review issues, including those related to sign-offs, lack of attendance, and large projects.

Sign-offs

Sign-offs can be problematic in sprint reviews. The first question to ask is whether sprint reviews are the proper venue to sign off on (approve) product backlog items. As I mentioned previously, before the sprint review even begins, the product owner must review the work to determine if it is done (meets the agreed-upon definition of done). The sprint review, therefore, should not be a formal approval or sign-off event; instead, the product backlog items should have already been "approved" by the product owner before the sprint review starts.

Let's say, however, that during the sprint review a senior-level stakeholder disagrees—he believes the product backlog item is not done. While that feedback is valuable, I would still say that if the product owner declared the original work done, it is done. In Chapter 9 I discussed how the product owner has to be the empowered central point of product leadership. For this to be true, the product owner must be in a position to definitively approve or reject work and can't have that authority usurped by a sprint review participant—no matter how senior.

That doesn't mean that the product owner should ignore comments about a feature not meeting stakeholder expectations. When this occurs, the proper course of action is to schedule a change to the feature by creating a new product backlog item to reflect the desired behavior requested by the senior stakeholder and to insert that item into the product backlog to be worked on in a future sprint. The product owner should also investigate to determine why he disconnected from the stakeholders regarding this story and make adjustments to prevent future misunderstandings.

Sporadic Attendance

The sprint review needs to be viewed as a critical inspect-and-adapt activity, one that is worth people's time to attend. Still, some organizations suffer from sporadic attendance.

One of the more common causes of sporadic attendance is that stakeholders have so much on their plates that other "higher-priority" commitments prevent them from attending sprint reviews. This is a strong indicator of organizational dysfunction—having so much concurrent work that stakeholders can't meet all of their commitments. In such situations I recommend that organizations stop working on the lower-priority products until such time as they are important enough for stakeholders to attend sprint reviews. If that day never arrives, those low-priority products, relative to the other products in the portfolio, are simply never valuable enough to work on.

Sometimes sporadic attendance is the result of people not believing that the Scrum team can produce anything worth reviewing in a few weeks' time. This is especially true when the organization first starts using Scrum. Stakeholders are accustomed to much longer periods between reviews, and the reviews they have attended heretofore might have been disappointing.

The best way to address this issue is to actually build a business-valuable, potentially shippable product increment every sprint. When teams do this, most people realize that these frequent reviews are worth their time and allow them to give fast feedback that the Scrum team can actually use.

Large Development Efforts

If you have a larger development effort with multiple Scrum teams, it might make sense to consider doing a joint sprint review. This is simply a review that includes the work completed by multiple highly interrelated teams.

There are several benefits to this approach. First, the stakeholders have to attend only one sprint review instead of several. Second, if the work was supposed to be integrated, it would make sense for the review to focus on the integrated work, not a collection of stand-alone increments. To achieve this goal, all teams need to make sure their definitions of done include integration testing, as they probably should anyway.

The downside to holding a joint sprint review meeting with more than one team is that it will probably take a bit longer and might require a larger room than any one team would have needed.

Closing

In this chapter I emphasized the purpose of the sprint review as a critical feedback loop during Scrum development. The sprint review involves a diverse set of participants, whose goal is to inspect and adapt the current product. Although the sprint review is an informal activity, the Scrum team does do minimal preparation to ensure a healthy, productive outcome. During the sprint review the Scrum team provides a synopsis of what took place and what was accomplished during the sprint. It also provides a demonstration of the product increment produced during the sprint. A vigorous discussion among the participants takes place; questions, observations, and suggestions are highly encouraged. Based on this discussion, the product backlog will be groomed and the release plan updated.

In the next chapter I will focus on the inspect-and-adapt activity for the process, the sprint retrospective.

Chapter 22

SPRINT RETROSPECTIVE

Scrum provides two inspect-and-adapt opportunities at the end of each sprint: the sprint review and the sprint retrospective. In the previous chapter I discussed the sprint review, where the team and stakeholders inspect the product itself. Let's now turn our attention to the sprint retrospective, where the Scrum team examines the process used to build that product.

I begin with an overview of the purpose of and participants in the sprint retrospective. I then describe the prework and major activities associated with a sprint retrospective, the most important of which occur after the sprint retrospective when the participants actually follow through on the improvements they identify.

Overview

In the preface to his book *Project Retrospectives*, Norm Kerth, the founder of the modern-day movement on retrospectives, summarizes the purpose of retrospectives by quoting a passage from *Winnie the Pooh* (Kerth 2001):

> *Here is Edward Bear, coming downstairs now, bump, bump, bump, bump, on the back of his head, behind Christopher Robin. It is, as far as he knows, the only way of coming downstairs, but sometimes he feels that there is another way, if only he could stop bumping for a moment and think of it.*

Sprint retrospectives give the whole Scrum team an opportunity to stop bumping along for a moment and think (see Figure 22.1). Inside the timebox of the retrospective, teams are free to examine what's happening, analyze the way they work, identify ways to improve, and make plans to implement these improvements. Anything that affects how the team creates the product is open to scrutiny and discussion, including processes, practices, communication, environment, artifacts, tools, and so on.

The sprint retrospective is one of the most important and least appreciated practices in the Scrum framework. It is important because it gives teams the chance to customize Scrum to their unique circumstances. It is underappreciated because some people have a misguided view that it takes time away from doing "real" design, build, and test work.

The sprint retrospective is a crucial contributor to the continuous improvement that Scrum offers. And while some organizations might wait to do a retrospective until the end of a large development effort, Scrum teams hold retrospectives each and

FIGURE 22.1   Edward Bear illustrating the need for a retrospective

every sprint (see Figure 22.2), allowing teams to take advantage of insights and data before they are lost.

Because a Scrum team meets at the end of each sprint to inspect and adapt its Scrum process, it can apply early and incremental learning throughout the development process and thereby significantly affect the outcome of the project.

In the rest of this chapter I describe a detailed approach for performing sprint retrospectives. However, don't let the details mislead you into believing that a sprint retrospective is a heavyweight, ceremonial process. A sprint retrospective can be as simple as the Scrum team members coming together to discuss questions such as

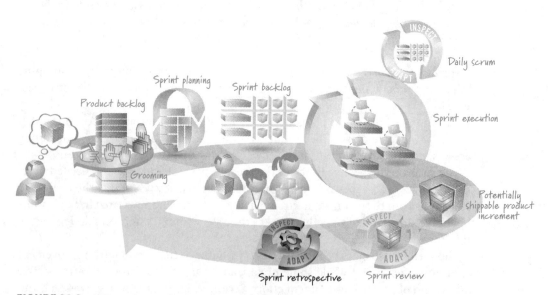

FIGURE 22.2   When the sprint retrospective happens

- What worked well this sprint that we want to continue doing?
- What didn't work well this sprint that we should stop doing?
- What should we start doing or improve?

Based on their discussions, team members determine a few actionable changes to make and then get on with the next sprint with an incrementally improved process.

Participants

Because the sprint retrospective is a time to reflect on the process, we need the full Scrum team to attend. This includes all members of the development team, the ScrumMaster, and the product owner. The development team includes everyone who is designing, building, and testing the product. Collectively, these team members have a rich and diverse set of perspectives that are essential for identifying process improvements from multiple points of view.

The ScrumMaster attends, both because she is an integral part of the process and also because she is the process authority for the Scrum team (see Chapter 10). Being an authority doesn't mean that the ScrumMaster should tell the team how to change its process. Instead, it means that she can point out where the team is not adhering to its own agreed-upon process and also be a valuable source of knowledge and ideas for the team.

Some argue that having the product owner at the retrospective might inhibit the team from being completely honest or revealing difficult issues. While this can be a risk in some organizations, the product owner is a critical part of the Scrum process and as such should be part of discussions about that process. If there is a lack of trust between the product owner and the development team, or there is a low level of safety so that speaking candidly isn't comfortable, perhaps the product owner should not attend until the ScrumMaster can help coach those involved toward creating a safer, more trusting environment.

Assuming trust and safety are reasonably in place, an effective product owner is critical to achieving the fast, flexible flow of business value and therefore should participate in the sprint retrospective. For example, the product owner is the channel or conduit through which requirements flow to the team. What if something is wrong with how requirements are flowing through the Scrum process? Perhaps PBIs are not well groomed by the start of sprint planning. In such cases it would be difficult for the Scrum team to brainstorm potential process improvements if the product owner were absent from the retrospective.

Stakeholders or managers who are not on a Scrum team, on the other hand, should attend a retrospective only if invited by the Scrum team. Although transparency is a core Scrum value, the reality is that many organizations have not yet achieved a level of safety to support non-Scrum team members regularly attending retrospectives. The team members must feel safe if they are to have an open and candid discussion without feeling inhibited by outsiders. If the team doesn't feel safe enough to reveal the real issues because outsiders are attending, the retrospective will lose its effectiveness.

Prework

Prior to the sprint retrospective there is some prework to complete (see Figure 22.3).

For short-duration sprints or for teams that are using a well-practiced, simple retrospective format, this prework should not require much, if any, time.

Define the Retrospective Focus

Each sprint retrospective should have a well-defined focus. The default focus is to review all relevant aspects of the process the Scrum team used during the current sprint. However, there are times when a team might select a different retrospective focus based on what is currently important to the team and where it is energetic about seeing improvement. For example:

- Focus on how to improve our skills with test-driven development (TDD).
- Focus on why we build what we think the customers want, but when they see it they frequently believe we misunderstood their desires or missed an important facet of the requirement.

Establishing and communicating the focus before the start of the retrospective allow the Scrum team to determine if any non-Scrum team members should be invited. In addition, knowing the focus before the start of the retrospective allows the team to select appropriate retrospective exercises and gives people time to gather and prepare any data needed to ensure a smooth performance of the retrospective.

Having the ability to define a specific focus can help long-lived, high-performance Scrum teams continue to extract measurable value from sprint retrospectives. For example, in one organization I coached there was a mature Scrum team whose

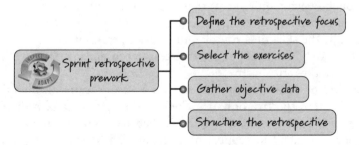

FIGURE 22.3   Sprint retrospective prework

members had been working well together for nearly three years. They had gone through many dozens of sprints together. They were starting to feel that doing a sprint retrospective focused on the just-completed sprint was often low value. One team member remarked, "For a long time the sprint retrospectives felt indispensable, and now they frequently just feel like process for the sake of process." What we ended up doing was performing shorter, more focused sprint retrospectives that allowed the team and invited outsiders to dig into very specific issues, going deep into root cause analysis. The result was that the team continued to learn and improve despite its considerable experience with Scrum. There is always room for growth; it just might require a more focused retrospective to uncover it.

Select the Exercises

Once we have established the focus and final participants for the upcoming retrospective, we can determine which exercises might help participants to engage, think, explore, and decide together. A typical retrospective includes the following exercises:

- Create and mine a sprint event timeline.
- Brainstorm insights.
- Group and vote on insights.

However, we might choose to vary these exercises to support a particular focus or set of participants. We might also decide to try new exercises to keep things fresh. See *Project Retrospectives* (Kerth 2001) and *Agile Retrospectives* (Derby and Larsen 2006) for additional exercises.

The participants don't have to decide exactly which exercises to use during pre-work. In fact, it might actually be better to select some exercises in a just-in-time fashion during the retrospective based on what the participants think would work best. At the same time, some exercises, especially those that require data or supplies, are best determined during the prework. Be prepared but stay flexible.

Gather Objective Data

Because a sprint retrospective is performed in a focused, short period of time (many teams establish a timebox), any legwork to collect needed data should be done before the retrospective begins.

We know both the focus and the exercise options for the upcoming retrospective, so we should have a good idea of what, if any, objective data should be gathered. Objective data is hard data (not opinions), such as what events happened and when, or counts of the number of PBIs that were started but not finished, or the feature burnup chart for the sprint illustrating the flow of completed work. At this point we are not organizing or analyzing any data; we are just collecting it so that it is available during the retrospective.

Structure the Retrospective

Like sprint reviews, retrospectives happen at the end of each sprint, often immediately following the sprint review, and generally should recur at the same place, day, and time each sprint. However, unlike for sprint reviews, you might occasionally need to vary the place, date, or time of a particular retrospective to better serve its focus, any non–Scrum team participants, or specific exercises you are planning to run. That's why I like to review the structure of the retrospective as part of the prework.

The exact length of the retrospective is influenced by factors such as how many people are on the team, how new the team is, whether any team members are located remotely, and so on. In my experience, teams new to Scrum have a tendency to budget too little time for their retrospectives. It's difficult to hold a meaningful sprint retrospective in less than 60 minutes. As a rule, I usually budget about 1.5 hours for the sprint retrospective when using two-week sprints, and proportionally more when using longer sprints.

The Scrum team should choose a sprint retrospective location that is most conducive to achieving a successful outcome. Some teams prefer to hold their retrospectives in the standard team area where their big visible charts are located. This gives them easy access to a wealth of relevant information. Others prefer to meet away from the standard team area, perhaps to introduce an environment with less emotional saturation where people might feel less inhibited and more likely to speak freely. Again, location doesn't matter nearly as much as the fact that you are meeting in a safe environment where team members feel free to speak their minds.

Although the ScrumMaster will often act as and can be quite effective as the facilitator for the sprint retrospective, any capable team member can fulfill the role of retrospective facilitator. There are also times when bringing in a skilled, neutral, outside facilitator might be the best solution to help team members either get started doing retrospectives or to assist them through a particularly difficult or sensitive retrospective where a closely aligned, internal facilitator may be far less successful. Alternatively, in organizations with multiple Scrum teams with different ScrumMasters, it is often helpful and enlightening to all involved to have the ScrumMaster of one Scrum team facilitate the retrospective of a different Scrum team. We should establish who is going to facilitate the retrospective during the prework.

Approach

Figure 22.4 illustrates the sprint retrospective activity.

Inputs to the sprint retrospective include the agreed-upon focus for the retrospective and any exercises and materials that the team might decide to use during the retrospective. In addition, most retrospectives require at least some precollected, objective data. And one piece of input every attendee will bring without fail is her

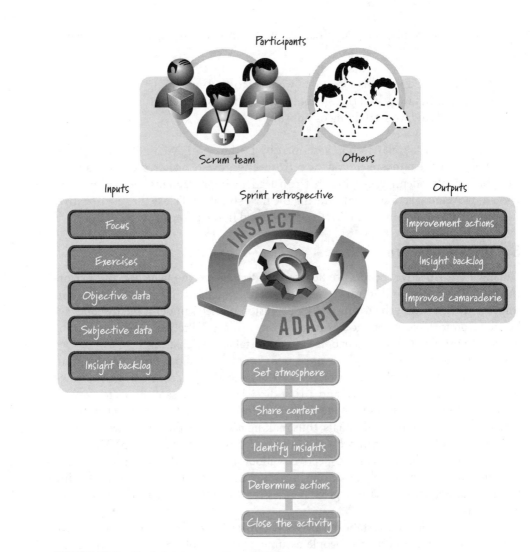

FIGURE 22.4   Sprint retrospective activity

own subjective data regarding the current sprint. Another retrospective input is a backlog of insights produced in previous retrospectives.

The outputs of the sprint retrospective include a set of concrete improvement actions that the team has agreed to perform in the next sprint. The outputs might also include a backlog of insights collected during the current retrospective that the team will not address in the upcoming sprint but might choose to address in the future. Team members should also expect improved camaraderie as an output from a retrospective.

While many retrospective approaches exist, most seek to answer the following questions:

- What worked well this sprint that we want to continue doing?
- What didn't work well this sprint that we should stop doing?
- What should we start doing or improve?

An approach (similar to one described by Derby and Larsen 2006) that I find useful is to set the atmosphere for the retrospective, create a shared context among the participants, identify insights that can lead to improvements, determine concrete improvement actions to take during the next sprint, and close the retrospective. These steps are shown in Figure 22.4 and explained in the paragraphs that follow.

Set the Atmosphere

During a retrospective, people are being asked to analyze the behavior and performance of their team and to make specific recommendations for how the team can improve itself. Putting the team (and by extension oneself) under a microscope can be an uncomfortable experience. So, a good way to start the retrospective is to establish an atmosphere that makes people feel comfortable participating.

People must feel it is safe to express their opinions without fear of retribution. Teams should have established ground rules, or a working agreement, which make it clear that expressing opinions and airing dirty laundry are safe things to do. It is helpful for the ground rules to make clear that the focus is on the organizational system and process, not the individuals, thus making it safe to explore what went wrong.

There will be times when problems are people problems; the retrospective is not the place to solve them. The retrospective is about improving the Scrum team's process, not about assigning blame or reprimanding individual behavior. When setting the atmosphere, ensure that the ground rules reinforce the concept of a blame-free environment.

It is also important to establish a precedent of active participation. We won't have a very effective retrospective if people assume a passive role. So, when setting the atmosphere, it's a good idea to get people talking just to prime the pump of participation. Some teams do something as simple as ask each participant to express in a few words her current feelings or energy level. It's not critical what question people are asked to answer, but that they are asked to say something to get in the mood of talking.

Share Context

A group of people can all experience the same event and yet interpret it quite differently. To successfully inspect the current sprint, it is important to get everyone on the same page so that they have a shared context.

To establish a shared context the participants must align their diverse individual perspectives (see the left side of Figure 22.5) into a shared team perspective (see the right side of Figure 22.5).

The left side of Figure 22.5 shows that each person might view the sprint differently based on her own experience during the sprint rather than have a more big-picture view of the sprint events, accomplishments, and shortcomings. If individual perspectives are allowed to dominate, the retrospective could degrade into a session of opinion debate rather than a session focused on actionable outcomes based on a shared context.

When establishing a shared context, therefore, it's imperative that you first ground the retrospective in an objective, big-picture view of the sprint. After getting everyone in a talking mood, share objective data, such as committed PBIs, PBIs completed, number of defects, and so on. (Exactly what specific objective data is relevant should be based on the retrospective focus.) While most of the objective data is typically gathered during the prework, some objective data can also be left for the participants to collect collaboratively during the retrospective. Doing this can help energize the team around the importance of that data. Whether done as part of the prework or as a group, gathering objective data is crucial for establishing a common foundation built on facts rather than opinions.

Just because we are grounded in objective data doesn't mean subjective data is irrelevant, however. Each person brings to the retrospective subjective data reflecting her interpretation of the sprint. If that subjective data is not exposed and discussed, participants might just assume that everyone else experienced the sprint in a similar

FIGURE 22.5 Aligning perspectives to create a shared context

way. This misalignment will make it difficult for people to understand one another's comments and suggestions.

There are a number of exercises that the participants can use to develop a shared context of both objective and subjective data. Two of the most common exercises are an event timeline and an emotions seismogram.

Event Timeline

Creating an **event timeline** is a simple yet powerful way to generate a shared artifact that visually represents the flow of events during a sprint. Events could include "Busted the build," or "Interrupted to fix production failure," or "Salina returned from holiday."

A common approach is to draw a timeline on a wall or whiteboard and have the participants put cards (or sticky notes) on the timeline representing meaningful events that occurred during the sprint (see Figure 22.6). Distributed teams could do the same exercise using an online-shared whiteboard.

The event cards are placed on the timeline in chronological order. This temporal view of events provides excellent visibility into the flow of activities during the sprint and also provides a context for quickly identifying missing or forgotten events.

To help visually categorize events, many teams use a variety of colored cards. Some do this to represent different event types (for example, green is a technical event, yellow is an organizational event, red is a personal event). Other teams use colors to represent feelings or energy levels (for example, green is a positive event, yellow is a neutral event, and pink or red is a negative event).

Emotions Seismogram

Many teams create an **emotions seismogram** as a complement to their event timeline. More commonly but mistakenly referred to as a seismograph, an emotions seismogram is a graphical representation of the emotional ups and downs of the participants over the course of the sprint (see Figure 22.7). Creating an emotions seismogram helps expand the shared context beyond the objective data (what happened) to include some subjective data (how the team felt about it).

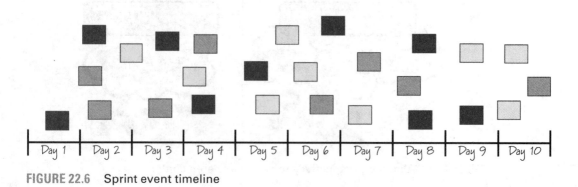

FIGURE 22.6   Sprint event timeline

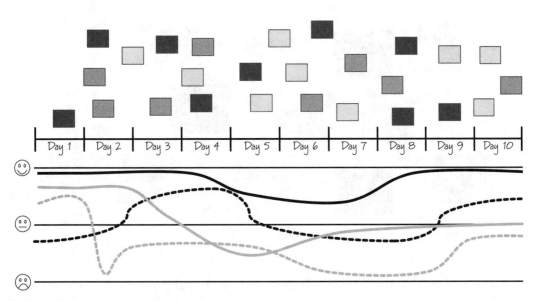

FIGURE 22.7   Emotions seismogram

To create the seismogram each participant is invited to draw a curve showing how she felt or what her energy level was like over the course of the sprint. It is frequently convenient to draw the seismogram directly under the event timeline so that the two sets of data can be visually correlated. Later, the participants can mine this data for interesting insights for process improvement.

Identify Insights

Once a shared context has been established, the participants can thoughtfully examine, understand, and interpret the data to identify process improvement insights. Doing this effectively requires a system-level (bigger-picture) focus. Focusing on just one aspect (having a more localized view) might cause teams to miss the bigger picture. A system-level focus also helps teams move past the superficial and identify the root causes of issues.

The participants should start by mining the shared context data. For example, they could look at their event timeline and emotions seismogram and ask the following questions to help uncover insights:

- What worked well?
- What didn't work well?
- Where are some opportunities to do things differently?

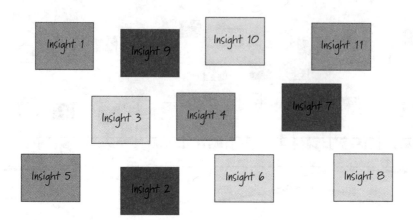

FIGURE 22.8   Retrospective insight card wall

Frequently participants are asked to brainstorm insights and then capture them on cards and place them on a shared wall or other surface so that everyone can see them (see Figure 22.8).

Another source for insights might be the team's **insight backlog**, a prioritized list of previously generated insights that have not yet been acted upon. If such a backlog exists, mine it to see which insights the participants would like to include and consider during the current retrospective. Any existing insights should be represented by cards and placed on the wall alongside the new insights.

Once the cards have been placed on the wall, the participants will need to organize them. To do this, many teams choose an exercise such as **silent grouping** to cluster the insights into meaningful groupings to indicate similar or duplicate cards (see Figure 22.9).

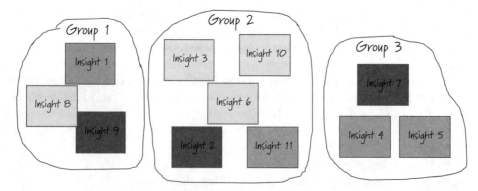

FIGURE 22.9   Insight cards clustered into similarity groups

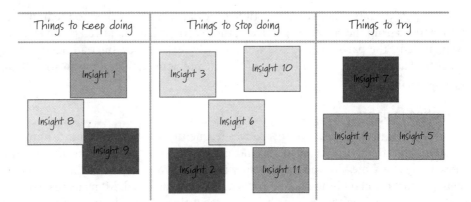

FIGURE 22.10   Insight cards placed into predetermined groups

During silent grouping, people collaboratively create the groupings without verbal discussion, relying only on the individual placement and movement of cards as a means of communicating and coordinating among the participants. Silent grouping is time efficient and effective.

Other teams prefer to divide the wall into category areas (such as things to keep doing, things to stop doing, things to try) before the retrospective begins. Then, as the insight cards are being created, the participants can place each card on the wall in the appropriate category (see Figure 22.10).

Even with preassigned categories, however, it is still effective and efficient to have the participants perform silent grouping to cluster similar cards within a category.

After creating a shared context and mining the data for insights, the participants should have identified many areas for improvement in their use of Scrum and, by extension, the way they work together to deliver value. Some of these insights might lead to deeper discussions among the participants to better understand underlying causes, or important patterns or relationships. When all the insights have been discussed and organized on the wall, it's time to determine what to do with all of the information.

Determine Actions

Insights are our ideas or perceptions of things that can be improved. To extract long-term value from these insights we need to move from discussing them to taking demonstrable actions to leverage them. For example, if the insight is "We're wasting too much time because the code management system keeps failing," the improvement action moving forward might be "Have Talya apply the vendor patches to the code management system to make it more stable." Talya, a member of the development team, can take this action in the next sprint.

The participants should also take time to review what happened to the improvement actions from the last retrospective. If those actions have not been completed (or even started), the participants need to know why before they start addressing new insights. They might choose to carry forward previous actions or prioritize them against the new insights they have just identified.

Selecting Insights

It is important to realize that retrospectives frequently identify many more improvement insights than the Scrum team and organization can digest and act on in a short period of time. So, the participants first need to determine which improvement insights to act on immediately and which can be deferred. Many teams have the participants prioritize the insights based on what they believe is most important or where they are most energetic about seeing improvement. Sometimes these two are not the same. We might agree that a particular improvement insight is important, but if there is no appetite to do the work required to leverage the insight, it might not be a good choice right now. If the participants are energetic about an insight, they are much more likely to take concrete actions to leverage it.

One popular way to prioritize insights is to use **dot voting**, as illustrated in Figure 22.11.

During dot voting, each participant is given a small number (perhaps three to five) colored dots. The participants then simultaneously place their dots on the improvement insight cards that they feel are the highest priorities to address. A person can put all of her dots on one card or spread them out over several cards. Once everyone has voted, the cards with the greatest number of votes should be considered first.

Exactly how many insights should the participants select to work on? Well, that depends on how much capacity the participants are able to dedicate to the insights and over what period of time.

Typically the period of time is the next sprint. So if the Scrum team is doing two-week sprints, it will likely consider insights that it can address over the next two-week

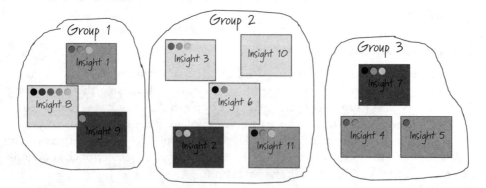

FIGURE 22.11   Example of dot voting

period. Even if an insight is too large to be fully addressed in the next sprint, the participants might choose to start working on it and make demonstrable progress against it.

The participants must also determine how much capacity they can dedicate to addressing insights during the next sprint (or whatever time period they are considering). If the team plans to dedicate time in the next sprint to actions from the previous retrospective, it will clearly affect the team's capacity for new actions identified in this retrospective.

Spending time working on insights, old and new, leaves less time for working on features. So, how much time should the team allocate today to address insights that can provide a larger payoff later? Answering that question really requires input from the product owner, which is one of the reasons it is important to have the product owner present at the retrospective. If the Scrum team doesn't specifically allocate time to work on improvement insights, a likely outcome is that insights won't get worked on.

Once we know the available capacity to work on insights, the participants can get a rough idea of which of the high-priority insights can be immediately addressed. However, the final decision can really be made only once the specific actions are determined.

Decide on Actions

At this point we have prioritized our insights and have some idea of the capacity we have to work on them. However, we get no measurable value from the retrospective until we define concrete, actionable steps to leverage our insights and improve the Scrum process.

Most actions will take the form of specific tasks that one or more Scrum team members will perform during the upcoming sprint. For example, if the insight is "It takes too long to determine when the code build breaks," the action might be "Have the build server send an email when the build is broken." This action requires task-level work on the part of one or more development team members. The team should determine who can do this work and how much time the work will take. Only then can the team be sure that working on a particular insight is doable within the available capacity.

Not all insights require specific task-level work. For example, an insight like "Be respectful to one another and show up to the daily scrum on time" should require little (if any) task-level work by the team. While there is a real action, "People should actually make the effort to show up on time," it will not reduce the team's capacity.

Sometimes the actions represent impediments that the ScrumMaster might own but someone else in the organization has to resolve. For example, the insight might be "We can't get PBIs done because we need the latest version of a third-party vendor's software to test against." The action might be "Nina will work with our procurement department to obtain the latest vendor update." So Nina, the ScrumMaster, will work with the procurement people to address the third-party vendor issue that is impeding the team from getting PBIs done. This action will start in the next sprint, will need some capacity from the ScrumMaster, and may require several sprints to be resolved.

When determining the proper actions, we need to remember that it might not be possible to immediately address the insight. Instead, we might need to *explore* the insight before we can actually make an improvement. In such cases the proper action might be to investigate and collect data during the next sprint so that we can better understand the problem.

For example, the insight might be "We're puzzled by why two components that are fully tested and have their own automated test suites fail when they are combined into a cross-component automated test suite where each component is still individually executed." At this point there isn't a specific action the Scrum team members can take to address this insight because they really don't understand what is going wrong. However, the team can create an action for specific team members to explore this issue in the next sprint, and the team can determine how much capacity to allocate for exploration.

Insight Backlog

As I mentioned earlier, many teams create an *insight backlog* (sometimes called an *improvement backlog*) to hold any issues that are identified during a retrospective but cannot be worked on immediately. The idea is that at the next sprint retrospective the participants can choose to use the insights in the backlog as candidates to be prioritized against new insights when determining where to focus time in the next sprint. Of course, the insight backlog should be groomed periodically to ensure that its contents remain valuable insights.

Other teams simply discard any insights that they choose not to work on in the next sprint. The thinking is that if an insight is truly important, it will be identified again at the next retrospective.

Close the Retrospective

Once the final improvement actions have been determined, the participants close out the retrospective. Many close by recapping what actions the team has decided to take based on what the participants learned. This might be as simple as describing each committed action item and who is going to work on it.

Closing is also a good time to appreciate people and their participation. Each participant should say a few kind words of appreciation regarding the contributions made by others. Be sure to also recognize any non–Scrum team members who took time out of their busy schedules to participate in the retrospective.

Finally, it's a good idea to spend a few minutes asking the team for suggestions to improve the team's approach to performing a retrospective. A retrospective is, after all, part of the Scrum framework and as such should also be subject to inspection and adaptation.

Follow Through

To ensure that what happens in the sprint retrospective does *not* just stay in the sprint retrospective, the participants should follow up on the actions they chose to complete. Some actions (such as that everyone shows up on time for daily meetings) need only to be reiterated and reinforced by the team members and the ScrumMaster. Others will need to be addressed during the forthcoming sprint-planning activity.

Frequently the easiest way to handle the improvement actions is to populate the sprint backlog with tasks corresponding to each action prior to bringing in new features. The team's available capacity to work on new features would then be adjusted downward by the estimated time these improvement tasks will take. Honestly, any approach that allows the team to make a good commitment at sprint planning while at the same time affording it the opportunity to work on the improvement actions is a good approach.

One approach that does *not* work is to have an "improvement plan" for the team that is separate from the work it will do each sprint. This two-pronged approach will almost always lead to the improvement plan being subordinate to the typical feature-driven sprint plan. To ensure that the improvement actions do take place, don't separate; integrate!

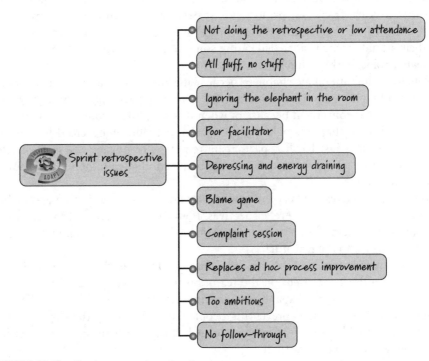

FIGURE 22.12   Sprint retrospective issues

Actions that do not require team member time will likely find a home on the ScrumMaster's impediment list. And actions that are destined for other teams or the organization as a whole can be placed into the appropriate backlog for the people who are expected to do the work; the ScrumMaster typically follows up with the external parties to help ensure that these actions actually get done.

Sprint Retrospective Issues

Sprint retrospectives are not without issues. Having worked with many organizations using Scrum, I have noticed a number of common issues (see Figure 22.12).

An unfortunate issue is when teams simply don't do the sprint retrospective, or when they do, attendance is low. The reasons for both tend to be similar. If people are assigned to multiple teams, scheduling conflicts could prevent them from attending. This is an organizational dysfunction that managers need to address. Or perhaps team members are just bored or disengaged, or they have not really bought into using Scrum. Others might think that doing anything other than their particular work isn't worth their time (for example, they believe that anything other than coding or testing is just wasteful). Often these issues stem from naiveté regarding Scrum and its focus on continuous improvement. Other times it's just the opposite—team members believe they have reached the pinnacle of Scrum usage and therefore have nothing further to learn from the sprint they just performed, from their teammates, or from their own success or failure. If people don't see the value of doing a retrospective or of their attendance, consider dedicating some of or the entire next retrospective meeting to exploring this value issue.

Sometimes low attendance happens because it is inconvenient for remote participants to join by phone or video conferencing. If remote participants find attending the retrospective inconvenient because of when it is scheduled, consider changing or rotating the time so that no single location is always inconvenienced. If it is inconvenient because it is just hard to participate remotely, reconsider the current telecom infrastructure and how the exercises are being conducted to better incorporate remote participants.

Some retrospectives are very busy but really don't achieve anything actionable. I call these the *all fluff, no stuff* retrospectives. If all we get is fluff, we're wasting our time. Consider bringing in an outside, experienced retrospective facilitator to help the participants get to the real stuff.

Other retrospectives are fascinating to observe. There is clearly a critical issue that is having a dramatic effect on the team, but nobody will even bring it up. To reuse the old adage, the participants are ignoring the elephant in the room. There is probably a safety issue that is preventing people from discussing the elephant. The ScrumMaster should take a leadership role in helping the team and organization address the safety impediment first.

Other times the retrospective is just poorly facilitated. The facilitator, perhaps a new ScrumMaster, is trying her best but it's clearly not working. Perhaps an outside facilitator should be used for a few retrospectives.

Some retrospectives are downright depressing and energy draining. Perhaps the sprints are not going well and people view the retrospective as an activity that just compounds the misery by making them relive it. Consider spending a bit more time to set the appropriate atmosphere at the start of the retrospective. Also, an outside facilitator might be more effective at helping people stay focused on positive improvements.

Frequently retrospectives are depressing because people start playing the blame game and finger-pointing. The facilitator must extinguish this behavior as soon as it occurs to prevent a cascade of finger-pointing.

Other times a retrospective can degrade into a complaint session. Perhaps some people view it as therapeutic to just come and complain about the way things are (or at least how they perceive things to be). They have no desire to improve, just the desire to complain. Consider inviting people to the retrospective who can actually effect real change. Then have a face-to-face dialogue with them instead of complaining in their absence.

Another unfortunate situation is where participants consider the retrospective to be *the* time to do process improvement, thereby diminishing ad hoc process improvement during the sprints. A retrospective is a great time for the team to reflect on a period of work and discuss how to make things better, but it was never intended to be the replacement for ad hoc process improvement. The ScrumMaster should proactively promote healthy ad hoc process improvements throughout the sprint.

Sometimes our desires are bigger than our abilities. New teams that are energized and focused on really getting better can frequently become overly ambitious and set improvement goals that are totally unrealistic. Doing so will only lead to a big letdown when the team fails to meet its ambitious goals. The ScrumMaster should be vigilant and remind the participants of their available capacity to do improvements and help them moderate their ambitions.

Perhaps the biggest issue of them all is when there is no follow-through to actually work on the improvement actions identified during the retrospective. If we're not going to follow through, there's no need to waste our time on retrospectives. The ScrumMaster has a leadership role in helping the team constantly improve its process. If there is no follow-through, the ScrumMaster needs to be aggressive about working with the team to identify the root cause and helping team members address the impediment.

Closing

Sprint retrospectives are a time for the team to reflect on how well it is using Scrum and to propose improvements. The retrospective is a collaborative activity among the Scrum team members (and any non–Scrum team members on an as-needed basis).

Once the retrospective prework is completed, the basic flow of the retrospective is to set the atmosphere to have a successful retrospective, get everyone on the same page by creating a shared context grounded in data, identify improvement insights, determine improvement actions, and then close the retrospective. After closing the retrospective, it is critical that the participants follow up and carry out the improvement actions so that the team is more effective during the next sprint. It is also important to keep a watchful eye out for issues that might prevent the retrospective from being successful and to quickly act on them.

Chapter 23

THE PATH FORWARD

In the first 22 chapters of this book, I have laid out the Scrum framework and explained what I believe to be essential Scrum. You should now understand the mechanics of using Scrum to deliver innovative solutions. You should also have a good sense of why Scrum prescribes particular roles, practices, artifacts, and rules. Now you are ready to define your path forward. In this chapter I discuss the idea that there is no universal, final target for your Scrum implementation; instead, you need to define your own unique route towards agility. I end by describing the role of best practices and how to use Scrum, with its iterative and incremental approach, as the basis for discovering your own path forward.

There Is No End State

Every organization has a vision for what it wants to achieve. Using Scrum can help organizations manage the work to achieve that vision. Being highly proficient with Scrum and thus being more agile, however, is not the end goal, but rather a means of more effectively and economically achieving business goals. So, how do you know when you're done with Scrum?

The thing is, there is no definition of done for a Scrum adoption or transition effort. There is no agile maturity model like CMMI (SEI 2010), where the goal is to try to reach level 5. Trying to define "done" for your Scrum implementation presumes that when you achieve that state, you can't get any better. This flies in the face of Scrum being a form of continuous improvement, where you are always working to better align your use of Scrum to the complex world in which you must develop products.

Worse yet, if we tried to define such an end state for the industry, it would further assume that the final target state would apply to every organization, even those that develop radically different types of products under very different circumstances.

To say, "I have finally achieved agility!" is a meaningless comment. As Mike Cohn nicely summarized, "Agile is not something you become, it's something you become more of" (Cohn 2010). There is no end state that you can call agile or Scrum. Instead, becoming more proficient with Scrum and more agile is a process of continuous, never-ending improvement aimed at improving your bottom line.

Discover Your Own Path

Just as no one can tell you where your Scrum implementation should end, no one can lead you down a predefined path that will guarantee success. Instead, you must learn, inspect, and adapt your way forward based on your organization's own unique goals and culture and the ever-changing complex environment in which you must operate. Trying to follow someone else's path and leveraging their learning might feel like the fast track to becoming agile. However, no two organizations, or even teams within an organization, are the same. Following someone else's path might well lead you to precisely the wrong location.

You can't circumvent your own learning process. Instead, you need to quickly close your own learning loops and inspect and adapt based on what you learn. I'm not suggesting that you ignore those who have preceded you down the agile path. Examine what they have done and how it worked for them, but discover your own path for becoming more agile.

Sharing Best Practices

If we aren't supposed to follow others' paths, how do best practices fit into the picture? Just as there is no one path to follow, there is no one set of best practices across all organizations.

When I'm asked to describe "best practices" that other organizations are using to become more agile, I give examples. However, I always provide the relevant context of the other organizations so that the people who are asking can evaluate whether it would be sensible to adopt a similar approach in their organization. Even when scaling up within a single organization, we need to be cautious about universally applying best practices. Many organizations try to describe what a successful Scrum team is doing, capture it, and then institutionalize it as a best practice. Doing so can be harmful, because these are individual team approaches that may not work for other teams.

You might notice I just used the word *approach* several times when referring to best *practices*. Let's talk for a moment about that distinction. Throughout this book I have used the term *practice* to mean a core or essential aspect of Scrum. An approach is a particular implementation of a Scrum practice. When people ask me about best *practices*, I take that to mean best *approaches*.

While two different teams or organizations have unique Scrum implementations, each should adhere to the same Scrum practices. Both, for example, should have Scrum teams made up of a product owner, ScrumMaster, and development team. Both should perform sprint planning, daily scrums, sprint reviews, and sprint retrospectives. However, I expect that each team (or organization) will have its own unique approaches to performing these practices. Let me illustrate by example.

The daily scrum is a core Scrum practice. If you don't do it, you aren't doing Scrum. During the daily scrum each team member updates and synchronizes with all other team members to get a shared picture of the full scope of work. But when the daily scrum starts, which person should provide his update first? Scrum doesn't define this. Each team will have its own approach.

For example, while working with a team in Vancouver, Canada, I learned of an interesting approach to deciding who speaks first. On this team, at the start of each daily scrum, the ScrumMaster would toss a toy stuffed moose into the air. Whoever caught the moose would speak first, and then the rest of the team members would speak in turn, moving to the left of the person who caught the moose. This simple, kind-of-silly-but-fun approach worked very well for the team in Vancouver.

As it turns out, the Vancouver team had a sister team in China that was formed some months after the Vancouver team had been established. A member of the China team asked the Vancouver team for a "policy or best practice" for determining who should speak first at the daily scrum. The Vancouver team told the person in China that in Vancouver they "tossed the moose" each daily scrum to figure that out. Apparently, tossing the moose took on a whole different meaning when translated into Chinese! An approach that worked well for the Vancouver team would not work at all for the China team. The China team adopted its own approach, as well it should.

Scrum defines core practices that must be followed. It is left to each team, however, to determine the approaches (or best practices) that work best. Approaches, therefore, are unique to each team, and they can and should be reused by other teams only if they make sense in the context of those other teams.

Using Scrum to Discover the Path Forward

Whether you are new to Scrum or are already using Scrum to develop products, you can use the principles of Scrum to help guide you on the path forward. Mike Cohn, in *Succeeding with Agile* (Cohn 2009), goes into great detail describing this approach, and I refer you to his excellent book for a detailed treatment of the topic.

I describe the essence of this approach with an example. In 2007 I was retained to train and coach a large, multinational organization on its adoption and use of Scrum. The organization had 100 IT members in New York City and 400 IT members in Mumbai, India. At any one time the IT organization had about 45 development efforts in flight.

The organization decided that any new team that was going to use Scrum should have a coach available to help it. With limited initial coaching capacity, it was unreasonable to transition the entire IT organization over to Scrum at once. So, as is typical in such environments, the organization selected a small number of pilot efforts to focus on first. The goal was to incrementally move other teams over to Scrum as the organization's Scrum coaching capacity increased via the on-the-job training of internal coaches.

These pilot efforts crossed the spectrum from simple systems maintenance to larger, new-product development. Based on this diversity, each Scrum team implemented its own version of the Scrum framework, using approaches aligned with the people on the team and the work they had to perform. A wiki was used to "syndicate" the approaches used by each team to assist with overall organizational learning and share what was working for other teams.

Several months into the adoption, it was time to scale the use of Scrum from the team level to the organizational level. At that point we created what Cohn calls an ETC or Enterprise Transition Community (Cohn 2009). In our case the ETC was called the Working Software Group. That group of managers and executives maintained a backlog of improvement-related items and ran three-week sprints against that backlog. The items in that backlog represented organizational change initiatives (such as "Update the compensation model to be more team focused") or significant impediments that were blocking one or more Scrum teams ("Improve server stability so that teams can complete their testing").

By working in sprints against this improvement backlog, the organization was able to iteratively and incrementally make progress down its own path to successfully adopting Scrum. There was no predetermined end state for the organization's use of Scrum. Trying to create one up front would have been as wasteful as trying to create a full, complete requirements specification for a totally new, never-been-built product that no one understood well.

Instead, the Working Software Group took input from the Scrum teams and stakeholders and made incremental improvements to the organizational structure to better align itself with agile values. Through continuous learning, inspecting, and adapting, the organization determined an appropriate path forward that was aligned with the overall organizational business goals.

This ETC-type pattern is quite common today. Many organizations realize that using Scrum to adopt Scrum is a sensible approach to iteratively and incrementally becoming more agile.

Get Going!

I am frequently amused when the same people who believe that it is not possible to get the requirements for a product correct up front, and therefore want to use Scrum for development, will in the next breath explain how they aren't quite ready to start using Scrum because they haven't worked out all of the details of their Scrum approach! This type of thinking is poorly aligned with fundamental Scrum principles.

When employing Scrum, you shouldn't worry about getting things perfect up front. You can't! And trying to be perfect up front will force you to guess at the expense of important learning that you will get only by applying Scrum and seeing what happens. In my experience, most teams' first couple of sprints aren't all that pretty. That's OK. My only expectation of any Scrum team is that it be better in the next sprint than it was in the previous sprint. So, don't delay getting started. Whatever you think you know now about your use of Scrum, imagine how much more you will really know after you start and finish the next sprint!

Also, don't expect your Scrum adoption to be problem free. I can guarantee that at some point your organization will encounter impediments that make performing Scrum difficult. Scrum makes visible the dysfunctions and waste that prevent organizations from reaching their true potential. What it does not do is tell organizations how to solve those issues. That hard work is up to the people in the organization.

The status quo is a powerful force. It is frequently easier for people to ignore Scrum or change Scrum than it is to change long-held organizational processes, rules, or behaviors. And a culture that is outright hostile toward being shown its dysfunctions will quickly extinguish the bright light that is exposing what lurks in the shadows. To counteract this tendency, be a steadfast and patient force for change in your organization. Understand that resistance to change is natural. Help overcome the worst of it by educating others about the principles that underlie Scrum and the goals you are trying to achieve. Work with them, rather than against them, to chip away at the obstacles that prevent your team, your product development effort, and your organization from realizing the full benefits of your Scrum implementation.

My hope is that this book has provided you with the essential Scrum knowledge to shine a bright light that will illuminate your path forward. I wish you the best of success on your journey with Scrum.

GLOSSARY

Overview

Entries in this glossary are arranged alphabetically. An entry may be a single word, such as *Scrum*, a phrase, such as *acceptance criteria*, or an acronym, such as *TDD*. If a term has more than one definition, the definitions are numbered.

The following cross-references are used to show a term's relationship to other terms in the glossary:

- *See* refers to a preferred term or to a term whose definition serves to define the term in question.
- *See also* refers to a related term.
- *Synonymous with* refers to a synonym or term with a nearly identical meaning.
- *Contrast with* refers to a term with a substantially different meaning.

Definitions

A

acceptance criteria. 1. The external quality characteristics specified by the product owner from a business or stakeholder perspective. Acceptance criteria define desired behavior and are used to determine whether a product backlog item has been successfully developed. 2. The exit criteria that a component or a system must satisfy in order to be accepted by a user, customer, or other authorized entity (IEEE 610).

acceptance test. 1. The testing carried out to verify that the acceptance criteria have been met. 2. A test that defines the business value each product backlog item must deliver. It may verify functional requirements or nonfunctional requirements such as performance or reliability. It is used to help guide development (Crispin and Gregory 2009). 3. Formal testing with respect to user needs, requirements, and business processes conducted to determine whether or not a system satisfies the acceptance criteria and to enable the user, customers, or other authorized entity to determine whether or not to accept the system (IEEE 610).

acceptance-test-driven development (ATTD). A technique in which the participants collaboratively discuss acceptance criteria, using examples, and then distill them into a set of concrete acceptance tests before development begins. Synonymous with *specification by example.*

accuracy. How close an estimate is to the actual value—the proximity of the measure to its true value. For example, estimating that the product will ship in October 2015 is accurate if the product ships any day during October 2015. Contrast with *precision.*

activity. 1. A Scrum practice that involves taking action or performing a process, for example, sprint-planning activity, daily scrum activity, sprint review activity, and sprint retrospective activity. 2. In a general sense, the work performed by the Scrum team members such as writing code, performing tests, creating estimates, and so on. See also *practice.*

adaptation. One of the three pillars of empirical process control; feedback is used to make an adjustment to the work product being developed or the process by which it is being developed. See also *empirical process control, inspection, transparency.*

agile. 1. A specific set of values and principles, as expressed in the Agile Manifesto (Beck et al. 2001). 2. An umbrella term used for a group of related approaches to software development based on iterative and incremental development. Scrum is an agile approach to development. See also *Extreme Programming, Kanban, Scrum.*

all-at-once product development. Doing all types of work (for example, analysis, design, coding, integrating, and testing) opportunistically within a single iteration.

all-before-any. A characteristic of a sequential development process, where the work product from a previous step in a process is transferred to the next step using a batch size of 100%. See also *batch size.*

anticipatory process. See *plan-driven process.*

approach. A specific way to realize a practice or activity. For example, Scrum specifies a sprint retrospective. How a team chooses to perform a sprint retrospective is its approach, which may be different from the approaches of other teams. See also *activity, practice.*

artifact. A tangible by-product produced during product development. The product backlog, sprint backlog, and potentially shippable product increment are examples of Scrum artifacts. See also *practice.*

assumption. A guess, or belief, that is presumed to be true, real, or certain even though there is no validated learning to know that it is true. Contrast with *validated learning.*

ATTD. See *acceptance-test-driven development.*

B

batch size. The cardinality of a set of items to be processed at some future step. See also *work in process.*

Boy Scout rule. 1. Always leave the campground cleaner than you found it. If you find a mess on the ground, clean it up regardless of who might have made the mess. 2. Every time you are in an area of the code doing work, always leave the code a little cleaner, not a little messier, than you found it. See also *technical debt.*

burndown chart. A graph that shows on the vertical axis the *quantity of work* (in either hours or product backlog item units) remaining over *time*, which is shown on the horizontal axis. Because less and less work should remain over time, the general trend in the graph is to burn down to a point where no work remains. We can show projected outcomes on burndown charts by calculating a trend line to see when work might be completed. Contrast with *burnup chart.*

burnup chart. A graph that shows the progress of work toward a *goal line* associated with a value on the vertical axis. As work is completed over *time* (the horizontal axis), the progress line moves up (burns up) to be nearer to the goal line. We can show projected outcomes on burnup charts by calculating a trend line to see when work might be completed. Contrast with *burndown chart.*

C

cadence. A regular, predictable rhythm or heartbeat. Sprints of consistent duration establish a cadence for a development effort. See also *synchronization.*

capacity. 1. The quantity of resources available to perform useful work. 2. A concept used to help establish a WIP limit by ensuring that we only start work to match the available capacity to complete work. See also *work in process.*

ceremony. A ritualistic or symbolic activity that is performed on well-defined occasions. Some people refer to the core Scrum activities of sprint planning, daily scrum, sprint review, and sprint retrospective as ceremonies. See also *activity, unnecessary formality.*

chaotic domain. 1. A situation that requires a rapid response. We are in a crisis and need to act immediately to prevent further harm and reestablish at least some order. 2. One of the domains in the Cynefin framework. See also *Cynefin.* Contrast with *complex domain, complicated domain, disorder domain, simple domain.*

chickens. A metaphor used by some Scrum teams to indicate that people are invested in the goal of the Scrum team, but at a level of involvement (not accountable) rather than commitment. Best used to refer to people outside of the Scrum team. Derived from an old joke about a chicken and a pig: "In a ham-and-eggs breakfast, the chicken is involved, but the pig is committed." Contrast with *pigs.*

chief product owner. The overall product owner within a product owner team on a large development effort. See also *product owner.*

commitment. The act of binding oneself to a course of action. Scrum encourages commitment. Commitment means that during both good times and bad, each team member is dedicated to meeting the team's collective goal. Contrast with *forecast.*

complex adaptive system. A system with many entities interacting with each other in various ways, where these interactions are governed by simple, localized rules operating in a context of constant feedback. Examples include the stock market, the brain, ant colonies, and Scrum teams.

complex domain. 1. A situation in which things are more unpredictable than they are predictable. If there is a right answer, we will know it only with hindsight. 2. One of the domains in the Cynefin framework. See also *Cynefin.* Contrast with *chaotic domain, complicated domain, disorder domain, simple domain.*

complicated domain. 1. A situation in which there might be multiple right answers but expert diagnosis is required to figure them out. 2. One of the domains in the Cynefin framework. See also *Cynefin.* Contrast with *chaotic domain, complex domain, disorder domain, simple domain.*

component team. A team that focuses on the creation of one or more components of a larger product that a customer would purchase. Component teams create assets or components that are then reused by other teams to assemble customer-valuable solutions. Contrast with *feature team.*

conditions of satisfaction. The conditions under which a product owner would be satisfied that a product backlog item is done. Conditions of satisfaction are acceptance criteria that clarify the desired behavior. See also *acceptance criteria.*

confidence threshold. 1. The definition of done for envisioning (product-level planning). 2. The set of information that decision makers need in order to have sufficient confidence to make a go/no-go funding decision for more detailed development.

continuous delivery. See *continuous deployment.*

continuous deployment. Deploying each new feature to users immediately after it is built, integrated, and tested. Synonymous with *continuous delivery, integration.*

continuous integration. A technical practice where members of a single team or multiple teams integrate their work as frequently as is practical. See also *integration, technical practices.*

cost of delay. The financial cost associated with delaying work or delaying achievement of a milestone. Cost of delay emphasizes the concept that time has a real financial cost, and to make economically sensible trade-offs it is important to know that cost.

cross-functional team. A team composed of members with all the functional skills (such as UI designers, developers, testers) and specialties necessary to complete work that requires more than a single discipline.

customer uncertainty. Uncertainty surrounding who the customers of a product are. See also *uncertainty*. Contrast with *end uncertainty, means uncertainty*.

Cynefin. A sense-making framework that helps us understand the situation in which we have to operate and decide on a situation-appropriate approach (Snowden and Boone 2007).

D

daily scrum. A synchronization, inspection, and adaptive planning activity that a development team performs each day. This core practice in the Scrum framework is timeboxed to no more than 15 minutes. Synonymous with *daily stand-up*. See also *inspect and adapt*.

daily stand-up. A common approach to performing a daily scrum whereby the participants stand for the entirety of the activity. Standing up promotes brevity and helps ensure that the activity does not exceed its timebox. See *daily scrum*.

DEEP. An acronym coined by Roman Pichler and Mike Cohn for remembering a set of criteria used to evaluate the quality of a product backlog. The criteria are *Detailed appropriately, Emergent, Estimated*, and *Prioritized*. See also *product backlog*.

defined process. A process with a well-defined set of steps. Given the same inputs, a defined process should produce the same output every time (within a defined variance range). Contrast with *empirical process control*.

definition of done. 1. A checklist of the types of work that the team is expected to successfully complete by the end of the sprint, before it can declare its work to be potentially shippable. A bare-minimum definition of done should yield a complete slice of product functionality, one that has been designed, built, integrated, tested, and documented and will deliver validated customer value. 2. Sometimes described as the acceptance criteria that apply to all product backlog items. Contrast with *definition of ready*.

definition of ready. A checklist of conditions that must be true before a product backlog item is considered ready to pull into a sprint during sprint planning. Contrast with *definition of done*.

development team. A self-organizing, cross-functional team of people who collectively are responsible for all of the work necessary to produce working, validated assets. One of the three roles that constitute every Scrum team. See also *cross-functional team, product owner, ScrumMaster, Scrum team*.

disorder domain. A dangerous state where we really don't understand or can't make sense of the situation we are in. Our goal is to get out of this domain. 2. One of the domains in the Cynefin framework. See also *Cynefin*. Contrast with *chaotic domain, complex domain, complicated domain, simple domain*.

done. See *definition of done*.

dot voting. A technique that allows participants to vote their preferences among a set of items by placing a colored dot on items that they believe are higher priority than other items. Items with more dots are higher priority than items with fewer dots. This technique is frequently used during the sprint retrospective activity. See also *sprint retrospective*.

E

economic filter. The decision criteria used by an organization to evaluate the economics of a proposed product in order to decide whether or not to fund it. Contrast with *strategic filter*.

emergence. 1. Individual, localized behavior that aggregates into global behavior that is disconnected from its origins. 2. An attribute of complex adaptive systems. 3. When applied to software development, recognizing that it is not possible to a priori determine the correct set of features, designs, or plans. Instead, over time as more information is learned, important information will emerge from the experience gained on prior work. See also *complex adaptive system*.

emergent opportunity. An opportunity that was previously unknown, or was deemed sufficiently unlikely to occur and therefore not worth spending money on at the time.

emotions seismogram. A graphical representation of the emotional ups and downs of team members over the course of a sprint. A technique frequently used during the sprint retrospective activity. See also *sprint retrospective*.

empirical process control. A style of work that leverages the principles of inspection, adaptation, and transparency. Contrast with *defined process*.

end uncertainty. Uncertainty surrounding what will be built (the product). See also *uncertainty*. Contrast with *customer uncertainty, means uncertainty*.

envisioning. An activity that captures the essence of a potential product and creates a rough plan for the creation of that product. Envisioning begins with the creation of a vision, followed by the creation of a high-level product backlog and frequently a product roadmap. Synonymous with *product planning*. See also *product roadmap*.

epic. A large user story, perhaps a few to many months in size, that can span an entire release or multiple releases. Epics are useful as placeholders for large requirements. Epics are progressively refined into a set of smaller user stories at the appropriate time. See also *feature, progressive refinement, theme, user story*.

essential Scrum. The values, principles, and practices of the Scrum framework combined with rules and proven approaches to applying Scrum practices. See also *approach, practice, rule, Scrum framework.*

estimation. A rough calculation of the value, number, quantity, or extent of something. In Scrum, we estimate the size of portfolio backlog items, product backlog items, and sprint backlog tasks. See also *forecast.*

event timeline. A visual, chronologically ordered depiction of the meaningful events that occurred over a period of time. A common technique used during sprint retrospectives. See also *sprint retrospective.*

exploitation. Making a decision based on the certainty of the information we currently possess. Contrast with *exploration.*

exploration. The act of acquiring or buying knowledge by performing some activity such as building a prototype, creating a proof of concept, performing a study, or conducting an experiment. Contrast with *exploitation.*

external stakeholders. Stakeholders who are typically external to the organization that is developing a product, for example, customers, partners, and regulators. See also *stakeholders.* Contrast with *internal stakeholders.*

Extreme Programming (XP). An agile development approach that is complementary to Scrum. Extreme Programming specifies important technical practices that development teams use to manage the flow of task-level work during sprint execution. See also *agile.*

F

fail fast. A strategy of trying something, getting fast feedback, and then rapidly inspecting and adapting. In the presence of high levels of uncertainty, it is often less expensive to start working on a product, learn whether we made a good decision, and if not, kill it fast before more money is spent. See also *fast feedback, inspect and adapt, pivot.*

fast feedback. A principle that states that feedback today is much more valuable than the same feedback tomorrow, because today's feedback can be used to correct a problem before it compounds into a much larger problem, and provides the ability to truncate economically undesirable paths sooner (to fail faster). See also *fail fast.*

feature. 1. A slice of business functionality that is meaningful to a customer or user. 2. Used by some to mean a medium-size user story that can and will be divided into a collection of smaller user stories that together will be implemented to deliver the value of a feature. See also *theme, user story.*

feature team. A cross-functional and cross-component team that can pull end-customer features from the product backlog and complete them. See also *cross-functional team.* Contrast with *component team.*

fixed-date release. A release that must be delivered on a known future date. The scope of the release, and possibly the cost, needs to be flexible. Contrast with *fixed-scope release*.

fixed-scope release. A release that must have a specific set of features. The date on which the features are delivered and/or the costs are flexible. Contrast with *fixed-date release*.

flow. 1. The smooth, steady movement of work through the development process to ensure that good economic value is delivered. 2. Avoiding idle work in economically sensible ways. 3. The opposite of big batch, big release, and big bang.

forecast. 1. Making statements, predictions, or estimations about events whose actual outcomes have not yet been observed. 2. The 2011 "Scrum Guide" term for what a development team generates during sprint planning. See also *estimation*. Contrast with *commitment*.

framework. See *Scrum framework*.

G

grooming. See *product backlog grooming*.

group. A collection of people who share a common label (the group name) but have not yet formed a team whose members have learned how to work together and trust each other. Contrast with *team*.

H

happened-upon technical debt. A status category for technical debt that represents debt that the development team was unaware existed until it was exposed during the normal course of performing work on the product. Contrast with *known technical debt, targeted technical debt*. See also *technical debt*.

I

ideal day. A unit for estimating the size of product backlog items based on how long an item would take to complete if it were the only work being performed, there were no interruptions, and all resources necessary to complete the work were immediately available. See also *ideal hour*. Contrast with *story point*.

ideal hour. A unit for estimating the size of the design, build, integrate, and test work, represented as sprint backlog tasks. Often referred to as an effort-hour, person-hour, or man-hour. See also *ideal day*.

idle work. Work that is not actively being pursued as it sits in some queue. Contrast with *idle workers*.

idle workers. People who have available capacity to do more work because they are not currently 100% utilized. Contrast with *idle work*.

impediment. A hindrance or obstruction to doing something. Frequently used to describe some issue or blocker that is preventing a team or organization from performing Scrum in an effective way.

implementable story. A user story that is sized small enough to fit nicely within a sprint. Synonymous with *sprintable story*.

incremental development. 1. Development based on the principle of building *some* before building *all*. 2. A staging strategy in which parts of the product are developed and delivered to users at different times, with the intention to adapt to external feedback. See also *iterative and incremental process, iterative development*.

incremental funding. Funding some of the product development without committing to funding all of it. Using incremental funding, we fund just the first small part of the development effort and revisit the funding decision after we have the critical validated learning we are paying to get from the first part. See also *confidence threshold, validated learning*.

information radiator. A visual display that presents up-to-date, sufficiently detailed, and important information to passersby in an easy, self-interpretable format.

innovation accounting. A measurement/accounting system that uses actionable metrics to evaluate how fast we are learning as a critical measure of progress toward converging on a business-valuable result (Ries 2011).

innovation waste. The lost opportunity to create an innovative solution. Frequently occurs when a prescribed solution is provided with a product backlog item.

in-process product. A product that is currently under development, already live in production, or currently being sold. See also *portfolio planning*.

insight backlog. A prioritized list of previously generated insights or process improvement ideas that have not yet been acted upon. The insight backlog is generated and used during sprint retrospectives. See also *sprint retrospective*.

inspect and adapt. 1. A common phase in Scrum that refers to the inspection and adaptation principles of empirical process control. 2. The principle of inspecting a product or process and making adaptations based on what is learned. 3. A key part of the learning loop. See also *adaptation, empirical process control, inspection, learning loop*.

inspection. One of the three pillars of empirical process control, involving thoughtful examination and processing of feedback to make adaptation decisions regarding the process or product. See also *adaptation, empirical process control, transparency.*

integration. The combining of the various components or assets of some or all of a product to form a coherent, larger-scope work product that can be validated to function correctly as a whole. See also *continuous integration.*

internal stakeholders. Stakeholders who are internal to the organization that is developing the product, for example, senior executives, managers, and internal users. See also *stakeholders.* Contrast with *external stakeholders.*

inventory. See *work in process.*

INVEST. An acronym coined by Bill Wake for remembering a set of criteria used to evaluate the quality of user stories. The criteria are *Independent, Negotiable, Valuable, Estimatable, Sized correctly* (small), and *Testable.* See also *user story.*

iteration. A self-contained development cycle focused on performing all of the work necessary to produce a valuable outcome. See also *all-at-once development, sprint.*

iterative and incremental process. A style of development that leverages both iterative development and incremental development. See also *incremental development, iterative development.*

iterative development. A planned rework strategy where multiple passes over the work are used to converge on a good solution. See also *incremental development, iteration, iterative and incremental process.*

J

just in time (JIT). A characteristic of a process whereby the assets or activities of a work stream become available or occur just as they are needed.

K

Kanban. An agile approach overlaid on an existing process that advocates visualizing how work flows through a system, limiting the work in process, and measuring and optimizing the flow of work. See also *agile, work in process.*

known technical debt. A status category for technical debt that represents the debt that is known to the development team and has been made visible for future consideration. Contrast with *happened-upon technical debt, targeted technical debt.* See also *technical debt.*

L

last responsible moment (LRM). A strategy of not making a premature decision but instead delaying commitment and keeping important and irreversible decisions open until the cost of not making a decision becomes greater than the cost of making a decision.

learning loop. A feedback loop focused on increasing learning. Generally follows these steps: make an assumption (or set a goal), build something (perform some activities), get feedback on what was built, and then use that feedback to inspect what was done relative to what was assumed.

lifecycle profits. 1. The total profit potential for a product over its lifetime. 2. In the case of portfolio planning, the total profit potential of the entire portfolio rather than a single product.

LRM. See *last responsible moment.*

M

means uncertainty. Uncertainty surrounding how something will be built. See also *uncertainty.* Contrast with *customer uncertainty, end uncertainty.*

minimum marketable features (MMFs). The smallest or minimum set of functionality related to a feature that must be delivered for the customer to perceive value (for it to be marketable). Contrast with *minimum releasable features.*

minimum releasable features (MRFs). 1. The minimum set of features that must be present in a release to make it viable—useful enough to end customers such that they want it and would be willing to pay for it. 2. Features composed from a collection of minimum marketable features. Synonymous with *must-have features.* See also *minimum marketable features.*

minimum viable product (MVP). A product that has just those features that allow the product to be deployed, and no more.

MMFs. See *minimum marketable features.*

MRFs. See *minimum releasable features.*

MVP. See *minimum viable product.*

Musketeer attitude. 1. All for one and one for all. 2. The attitude among members of a team that they are all in the same boat and that they will win or lose together as a team.

must-have features. The set of features that must be present in the upcoming release for the release to be viable. Synonymous with *minimum releasable features.* Contrast with *nice-to-have features, won't-have features.*

N

naive technical debt. A form of technical debt that accrues due to irresponsible behavior or immature practices on the part of the people involved. Contrast with *strategic technical debt, unavoidable technical debt.* See also *technical debt.*

nice-to-have features. Features that are targeted for the upcoming release but could be excluded if there are insufficient resources to finalize their development. Contrast with *must-have features, won't-have features.*

nonfunctional requirement. 1. A requirement that does not relate to functionality but to attributes such as reliability, efficiency, usability, maintainability, and portability, which product backlog items must possess in order to be fully accepted by the stakeholders. 2. Each nonfunctional requirement is a candidate for inclusion in the definition of done. See also *definition of done.*

P

PBI. See *product backlog item.*

persona. 1. A user archetype, synthesized from the ethnographic data of real users, that helps guide decisions about product features, navigation, interactions, and visual design. 2. A fictitious person that is the prototypical instance of a particular user role. See also *user story.*

pigs. A metaphor used by some Scrum teams to indicate that people are invested in the goal of the Scrum team at a commitment level (accountable for the outcome). Most people consider the members of the Scrum team to be pigs. See also *Scrum team.* Contrast with *chickens.*

pivot. 1. To change directions but stay grounded in what we have learned. 2. A structured course correction designed to test a new fundamental hypothesis about a product, strategy, and engine of growth (Ries 2011).

plan-driven process. A style of development that attempts to plan for and anticipate up front all of the features a user might want in the end product and to determine how best to build those features. The work plan is based on execution of a sequential set of work-specific phases. Synonymous with *anticipatory process, predictive process, prescriptive process, sequential process, traditional development process, waterfall process.*

Planning Poker. A consensus-based technique for the relative sizing of product backlog items.

point inflation. The unfortunate behavior of inflating the value of product backlog size estimates in an attempt to conform to or optimize an unwisely conceived measure (such as achieving a target velocity).

portfolio backlog. A backlog composed of products, programs, projects, or high-level epics. See also *portfolio planning.*

portfolio planning. An activity for determining which products (or projects) to work on, in which order, and for how long. Sometimes referred to as portfolio management.

potentially shippable product increment. Results that are completed to a high degree of confidence and represent work of good quality that is potentially shippable to end customers at the end of a sprint. Being potentially shippable does not mean the results will actually be delivered to customers. Shipping is a business decision; potentially shippable is a state of confidence.

practice. The way in which a principle is supported or realized. For example, the principle of demonstrating progress is supported by the sprint review Scrum practice. See *activity, artifact, role, rule.* See also *principle, values.*

precision. How exact an estimate is. For example, saying a product will ship on October 7, 2015, is more precise than saying a product will ship in October 2015. Contrast with *accuracy.*

predictive process. See *plan-driven process.*

prescriptive process. See *plan-driven process.*

principle. A fundamental truth or belief that serves as the foundation for how we approach product development. An example Scrum principle is to demonstrate progress frequently. See also *practice, values.*

principle of least astonishment. Acting or developing work products in a way that is least likely to startle those around you.

product. 1. The result of a product development effort. 2. A good or service consisting of a bundle of tangible and intangible attributes that satisfies consumers and is received in exchange for money or some other unit of value. 3. Typically a longer-lived, more stable artifact against which organizations might conduct one or more projects. See also *product development effort.* Contrast with *project.*

product backlog. A prioritized inventory of yet-to-be-worked-on product backlog items. See also *product backlog item.*

product backlog grooming. The activities of writing and refining, estimating, and prioritizing product backlog items.

product backlog item (PBI). 1. An item such as a feature, defect, or (occasionally) technical work that is valuable from the product owner's perspective. 2. An item in the product backlog. See also *product backlog.*

product development effort. The full scope of work performed to create or enhance a product or service. Contrast with *project.*

product owner. The empowered central point of product leadership. One of the three roles on a Scrum team; the single voice of the stakeholder community to the Scrum team. The product owner defines what to do and in what order to do it. See also *Scrum team.*

product owner proxy. A person enlisted by the product owner to act on his behalf in particular situations. See also *product owner.*

product planning. See *envisioning.*

product roadmap. A description of the incremental nature of how a product will be built and delivered over time, along with the important factors that drive each individual release. Useful when developing a product that will have more than one release. See also *envisioning.*

product vision. A brief statement of the desired future state that would be achieved by developing and deploying a product. A good vision should be simple to state and provide a coherent direction to the people who are asked to realize it. See also *envisioning.*

progressive refinement. To disaggregate, in a just-in-time fashion, large, lightly detailed product backlog items into a set of smaller, more detailed items.

project. 1. A temporary endeavor undertaken to create a unique product, service, or result (PMI 2008). 2. An effort that completes when its objectives have been obtained. Compared with a life of a product, a project is shorter in duration. Frequently multiple projects are performed over the full cradle-to-grave lifecycle of a product. Contrast with *product.*

project chartering. The set of up-front work needed to define a project at a sufficient level of detail that a funding decision can be made. Synonymous with *project inception, project initiation.*

project inception. See *project chartering.*

project initiation. See *project chartering.*

Q

queue. A holding place for items (an inventory) as they wait for the next action in a work stream. See also *inventory, work in process.*

R

refactoring. A technique for restructuring an existing body of code by improving/simplifying its internal structure (design) without changing its external behavior. Refactoring is one of the principal techniques for managing technical debt. See also *technical debt, technical practices.*

relative size measure. A means of expressing the overall size of an item where the absolute value is not considered, but the relative size of an item compared to other items is considered. For example, an item of size 2 is half the size of an item of size 4, but we have no idea how big an item of size 2 or 4 is in some absolute sense. See also *ideal day, story point.*

release. 1. A combination of features that when packaged together make for a coherent deliverable to customers or users. 2. A version of a product that is promoted for use or deployment. Releases represent the rhythm of business-value delivery and should align with defined business cycles.

release goal. A clear statement of the purpose and desired outcome of a release. A release goal is created by considering many factors, including the target customers, high-level architectural issues, and significant marketplace events. See also *release.*

release plan. 1. The output of release planning. On a fixed-date release, the release plan will specify the range of features available on the fixed future date. On a fixed-scope release, the release plan will specify the range of sprints and costs required to deliver the fixed scope. 2. A plan that communicates, to the level of accuracy that is reasonably possible, when the release will be available, what features will be in the release, and how much will it cost. See also *fixed-date release, fixed-scope release.*

release planning. Longer-term planning that answers questions like "When will we be done?" or "Which features can I get by the end of the year?" or "How much will this cost?" Release planning must balance customer value and overall quality against the constraints of scope, schedule, and budget. See also *release plan.*

release train. An approach to aligning the vision, planning, and interdependencies of many teams by providing cross-team synchronization based on a common cadence. A release train focuses on fast, flexible flow at the level of a larger product. See also *scrum of scrums.*

retrospective. See *sprint retrospective.*

risk. 1. The likelihood that an event will be accompanied by undesirable consequences. Risk is measured by both the probability of the event and the seriousness of the consequences. 2. Any uncertainty that is expected to have a negative outcome for the activity. See also *uncertainty.*

role. A cohesive set of responsibilities that may be fulfilled by one or more people. The three Scrum roles are product owner, ScrumMaster, and development team. See also *practice, principle.*

rule. A common practice or generally reliable method of action in a particular situation. A rule may be broken when the pragmatics of a situation dictate that a different course of action should be pursued. The Scrum framework includes rules. See also *essential Scrum, Scrum framework.*

S

Scrum. A term borrowed from the sport of rugby. 1. A lightweight agile framework for managing complex product and service development. 2. An iterative and incremental approach to developing products and managing work. See also *agile, Scrum framework.*

Scrum framework. A collection of values, principles, practices, and rules that form the foundation of Scrum-based development. See also *Scrum.*

ScrumMaster. The coach, facilitator, impediment remover, and servant leader of the Scrum team. The ScrumMaster is one of the three roles on a Scrum team. The ScrumMaster provides process leadership and helps the Scrum team and the rest of the organization develop their own high-performance, organization-specific Scrum approach. See also *Scrum team, servant leader.*

Scrummerfall. See *WaterScrum.*

scrum of scrums (SoS). An approach to coordinating the work of multiple Scrum teams wherein one or more members of each Scrum team come together to discuss and resolve inter-team dependency issues. See also *release train.*

Scrum team. A team composed of a product owner, ScrumMaster, and development team that works on a Scrum development effort. See also *development team, product owner, ScrumMaster.*

self-organization. 1. A bottom-up emergent property of a complex adaptive system whereby the organization of the system emerges over time as a response to its environment. 2. A property of a development team that organizes itself over time, without an external dominating force applying traditional top-down, command-and-control management. 3. Reflects the management philosophy whereby operational decisions are delegated as much as possible to those who have the most detailed knowledge of the consequences and practicalities associated with those decisions. See also *complex adaptive system, emergence.*

sequential process. See *plan-driven process.*

servant leader. 1. A person who achieves results for her organization by giving priority attention to the needs of her colleagues and those she serves. 2. A philosophy and practice of leadership based on listening, empathy, healing, awareness, persuasion, conceptualization, foresight, stewardship, commitment, and community building. See also *ScrumMaster.*

silent grouping. A facilitation technique for getting people to group related items without talking, relying only on the individual placement and movement of items (typically cards or sticky notes) as a means of communicating and coordinating among the participants. A technique frequently used during the sprint retrospective activity. See also *sprint retrospective.*

simple domain. 1. A situation in which everyone can see cause and effect. Often the right answer is obvious and undisputed. 2. One of the domains in the Cynefin framework. See also *Cynefin*. Contrast with *chaotic domain, complex domain, complicated domain, disorder domain.*

single-piece flow. A state where items are produced one at a time and flow (are pulled) through the development process as a single unit.

solution. A product or a service that results from a development effort.

SoS. See *scrum of scrums.*

specification by example. See *acceptance-test-driven development.*

sprint. A short-duration, timeboxed iteration. Typically a timebox between one week and a calendar month during which the Scrum team is focused on producing a potentially shippable product increment that meets the Scrum team's agreed-upon definition of done. See also *definition of done, iteration, potentially shippable product increment.*

sprintable story. See *implementable story.*

sprint backlog. 1. An artifact produced at a sprint-planning meeting and continuously updated during sprint execution that helps a self-organizing team better plan and manage the work necessary to deliver on the sprint goal. 2. A list of the product backlog items pulled into a sprint and an associated plan for how to achieve them—frequently expressed in terms of tasks that are estimated in ideal hours. See also *ideal hour, sprint planning, task.*

sprint demo. 1. An activity of a sprint review where the completed (done) product backlog items are demonstrated with the goal of promoting an information-rich discussion between the Scrum team and other sprint review participants. 2. A term that is frequently used synonymously to refer to the entire sprint review. See also *sprint review.*

sprint goal. A high-level summary of the goal the product owner would like to accomplish during the sprint. Frequently elaborated through a specific set of product backlog items.

sprint planning. A time when the Scrum team gathers to agree on a sprint goal and determine what subset of the product backlog it can deliver during the forthcoming sprint. During sprint planning, a sprint backlog is produced to help the team acquire confidence that it can deliver the committed product backlog items. See also *sprint backlog, sprint goal.*

sprint retrospective. An inspect-and-adapt activity performed at the end of every sprint. The sprint retrospective is a continuous improvement opportunity for a Scrum team to review its process (approaches to performing Scrum) and to identify opportunities to improve it. See also *inspect and adapt, sprint review.*

sprint review. An inspect-and-adapt activity that occurs after sprint execution where the Scrum team shows to all interested parties what was accomplished during the sprint. The sprint review gives everyone with input in the product development effort an opportunity to inspect what has been built so far and adapt what will be built next. See also *inspect and adapt, sprint demo.*

stakeholder. A person, group, or organization that affects or can be affected by an organization's actions. See also *external stakeholders, internal stakeholders.*

stakeholder value. The value that a solution delivers to stakeholders. Sometimes used interchangeably with customer value. See also *stakeholder.*

story. See *user story.*

story mapping. 1. A technique that takes a user-centric perspective for generating a set of user stories. Each high-level user activity is decomposed into a workflow that can be further decomposed into a set of detailed tasks. 2. A two-dimensional representation of a traditional one-dimensional product backlog list. See also *product backlog, user story.*

story point. A measure of the relative size of product backlog items that takes into account factors such as complexity and physical size. Typically determined by engaging in Planning Poker. See also *ideal day, Planning Poker, relative size measure.*

strategic filter. The decision criteria used by an organization to evaluate whether a proposed product meets the strategic criteria to move forward for additional consideration. Contrast with *economic filter.*

strategic technical debt. A form of technical debt that is used as a tool to help organizations better quantify and leverage the economics of important, often time-sensitive, decisions. Sometimes taking on technical debt for strategic reasons is a sensible business choice. Contrast with *naive technical debt, unavoidable technical debt.* See also *technical debt.*

sustainable pace. The appropriately aggressive pace at which a team works so that it produces a good flow of business value over an extended period of time without getting burned out.

swarming. A behavior whereby team members with available capacity and appropriate skills collectively work (swarm) on an item to finish what has already been started before moving ahead to begin work on new items. See also *T-shaped skills.*

synchronization. Causing multiple events to happen at the same time. Frequently used to ensure that multiple Scrum teams work together in a coordinated way by starting and ending their sprints on the same days. See also *cadence.*

T

tacit knowledge. Unwritten and unspoken knowledge (including insights, intuitions, and hunches) that is hard, but not impossible, to articulate with formal language. The opposite of explicit or formal knowledge. Sometimes referred to as "know-how."

targeted technical debt. A status category for technical debt that represents debt that is known and has been targeted for servicing by the development team. Contrast with *happened-upon technical debt, known technical debt.* See also *technical debt.*

task. The technical work that a development team performs in order to complete a product backlog item. Most tasks are defined to be small, representing no more than a few hours to a day or so of work.

task board. An information radiator used during sprint execution to communicate the progress and flow of task-level work within a sprint. See also *information radiator, task.*

TDD. See *test-driven development.*

team. A small, cross-functional collection of diverse, collaborating people who are aligned to a common purpose and goal. Team members trust each other and work together to achieve the goal, holding themselves mutually accountable for the outcome. Contrast with *group.*

technical debt. 1. A term used to describe the obligation that a software organization incurs when it chooses a design or construction approach that is expedient in the short term but that increases complexity and is more costly in the long term. 2. A metaphor that facilitates the communication between business and technical people regarding implementation artifact inadequacies. See also *naive technical debt, strategic technical debt, unavoidable technical debt.*

technical practices. The specific practices or techniques that are used during sprint execution to properly perform the work required to deliver features that have manageable levels of technical debt and meet the Scrum team's definition of done.

technical stories. A "user" story (product backlog item) that delivers no perceived end-user value but does deliver important architecture or infrastructure needed to deliver future user value. See also *user story.*

technique. A defined procedure that is used to perform some or all of an activity or support an approach. See also *activity, approach.*

test-driven development (TDD). 1. An evolutionary approach to development based on writing a failing automated test before the functional code that makes the test pass. Once the code is written to pass the test, the cycle is then repeated, including refactoring the existing code to ensure a coherent cross-functional design. The goal of test-driven development is specification and not validation—to think through a design before code is written, to create clean code that always works. 2. An example of test-first development. See also *refactoring, technical practices, test-first development.*

test-first development. A technical practice where the tests are written before the development is performed. An example is test-driven development. See also *technical practices, test-driven development.*

theme. A collection of related user stories. A theme provides a convenient way to indicate that a set of stories have something in common, such as being in the same functional area. See also *epic, user story.*

timebox. A fixed-length period of time during which an activity is performed. In Scrum, sprints are timeboxed iterations where a team works at a sustainable pace to complete a chosen, WIP-limited set of work. See also *sprint, timeboxing.*

timeboxing. A time management technique that helps organize the performance of work and manage scope. See also *timebox.*

traditional development process. See *plan-driven process.*

transparency. One of the three pillars of empirical process control; open access to the unbiased information required for inspection and adaptation. See also *adaptation, empirical process control, inspection.*

T-shaped skills. A metaphor used to describe a person with deep vertical skills in a specialized area (such as UX design) as well as broad but not necessarily very deep skills in other relevant areas (such as testing and documentation). Team members with T-shaped skills better enable swarming behavior. See also *swarming.*

U

unavoidable technical debt. A form of technical debt that is usually unpredictable and unpreventable and accrues through no fault of the team building the product. Contrast with *naive technical debt, strategic technical debt.* See also *technical debt.*

uncertainty. Something that is not known or established. Often considered synonymous with risk but is actually broader in scope because uncertainty includes both risks (negative outcomes) and opportunities (positive outcomes). See also *risk.*

unknown unknowns. The things that we don't yet know that we don't know.

unnecessary formality. 1. A ceremony that has a real cost but delivers little or no value (a form of waste). 2. Process for the sake of process. See also *ceremony, waste.*

user role. 1. The name for a class of product users. 2. One of the key elements of a user story that defines the recipient of the value delivered by a user story. See also *user story.*

user story. A convenient format for expressing the desired business value for many types of product backlog items. User stories are crafted in a way that makes them understandable for both business people and technical people. They are structurally simple and typically expressed in a format such as "As a <user role> I want to achieve <goal> so that I get <benefit>." They provide a great placeholder for a conversation. Additionally, they can be written at various levels of granularity and are easy to progressively refine. See also *epic, progressive refinement, theme, user role.*

user-story-writing workshop. A workshop lasting from a few hours to a few days where a diverse team of participants collectively brainstorms desired business value and creates user story placeholders for what the product or service is supposed to do. See also *user story.*

V

validated learning. A term proposed by Ries (2011) to describe the progress made when important assumptions have been confirmed or refuted by subjecting each assumption to one or more customer validation tests. Contrast with *assumption.*

values. 1. Those things that we hold dear or precious. 2. The foundation of a shared operating agreement among members of a team. Core Scrum values include honesty, openness, courage, respect, focus, trust, empowerment, and collaboration.

variability. The spread or dispersion of a set of data representing non-identical outcomes. In manufacturing, variability is always waste. In product development, some variability is necessary to develop innovative solutions. See also *waste.*

velocity. A measure of the rate at which work is completed per unit of time. Using Scrum, velocity is typically measured as the sum of the size estimates of the product backlog items that are completed in a sprint. Velocity is reported in the same units as product backlog items—usually story points or ideal days. Velocity measures output (the size of what was delivered), not outcome (the value of what was delivered).

W

waste. Any activity that consumes resources and produces no added value to the product or service that a customer receives.

waterfall. A term referring to the graphical depiction of a development process in which the sequential phases of work are shown flowing steadily downwards like a cascading waterfall. See also *plan-driven process.*

waterfall process. See *plan-driven process.*

WaterScrum. Overlaying waterfall-style development on the Scrum framework. An example would be performing an analysis sprint, followed by a design sprint, followed by a coding sprint, followed by a testing sprint. Synonymous with *Scrummerfall*.

weighted shortest job first (WSJF). An economically optimal algorithm for scheduling work in an environment where both the cost of delay and the duration vary among the work items. See also *cost of delay*.

WIP. See *work in process*.

won't-have features. The set of features that are specifically declared to not be in the upcoming release. Contrast with *must-have features, nice-to-have features*.

work in process (WIP). Work that has entered the development process but is not yet finished and available to a customer or user. Refers to all assets or work products of a product or service that are currently being worked on or waiting in a queue to be worked on.

WSJF. See *weighted shortest job first*.

X

XP. See *Extreme Programming*.

REFERENCES

Adkins, Lyssa. 2010. *Coaching Agile Teams: A Companion for ScrumMasters, Agile Coaches, and Project Managers in Transition.* Addison-Wesley Professional.

Anderson, David J. 2010. *Kanban.* Blue Hole Press.

Appelo, Jurgen. 2011. *Management 3.0: Leading Agile Developers, Developing Agile Leaders.* Addison-Wesley Professional.

Beck, Kent, Mike Beedle, Arie van Bennekum, Alistair Cockburn, Ward Cunning-ham, Martin Fowler, James Grenning, Jim Highsmith, Andrew Hunt, Ron Jeffries, Jon Kern, Brian Marick, Robert C. Martin, Steve Mellor, Ken Schwaber, Jeff Suther-land, and Dave Thomas. 2001. *Manifesto for Agile Software Development.* www.agilemanifesto.org/.

Beck, Kent, and Cynthia Andres. 2004. *Extreme Programming Explained*, 2nd ed. Addison-Wesley Professional.

Boehm, Barry W. 1981. *Software Engineering Economics.* Prentice Hall.

Brooks, Frederick P. 1995. *The Mythical Man-Month: Essays on Software Engineering*, 2nd ed. Addison-Wesley Professional. (Originally published in 1975.)

Cohn, Mike. 2004. *User Stories Applied: For Agile Software Development.* Addison-Wesley Professional.

———. 2006. *Agile Estimating and Planning.* Addison-Wesley Professional.

———. 2009. *Succeeding with Agile.* Addison-Wesley Professional.

———. 2010. Agile 2010 keynote presentation.

Cook, Daniel. 2008. "The Laws of Productivity: 8 productivity experiments you don't need to repeat." Presentation found at http://www.lostgarden.com/2008/09/rules-of-productivity-presentation.html.

Crispin, Lisa, and Janet Gregory. 2009. *Agile Testing: A Practical Guide for Testers and Agile Teams.* Addison-Wesley Professional.

Cunningham, Ward. 1992. "The WyCash Portfolio Management System," OOPSLA 1992 experience report. OOPSLA '92, Object-Oriented Programming Systems, Lan-guages and Applications, Vancouver, BC, Canada, October 18–22.

Denne, Mark, and Jane Cleland-Huang. 2003. *Software by Numbers: Low-Risk, High-Return Development*. Prentice Hall.

Derby, Esther, and Diana Larsen. 2006. *Agile Retrospectives: Making Good Teams Great*. Pragmatic Bookshelf.

Fowler, Martin. 2009. "Technical Debt Quadrant." Bliki entry found at http://martinfowler.com/bliki/TechnicalDebtQuadrant.html.

Fowler, Martin, Kent Beck, John Brant, William Opdyke, and Don Roberts. 1999. *Refactoring: Improving the Design of Existing Code*. Addison-Wesley Professional.

Goldberg, Adele, and Kenneth S. Rubin. 1995. *Succeeding with Objects: Decision Frameworks for Project Management*. Addison-Wesley Professional.

Grenning, James. 2002. "Planning Poker." www.objectmentor.com/resources/articles/PlanningPoker.zip.

Highsmith, Jim. 2009. *Agile Project Management: Creating Innovative Products*, 2nd ed. Addison-Wesley Professional.

Hohmann, Luke. 2003. *Beyond Software Architecture*. Addison-Wesley Professional.

IEEE. 1990. IEEE Std 610.12-1990 (revision and designation of IEEE Std 792-1983). IEEE Standards Board of the Institute of Electrical and Electronics Engineers, New York, September 28, 1990.

Jeffries, Ron. 2001. "Essential XP: Card, Conversation, Confirmation." http://xprogramming.com/articles/expcardconversationconfirmation/.

Katz, Ralph. 1982. "The Effects of Group Longevity on Project Communication and Performance." *Administrative Science Quarterly* 27: 81–104.

Kennedy, John Fitzgerald. 1961. Special Message to the Congress on Urgent National Needs, May 22.

Kerth, Norm. 2001. *Project Retrospectives: A Handbook for Team Reviews*. Dorset House.

Larman, Craig, and Bas Vodde. 2009. "Lean Primer." Downloadable from www.leanprimer.com/downloads/lean_primer.pdf.

Laufer, Alexander. 1996. *Simultaneous Management: Managing Projects in a Dynamic Environment*. American Management Association.

Leffingwell, Dean. 2011. *Agile Software Requirements: Lean Requirements Practices for Teams, Programs, and the Enterprise*. Addison-Wesley Professional.

McConnell, Steve. 2007. "Technical Debt." Blog entry found at http://blogs.construx.com/blogs/stevemcc/archive/2007/11/01/technical-debt-2.aspx.

Mar, Kane. 2006. "Technical Debt and the Death of Design: Part 1." Blog entry found at http://kanemar.com/2006/07/23/technical-debt-and-the-death-of-design-part-1/.

Martin, Robert C. 2008. *Clean Code: A Handbook of Agile Software Craftsmanship*. Prentice Hall.

Page, Scott. 2007. *The Difference: How the Power of Diversity Creates Better Groups, Firms, Schools, and Societies*. Princeton University Press.

Patton, Jeff. 2008. Example of incremental releasing. Personal communication.

———. 2009. "Telling Better User Stories: Mapping the Path to Success." *Better Software*, November/December, 24–29.

Pelrine, Joseph. 2011. "Is Software Development Complex." Guest blog entry found at http://cognitive-edge.com/blog/entry/4597/is-software-development-complex.

Pichler, Roman. 2010. *Agile Product Management with Scrum: Creating Products That Customers Love*. Addison-Wesley Professional.

PMI. 2008. *A Guide to the Project Management Body of Knowledge (PMBOK® Guide)*, 4th ed. Project Management Institute, Inc.

Poppendieck, Mary, and Tom Poppendieck. 2003. *Lean Software Development: An Agile Toolkit*. Addison-Wesley Professional.

Putnam, Doug. 1996. "Team Size Can Be the Key to a Successful Project." An article in QSM's Process Improvement Series. www.qsm.com/process_01.html.

Putnam, Lawrence H., and Ware Myers. 1998. "Familiar Metrics Management: Small Is Beautiful—Once Again." *IT Metrics Strategies* IV:8: 12–16. Cutter Information Corp.

Reinertsen, Donald G. 2009a. "Types of Processes." Guest blog entry found at www.netobjectives.com/blogs/Types-of-Processes.

———. 2009b. *The Principles of Product Development Flow: Second Generation Lean Product Development*. Celeritas Publishing.

Ries, Eric. 2011. *The Lean Startup: How Today's Entrepreneurs Use Continuous Innovation to Create Radically Successful Businesses*. Crown Business.

Schwaber, Ken. 1995. "Scrum Development Process." In *OOPSLA Business Object Design and Implementation Workshop*, ed. J. Sutherland et al. Springer.

———. 2004. *Agile Software Development with Scrum*. Microsoft Press.

Schwaber, Ken, and Mike Beedle. 2001. *Agile Software Development with Scrum*. Prentice Hall.

Schwaber, Ken, and Jeff Sutherland. 2011. "The Scrum Guide." Downloadable at www.scrum.org.

SEI. 2010. "CMMI for Development, Version 1.3." Software Engineering Institute, Carnegie Mellon University. Downloadable at www.sei.cmu.edu/library/abstracts/reports/10tr033.cfm.

————. 2011. Second International Workshop on Managing Technical Debt, May 23. Colocated with ICSE 2011, Waikiki, Honolulu, Hawaii. Downloadable at www.sei.cmu.edu/community/td2011/.

Smith, Preston G., and Donald G. Reinertsen. 1998. *Developing Products in Half the Time: New Rules, New Tools.* Van Nostrand Reinhold.

Snowden, David J., and Mary E. Boone. 2007. "A Leader's Framework for Decision Making." *Harvard Business Review*, November.

Staats, Bradley R. 2011. *Unpacking Team Familiarity: The Effects of Geographic Location and Hierarchical Role.* University of North Carolina at Chapel Hill.

Takeuchi, Hirotaka, and Ikujiro Nonaka. 1986. "The New New Product Development Game." *Harvard Business Review*, January, 137–146.

Tuckman, Bruce W. 1965. "Developmental Sequence in Small Groups." *Psychological Bulletin* 63: 384–399. The article was reprinted in *Group Facilitation: A Research and Applications Journal*, no. 3, Spring 2001.

VersionOne. 2011. "The State of Agile Development: Sixth Annual Survey." Posted as a downloadable PDF in the Library of White Papers on www.versionone.com.

Wake, William C. 2003. "INVEST in Good Stories, and SMART Tasks." www.xp123.com.

Wheelwright, Steven C., and Kim B. Clark. 1992. *Revolutionizing Product Development: Quantum Leaps in Speed, Efficiency, and Quality.* The Free Press.

Wiseman, John "Lofty." 2010. *SAS Survival Guide: For Any Climate, in Any Situation*, rev. ed. Collins Reference.

INDEX

A

Absolute sizes, vs. relative sizes in estimation, 125–128

Acceptance criteria
conditions of satisfaction related to product backlog, 77
defined, 401
definition of ready and, 110
product owner defining and verifying, 169–170
user stories containing confirmation information, 85–86

Acceptance-test-driven development (ATTD), 85–86, 402

Acceptance tests
conditions of satisfaction expressed via, 85
defined, 401
product owner responsibilities and, 169
verifying conditions of satisfaction, 77

Accountability, of product owner, 173

Accrual of technical debt, managing, 149–152

Accuracy
defined, 402
vs. precision in estimation, 125, 274–275

Actions, resulting from retrospective
deciding what action to take, 389–390
determining possible actions, 387–388
follow through on, 391–392
as output of sprint retrospective, 381
selecting insights to act on, 388

Activities
defined, 402
overview of, 16–18

Adaptation. *See also* Prediction and adaptation principle, in agile development
balancing predictive work with adaptive work, 43–44
based on product review, 371

daily scrum as inspect-and-adapt activity, 354
defined, 402
discovering your own path forward, 396
and exploration in approach to development, 39–40
as focus of planning rather than conformance, 249–251
leveraging variability, 35–36
plan-driven development compared with agile development, 59
responsibilities of development team, 197–198
sprint retrospective and, 375
sprint review and, 363

Agile development
concerns about adopting, 225
defined, 402
managers promoting agile values, 233–234
no end state in, 395
overview of, 1–3
plan-driven approach compared with, 59–60
product backlog in, 1
sharing best practices, 396–397

The Agile Manifesto (Beck), xxxi, 30, 204–205, 210

Agile principles
accepting that you can't get it right up front, 38–39
adapting to real-time information and replanning based on, 54
adaptive, exploratory approach, 39–40
balancing predictive work with adaptive work, 43–44
batch sizes in, 48–49
cost of change and, 40–43
cost of delays and, 52–54

427